Women
and
World Religions

Women
and
World Religions

Lucinda Joy Peach
American University

Prentice
Hall

Upper Saddle River, New Jersey 07458

Library of Congress Cataloging-in-Publication Data

PEACH, LUCINDA J., [date].
  Women and world religions / LUCINDA JOY PEACH
    p. cm.
  Includes bibliographical references and index.
  ISBN 0-13-040444-6
  1. Women and religion. I. Title.
  BL458.P43 2002
  200'.82—dc21   2001036862

VP, Editorial Director: *Charlyce Jones Owen*
Acquisitions Editor: *Ross Miller*
Assistant Editor: *Katie Janssen*
Editorial Assistant: *Carla Worner*
Editorial/Production Supervision: *Joanne Riker*
Prepress and Manufacturing Buyer: *Sherry Lewis*
Director of Marketing: *Beth Gillett Mejia*
Marketing Manager: *Chris Ruel*
Cover Art Director: *Jayne Conte*
Cover Designer: *Bruce Kenselaar*

This book was set in 10/12 Palatino by East End Publishing Services, Inc. and was printed and bound by Courier Companies, Inc. The cover was printed by Phoenix Color Corp.

Printed in the United States of America

10 9 8 7 6 5 4

ISBN 0-13-040444-6

Pearson Education LTD., *London*
Pearson Education Australia PTY, Limited, *Sydney*
Pearson Education Singapore, Pte. Ltd
Pearson Education North Asia Ltd, *Hong Kong*
Pearson Education Canada, Ltd., *Toronto*
Pearson Educación de Mexico, S.A. de C.V.
Pearson Education -- Japan, *Tokyo*
Pearson Education Malaysia, Pte. Ltd
Pearson Education, *Upper Saddle River, New Jersey*

Contents

Preface xi

Acknowledgments xiii

Chapter 4

Women and Other Asian Religious Traditions 101

Chapter 5

Women and Judaism 157

Women and Christianity   201

Women and Islam   249

Women and African Religions 299

Women and Goddess-Centered Religions 349

Preface

The primary focus of *Women and World Religions* is "actual" women in world religions, as opposed to goddesses or other images and symbols of females and the feminine found in religious myths, art and scriptures. Even when women's relationship to religion is considered in other world religions texts, the experience and status of real women's lives has often been ignored. *Women and World Religions* rectifies this.

The understanding of "world religions" used in this text—that is, those religions which are represented by people living in more than one limited region in the world—also differs from the more traditional understanding that the term only encompasses the "big five" traditions of Christianity, Judaism, Islam, Buddhism, and Hinduism. In addition to chapters covering each of these traditions, *Women and World Religions* includes religions that have had an impact outside of their place of origins, including Taoism, Confucianism, Shinto, African indigenous and tribal religions, and goddess-centered religions from different parts of the world.

The Introduction addresses the questions, *Why focus on women and religion?* and *What does a gender perspective contribute to the study of religion?* It also considers some important commonalities and differences in women's religious experience including: *How have women practiced religion? How have their religious beliefs and practices differed from those of men, if at all? How have women been treated differently than men in religious settings,* and *What effect, if any, has gender segregation and discrimination had on women's religious experiences?*

Succeeding chapters demonstrate how women from very different cultures and regions of the world have thought about, acted, and been treated as members of their religious tradition and culture. Introductory text for each chapter provides an overview of the religious tradition, describes some of the more important aspects of the relationship of female-gendered and feminine images and symbols to "real" women, and discusses women's relationship to the tradition and the changes in the religious status of women in that tradition. Following this material are essays that reflect real women's experiences in the religious tradition. The chapters end with questions for class discussion and references for further study and exploration of women in the religious tradition covered.

In addition to informing the reader about women's experience in the variety of world religious traditions, another goal of the text is to reveal a number of striking similarities and differences among women in different religious traditions and illuminate how the study of women's experience in religion can enrich the study of religion altogether.

Acknowledgments

First, I would like to acknowledge my dear departed college professor Teresina Havens, who first introduced me to the topic of women and world religions when I was an undergraduate at the University of Massachusetts—she indulged my interest with her willingness to conduct independent study courses with me and by advising me to pursue further study in religion rather than go to law school (advice which I ignored in the short term, but finally heeded!). The second acknowledgement is for professors Mary Jo Weaver and Jan Nattier who taught me more theoretically-sophisticated and critically-informed methods of thinking about women in religious traditions during my graduate studies in religion at Indiana University in Bloomington (*after* law school at New York University and a brief stint practicing law).

Third, I kindly acknowledge the assistance of all the people at Prentice Hall who facilitated the publishing of this text: my initial acquisitions editor Karita France and sales representative Allyson Williams for their initial encouragement and enthusiasm for the project; my current editor Ross Miller for his good natured acquiescence to proposed last-minute revisions and my assistant editor Katie Janssen, who has been a joy to work with, and an unflagging source of suggestions and constructive feedback; to the Prentice Hall reviewers Nancy A. Hardesty at Clemson University and E. Ann Matter, University of Pennsylvania; and to Joanne Riker and East End Publishing Services for their competent and cheerful editorial production services (as well as Joanne's suggestions for New York City theatre!).

LJP

Women
and
World Religions

Introduction

∿

Preliminary Considerations: Why Study Women and World Religion?

The title *Women and World Religions* was deliberately chosen for the volume to emphasize that the primary focus is on "actual" women, as opposed to goddesses or other images and symbols of females and the feminine found in religious myths, art, and scriptures. Although the gender ideology and symbolism are relevant here to the extent that they help us understand how women have been viewed within and outside of their religious traditions as well as how they have viewed themselves, the main subject of this text is on actual women, not myths or symbols.

A preliminary question for consideration is, *Why focus on women and religion at all?* What makes it necessary, or even important or interesting, to look at *women's* religious experience apart from that of men? One reason is that, like the rest of history and cultural development, *women* make up over half of the world's population, and yet their *experiences and contributions have mostly been ignored, especially historically*. Religious traditions have almost all been **androcentric**, that is, established and developed by men from male perspectives and focused on the experiences of men.

Even more significantly, however, world religions are all **patriarchal** and **sexist** in origins, development, leadership, authority, and power. That a religion is "patriarchal" means literally that it is "ruled by the fathers." The term is generally used today to refer to male domination, usually in a hierarchical and gender-stratified manner, with men occupying the more significant and valued positions, and women the secondary, subordinate ones. That a religion is "sexist" means that it privileges men and male experience as superior and devalues or denigrates those of women as inferior. Because religious beliefs are generally highly valued within a culture, sexist religious beliefs that are presented as representing the "divine will" are used to legitimate patriarchy and sexism in society. As Susan Sered tells us, religion has a crucial role in presenting patriarchy as inevitable, inescapable, and ultimately correct (Sered 1999, 4).

In addition, the patriarchy and sexism of religious traditions has resulted in **gender differentiation** and **gender segregation**. Regarding the former, gender has often been used as a way of categorizing different aspects of experience in a dualistic manner, associating certain attributes or aspects as "female" and others as "male," with the former signifying what is inferior and the latter what is superior, such as earth/heaven, nature/culture, emotion/reason, weak/strong, yin/yang, dark/light, moon/sun, practical/theoretical, feeling/intellect. The result is often **gender ideology** which naturalizes ideas about how men and women both are and ought to be, ideas that develop out of cultures, but which are legitimated as part of divine law or God's will.

Gender segregation functions to separate and divide religious activities and experiences on the basis of gender, designating certain activities as appropriate or even mandated only for women, and others only for men. As we will see, gender segregation has operated to prohibit women from access to places of worship, from learning religious texts and practices, or taking leadership roles, and required them to perform certain additional tasks to purify themselves which men are not required to do. Gender segregation is often justified by taboos regarding menstruation and/or childbearing functions. Whether gender segregation is explained or justified in terms of the inferiority of women and superiority of men or as simply offering "complementarity of sex roles" of equivalent value and worth, it almost always functions to disadvantage women.

Gender segregation has resulted in women being excluded from the formulation of religious doctrine and practice, from participation in the central religious rituals of the tradition, and from spaces designated as sacred, especially during certain times such as menstruation or childbearing. They have often been excluded from opportunities for religious training and education, from the ability to become full-time religious specialists, such as nuns or priests, either formally or because of the inferior resources afforded to women for those roles, and from opportunities for leadership in their religious communities.

Because aspects of all world religions have been sexist and patriarchal and have used gender differentiation and segregation, the experiences of women in relation to religion have differed markedly from those of men. In addition, because women's experience has so often been ignored or over-looked in religious traditions, it is either assumed to be the same as men's or at least as homogeneous with that of other women. Thus, another reason to focus on women and religion is to examine the differences among the statuses and experiences of women within the same religious tradition, as well the differences between men's and women's status and experiences. The male bias of religious traditions sometimes means, though, that it is difficult to find sources that shed light on women's religious lives, especially historically.

Although all the major world religions traditionally have been andro-centric, sexist, and patriarchal, women have nonetheless had a significant influence, both within their own gender-differentiated or -segregated "separate spheres," as well as on the larger tradition. Consequently, this textbook will explore how women from many parts of the world have thought about, acted, and been treated as members of a religious tradition and community. It will therefore address such questions as, How have women practiced religion? How have their beliefs differed from those of men, if at all? How have women within the major world religions negotiated their spiritual lives within traditions that are not only male dominated, but also sexist and patriarchal? Have they successfully carved out a "separate sphere" for their own spiritual activities, or are their religious lives in large part defined for them by male leaders?

Having established several important reasons for studying *women* and religion, it must also be noted that such a study is a hugely ambitious undertaking, even when we limit ourselves to "world religions," that is, those religions which are represented by peoples living in more than one geographical region or cultural area in the world. This is a slightly more expansive interpretation than the classic definition of "world religions" as comprised of only Christianity, Judaism, Islam, Buddhism, and Hinduism. It also includes religions that have had an impact outside their place of origins, but not quite as extensive an influence as these world religions. Thus, in addition to the five main religions, this text also includes a number of Asian religions, including Taosim, Confucianism, and Shinto, African indigenous tribal religions, and Goddess religions from a number of different parts of the world. Covering such a vast amount of ground means that some generalizations will be made that do not apply universally, and that some exceptions to these generalizations will be overlooked.

Similarities and Differences in Women's Experience

There are a number of striking similarities and differences running through the descriptions of women's relationships to the religious traditions discussed in this volume.

Similarities

There are two striking similarities running through many religious traditions which present something of a paradox. On the one hand, women are almost always regarded as secondary or inferior to the men in the tradition, even where this is described in terms of them being "complementary" gender roles rather than those of superior and inferior. The dominant religous symbols are, more often than not, male gendered. The main textual sources and interpretations of those sources are almost exclusively written and controlled by men. Men predominate as the spiritual leaders, often occupying all significant leadership roles within the religion. This usually tends to be the case in religions which are more formally established and institutionalized than in less formally organized and structured ones, as we will see.

In short, the power and authority within religions is generally held predominantly, if not exclusively, by men. The exclusion of women from interpretation of sacred texts, the exclusive use of male-gendered language to refer to God or the divine, and the exclusion of women from full ordination as renunciants or formally recognized spiritual leaders, transcend a single world religion. In addition, although little research has yet been done on the topic, women-identified or lesbian women have been especially singled out for denigration by religious institutions, which have generally demanded female obedience and subordination to the authority of males, both sexually and otherwise.

On the other hand, women have found solace, inspiration, nurturance, sustenance, and spiritual growth and meaning within the confines of these sexist and patriarchal religious traditions. They have carved out spheres for their own practice, devotion, and even authority, within every religion described here. Whether formal or informal, women's religious roles frequently provide the fundamental support necessary for the maintenance and growth of the tradition. Women dominate many of the religious gatherings and worship services of many faith traditions and provide the ongoing labor, caring, and financial support necessary to maintain the religion.

In turn, religion has provided women with a space within which they have relatively more freedom and authority than is often available to them in many other spheres of social life. Devoting their lives to religious practice has often liberated women from a choiceless existence as wife and mother and provided them with the material support necessary to live relatively independent and autonomous lives. Ironically, the choices made available to women who commit themselves to foresaking "worldly" existence for a spiritual life often occur in the face of messages from those very religious traditions that tell women that they best fulfill their religious obligations and spiritual fulfillment through marriage and childbearing.

To some extent, this paradox is breaking down in the face of modernity. Increasingly, religious women are challenging the sexist and patriarchal dimensions of their religions of origin. Some of these women are abandoning these religions for alternative religious traditions, "new" women-centered or women-friendly religions such as Wicca or Goddess spirituality, or altogether. Others are calling for reforms, ranging from modest to radical, in the way traditional religious traditions relate to women adherents. In almost every religion included in this volume, as we will see, there have been feminists advocating changes to improve the status of and roles for women in their religious institutions.

Differences

Not only does the experience of women within different religious traditions vary widely, but the experience of different women within the *same* religious tradition is often radically different, depending on a number of factors, especially cultural and regional differences, but also class status, age, childbearing (both capacity for and the actuality of), marital status, sexual orientation, geographical location (both First World versus Third World as well as rural versus urban), and political affiliation. These differences may result in women sharing a common religion having little in common with one another, for example, Egyptian and European Christian women.

Since religion is an aspect of culture, it is impossible to adequately study religion in the abstract, removed or out of context from a given cultural context. However, shared religious beliefs and practices may be more significant than cultural or regional differences. For example, it may make an Egyptian Christian woman's experiences more understandable to a European Christian woman than to an Egyptian Muslim woman. One important demarcation of regional and cultural differences is between the so-called Third World or developing countries and the First World or (post)industrialized countries. Because of disparities which result in people in the First World having relatively greater income, wealth, education, and general access to resources than people in the Third World, as well as the legacy of colonialism which subjugated the latter to the former, in general we will find that Third World women have had fewer opportunities to participate in, and thus to change, their religious traditions than First World women.

Also, in general, feminist initiatives to improve women's status in religion have begun in First World countries and later been implemented in Third World situations. For instance, many (especially Christian) citizens of Third World countries attend theological school in Western countries, thereby adopting different cultural traditions which they then bring back to their congregations. Despite these differences, international organizations in many religious traditions often facilitate interaction and understanding among women of diverse cultural and regional backgrounds who share a religious tradition. For example, women monastics in Christianity and Buddhism have international networks within which to share ideas and experiences, and to facilitate travel to other cultures and thereby enhance women's knowledge of other forms of practice and opportunities for women in their larger religious tradition.

In addition to cultural and regional differences, class differences may play an important role in determining women's status and experience within a religious tradition. Just as elite women generally have had relatively more access to education and political power than poor women cross-culturally and throughout history, elite religious women have had greater opportunities for religious education, training, leadership, and participation in their traditions.

A further significant difference is how women have chosen to respond to the patriarchy, sexism, and gender segregation of their religious traditions. Even in contemporary times, when many women have had some degree of choice about their religious affiliations, especially in Western countries, many have chosen to remain faithful to patriarchal and sexist religious traditions. Although sometimes this adherence (or conversion) has been influenced by factors supplemental to religious faith alone, such as nationalist loyalty or political struggles for ending colonial domination or influence, it sometimes appears to be based on less tangible factors of faith and commitment to one's culture and traditions.

Similarities within Differences
and Differences within Similarities

One of the fascinating aspects of studying women and world religions is that we discover differences within the similarities and similarities within the differences. As an example of the former, although most religions segregate women from men in certain aspects of practice and ritual, this segregation has very different impacts in different traditions. In many aboriginal and Native American religions, for example, gender segregation served to give both men and women vitally important roles to play in maintaining the religious life of the community. With the advent of colonialism, however, these roles often became the basis for hierarchy and sexist treatment of women.

In the postcolonial era, many women choose to support independence or nationalist movements spearheaded by men of their society and in the process reject "Western" notions of equality for women based on individual rights. For example, in Iran, many educated Islamic women voluntarily took back the wearing of the veil, a traditional Islamic practice for women, as a symbol of solidarity against Western imperialism. Wearing of the veil had been banned by the Western-supported reign of the Shah prior to the Islamic Revolution which installed the Ayatollah Khumanei as both spiritual and secular leader of Iran. The maintenance of religious tradition in this case, as in several others throughout the Middle East, Africa, and Asia, is often viewed as a bulwark against Westernization and the secularization of society.

As an example of the similarities among the differences in women's experiences, although symbols of women and the feminine have had a wide variety of different meanings and functions in different religious traditions, they have all functioned similarly to shape and define "ideal" roles and normative behavior for actual women.

Outline of Chapter Organization

Each chapter will focus on a specific religious tradition and will include the following dimensions:

I. Overview of the Religious Tradition

II. Relationship of Female-Gendered and Feminine Images and Symbols to "Real" Women

III. Women's Relationship to the Religion

    A. Women-Specific or Distinctive Aspects of the Tradition

    B. Gender-Based Segregation and Inequalities

    C. Women's Access to Religious Training and Education and Opportunities for Leadership Roles

    D. Well-Known and/or Influential Women in the Tradition

IV. Changes in the Status of Women, Both Historically and in Terms of Future Prospects

V. Selection of Essays

VI. Questions for Discussion

VII. References and Materials for Further Study

    A. Books and Articles

    B. Internet and Media References

Further description of each of the sections follows.

Overview of the Religious Tradition

This section of each chapter will provide a very brief background of the major outlines of the religion, including some description of regional, cultural, and sectarian variations in the tradition. This background will provide a context for discussing women's status and experience within the religious tradition.

Relationship of Female-Gendered and Feminine Images and Symbols to "Real" Women

Determining what this relationship is can be tricky and paradoxical. Many commentators have assumed, often wrongly, that positive images and symbols of women in a religous tradition mean that women are highly regarded and well treated within that tradition. Instead, often there is a lack of direct correlation, or even a direct contradiction between the status and value accorded by a religion to female images and symbols, and the actual status of women within that religious tradition. This is especially evident in Christianity, Hinduism, and Buddhism.

Women's Relationship to the Religion

This will include specific information about how women are viewed, and view themselves, within the tradition.

Women-Specific or Distinctive Aspects of the Tradition. These may include specific roles, rituals, practices, ceremonies, liturgies, sacred texts, prayers, and so forth, that are specific or distinctive to women. Sometimes these will be religious practices that have been designed by men *for* women, but in other instances, they reflect the independent or self-generated efforts of women.

For example, ritual is often a sphere in which women are given greater power and autonomy within a religious tradition, especially when there are women's organizations within the larger religious institution. In addition, as Rosiland Hackett points out in her essay "Women in African Religions" (included in Chapter 8), ritual often reflects a culture's views about gender and also provides an important context to look for evidence of women's power and authority outside of public officeholding (Hackett 1994, 63).

To foster comparative analysis, this section of each chapter will note some of the important variations among women within the religious tradition and across traditions in terms of their status and experience.

Gender-Based Segregation and Inequalities. It is important to note that separate gender roles and duties for men and women within a religious tradition need not *necessarily* or *inherently* be negative or disadvantaging to women. In some traditions, notably aboriginal Australian and Native American, women's roles were regarded as important and integral to the efficacious functioning of religious ritual and practice. However, in the majority of religious traditions that do draw sharp distinctions between religious roles based on gender, women have a distinctly secondary or inferior place.

Women's Access to Religious Training and Education and Opportunities for Leadership Roles. As we will see, women's access to religious training and leadership has varied widely across and within the religions we will be exploring. Despite the prevalence of patriarchal and sexist religious institutions which exclude women from most formal religious training and leadership status, many women have been able to gain some religious training and authority within gender-segregated groups or ritual practices. This is especially the case in folk religions or more marginal practices or traditions involving spirit mediums and healing practices.

Well-Known and/or Influential Women in the Tradition. Despite the general subordination and marginalization of women within the world's religions, some exceptional women have managed to rise to prominence in all of them. Thus, we will be taking a brief look at who these women were or are in each tradition, and what enabled them to succeed in spite of a sexist and patriarchal environment.

Changes in the Status of Women, Both Historically and in Terms of Future Prospects

In all the religions covered in this text, the status of women has shifted over time, although not always in the direction of improving women's status or establishing their equality with men. In some cases, women have gained more opportunities, privileges, and access to spiritual training and authority as time went on. In other cases, their lives have become more limited and restricted.

In recent decades, especially, with the rise of fundamentalist movements in many religious traditions, especially Christianity, Islam, and Hinduism, the status of women has distinctly deteriorated. Often forced into strictly gender-segregated roles, limited to the domestic sphere of childbearing and rearing, deprived of opportunities for education, and the opportunity to earn their own incomes, women in fundamentalist traditions are being used to reinforce male political agendas. "Used" does not necessarily mean that they are being forced against their will. In some cases, women may actually approve of and affirm these changes, both for themselves and other women. Nonetheless, the fact remains that the decision to revert to "traditional" gender-differentiated and gender-segregated roles and functions has almost always been made by men without the participation of or input from women.

Moreover, fundamentalist movements are often used by governments to control political groups and preserve an unstable regime against fragmentation in a religiously pluralistic polity. Women in nationalist and similar contexts are often treated as "symbols" of the nation, where preserving their "purity" and "integrity" against corruption by Westernizing or modernizing forces becomes paramount. Thus, a continuing issue running throughout the chapters in this volume is whether the religious tradition under consideration is, on balance, liberating or oppressive for women.

This part in each chapter will include a discussion of some of the major factors that have influenced the change in women's religious status and roles. In some cases, changes have taken place as a result of larger social forces of modernization. In others, it has come about as a result of organized efforts, sometimes by men, and sometimes by women, sometimes working alone, and sometimes within groups. In some cases, the status of women has changed as a simple result of modernization of the surrounding society. As more women are becoming wage earners, for example, working for a salary outside the home, traditional religious prescriptions concerning matters such as keeping women segregated in the home, or with roles restricted to those of wife and mother, are necessarily changing. The greater opportunities afforded to women and girls to obtain an education also facilitates this process.

In other cases, the impetus for change has come about as a result of the deliberate efforts of women dissatisfied with their status and roles within their religious communities. In some of these cases, the impetus has been "imported," for example, by women who have studied abroad and brought feminist ideas back to their home communities, as is the case with many African and Asian Christian women who study at European or North American theological schools. Or the impetus may come from Western women, who perceive that the status of women within a Third World society warrants improvement, as is in part the situation with the movement to restore full ordination for women in Buddhist countries.

In most cases, feminist religious scholars and practitioners have been developing programs to reform or otherwise eliminate the patriarchal, sexist, and gender-stratified aspects of their religious traditions, and to implement practices and policies that are gender-inclusive and egalitarian. The nature or shape of those changes varies widely, however. There is no single model of how women *should* relate to the limitations and exclusions that have been imposed upon them by a religious tradition. The kinds of strategies that have been adopted by women in Western religions and countries may not be appropriate for women in other religious and cultural contexts. For example, nationalism and family ties, which are not signficant concerns for women in First World countries, often present complications to feminist reform agendas in non-Western religions and Third World countries.

These changes can be usefully categorized if we imagine the possible range of changes as a continuum, with the different types occupying some point along it. The continuum has *rejection* of the religion at one end and *maintaining the status quo* at the other. At the intermediate points are *reformist, radical revisionist,* and *revolutionary* proposals for changes. At the reformist end, efforts are made to include women as equal partners with men in the religious life of their communities. And this, of course, may take a variety of forms itself. It may or may not mean rewriting liturgies, prayers, and sermons, introducing gender-neutral or female-gendered symbols, promoting women to leadership roles they have been excluded from, or eliminating aspects of the tradition, like certain texts, which are disrespectful or disadvantaging to women. Generally, reformist strategies do not involve significant revisions of the tradition as a whole, which alter its fundamental core (however that is defined by members of that tradition). We will see calls for reinterpreting the Qur'an as an example of reform in the chapter on women and Islam.

At a point further along the continuum are agendas for more *radical revisionist* or *revolutionary* changes, such as establishing or affirming the existence of existing separate, often parallel, institutions for women within the tradition to enable them to have a separate space free of male domination and oversight, or replacing sacred scriptures with new texts that have eliminated their sexist bias. Examples of this strategy appear in the chapters on women in Judaism and Christianity.

A final strategy is *rejectionist* in its approach: Having determined that a religious tradition is sexist and patriarchal to the core and can never be modified sufficiently to encompass the needs and interests of women as full partners in religious life, proponents of this third strategy leave their religious traditions behind. Some adopt membership in other established religious traditions that are considered to be less sexist and patriarchal. Others become involved with "women's religions," like the Wiccan or Goddess religions that we will explore in Chapter 10. And still others reject religion completely and become secularists.

Just as other aspects of women's religious experience evade generalization, so does an assessment of the prospects for women's full equality in traditional religions in the future. In some cases, as in many Christian and Jewish institutions, several steps have been taken to grant women equal partnership with men, including the opening of opportunities for spiritual leadership, participation in the formulation of theology, liturgy, and so on. In other cases, it seems as though the status of women is worse now than when the religion was established, as is the case of women under the Islamic Taliban regime in Afghanistan. It is likely that tensions, if not outright conflicts, between men and women in religious communities will continue into the future.

Selection of Essays

Despite the effort to find essays that at least touch on each of these areas, the scope and depth of coverage of each of these topics varies somewhat from chapter to chapter. This is inevitable in an anthology of already published essays that were written for a variety of purposes and audiences. Nonetheless, to the extent possible, consistency in coverage will be provided in the introductory essays to precede the reading selections for each chapter.

Questions for Discussion

The following are some overarching questions about the status and experience of women in religion in general to consider as you read the chapters to follow:

1. How have women's religious beliefs and practices differed from those of men, if at all?
2. To what extent can a religious tradition be changed to eliminate inequalities based on gender? Another way of asking this is, Are there limits to reforming religious traditions to ameliorate gender-based inequalities? Are patriarchy and sexism inherent in or essential to religious traditions (or to traditional religions)? To what extent can a religion be changed without becoming a new religion? Consider changes in ritual, symbolism, institutional structures, basic beliefs, liturgies, music, and so on. Can a religion remain "traditional" with the introduction of symbols of the Goddess, either alongside of or to replace those of a male God? How about replacing androcentric or male-centered God language?
3. On balance, would you say that religious membership or participation is liberating or oppressive for the women involved?
   - For what reasons?
4. What are the most effective strategies for empowering women within religious traditions?
   - Through reform of existing religious institutions, practices, symbol systems, rituals, and so on?
   - Through the establishment of "parallel" institutions, rituals, or symbol systems?
   - Through incorporating "feminine" or "feminist" elements into the tradition, such as the addition of goddess symbolism in addition to or in substitution for male god symbolism?
   - Through rejection of existing institutions and formation of separate women's religious communities?
5. What factors influence women's conversion from one religion to another, or to religion from no religion?
   - Should such conversions be viewed as empowering for the women in question?

In addition, for each religion in the chapters to follow, the following are some general questions for discussion to assist in both clarifying your understanding of the status and experience of women in that tradition, and, more broadly, for making comparisons across different religious traditions. Questions for discussion that are specific to particular traditions can be found at the end of each chapter.

1. What significant similarities and differences do you find between men's and women's experiences in the tradition?
2. What significant similarities and differences do you find among women in their status and experience in the tradition?
   - What do you think are the major factors that account for the differences you find?
3. How have women negotiated their spiritual lives in the face of the male domination, sexism, and patriarchy of the tradition? This requires thinking about matters such as the following:
   - Have women successfully carved out a "separate sphere" for their own spiritual activities, or are their religious lives in large part defined for them by male leaders?
   - How have women been subjects and how have they been objectified by/in the tradition?
   - Do women have equal status as either participants or leaders in the tradition?
   - If not, why not?
   - If women do have leadership roles, are they restricted to women who fit a particular profile, for example, married or unmarried, with or without children, young or old, domestically or foreign/Western educated, from a particular social class and/or economic status?
4. How has the status of women in the tradition changed over time?
   - Would you say that it is better today than historically?
   - What do you think are the major factors that account for these changes?
5. What recommendations can you make for further improvements in the status of women in this tradition?
   - What is the likelihood of these changes being implemented in the near future (the next five to ten years)?
6. What factors determine the relationship between female gender imagery and the status of "real" women in religious traditions?

References and Materials for Further Study

What follows are some general references on women and world religions.

Books and Articles

Ferguson, Marianne. 1995. *Women and Religion*. Upper Saddle River, NJ: Prentice Hall.

Flinders, Carol Lee. 1998. *At the Root of This Longing: Reconciling a Spiritual Hunger and a Feminist Thirst*. San Francisco: HarperSan Francisco.

Franzmann, Majella. 2000. *Women and Religion*. New York: Oxford University Press.

Gross, Rita. 1998. *Feminism and Religion*. Boston: Beacon Press.

Hackett, Rosiland. 1994. "Women in African Religions, in Arvind Sharma, ed., *Religion and Women*. Albany: State University of New York Press.

Haddad, Yvonne Yazbeck and Ellison Banks Findly, eds. 1985. *Women, Religion, and Social Change*. Albany: State University of New York Press. Includes essays on women in African, Native American, Chinese religions, Islam, Christianity, Judaism, Buddhism, and Hinduism.

Holm, Jean. 1994. *Women in Religion*. London: Pinter Publishers.

King, Ursala. 1995. *Religion and Gender*. Oxford, UK: Blackwell Publishers.

Paper, Jordan. 1997. *Through the Earth Darkly: Female Spirituality in Comparative Perspective*. New York: Continuum Press.

Sered, Susan. 1999. *Women of the Sacred Groves: Divine Priestesses of Okinawa*. New York: Oxford University Press.

———. 1994. *Priestess, Mother, Sacred Sister: Religions Dominated by Women*. New York: Oxford University Press.

Sharma, Arvind, and Katherine Young, eds. 1999. *Feminism and World Religions*. Albany: State University of New York Press.

Sharma, Arvind, ed. 1994. *Today's Woman in World Religions*. Albany: State University of New York Press.

Wessinger, Catherine, ed. 1996. *Religious Institutions and Women's Leadership: New Roles Inside the Mainstream*. Columbia: University of South Carolina Press.

Young, Serinity, ed. 1999. *Encyclopedia of Women and World Religion*. Vols. 1, 2. New York: Macmillan Reference. Provides excellent overviews by leading scholars of all the major religious traditions and many minor ones as well, in addition to a wide range of other topics, such as religious music, ritual, religious symbolism.

Young, Serinity. 1993. *Anthology of Sacred Texts By and About Women*. New York: Crossroad.

Internet and Media References

Academic Info Religion: Women & Religion—Bibliographies Web Site:
http://www. academicinfo.net/religwombibs.html.

Bibliography on Women and Religion Web Site:
http://www.nd.edu/~archives/lau_bib.
Extensive bibliography of books on women and religions.

Celebration of the Feminine Divine Web Site:
http://music.acu.edu/www/iawm/pages/reference/divine.html.
Texts, hymns, and poetry on the feminine divine from East and West, from ancient times to the eighteenth century.

Other Women's Voices: Translations of Women's Voices Before 1600.
http://www.akron.infi.net/~ddisse/.
The site offers an introduction to over 80 women who wrote a substantial amount before 1600 and whose work (or at least a good part of it) has been translated into modern English.

Scovill, Nelia Beth. "The Liberation of Women: Religious Sources." *The Religious Consultation on Population, Reproductive Health and Ethics:*
http://www.consultation.org/consultation/libpub.htm#Introduction.

chapter 2

Women and Hinduism

Overview

The term "Hindu" was used by Western colonialists beginning in the late eighteenth century to refer to the non-Muslim religions in India. There is no equivalent word in any Indian language. The religious tradition (or, more accurately, traditions) now known as Hinduism began in India and spread to other South Asian countries, especially Sri Lanka and Nepal. Hinduism is a difficult religion to describe, in part because the term is used to refer to an immense number of different texts and practices, both culturally and historically. The differences are so vast that there is an ongoing dispute about whether Hinduism is a monotheistic or a polytheistic religion. Although there are many different gods and goddesses (prominent among them the gods *Brahman, Siva, Vishnu* (who himself has many different forms, including Krishna, and Rama) and the goddesses *Durga, Sita,* and *Lakshmi*), those promoting a monotheistic view argue that all of these are merely different forms or manifestations of the "one God," *Atman.*

It is also difficult to date the different periods of Indian religious literature because of what was basically an oral tradition for generations, indeed, one in which the written word was treated disparagingly. For the sake of providing some signposts to the historical development of the tradition, however, the vast heritage of Hinduism can be categorized in terms of three main time periods. These are the ancient Vedic religion of the *Brahmins,* the Aryan invader tribes to North India (approximately 1500 to 500 B.C.E.); the classical period of the *Upanishads* and great Indian epic *Mahabharata* (from 500 B.C. onward), and devotional movements, which began somewhere between 500 and 1000 C.E. and continue to the present.

During the Vedic period, hymns and commentaries describe elaborate rituals that were conducted to supplicate the gods and maintain the order of the cosmos. In "Essence and Existence: Women and Religion in Ancient Indian Texts," Julia Leslie argues that the movements that arose during the second and third periods created a backlash of Vedic orthodoxy. This backlash not only attempted to return to original Vedic ritual practices but also severely curtailed women's participation in these practices. She describes how women's religious roles became increasingly limited as Hinduism developed from the original Vedic period through the classical.

In the third period, however, devotionalism (*bhakti*) opened religious practice to women. Freed from adherence to strictly defined social roles or ritual practices prescribed in accordance with one's gender, caste, or ethnicity, devotional movements, which focus simply on pure love for and devotion to God—modeled on the love of a woman for a man—enabled women to participate in religious practices in unprecedented ways. Devotional movements were also identified with women because of their emphasis on passion and the emotions, characteristics of humanity that already had been gendered female in earlier periods of the Hindu tradition.

Two prominent forms of devotional movements are *Vaishnavism* (devotion to the god *Vishnu*) and *Saivism* (devotion to the god *Siva*), both prominent gods of the Hindu pantheon. Among the different sects of *Vaishnavism*, the worship of *Vishnu's* manifestation of *Krishna* is one of the most prominent. The model for the devotee of *Krishna* is that of the female cowherds who abandoned their husbands and families out of overpowering love for *Krishna*, especially that of his lover *Radha*.

Relationship of Female-Gendered and Feminine Images and Symbols to "Real" Women

Religious images and symbols of women and the feminine date back to the earliest strata of Hindu teachings, in the ancient Vedic texts. Women are identified with nature because of the auspicious life-giving powers of both, and nature is identified as female. In fact, the land of India itself came to be seen as a goddess, still extant in the cult of *Bharat Mata*, or "Mother India" (see Findly 1999, 424).

The Hindu word *Devi* is the generic name for goddess. Goddesses play central roles in Hinduism, contrary to the Western, monotheistic traditions of Judaism, Christianity, and Islam that we will encounter in later chapters. For example, the deities who rule wealth and commerce (*Lakshmi*), strength and protection (*Durga*), and education, art, and spiritual knowledge (*Saras-*

vati) are all female. As in other traditions where goddess worship is a feature, however, Hindu goddesses bear a complicated relationship to real women.

In part, goddesses are promoted as idealized versions of real women, and as models and ideals for women to emulate. For example, the ancient Vedic goddess *Usha*, "the Dawn," is a symbol of "youthful loveliness" who is constantly being reborn. She represents nature as a frame for human emotions, and the natural world as a reflection of man's moods and passions.

In the early *Upanishads*, Brahman is manifested in three modes—as Lord, self, and Nature. As Nature (*Prakriti*), Brahman is the female field of enjoyment or involvement of the self. *Prakriti* consists of three elements: fire, water, and earth. She continuously produces manifold offspring through the impetus of *Sakti*—the female power of the Lord, the active self-power of the divine. In the later *Upanishadic* period, the epic narrative *Bhagavad Gita* expresses an ambivalence in the traditional Hindu attitude toward women, who are portrayed in dichotomous stereotyped terms as whores and virgins, sexual seductresses, and wives and mothers.

The complete devotion, obedience, and service of *Sita,* one of the most beloved of the Hindu goddesses, to her husband *Rama* is held up as a role model for women to emulate, especially young brides. Other goddesses of this type include *Savitri,* whose talents are able to bring her husband back from the dead, *Lakshmi,* the wife of the god *Vishnu,* and *Parvati,* wife of the god *Siva* (see Findly 1999, 420). Indeed, Mohandas Gandhi held up goddesses like *Sita, Damayanti,* and *Draupadi*, all extremely devoted to their husbands, for women to emulate.

In other cases, however, the relationship between goddesses and actual women is an inverse one. For example, the goddess *Durga* appears in the classic epic narrative *Mahabharata*, both as Krishna's sister, a virgin who upholds heaven by her chastity, and as a woman who delights in wine, meat, and animal sacrifices. *Durga* also appears as the wife of the god *Siva* named *Uma.* In both forms, she is the slayer of the Buffalo demon.

The goddess *Kali*, "the Dark one," *Sakti*, the female power, consort of *Siva*, is the active female energy that complements *Siva's* pure passive intelligence. *Sakti* is the central power that activates *Prakriti*, the female manifestation of *Brahman* as Divine Mother who also becomes the Destroyer as *Kali.* Worshipers of this powerful form of *Devi* are *Saktas*, devotees of the divine creative *Sakti* present in all things. To the extent that goddesses like *Kali* are fierce and powerful, it may mean that actual women are viewed as weak, gentle, and lacking in power. To the extent that goddesses act in the outside world without constraint or limitation, it may also mean that real women are subjected to a number of restrictions on their ability to move about freely, especially without a male escort outside the home.

It is possible that this seeming disparity can be explained on the basis that goddesses who are married, such as *Lakshmi*, the goddess of Prosperity, are considered benign, whereas those who are alone—such as *Kali*—are viewed as dangerous. Thus, marriage—control by a man—reins in women's power, whereas a woman outside the bonds of marriage is untamed and capable of doing harm. However, given the limited study of women in Hinduism that has been conducted to date, it is difficult to know how actual women relate to these goddess symbols. As Leslie Orr points out, "given the lack of evidence, it is impossible for us to know whether, for example, goddesses have actually served as 'models' (or 'antipodes') for Hindu women at a point in their history—something that seems to be assumed by many scholars" (Orr 1999, 244).

Women's Relationship to Hinduism

Women-Specific or Distinctive Aspects of the Tradition

To make an obvious statement, Hinduism is a strongly gendered religion, as the essays selected for this chapter will reveal. It is also a strongly sexist and patriarchal tradition. At the same time, many Hindu women have found deep meaning and significance in Hindu beliefs and practices. It is therefore important not to be dismissive of this tradition as having nothing positive to offer to women. Despite the male dominance and patriarchy of the Hindu tradition, at various points in history women participated in the development of the religion. During the *Vedic* period, for example, some women participated in composing hymns. In the *Upanishadic* period there were women philosophers. At a later time, some women were able to renounce lives as householders and become renunciants, tantric practitioners, or ascetics (see Findly 1999, 421).

With respect to ritual, women were excluded from the public ritual expressions of religious life during the early *Vedic* period, especially from performing the sacrificial *srauta* rituals, which were understood to be necessary for the maintenance of the universe. At the same time, their mediational role was nonetheless viewed as essential to the efficacy of certain rituals, especially those involving fertility and sexuality. In addition, women were given responsibility for performing *vratas*, vowed observances—especially ritual fasts—viewed as efficacious for bringing about prosperity, marital harmony, and so on, which accrue benefit to the entire household (see Findly 1999, 422). In modern Hinduism, wives both assist their husbands in the performance of rituals and maintain the household ritual shrines, which require daily attention. Women (and to a greater extent, lower-caste women) also now have more public roles as temple attendants, devotional singers, mediums for goddesses or spirits, and as *devadasis*, the subject of the selection by Kay Jordan.

Because bearing children is so vital to women's having a respectable social status in Hindu society, childless women spend much energy in ritual activities designed to enhance their fertility, including those designed to ward off obstructing spirits who may be preventing them from becoming pregnant. They also vow to go on pilgrimage, perform rituals at the temple regularly, or make some other offering if their desire for healthy children is fulfilled (see Feldhaus 1999, 425).

Gender-Based Segregation and Inequalities

There are a number of ways in which Hinduism functions on the basis of gender categories which limit the freedoms and autonomy of women. Here, we will look at how these categories function with respect to women's bodies and family life.

Women's Bodies. In general, Hinduism views women's bodies as polluted, the result of past negative karma. While temporary sources of pollution, especially from menstruation, sexual activity, and childbirth, can be remedied by performing the appropriate rituals, permanent pollution, such as is thought to result from being a prostitute or a midwife, can only be purified by the soul obtaining a new body in a future life (we will see a similar view of the female body in the chapter on Buddhism).

Women's bodies also came to be seen as corrupted by interacting with others from lower castes. For example, the *Bhagavad Gita* explains that when intermingling of castes occurs, a family decays, its religious laws are destroyed, lawlessness prevails, and the women are corrupted.

Evidence for the practice of the seclusion of women dates back to the Vedic period, but it was strengthened by the Muslim practice of *purdah*, introduced when Muslims entered India in substantial numbers beginning in the second millenium and again as rulers from the early thirteenth century. The rationale for secluding women is tied to the honor and respectability of the family. The extent of veiling depends on local cultural custom and is usually not practiced until after a woman is married.

Family Life. Traditional Hindu culture discriminates against females in a number of ways. Girls were not, and many still are not, given the same opportunities for education as boys (viewed as an essential part of spiritual training for males), and so married earlier than boys. Although earlier in the *Upanishadic* period, initiation into *Vedic* studies (*upanayana*) was available to girls, by the sixth or seventh centuries C.E., marriage came to be viewed as the complementary *upanayana* for girls (indeed, the only significant rite of passage in a woman's life), who generally married between eight and ten years old to a husband whom her father had arranged for (indeed, arranged marriages still take place in some parts of South Asia, although they are far less common than they once were). Unlike the heterodox traditions of Buddhism and Jainism, where women could renounce domestic roles for spiritual ones as nuns, in Hinduism it was expected that all young women would marry and, if fertile, bear children.

By the time of the *Dharma-Sastras* (approximately 200–232 B.C.E.), which established specific codes of conduct for males and females of the different castes, females were viewed as acquiring spiritual merit through their husbands. Females were expected to marry males in the same or higher caste (*varna*), called *anuloma*, meaning "with the grain." Females who married a male in a caste below them—*pratiloma* ("against the grain")—brought disgrace to their family. In contrast, Brahman males could marry down, but their wider choices meant a reduction in the choices for upper-class women. Divorce was not possible, although a married man could take a second wife in certain circumstances, for example, if his first wife was barren.

At the same time that marriage came to be viewed as such a seminal event, it also represented misfortune for the bride's family, not only for the loss of wealth and property that paying her dowry required (in recent years, more and more Hindu brides are being killed by their husbands or his family in so-called "dowry deaths" because the woman's family is unable to pay satisfactory dowries), but also because of the loss of labor in the family household. Female infanticide has been practiced since ancient times, and in modern India, female fetuses are aborted at such an alarmingly high rate that international development organizations report that the practice of amniocentesis (to determine the sex of a fetus) has resulted in *millions* of "missing" females in India (and other parts of South Asia as well) (see Seager 1997).

Married women were (are) subject to the control of their husbands and their husband's parents, with whom the married couple often lives (often creating much stress and anxiety for the new bride). The purpose of marriage is for the wife to devotedly serve and give pleasure to the husband and to bear and raise children, particularly sons.

At a husband's death, Hindu women were generally not allowed to remarry. Ideal Hindu wives were obligated to end their own lives when their husbands died through the practice of *sati*, or throwing themselves on their husband's funeral pyre (and being burned alive), which tradition held would turn them into goddesses and her location of death a site of pilgrimage.[1] During the era of British colonialism in India, *sati* was outlawed, but it continues in isolated instances even today, as illustrated by the Roop Kanwar case in 1987 (see Findly 1999, 420). Widows are entitled to financial support from their husband's family, but only as long as they remain celibate.

The *Manava-dharma-Sastra* or "Laws of Manu" (approximately 250 B.C.E. to A.D. 100) established particularly onerous restrictions on women's lives. Some of the prescriptions are as follows:

- Day and night must women be kept in dependence by males of their families.
- A woman is never fit for independence.
- Women must particularly be guarded against evil inclinations.
- By guarding his wife carefully, a man protects the virtue of his family, himself, and his ability to acquire merit.
- Wives who bear children, who are "worthy of worship and irradiate their dwellings," and who secure many blessings are not different from one another.

These prescriptions for women's roles and activities suggest how restricted Hindu women's lives have been, at least *ideally*, within the Hindu world view.

Women's Access to Religious Training and Education. As noted above, in traditional Hindu culture, women and girls have had only limited access to religious education (or formal education of any kind, for that matter), as they were viewed as preparing for lives as wives and mothers, where formal education would be wasted on them. The first schools for girls were opened by Christian missionaries during the colonial period, but they were viewed suspiciously. The movement for educating girls did not gain momentum until the second half of the nineteenth century. In the modern era, however, the Indian government has made efforts to ensure that Hindu girls and women have opportunities for education. More Hindu women are taking an interest in their religious tradition and becoming Hindu scholars and theologians.

Opportunities for Leadership Roles. Archeological evidence is revealing that Hindu women were involved in religious life to a far greater extent than was once thought. Traditionally, however, these opportunities have been very limited, especially in the public spaces of Hindu temples. This has changed somewhat, as the following section suggests. In any event, women have traditionally been, and still are, mainly responsible for keeping the household shrines, which every observant Hindu family should have, and making offerings daily.

Well-Known and/or Influential Women in the Tradition

There is evidence of philosophically trained women during the *Upanishadic* period, including Maitreyi and Gargi Vacaknavi. Not surprisingly however, it is in the *Bhakti* tradition that women have been most recognized for their spirituality and revered as saints. One of the best known women in the *Vaishnavite* devotional tradition is the sixteenth-century poet saint Mirabai, whose life of devotion is depicted in her many passionate poems of love and devotion to *Krishna* (Leslie 1983, 103). Others are the ninth-century Antal and the seventeenth-century Bhina Bai.

Among *Saivite* worshippers, one of the most famous is Akka Mahadevi of Karnataka, who became a wandering ascetic, renouncing her husband and escaping from his family's efforts to restrain her out of her love for and devotion to *Siva* (Leslie 1983, 105–6). Others are the Tamil forest-dwelling Karaikkal Ammaiyar in the sixteenth century and the brahman Lalla Ded of Kashmir who practiced tantra. In recent years, it has become more common for yogis, swamis, and other male spiritual masters to pass their mantle to their wives or female disciples (see Johnsen 1994).

The development of Tantric practices also gave goddesses (and seemingly women as well) a much more prominent role in religious practice. For example, in Tantric sexual practices, the yogi viewed his consort as the Goddess *Devi*. In fact, if the yogi is not able to perceive his consort as *Devi*, having sex with her is an impure act. At first, the practitioner of Tantra worships the goddess as external in the temple (as God's body in the world) but gradually comes to identify her with himself and then prepares for higher tantric practices. These practices suggest a positive valuation of the female principle, if not for women themselves.

Changes in the Status of Women

Historically

The development of the path of devotion (*bhaktimarga*) revolutionized women's religious life. In the section of the *Mahabharata* known as the *Bhagavad Gita*, *Krishna* finally breaks free of later *Upanishads'* emphasis on yoga and declares that salvation is available to **anyone** who worships him—including women, *sudras*, or the wicked. This represented a complete break from the earlier tradition in which dharma texts specified that women and *sudras* were excluded from studying the Vedas. The *Krishna* of the next stage of written Hindu texts, the *Puranas*, places emphasis on emotional experience, which is associated with females and thus gives women a more legitimate and "natural" role as worshippers. The *Bhakti* tradition overthrows traditional religious distinctions based on caste, gender, and age and enables women and outcastes complete access to the divine. In the form of *Krishna-Gopala*, the image of *Krishna* frequently used is that of a passionate woman longing for the embrace of her lover, to symbolize union of the soul with God.

British colonialism had a significant impact on the status of women in Hindu society in India. The colonial government viewed itself as the salvation of Hindu women from oppressive conditions. Among other legal measures, the British outlawed the traditional Hindu practice of *sati*, or burning the wife alive on her husband's funeral pyre. Indian feminist scholars in recent years, however, question the motives of the colonial government in improving the status of women and speculate that gender inequalities were used more as an excuse for the British to impose their will upon the Indian people than as the opportunity to actually improve the status of women.

In recent times, women have had some opportunities to enter traditionally male-only preserves, including becoming ascetics (spiritual seekers who renounce worldly life, families, possessions, etc., and live a minimal existence with only bare essentials and dependent upon the generosity of others for basic needs), becoming gurus, studying the Vedas, and performing Vedic rituals. In addition, there are now sections of some ashrams designated for women, also a change from traditionally male-only participants (Young 1994, 14).

Innovations in Hindu women's religious practices have also occurred in the temples that have been established in the West. Women have more active roles in the temples, for example, as administrators. Some women have innovated ritual processions, carrying a goddess statue, which is exclusively a male role in India. The taboos prohibiting menstruating women from the temples have also been relaxed in the West, and many rituals that were traditionally practiced in the home are now practiced in the temple (see Narayanan 1999, 429).

Future Prospects

To some extent, the opportunities for continued improvements in the status of and opportunities for women in Hinduism are dependent on larger political and social forces. If these forces continue to broaden opportunities for women generally, religious institutions will probably follow suit in expanding opportunities for women. However, the status of Hindu (and other religious) women in India is currently in question, as the Hindu revival movement battles for political control of the (now secular) state. If Hindu forces are successful, they are likely to reinstitute religious laws, which are oppressive to women in several respects, especially in the areas of family laws and reproductive rights.

In addition, as the South Asian economy weakens, it is likely that Hindu women now working in the labor market will be forced to return to their homes to enable men to have these jobs. Once back in the restrictive space of the domestic sphere, it is possible that traditional religious restrictions on women's mobility and ability to control their reproductive lives will be reinstituted and/or strengthened (Young 1994, 21). On the other hand, the Internet has opened up numerous avenues for accessing spiritual knowledge which were previously closed to women. It is possible then that such modern technology will revolutionize Hindu women's experience in a positive way.

The selections which follow examine the status of women in different aspects and distinctly different time periods of the Hindu tradition. The first essay, "Essence and Existence: Women and Religion in Ancient Indian Texts" by Julia Leslie, describes what we may be able to understand about the lives of Hindu women from the earliest eras of the tradition by studying the classical Hindu religious texts, especially those of the *Vedas* and *Upanishads*. Kay Jordan's essay "Devadasi Reform: Driving the Priestesses or the Prostitutes Out of the Hindu Temples?" examines the debate over the movement in nineteenth- and twentieth-century India to eliminate the tradition of "devadasi," girls and young women who are "donated" to a temple, usually for the purpose of becoming the "wife" of the god of that temple, and in many cases becoming a prostitute as a result. The third essay in this chapter, by Vanaja Dhruvarajan, "Religious Ideology, Hindu Women, and Development in India," discusses the negative religious beliefs about women that obstruct the benefits of development programs from flowing to women in contemporary India. Together, these three essays give us a broad historical overview of the status and roles of Hindu women.

Note

1. The religious rationale for the practice had been that the passive "soil" of the wife is subsumed under the active agency and "seed" of the husband upon marriage. When the husband dies, the wife is also dead spiritually, since she is part of him.

Essence and Existence: Women and Religion in Ancient Indian Texts

Julia Leslie

Introduction

Imagine the individual as a nut. The kernel hidden inside is the transmigrating soul or self, the essence or religious potential of the individual. The outer shell combines the circumstances of birth, personality, and all the existential trappings of a particular lifetime. Femaleness is evidently to do with 'existence' not 'essence'. But how far is it seen to impinge upon and even define the soul's potential in Indian religious texts?

The aims of this paper are fourfold: to draw a simplified chronological map of ancient Indian religion; to place in that context what we know of the religious opportunities open to women; where possible, to find a female voice to put the case for women; and, finally, to investigate the tensions of 'existence' versus 'essence' in relation to women.

The story of Sulabhā illustrates the problem. She is described in India's great epic, the *Mahābhārata*, (XII. 321) as a woman far advanced in religious knowledge. When she hears of the great learning of Janaka, king of Mithila, she decides to find out if he is truly enlightened. Assuming the form of a beautiful woman, she goes to Janaka's court and begs him to share his knowledge. Janaka does so, and concludes his discourse with the claim that he is indeed enlightened: 'Free of all attachment, my soul fixed on the supreme truth, I regard all creatures equally.' But Sulabhā is not so easily satisfied. By means of her yogic powers, she enters his mind to test his claim for herself. Aghast, Janaka denounces her for attempting to seduce and humiliate a righteous man. 'However beautiful you are,' he declares, 'this union is unlawful. You have no right to pollute me with your touch.' Sulabhā is unabashed. 'Only one who still confuses soul and body (essence and existence) could talk like that,' she replies.

> True, our bodies should not touch, but I have not touched you with any part of my body. I rest in you like a drop of water on a lotus leaf, without permeating it in the least. How can you distinguish between souls which are in essence the same? How can you call the contact of two enlightened beings unlawful?

From Pat Holden, ed., 1983. *Women's Religious Lives*. London: Croom Helm, pp. 89–112 (excerpted). Reprinted with permission.

Sulabhā concludes that anyone so obsessed with the external fact that she is a woman cannot be enlightened.

This is precisely the problem I wish to investigate. How far is the kernel (the individual soul) defined by its outer shell (the existential fact of being a woman)? As the story of Sulabhā demonstrates, it is a problem of which Indian religious thinkers were well aware....

I Vedic Religion

Vedic religion (i.e. the beliefs and practices of the Aryan tribes in northern India, often called Brahmanism) was marked by polytheism (invoking gods for specific purposes), fire sacrifices, ecstasy (perhaps involving hallucinogens such as soma), and a powerful priesthood in charge of religious knowledge and ritual. Education in the form of Vedic studies was the necessary preliminary to any kind of religious activity. But were women initiated into Vedic studies? The little evidence available suggests that they were. There are many references to female scholars, poets and seers, to women taking the rite of initiation and wearing the sacred thread, the mark of the initiated. Once embarked on the religious life, then, were women allowed to act as priests? Were they permitted to invoke the gods on their own behalf or for others, to chant sacred texts and formulae, to offer fire and soma sacrifices? Again, the rather sparse evidence suggests that they were.

Several hymns of the RgVeda (abbreviated RV) are ascribed to female seers, some of them describing the priestly activities of the women concerned. In RV.X.39, for example, Ghosā invokes the twin sun gods on behalf of the people with the stirring words:

> As 'twere the name of father, easy to invoke, we all assembled here invoke this Car of yours,
> O Aśvins ...
> Awake all pleasant strains and let the hymns flow forth ...
> O Aśvins, bestow on us a glorious heritage, and give our princes treasure fair as Soma is ... (v. 1–2)

In RV.VIII.80, Apālā describes how she herself plucks the sacred soma, presses it, and offers it with invocations to the god, Indra, saying:

> Drink thou this Soma pressed with teeth, accompanied with grain and curds, with cake of meal and song of praise. (v. 2)

In RV.V.28, Viśavavārā invokes and offers sacrifice to Agni, god of fire. She conducts the ceremony herself, pouring oil with the sacrificial ladle, and declaring:

Thy glory, Agni, I adore, kindled, exalted in thy strength. (v.4)

There is no suggestion in any of these examples that being a woman might disqualify one from ritual acts.

However, both Ghosā and Apālā are described as having some skin disease, possibly leprosy. This might have placed them in a different category from the other women of their time. It is also impossible to prove the historicity of any of these seers, male or female. Nonetheless, the little evidence we have does suggest that women could both receive religious education and conduct ritual sacrifice. In view of later developments, this is important.

II The Classical Period

A: The Pursuit of Knowledge

The Classical period marks a radical change in the Indian religious approach. The worship of many gods was replaced by an increasing tendency to reduce everything to one ultimate truth; external sacrifice by the inner ritual of self-control (yoga, meditation etc); ecstasy by the pursuit of esoteric knowledge ('seeing things as they really are'); the emphasis on the priest hood reinforcing the social hierarchy by that on the individual outside society's demands. Although the Upanisads are strictly speaking Vedic texts and the two great Upanisads probably older than the Buddha, it is likely that they are records of the same spiritual turmoil from which Buddhism and Jainism arose.

1. The Upanisads For the Upanisads, esoteric knowledge means the knowledge of Brahman which alone can release the individual from the endless cycle of births and deaths. Our concern here is to discover whether women were both considered capable of attaining this knowledge and allowed to pursue it. Once again, the literature available provides markedly little evidence for the religious involvement of women. What there is, however, suggests that religious pursuits were not yet barred to them.

The story of the sage, Yājñavalkya, and his two wives demonstrates that, from the religious point of view, there were two kinds of women. Kātyāyanī is described as 'possessing only a woman's knowledge'. Maitreyī, however, is 'one who discourses on (the knowledge of) Brahman'. When Yājñavalkya decides to renounce the life of the householder and become a forest hermit, he offers to divide his wealth between his two wives. Kātyāyanī agrees. The Brhadāranyaka Upanisad continues:

But Maitreyī said: "If, sir, this whole earth, filled as it is with riches, were to belong to me, would I be immortal thereby?" 'No,' said

Yājñavalkya. 'As is the life of the rich, so would your life be. For there is no hope of immortality in riches.' And Maitreyī said: 'What should I do with something that does not bring me immortality? Tell me, good sir, what you know.' (Br. Up. II.4.2–3.)

Without a second thought, Yājñavalkya complies.

The story of Gārgī is even more persuasive (Br. Up. III.6,8). In a public debate in which she is the only woman mentioned, Gārgī repeatedly questions the great Yājñavalkya. Her persistence and perspicacity finally elicit from him one of the finest definitions of Reality that we have (Br. Up. III.8.11). We may conclude that Gārgī was sufficiently learned in religious matters to be taken seriously, and that such learned women were permitted to display their knowledge and debating skills in a predominantly male public gathering.

Yājñavalkya does not question either Maitreyī's or Gārgī's capacity to understand religious truth, nor does he deny their right to pursue it, either in private or in public. But it must be added that the epithet applied to Kātyāyanī indicates the apparently equally current notion that religious knowledge is somehow not the property of women. It is this idea that takes increasing precedence in later Hindu literature....

B: Right Action

The upsurge of Buddhism and other ascetic sects provoked a counter-reaction on the part of orthodox brahmanism. The importance of knowledge is replaced by that of action: either correct ritual action as laid down by the Vedic Commentators, or appropriate human action within society as ordained by cosmic law (*dharma*) and interpreted for men by the lawgivers. The religious goals for both approaches are the same: release from the cycle of births and deaths: or, failing that, heaven and a good rebirth in the next life. But were both these goals considered attainable by women as well as by men?

1. The Vedic Commentators and Ritual Action   In an effort to stem 'heretical' thought, the Vedic Commentators (by which I mean primarily the Mīmāmsā school of Vedic exegesis) devoted themselves to resuscitating the ancient traditions and ideals of the already distant Vedic past. In relation to women, however, their concern was not merely to turn back the clock. The religious education and opportunities left open to women in Vedic times are repeatedly curtailed, and Vedic references to them redefined....

A woman's right to perform sacrifice is abolished altogether.

Even the rights of the wife taking part in the joint sacrifice with her husband, a tradition much in evidence in Vedic literature, are whittled away. In both Vedic and epic times, the wife's participation in the joint sacrifice is a religious necessity. According both to the grammarian, Pānini (IV.1.33), and to

Jaimini (VI.1.17–21), patnī (the word used to refer to the chief wife of equal caste) means 'female owner', and thus one who is qualified to take an equal share in the joint sacrifice. But later commentators insist first, that all injunctions for joint sacrifice expressed in the masculine form refer to the husband alone; and secondly, that those expressed in the feminine form should be reinterpreted according to what is considered 'proper' for women. For example, the invocation of blessings often ascribed to the wife involves Vedic mantras; but women are now redefined as unworthy of Vedic education. In relation to women, therefore, such references must be reinterpreted to mean 'bathing' or some equally unimportant activity (Jaiminīya-sūtra VI.1.24; Sabarabhāsya). The wife's religious role even in the joint sacrifice thus becomes increasingly passive and insignificant, covering such things as looking after the implements her husband alone can use. We have come a long way from the female seers of the RgVeda.

2. The Lawbooks and Human Conduct   The lawbooks take this trend even further. Religious education and ritual are categorically denied to women. No sacramental rite with sacred texts may be performed for women for they are weak, impure, and have no knowledge of Vedic literature (Manusrarti IX.18). No sacrifice, no vow and no fast may be performed by a woman independently of her husband (V.155), or she will go to hell (XI.36).

The emphasis has changed from knowledge and ritual to conduct: the concepts of dharma and svadharma. Dharma is the law of the cosmos, the principle underlying all creation. It is both descriptive and prescriptive: what is and what ought to be. Svadharma (own dharma) is this same cosmic law reflected in human existence. This too is both descriptive and prescriptive: what is (i.e. the duties and functions ordained by one's birth and circumstances) and what ought to be. Hence one's religious duty is to fulfil the obligations of one's current existence. Svadharma, the religious duty of every individual is also referred to as varnāśramadharma, the duty of one's class (varna) and stage (āśrama) in life.

The theory of class is briefly detailed in, for example, the *Baudhayāna Dharmasūtra*. Brahmins are expected to study the Vedas, teach, and perform sacrifices. The warrior class should study the Vedas, perform sacrifices and carry arms. The merchant or artisan class should study the Vedas, perform sacrifices, cultivate the soil, tend cattle and do business. The lowest class (śūdras) are required merely to serve the three higher classes.

It is often assumed that this hierarchy is applicable to both sexes. But a glance at the religious literature on the subject of class in relation to women soon reveals that it is not. Women of whatever class are increasingly relegated to the inferior status of śūdras. In Vedic literature, the four-class hierarchy is mentioned only once, right at the end of the RgVedic period (RV.X.90). In the Upanisads, the four classes are mentioned but do not yet form a rigid system. The oft-repeated question of the Upanisadic era is rather: Who is the real brahmin? The answer is unambiguous: he who sees things as they really are. In matters of religious truth, both class and sex are irrelevant. Buddhist literature shows the beginning of the downward trend: while the hierarchy of class is overruled by monastic values, that of sex is not. For the Vedic Commentators, however, both class and sex are crucial: śūdras and women are excluded from all religious ritual. From now on, women are openly grouped together with the lowest class. The lawbooks make this fact quite plain: the three higher classes are defined as having the right to study the Vedas and offer sacrifice; women, regardless of the class they are born into, are forbidden to do either. For example, Manu's instructions on the ritual purification of the body read that the three higher classes should sip water three times and wipe their mouths once; but that a woman and a śūdra should perform each action only once (V.139).

The theory of the four stages of life are equally clear-cut and equally inappropriate for women. The first stage is that of the student of the Vedas, a long and intense period of religious instruction with a teacher. This is followed by marriage and the assumption of the duties of the householder. The birth of one's first grandson heralds the third stage, that of the forest hermit. The fourth begins when the renunciate performs his own funeral rites while still alive to indicate his total rejection of the world.

Once again, we must ask how far this admittedly idealised hierarchy was seen to be applicable to women. As we have seen, the first stage of religious education was apparently open to women in Vedic times, but closed to them by the later commentators and lawgivers. With the gradual extension of the study period to 12–16 years and the simultaneous drop in the age of marriage for girls, it became impossible for women to do both. Perhaps for a while there were two kinds of women (like Maitreyī and Kātyāyanī in the Upanisads), but it seems that marriage became increasingly crucial. The religious education of women was dropped. By the time of Manu, a girl's wedding ceremony is described as equivalent in religious terms to the boy's rite of initiation; hence the way a married woman wears her saree draped across her left shoulder may be likened to the wearing of the sacred thread. The service of wife to husband is seen to parallel the boy's period of study and service with his teacher. Domestic duties incumbent on the wife correspond to the sacrificial ritual required of the male householder in the second stage.

The last two stages of hermit and renunciate are gradually barred to women. There are frequent epic references to women hermits such as Sulabha, who are described as possessing great knowledge and yogic powers. The *Mahābhārata* even mentions special hermitages for women ascetics. But Manu in his section on forest hermits tells us only that a man becoming a hermit may either commit his wife to his son's keeping or take her with him (VI.3). There is no suggestion that she may take up this stage on her own behalf. For Manu, no woman may ever leave her home to take up the ascetic life (V.149). She must always be controlled by a man: by her father in childhood, by her husband after marriage, by her son after her husband's death (V.148). This is undoubtedly the kind of prejudice the Buddha faced when he was considering the admission of women into his monastic order. In this context, his reluctance is hardly surprising. Even more important perhaps, from the orthodox male point of view, 'female ascetic' is simply a contradiction in terms. For women are wholly identified with the social, familial and sexual world that the (male) ascetic must renounce.

For the ancient lawgivers, then, religious goals and means vary according to the status of the individual. Release may be attained only by male brahmins who fulfil the duties of class and stage and whose lives therefore culminate in the purity of renunciation. Heaven and a good rebirth in the next life may be attained by all other men who fulfil their ordained functions. Women, of whatever class, now constitute an entirely separate category. They may attain heaven and a good rebirth (as a man perhaps) if they fulfil not the dharma of class and stage but the dharma of women. This is to be found in the male-related roles of daughter, wife, mother and widow, and all the obligations that these entail.

The role of wife is of paramount importance. The Visnusmrti intones:

> Obedience to her Lord is the only way for a woman to obtain bliss in heaven. (XXV.15)

This all-important role is perhaps best symbolised by the epic heroine, Sitā, for whom her husband is the incarnation of supreme law in her life, the definition of her religious duty, a god to be appeased (Rāmāyana). The role of mother comes a close second, and is as emotively described. For women must provide their husbands with sons to perform the necessary funeral rites. Without these regular offerings, one's ancestors (literally 'fathers') suffer pangs of hunger in the interim 'world of the fathers'. As social requirements crystallise into religious duty, women become totally dependent on their menfolk for salvation.

If we return once more to the image of the nut with which we began, we find that the outer shell protecting the kernel is now, for women, in two halves. The dark half is the polluted and inherently evil nature of women. For according to Manu, women are naturally lustful, heartless, disloyal, malicious, and so on. These accusations are seen to be proved by the fact of menstruation, a powerful symbol of guilt and pollution throughout Indian literature. If a woman indulges this half of her existential self (i.e. is disobedient etc.), she will go to hell. The bright half of the outer shell is provided by the idealised female roles prescribed by the dharma of women. A woman's religious progress is measured by the degree of her success in these male-related roles; that is, by the existence and continued health of her husband and sons, and by her devotion to them. The propaganda to this effect is persuasive: the truly religious (i.e. virtuous) woman may in this life wield astounding powers, and in the next enjoy the rewards of heaven....

III Devotional Religion

My third general phase of Indian religion is radically different from and opposed to the preceding ones. For devotional religion (bhakti) entails neither
correct ritual practice nor esoteric knowledge, nor even the fulfilment of the
obligations of one's birth and station. It requires only an intense personal relationship with a single supreme God, usually Visnu or Śiva. As long as this
relationship is direct, constant and deeply emotional, the exact form it takes
is less important. Rāvana, for example, retains to the end a fierce hatred of
and opposition to Rāma (an incarnation of Visnu), yet this very ferocity related to God takes him to heaven. Love, however, is the most appropriate
emotion. This may be interpreted in any number of ways: the love of a
mother for her child (as in the worship of the baby Krsna, another incarnation of Visnu), of a child for his parent, of a servant for his master or mistress,
of brothers (as in Laksmana's love for his brother, Rāma), and so on. The only
kind of relationship that is consistently ruled out as a form of worship is devotion to the Goddess on the part of a male devotee identifying himself as
her lover or husband. But the most intense and therefore most effective love
of all is that of a woman for a man. For in devotional terms, both men and
women are spiritually female and God is the only male. While one of the
(male) Vaisnavite Alvārs describes his languishing soul as 'a beautiful
maiden', Mahādevī praises Śiva as one 'for whom men, all men, are but
women, wives'. For though men and women are now equal in the eyes of
God, the male-female hierarchy remains. In the devotional ideal of the agony
and ecstasy of love, the soul of the devotee (whether male or female) must
burn for God as a lovelorn woman burns for her man.

Unlike the bhakti of the Bhagavad Gītā which is strictly controlled and
virtually synonymous with yoga, bhakti proper (such as in the 9th century
Bhāgavata Purāna) is a religion of the heart and passions. The intellectual
bias of Classical religion is swept away: the study of the Vedas and Sanskrit
is replaced by hymns and poems in the vernacular to be sung by all regardless of education or status. The social hierarchies of class, caste and sex are ignored by the doctrine of the grace of God. Salvation in the form of union with
God is now open to all, even women and śūdras, through the practice of
whole-hearted, often abject, devotion. I shall limit my account to two particularly striking forms, one each from Vaisnava and Śaiva devotionalism.

1. Devotion to Visnu

The devotional worship of Visnu is perhaps best exemplified by the
erotic passion of the gopīs (female cowherds) for Krsna in the form of an
amorous and mischievous young man. The gopīs represent the amoral in-
toxication of devotional love: all married women, they abandon husbands,
homes and children without a backward glance in order to seek out their

God. This overpowering devotion takes two main forms. For Caitanya, the devotee identifies himself with Radha, Krsna's favourite gopī, and longs to experience union with Krsna as she did. For Jayadeva, the devotee identifies himself with the other less fortunate gopīs, longing instead to witness that glorious union....

The earliest woman saint in this tradition, however, is probably Antal (6th century A.D.), the only woman among the twelve Alvārs. Her fervent Tamil poems depict the gopīs' total surrender to Krsna as bridegroom, while her Song Divine is still sung daily in Vaisnava shrines. But perhaps Mīrābāi (16th century A.D.) is the most famous woman poet-saint of the tradition. Widowed early, her life of devotion repeatedly obstructed by in-laws more concerned with the orthodox ideals of stridharma, Mīrābāī's early poems sing only of the pain of separation from her Lord Krsna. Later, when her devotion bears fruit, she sings of union and joy: 'My Beloved lives in my heart!' Ostracised at first for her refusal to immolate herself on her husband's pyre in accordance with Rajput custom, Mīrābāī is at last regarded as a saint.

It becomes clear from the literature that, for the female devotee, the Vaisnava path of devotion often takes shape as an uneasy combination of bhakti and stridharma. The gopī model is followed only in part: externally, social conventions are kept; internally, they are broken by the 'illicit' love of God. Bahinabāi, the 17th century Mahārāstrian brahmin saint flouts caste rules by accepting a śūdra as her teacher; yet she discourses in a most orthodox manner on the duties of a woman to obey her husband, control her sexual appetite, and perform her household duties. The example of the gopīs seems to be more a metaphor than a genuine goal. Yet many saintly women are recorded as having resisted the contrary demands of stridharma. Mīrābāī refuses to let herself be burned, the only acceptable widowhood in her community. In one legend, a Kerala saint, determined to resist her family's plans for an arranged marriage, is saved by the intervention of her God who steps out of the image she worships so fervently. Another Kerala saint, rebuked for reciting the Lord's name when she is menstruating, replies unabashed that life may desert her at any moment, even during her period, and she wishes at all costs to be prepared. In yet another tale, a 19th century Andhra saint refuses to shave her head when her husband dies: when the priests shave her by force, her luxuriant hair, symbol of uncensored femaleness, grows back at once. Such stories as these demonstrate that the unimpeded passion of the gopīs in their pursuit of God had to come to terms in one way or another with the orthodox demands of stridharma in real life.

2. Devotion to Śiva

Śaiva devotionalism, unlike the gopī model, is more applicable to the saint-ascetic outside society. Perhaps the earliest female mystic in this tradition is Kāraikkālammaiyār (6th century A.D.), one of the sixty-three

Nāyanārs. She left three Tamil treatises expressing a profound love for God as 'Father' or 'Lord'. Although married, she was so intoxicated by her love for Śiva, so totally absorbed in Him, that she was held to be possessed.

In Viraśaiva devotionalism in particular, the relationship with God, though equally important, is at the same time often less personal, less emotional and more abstract than in the Vaisnava version. While importance is given to the teacher and the community of saints, their model and ideal is the wandering ascetic mystic. Within this framework, the hierarchies of class, caste and sex are accepted as social facts but are never regarded as barriers to religious progress. Devara Dasimayya, a renowned male Virasaiva mystic, demands in one of his poems:

> Did the breath of the mistress
> have breasts and long hair?
>
> Or did the master's breath
> wear sacred thread?
>
> Did the outcaste, last in line,
> hold with his outgoing breath
> the stick of his tribe?
>
> What do the fools of this world know
> of the snares you set,
>
> O Rāmanātha?

For, as he explains elsewhere,

> If they see
> breasts and long hair coming
> they call it woman,
>
> if beard and whiskers
> they call it man:
>
> but, look, the self that hovers
> in between
> is neither man
> nor woman
>
> O Rāmanātha.

Here at last the distinction between the kernel and the outer shell is clear.

The woman's voice is provided by Mahādevī (12th century A.D.). Married against her will to a powerful and worldly man, Mahādevī endeavours to combine the dharma of women with devotion to God. But when her husband jealously obstructs her worship of Śiva, she leaves him to become a wandering ascetic. Whereas the gopīs' love for Krsna is seen as illicit and that owed their husbands as lawful, Mahādevī regards Śiva as her true husband. She exclaims contemptuously in one of her poems:

> Take these husbands who die,
> decay, and feed them
> to your kitchen fires!

For her only goal is Śiva. Since for this end being a woman is irrelevant, Mahādevī breaks all the rules laid down by strīdharma. One poem describes how she must escape the 'traps' set by her in-laws to guard her, all the social conventions that prevent her from following her God. She casts even her clothes aside, wandering naked through the forest. She explains:

> To the shameless girl
> wearing the White Jasmine Lord's
> light of morning,
> you fool,
> where's the need for cover and jewel?

When men molest her in the forest, she speaks movingly of their futile obsession with the physical:

> O brothers, why do you talk
> to this woman,
> hair loose,
> face withered,
> body shrunk?

> O fathers, why do you bother
> with this woman?
> She has no strength of limb,
> has lost the world,
> lost power of will,
> turned devotee,

> she has lain down
> with the Lord, white as jasmine,
> and has lost caste.

Mahādevī reaches the great community of saints, is cross-examined by their teacher, then accepted among them. Before long, intoxicated by devotion, she wanders off again in search of Śiva's holy mountain. At last, she finds it, and Him, and dies. She is in her early twenties.

I shall conclude by moving away from the more extreme examples of such as Mahādevī towards a more representative female point of view. This is persuasively supplied by the story of Cūdālā, taken from the Yoga Vāsistha (ca. 1300). Queen Cūdālā conscientiously performs all the duties entailed by having a husband, a household and a kingdom. But even as she does so, she realises the pointlessness of worldly things. She sees the Truth and becomes enlightened. But when she seeks to share this knowledge with her pleasure-loving husband, he co mmands her to be silent. Recognising that he will never learn from her, Cūdālā asks the court brahmins to preach to him instead. At last, their words prevail and the king too sees the futility of pleasures. Unlike his wife, however, he renounces everything to become a hermit in the forest. Cūdālā does not try to stop him. Instead, she uses her yogic powers to watch over him in secret. She sees that he is now as attached to his hermit existence as he had been to his throne, and that he is as far from enlightenment as ever. She knows he needs guidance but realises that he still cannot accept it from her. So she assumes the body of a young monk (thus demonstrating the irrelevance of her external form), goes to him in the forest, and eventually brings him to an understanding of the Truth. The king attains liberation and returns to his kingdom. There the enlightened couple rule together perfectly for thousands of years. The story ends with the appropriate accolades both to Cūdālā's wifely devotion (according to the dharma of women) and to her wise spirituality. This is the ideal Indian compromise between outer and inner, between kernel and shell.

Postcript

An article in *Kesarī*, a Marathi daily newspaper on 6 November 1981 describes a meeting between a Vedic scholar from Germany and the highly revered religious leader, Śankaracārya Candrasékharendra Sarasvatī of the Kancī Kāmakoti Pith. On being informed that she was learning to recite the Vedas; the Śankaracārya ruled that as a woman she had no right to do so: only Hindu men who had undergone initiation had that right.

References

Abbott, J. E. (tr.) *Bahinā Bāī, A Translation of her Autobiography and Verses*. Poona, Scottish Mission Industries Co. Ltd, 1929.

Alston, A. J. (tr.) *The Devotional Poems of Mīrābāī*. Delhi, Motilal Banarsidass, 1980.

Altekar, A. S. *The Position of Women in Hindu Civilisation*. Delhi, Motilal Banarsidass, 2nd edition 1959, 3rd reprint 1978.

Atharva Veda. See Bloomfield, M. 1897.

Basham, A. L. *The Wonder That Was India.* 2nd edition 1967, London, Fontana, 1974.

Bhagavata Gita. See Zaehner, R. C., 1966.

Bhagavata Purāna. See Burnouf, E., 1800; Sanyal, J. M., 1952.

Bloomfield, M. (tr.) *Hymns of the Atharva Veda, together with Extracts from the Ritual Books and Commentaries.* 1897. Delhi, Motilal Banarsidass, 1978.

Bühler, G. (tr.) *The Laws of Manu, Translated with Extracts from Seven Commentaries.* 1886. Delhi, Motilal Banarsidass, 1979.

——. (tr.) *The Sacred Laws of the Aryas, as Taught in the Schools of Apastamba, Gautama, Vāsishtha and Baudhāyana.* Part I 1879, Part II 1882. Delhi, Motilal Banarsidass. Part I 1975, Part II 1965.

Burnouf, E. (ed. and tr.) *Le Bhagavata Purāna ou L'Histoire Poétique de Krīchna.* 5 vols. Paris, 1840–98 (Vol V. tr. M. Hauvette-Besnault and Le P. Roussel).

Chatterji, K. C. (Sanskrit text and tr.) *Patañjali's Mahābhāsya: paspasahnika.* (introductory chapter). Calcutta, A. Mukherji, 1957.

Filliozat, P. (Sanskrit text and tr.) *Le Mahābhāsya de Patañjali avec le Pradīpa de Kaiyata et L'Uddoyota de Nāgesa, Adhyaya I, Pāda I, Ahnika 1–4.* Pondechery, *Publications de L'Institut Français d'Indologie* No 54, 1, 1975.

Griffith, R. T. H. (tr.) *The Hymns of the RgVeda.* 1889. Revised 2nd edition, Delhi, Motilal Banarsidass, 1973.

Hardy, F. *Emotional, Krsna Bhakti.* Oxford University D.Phil. thesis, 1976.

Jacobson, D. 'The Chaste Wife' in S. Vatuk (ed.) *American Studies in the Anthropology of India.* Delhi, 1978.

Jaini, P. S. *The Jaina Path of Purification.* Berkeley etc, University of California Press, 1979.

Jayal, S. *The Status of Women in the Epics.* Delhi, Motilal Banarsidass, 1966.

Jha, G. *Pūrya-Mīmāsā in its Sources.* Benares, Benares Hindu University. 1942.

Jolly, J. (tr.) *The Institute of Vishnu.* 1880. Delhi, Motilal Banarsidass, 1977.

——. (tr.) *The Minor Lawbooks.* 1889. Delhi, Motilal Banarsidass, 1965.

Kane, P. V. *History of Dharmaśāstra (Ancient and Mediaeval Religious and Civil Law in India),* 5 vols. 1930–62. 2nd edition, Poona, Bhāndarkar Oriental Research Institute, 1968–77.

Leslie, I. J. *The Religious Role of Women in Ancient India.* Oxford University M.Phil. thesis, 1980.

Madhavananda, Swami and Majumdar, R. C. (eds.) *Great Women of India.* Almora, Advaita Ashrama, 1953.

Mahābhārata. See van Buitenen, J. A. B., 1973–78; Roy, P. C. 1919–35; Narasimhan, C. V., 1964.

Manusmarti. See Buhler, G., 1886.

Mirābāī. See Alston, A. J., 1980.

Monier-Williams, Sir Monier. *A Sanskrit-English Dictionary, etymologically and philologically arranged with special reference to cognate Indo-European Languages.* 1899. Oxford, Oxford University Press, 1976.

Narasimhan, C. V. *The Mahābhārata, an English version based on selected verses.* New York etc, Columbia University Press, 1965.

Nikhilananda,. Swami (tr.) *The Gospel of Sri Ramakrishna.* 1942. New York, Ramakrishna-Vivekananda Center, 1973.

O'Flaherty, W. D. (tr.) *The Rig Veda, an anthology.* Harmondsworth, Penguin, 1981.

Oldenberg, H. (tr.) *The Grihva-Sūtras, Rules of Vedic Domestic Ceremonies.* Vol. I, 1886; Vol. II, 1892. Delhi, Motilal Banarsidass, 1967.

Patañjali. See Chatterji, K.C., 1957; Filliozat, P., 1975.

Pānini. See Vasu, S. C., 1891.

Radhakrishnan, S. (Sanskrit text and tr.) *The Principal Upanisads.* 1953. London, George Allen and Unwin Ltd., 1974.

Ramanujan, A. K. (tr.) *Speaking of Siva.* 1973. Harmondsworth, Penguin, 1979.

Rāmāyana. See Shastri, H. P., 1953–59.

RgVeda. See Griffith, R. T. H., 1889; O'Flaherty, W. D., 1981; Shastri, S. R., 1952; Upadhyaya, B. S., 1974.

Roy, M. *Bengali Women.* Chicago etc., University of Chicago Press, 1975.

Roy, P. C. *The Mahabharata of Krishna Dwaipayana Vyasa.* 12 vols. 2nd edition (Revised by E. H. Haldar). Calcutta, Oriental Publishing Co. (undated).

Śabarabhsāya. See Sandal, M. L., 1923–25; Jha, G., 1942.

Sandal, M. L. *The Mīmāmsā Sūtras of Jaimini.* (text, tr. and comm. of Chapters I–XII.) Allahabad, 1923–25. New York reprint, 1974.

Sanyal, J. M. *The Srimad Bhagabatam of Krishna-Dwaipayana Vyasa.* 5 vols. 2nd edition, Calcutta, D. N. Bose, 1952.

Shastri, H. P. (tr.) *The World Within the Mind (Yoga-Vasishta.)* 1937. 5th edition, London, Shanti Sadan, 1971.

———. (tr.) *The Ramayana of Valmiki.* 3 Vols. London, Shanti Sadan, 1953–59.

Shastri, S. R. *Women in the Vedic Age.* Bombay, 1952.

Siegel, L. *Sacred and Profane Dimensions of Love in Indian Traditions as Exemplified in the Gitagovinda of Jayadeva.* Delhi etc., Oxford University Press, 1978.

Singer, M. (ed.) *Krishna: Myths, Rites and Attitudes.* 1966 Chicago and London, University of Chicago Press, Phoenix edition 1968, 1971 reprint.

Upadhyaya, B. S. *Women in RgVeda.* 1933. 3rd edition, Delhi, S. Chand and Co. (Pvt.) Ltd., 1974.

Upanisads. See Zaehner, R. C., 1966; Radhakrishnan, S., 1953.

van Buitenen, J. A. B. (tr.) *The Mahābhārata.* Vols 1–3 (incomplete). 1973–78 Chicago and London, University of Chicago Press, Phoenix edition 1980–81 (2 vols.).

Vasu, S. C. (tr.) *The Ashtādhyāyī of Pānini.* 2 vols. 1891. Delhi, Motilal Banarsidass, 1977.

Visnusmrti. See Jolly, J., 1880.

Warner, M. *Alone of All Her Sex: The Myth and the Cult of the Virgin Mary.* 1976. London etc., Quartet Books, 1978.

Yoga Vasistha. See Shastri, H. P., 1971.

Zaehner, R. C. (tr.) *Hindu Scriptures.* 1938. 2nd edition 1966. London and Toronto, J. M. Dent and Sons Ltd., 1977.

Devadasi Reform:
Driving the Priestesses or the Prostitutes
Out of Hindu Temples?

Kay K. Jordan

The devadasis of India have been characterized by some as Hindu priest-esses and by others as prostitutes. The characteristic common to all devada-sis is that they were women dedicated by their parents or by themselves to serve a deity. These dedications often came about as expressions of gratitude to a deity for the conception or safe delivery of a child or the recovery of a family member from serious illness. The dedication ceremony of a devadasi included a symbolic marriage to the god whom she would serve. All women given in marriage to gods were called *nityasumangali* or ever-auspicious women, because they could never be widowed. As omens of good luck they were asked to dance in marriage processions and to string some of their own beads into the bridal tali which was tied around the bride's neck at the cli-mactic moment of a south Indian wedding. Although forbidden to marry and dwell with mortals, these auspicious women were not expected to re-main chaste. The Hindu *Śāstras* did not regard the devadasis as prostitutes.[1]

Although the devadasis were perceived as positive symbols during the reign of the Hindu kings, changes in both the perception and activities of these missionaries occurred in the nineteenth and twentieth centuries. Criti-cism by foreign journalists of the association of religion and sexual promiscu-ity embarrassed the Indian westernized elite. The loss of both royal patronage and the decline of patronage of wealthy zamindars, the redistribution of wealth away from the temples, urbanization and industrialization also caused changes in the activities of the devadasis and attitudes toward them.

Originally, the word "devadasi," which literally translated means "maidservant of the god," referred to rigorously trained South Indian temple dancing women who served in prestigious temples. These devadasis were actually an occupational group rather than a caste. Acceptance as a devadasi was contingent not upon birth but rather upon initiation through the dedica-tion ceremony and proficiency as a dancer or singer.[2] Social and legal re-formers have chosen to broaden the usage of the term "devadasi" by applying it to any woman dedicated to a deity. The names and duties of women dedicated to serve deities in other parts of India and other sectors of

Kay Jordan, "Devadasi Reform: Driving the Priestesses or the Prostitutes Out of Hindu Tem-ples?" in Robert Baird, ed., *Religion and Law in Independent India* (New Delhi, India: Manohar Publishers, 1993), pp. 257–78 (excerpt).

society varied widely. They were known as *bhavins, naikins, jogtins, basavis, kasbis, maharis, bogam sani, khudikàr,* and *aradhini.* Most of the women being dedicated as devadasis today come from the lower castes and have little or no official temple duties.

The purpose of this essay is to discuss the paradoxical impact of reform legislation on the religious and social status of the devadasis. My thesis is that reform legislation prohibiting devadasi dedication in some cases significantly deprived women of religious status while in other cases such legislation has served to alleviate the exploitation of women. This legislation, which is the result of the secularization of Indian society, restricts the expression of certain Hindu religious beliefs such as the idea that one may gain religious merit by dedicating a daughter to serve a deity or that an individual gains religious merit through such service.

Both before and after independence, the government of India has worked to eliminate devadasi dedication and service as an expression of Hindu piety. The provincial legislatures of Madras and Bombay passed laws aimed at gradually phasing out the devadasis from the Indian religious scene in 1929 and 1934, respectively. Immediately after independence in 1947, the Madras Legislature passed a law banning devadasi dedication. The legislatures of Karnataka and Andhra Pradesh enacted new legislation in 1982 and 1987 respectively because the earlier laws were only partially effective.

Scholars differ in their assessment of whether the prevention of dedication legislation represented a significant denial of religious freedom. J. D. M. Derrett, noting that "the lives of these women did not disturb the Hindu conscience for more centuries than can be counted . . . until missionary-inspired education made Hindus self-conscious about it,"[3] criticized this legislation. To the contrary, Donald Eugene Smith, defending the secularization of the Indian state, argued that while the practices of *sati* and *devadasi* "may have some basis in Hindu religion… the state still has constitutional power to ban them"[4] for the sake of public order, morality and health.

The changes in the legal and religious status of the devadasis reflect the secularization of Indian society. "Secularization" refers to a process by which practices and institutions previously viewed as religious cease to be so regarded and to "a process of differentiation which results in the various aspects of society, economic, political, legal and moral, becoming increasingly *discrete* in relation to each other."[5] Increasingly over the past one hundred years, Indian ideas and institutions have been critiqued or validated by their rationality and benefit to individuals in the temporal world without regard for their connection to the sacred or any concept of the afterlife. Secularization has denied the divine origin of Hindu law and shifted the power of defining social and religious norms and values from brahmins and kings, whose power was divinely mandated, to the governing elite of India who derive their power from the people. Hence, secularization has affected the issue of devadasi dedication by devaluing the connection of the devadasi to the sacred and by giving a secular government the power to regulate religious expression. . . .

Devadasis in Independent India

Before discussing recent devadasi reform legislation we should assess the impact of the 1934 Bombay Prohibition of Devadasi Dedication Act and the 1947 Madras Prohibition of Devadasi Dedication Act and of less direct attacks on the devadasis, such as the withdrawal of government patronage. It appears that devadasi reform legislation effectively ended the dedication and service of temple dancing girls in many prestigious temples, but that such legislation was ineffective in preventing the dedication of low caste women to village temples. Recent literature suggests that devadasi reform has, in some cases, deprived women of religious status and income, but in others has rescued them from exploitation.

Contemporary scholarship presents us with two contrasting portraits of the devadasi. The writings of Marglin, Srinivasan, and Kersenboom-Story describe the devadasis as skilled dancers and ritual specialists who were once revered by society. The publications of the Joint Women's Programme, Shankar's study, and that of Rozario, Rasool, and Kesari present them as low caste and untouchable women exploited by higher castes who lure them into prostitution sanctioned by superstitious religious beliefs. These contrasting portraits complicate the assessment of whether or not devadasi reform legislation unnecessarily restricted religious freedom.

Devadasis Deprived of Religious Status
by Reform Legislation

Let us review the literature which portrays the devadasi as a skilled and dignified ritual specialist who lost status and income because of the passage of devadasi reform legislation. Marglin's study of the devadasis at the Jagganatha temple at Puri asserts that only girls from the castes permitted to give water to brahmins were allowed to become devadasis. In other words, only members of the upper three castes could become devadasis and both *sudras* and untouchables were categorically excluded from such service.[6] These devadasis were not required to remain chaste. Ideally, either the king or brahmin priests might become their paramours. Actually they were permitted to have sexual relations with any member of the water-giving castes of Puri.[7] These devadasis were not considered prostitutes (women who earn their living through the sale of sexual favors), instead they were supported by the patronage of the king. Even when their lovers brought them significant gifts, these gifts were not considered payment for sexual favors.[8] Marglin denied that "temple prostitution" or "ritual intercourse" was practiced by these devadasis, who would never have considered polluting the temple by having intercourse within it.[9]

No laws restricting devadasi dedication have been passed in Puri, but the withdrawal of government patronage has almost completely eliminated devadasi temple service. One devadasi, who desires to carry on the tradition can barely scrape together the money for the flowers and food required by her part in the festival drama of the birth of Krishna.[10] According to Marglin, these devadasis experienced an immediate decline in status when royal patronage ended with the death of Ramcandra Dev in 1958. At about this time, the state took over management of the temple and the pilgrims ceased to pay attention to the devadasis.[11] Although these devadasis were the legitimate heirs to ritual status and the repository of an artistic tradition, representatives of the National Academy of Music and Dance from Delhi visiting Puri snubbed them.[12] The devadasis interviewed by Marglin were seeking husbands for their daughters instead of dedicating them to temple service, because of the lack of support for preserving and maintaining the devadasi tradition.

The dignity of the devadasis of Tamil Nadu described by Amrit Srinivasan is equal to that of the devadasis of the Jagganatha Temple at Puri. These devadasis were not prostitutes in the ordinary sense of the word. Their mothers and grandmothers exercised considerable power in the selection of their lovers, who were generally brahmins or members of the landed and commercial elite. Liaisons with Muslims, Christians or lower caste men were forbidden. Patrons drew status from their association with the devadasis because these women were married to divine husbands. These devadasis functioned as ritual specialists who attracted patronage to the temple through their skill and beauty. Srinivasan's field research did not uncover any evidence of ritual intercourse or tantric practices.[13]

The impetus for devadasi reform, according to Srinivasan, came from two sources: (1) devadasi males who were involved in the anti-Brahmin movement and (2) from Indian nationalists and upper caste women. The men of the devadasi community felt emasculated by matriarchal control of family resources and overshadowed by the prestige of their sisters.[14] During the centuries when the sexual freedom of the devadasis was culturally and religiously acceptable, high caste married women never studied dance for fear that it would damage their reputations. Nationalists, largely composed of upper caste Hindus, supported devadasi reform so they could promote *Bharata Natyam* as an Indian art form free of its association with sexual promiscuity.[15] Hence, Srinivasan asserted that devadasi reform legislation served the needs of the devadasi males and those of the revivalists, but displaced the only female ritual specialists in the Hindu tradition. The high social status of the devadasis, their high degree of artistic talent, and their social acceptance is evidenced by the ease with which many of them married into high caste familes.[16]

Saskia Kersenboom-Story emphasized the cultural and religious importance of the devadasi as a *nityasumangali*, or ever-auspicious woman. The function of a devadasi *nityasumangali* was to protect people from danger and to radiate an energy which helped them to gain wealth, preserve good health, obtain children, and secure marital happiness.[17] According to Kersenboom-Story, confusion regarding the character and activities of the devadasis was rooted in misuse of the term "devadasi." Denying that all women married to deities, who might be *nityasumangalis* could rightfully be called devadasis, she asserted that only women members of the *melakkaran* caste dedicated to deities could properly be called devadasis. Some of the devadasis she interviewed were either formally married to brahmins or "wives on the basis of affection" of brahmins.[18]

Like Marglin and Srinivasan, Kersenboom-Story thought that the decline of royal patronage contributed substantially to the demise of the devadasi tradition. Her assessment of the reform movements is that while "they succeeded in desstroying [*sic*] the most prominent and refined class of *nityasumangalis*," they did not destroy the cultural need for a female symbol of auspiciousness. Hence, the cruder forms of the *nityasumangali* such as the low caste *basivis* (*basavis*) and *Ellamadasis* (*Yellamadasis*) continue to exist and the highly skilled artists who represent the devadasi tradition have been deprived of the temple as the platform and context for expressing their artistry.[19]

In the writings of Marglin, Srinivasan, and Kersenboom-Story, we see a portrait of the devadasis as highly skilled and culturally valued female ritual specialists. We wistfully view their departure from Hindu temples, brought about by devadasi reform legislation and the end of royal patronage.

Other "Devadasis" and the New Reform Legislation

Other recent studies of the "devadasis" suggest that in spite of laws banning devadasi dedication, many girls and women from untouchable castes are dedicated to deities and exploited as prostitutes. One such study was prepared by the Joint Women's Programme, a group which played a significant role in establishing the need for new and effective devadasi reform legislation in Karnataka and Andhra Pradesh. This organization compiled informative reports, met with government officials and held press conferences in support of such legislation.[20] Recent studies by Jogan Shankar and Sister Rita Rozario along with Javeed Rasool and Pradeep Kesari also support the image of the contemporary devadasi as a low caste female dedicated to serve a deity who will probably earn her living as a prostitute.[21]

The government of Andhra Pradesh estimates that there are about 16,000 devadasis in that state.[22] In the Satara District of Maharashtra, as many as 5,000 women may have been dedicated to Krishna by the Mahanubhav sect. The total number of girls in the Maharashtra-Karnataka border area dedicated to Yellamma, Hanuman and Khandoba temples may be as high as 250,000.[23] As many as 5,000 girls are dedicated annually to the goddess Yellamma and later sent to brothels in Bombay and Pune. In the town of Nipani in Belgaum District 200 out of the town's 800 prostitutes are devadasis. The harijan community of Athani (total population 30,000), consists of 5,000 persons divided into 500 families out of which 98% of the families practice religiously sanctioned prostitution.[24] In Yellampura village in Belgaum District (total population 5,700) there were 85 devadasis all from groups identified by the government as scheduled castes. Thirty-nine of these devadasis practiced prostitution.[25] Only a portion of the girls and women dedicated to village deities wind up in urban areas, many of them continue to live in small cities and rural areas where they also practice prostitution. No estimate of the total number of devadasis in India is available. However, it is noteworthy that according to the study completed by Rozario, Rasool, and Kesari which sampled 1100 randomly selected persons who lived in red light districts, public and private rescue homes, areas where girls are often dedicated to deities and later become prostitutes and locations where prostitutes are often recruited, 22.7% of the sample practiced prostitution with some sort of religious sanction.[26]

Some of the low caste women dedicated to deities are called *"basavis."* A *basavi* is generally the child of parents who dedicated their daughter to serve a god because they had no son. According to customary law, a daughter dedicated as a *basavi* and her children are the legitimate heirs to her father's property. A *basavi*, who is permitted to take a regular lover, is forbidden to marry and her children are regarded as belonging to her father's family rather than that of their biological father. Under normal circumstances, the property of a man lacking a son reverts to his male relatives. The term *"basavi"* originally referred to a bull who runs free and may be rooted in the old village custom whereby Hindus sometimes dedicated a breeding bull for village use after the death of a family member.[27] The term "basavi" now refers to a woman who is sexually available.[28]

The girls and women dedicated to Yellamma are categorized as either being devadasis, who cater to men's sexual needs, or as *jogtis*, who serve the goddess without catering to men.[29] The goddess Yellamma, whose full name is Yellamma-Renuka, is popular among low caste people because she is supposedly comprised of a high caste and a low caste woman. One version of the Yellama-Renuka story is that Renuka used to fetch water for the rituals performed by her husband, the sage Jamadagni, in a pitcher of sand balanced upon a snake which served as a head-rest for the pitcher. One day when Renuka went to fetch water she was distracted by handsome Gandharvas frolicking in the water. For an instant, she thought about how she might have married a Gandharva and lived in luxury. Immediately the pitcher of sand, which had been held together by her virtue, crumbled in her hand. Her husband grasped what had happened and ordered his sons to behead Renuka. The two elder sons refused but the youngest, twelve-year-old Parushurama, obeyed. After the deed was done, Jamadagni offered three boons to Parashurama, who immediately asked for the restoration of his mother to life. Jamadagni told the boy to fetch the head of a Matangi woman (a particular untouchable caste) and place it upon the trunk of his mother's body. At once, she came to life and thereafter has been worshipped as Yellamma-Renuka. Since that day, members of the Matangi clan and other untouchable castes have offered their daughters to her for use by her son Parashurama.[30]

The reasons people continue to practice devadasi dedication can be divided into the following four categories: caste exploitation, religious beliefs, economics, and lack of education....

Caste Exploitation Devadasi dedication gives upper castes access to lower caste women and even provides religious sanction for it. The cost of the devadasi dedication ceremony is usually born by a wealthy patron who has the right to spend the first night with the newly dedicated devadasi. According to the Joint Women's Programme, the prevalence of devadasi dedication among low caste groups destroys the self-esteem of their women because this practice is contrary to the usual Hindu emphasis on chastity in women.[31]

Religious Beliefs Impoverished low caste parents, who wish to offer the best they have to the goddess, dedicate their daughters out of sincere religious commitment.[32] The devadasis themselves believe they are serving the goddess. The dedication ceremony makes it possible for them to practice prostitution without being socially ostracized by other castes and also for society to regard their children as legitimate. Although their religious duties are generally negligible, their acceptance as auspicious women in high caste homes on particular ritual occasions gives them a sense of importance and self-worth.[33] Other religious beliefs which perpetuate devadasi dedication include fear that the goddess will be angry if at least one daughter is not dedicated, belief in the sanctity of religious vows, belief that the goddess specifically chooses some women by causing a jat or knot to grow in their hair. An aging devadasi may influence parents to dedicate a daughter by soothsaying and oracles which are sometimes motivated by a bribe from a patron or by that devadasi's need to adopt a daughter to care for her in her old age. Shankar blames the oppressive patriarchal ideology of Hinduism for the persistence of devadasi dedication.[34] . . .

Devadasi Reform and Religious Freedom

Does devadasi reform legislation violate the provisions of the Indian Constitution which guarantee freedom of religious expression to both individuals and groups? Devadasi reform legislation definitely prevents women from voluntarily dedicating themselves to serve a deity and also restricts the freedom of religious expression of parents who sincerely believe that dedicating a daughter to serve a deity protects them from divine wrath, brings about blessings in this life, or contributes to their salvation.

Article 25 of the Indian Constitution guarantees all citizens freedom of religious belief and expression with certain limitations. It states:

Art. 25   (1) Subject to public order, morality and health and to the other provisions of this Part, all persons are entitled to freedom of conscience and the right freely to profess, practice and propagate religion.

(2) Nothing in this article shall affect the operation of any existing law or prevent the state from making any law—

(a) regulating or restricting any economic, financial, political or other secular activity which may be associated with religious practice;

(b) providing for social welfare and reform or the throwing open of Hindu religious institutions of a public character to all classes and sections of Hindus.[35]

While devadasi reform legislation restricts the free expression of religion, such legislation is in accord with the Indian Constitution which specifies that religious freedom is guaranteed subject to "public order, morality and health." From the viewpoint of the government, the prostitution of the devadasis was a violation of commonly accepted norms of morality. Another limitation on the free expression of religion is that the state shall not be precluded from "providing for social welfare and reform." The government could easily justify banning devadasi dedication as a means of reducing the incidence of prostitution in India and thereby reforming and benefitting society.

The Preamble of the Indian Constitution affirms the dignity of every individual; guarantees social, economic and political justice; equality of status and opportunity; as well as liberty of thought, expression, belief, faith and worship.[36] The practice of devadasi dedication limits the freedom of individuals and also diminishes the the dignity of women. In most instances, devadasis are dedicated by their parents and are thereby prevented from later choosing to marry or lead a life more attuned to the generally accepted moral norms of society. The prostitution which so often follows devadasi dedication makes sex a commodity to be purchased rather than the expression of a relationship between two persons and diminishes the dignity of the woman who sells herself or is sold by others.

The ban on devadasi dedication is also in accord with Article 46 of the "Directive Principles of State Policy," which states that "the State shall promote with special care the educational and economic interests of the weaker sections of the people, and in particular, of the Scheduled Castes and the Scheduled Tribes, and shall protect them from social injustice and all forms of exploitation.[37] The term "scheduled castes" refers to those groups who have traditionally experienced social discrimination. Most of the girls and women dedicated as devadasis today belong to scheduled castes. The poverty and ignorance prevalent in these castes cause parents to dedicate daughters to serve deities. Legislation banning such dedication reduces the exploitation of these castes who are giving up their women to lives of prostitution in which they will be exploited by procurers and customers. Hence, again we see that restricting the practice of devadasi dedication is in accord with the Indian Constitution.

Conclusion

Society's perception of the devadasis and, in fact, the identity, character and activities of the devadasis have changed significantly over the past century. In the late nineteenth century, the British colonial court system acknowledged them as a distinct and identifiable group of women possessing their own customary law of adoption and inheritance. British colonial officials refused to pass reform legislation specifically directed at the devadasi community because a significant number of Hindus regarded them as an essential part of their religious tradition. The Indian westernized elite pressed for devadasi reform because they believed they had the right to distinguish between appropriate and inappropriate expressions of the Hindu tradition.

The reform legislation passed by provincial legislatures along with the decline of royal patronage drove the devadasis who might be considered to be Hindu "priestesses" from prestigious temples. There can be no doubt that these women lost religious status and that the Hindu tradition lost a powerful symbol of feminine auspiciousness.

The goal of recent devadasi reform legislation is to eliminate religiously sanctioned prostitution which involves the exploitation of the impoverished and illiterate lower castes by educated and economically secure persons belonging to higher castes. While this legislation restricts the religious freedom of parents who wish to dedicate daughters to a deity and that of women who feel called to dedicate themselves to a deity, such limitations are in accord with the Indian Constitution. The secularization of Indian society has caused the government to assume the authority to distinguish appropriate expressions of religion from inappropriate expressions. The government of India, like other modern nations, is more concerned with the temporal well-being of its citizens than their spiritual well-being. While prohibiting devadasi dedication which frequently leads to prostitution, premature aging, and death from sexually transmitted diseases may limit the free expression of religion, it certainly contributes to the temporal well-being of potential victims of this custom. With proper enforcement, the new legislation may succeed in driving religiously sanctioned prostitution from Hindu temples.

Devadasi reform legislation has indeed had a paradoxical impact on the role of women in the Hindu tradition. On the one hand, it is sad that there are no female ritual specialists in Hindu temples and that the devadasi is fast fading as a symbol of feminine auspiciousness. On the other hand, it is good that low caste girls and women will no longer be dedicated for the purpose of satisfying the lust of upper caste men.

Notes

1. K.K. Pillay, *The Sucindram Temple* (Adyar, 1953), p. 287.
2. Amrit Srinivasan, "Reform and Revival: The Devadasi and Her Dance," *Economic and Political Weekly* 20/44 (November 2, 1985), p. 1869.
3. J. Duncan M. Derrett, *Religion, Law and the State in India* (London, 1968), p. 452.
4. Donald Eugene Smith, *India As a Secular State* (Princeton, N.J., 1963), p. 4.
5. M.N. Srinivas, *Social Change in Modern India* (Berkeley, 1966), p. 119.
6. Marglin, Frederique Affel. 1985. *Wives of the God-King: The Rituals of the Devadasis of Puri* (Delhi 1985).
7. *Ibid.*
8. *Ibid.*
9. *Ibid.*, p. 90.
10. *Ibid.*, p. 39.
11. *Ibid.*, p. 87.
12. *Ibid.*, p. 34.
13. Srinivasan, *Loc. cit.*, 1869–70.
14. *Ibid.* p. 1873.
15. *Ibid.*, pp. 1874–75.
16. Amrit Srinivasan, "Temple 'Prostitution' and Community Reform: An Examination of the Ethnographic, Historical and Textual Content of the Devadasis of Tamil Nadu, South India" (Unpublished Ph.D. diss., Cambridge University, 1984), pp. 2, 16.
17. *Ibid.*, p. 205.
18. Kersenboom-Story, Sashia, 1987. *Nityasumangali: Devadasi Tradition in South India*. Delhi: Motilal Banarsidass,
19. *Ibid.*, p. 207.
20. Joint Women's Programme (JWP), 'The Devadassi Problem," *Banhi* (1981/2) and JWP, "Prostitution with Religious Sanction," *Banhi* (1989).
21. Sr. M. Rita Rozario, Javed Rasool, and Pradeep Kesari, *Trafficking in Women and Children in India: Sexual Exploitation and Sale* (New Delhi, 1988), pp. 53–54. Jogan Shankar, *Devadasi Cult: A Sociological Analysis* (New Delhi, 1990).
22. Shanker, *Loc. cit.*, p. 49.
23. *Ibid.*, pp. 16–17, 18.
24. Rozario, Rasool, and Kesari, *Loc. cit.*, pp. 53–54.
25. Shanker, *Loc. cit.*, pp. 98–99, 106.
26. *Ibid.*, p. 47.
27. Fred Fawcett, "On Basivis: Women Who Through Dedication to a Deity Assume Masculine Privileges," *Journal of the Anthropological Society of Bombay*, vol. II, 1892, p. 322.
28. For further discussion of *basavis*, see Rozario, Rasool, and Kesari, *Loc. cit.*, p. 81

and JWP, "Venkatasani," and "The Basavi Cult," in "Prostitution with Religious Sanction," *Banhi* (1988), pp. 49–61, pp. 1–20.

29. JWP, "The Devadasi Problem," *Loc. cit.*, p. 7.
30. Rozario, Rasool, and Kesari, *Loc. cit.*, p. 52.
31. JWP, "The Devadasi Problem," *Loc. cit.*, pp. 12, 31.
32. Shanker, *Loc. cit.*, p. 125.
33. *Ibid.*, p. 124.
34. *Ibid.*, p. 163.
35. Quoted in Smith, *Loc. cit.*, p. 135.
36. G.C. Venkata Subbarao, *Computerised Constitution of India* (Hyderabad, 1985), p. 1.
37. Quoted in Shankar, *Loc. cit.*, p. 89.

Religious Ideology, Hindu Women, and Development in India

Vanaja Dhruvarajan

Development efforts in modern India have largely failed to help women because of the male-centered religious ideology of pativratya. This ideology encourages the adoption of a submissive and dependent position by Hindu women. There is a lack of political will to transcend this ideology because the status quo is beneficial to those in positions of power and privilege. Unless women who will be the beneficiaries of change demand it, changes in related policies and programs will not come about. This article proposes a series of action programs informed by the ideal of gender equality in order to diminish this oppressive ideology and empower women to demand necessary changes.

For the first time in India's history, gender equality has claimed legitimacy, since women's equality rights have been enshrined in the constitution.

From *Journal of Social Issues*. 46:3:1990, pp. 57–69. Reprinted with permission of the Society for the Psychological Study of Social Issues and Vanaja Dhruvarajan.

Prior to this event the possibility of equality for women was not debatable and in many contexts was even considered sacrilegious. Since India became a republic, informed by the tenets of egalitarian ideology, various legal changes have been brought about through the efforts of enlightened leadership (ICSSR, 1975). These laws define many rights of women, including inheritance of property; provision of opportunities in the educational and occupational spheres; political rights to vote, run for office, and hold office; and rights of divorce and custody (Desai & Krishnaraj, 1987). These laws have provided a conducive atmosphere for women to become equal participants in the developmental process and beneficiaries of various efforts on the part of the Indian government. Even though the legal reforms have a long way to go to ensure absolute equality with men and to provide an efficient framework for the realization of gender equality, important beginnings have been made in opening opportunity structures for women in the eyes of the law.

Nevertheless, after more than 30 years, the impact of these reforms on the realization of gender equality remains uncertain. The demographic trends suggest that in many instances conditions for women are worse than before. While some segments of the female population, particularly those in the middle and upper middle classes in urban areas, have derived some benefits from the developmental efforts, other segments have suffered (Dhruvarajan, 1989). The female-to-male sex ratio has gone down for most age groups. The unemployment rate among women especially in the rural areas has gone up since men are consistently favored for upgrading of skills. Female fetus abortions are on the rise because more efficient technology is available to achieve this objective. Neglect of female children is still very prevalent. "Dowry deaths" (in which educated young men raise their financial position by finding ways to kill their wife and then keeping her dowry), and violence against women in general are on the rise (Desai & Krishnaraj, 1987).

There seems to be a tremendous lack of political will to implement laws that promote gender equality. This is revealed by the fact that egalitarian values and ideals have not become part of the public discourse. The police are slow in responding to calls for help in cases of domestic violence. Dowry deaths are dismissed as suicides. The laws referring to property inheritance remain vague, and efforts are not made to define them clearly and implement them systematically. The media portrayal of ideal relationships between men and women romanticizes the subordination of women. The curriculum in schools and colleges remains dated—the old assumptions about gender inequality are not questioned. Even the simple effort to inform all students regarding their citizenship rights is not carried forth. Students are not made aware of the structure of the constitution and of the laws that promote gender equality. Equal pay for work of equal value is not consistently implemented. By and large men and women are steered into gender-stereotyped jobs. Training for upgrading of skills for management positions is routinely reserved for men. Day care facilities for workers with young children are rarely provided (Desai & Krishnaraj, 1987; ICSSR, 1975; Lebra, Poulson, & Everett, 1984).

The reason for this state of affairs is that a distinction is made between public and private spheres. The notions of privacy and sanctity of private life place it beyond the purview of secular laws. India is a secular state; in political terms, this does not mean that religion is outlawed but rather that the state ensures the coexistence of multiple religious ways of life. Private life is governed by religious precepts, and public life is governed by secular laws. The family system is patriarchal, patrilineal, and patrilocal. Women have been consistently denied economic self-reliance. Marriage is considered a must for all women, which means that the wife/mother role is the only legitimate role available for women. Men are in charge of productive labor, while women's duty is considered to be reproductive labor, which is unremunerated and devalued. Women's participation in the public sphere is a function of and is circumscribed by their position in the family.

Religious Ideology

The Hindu religious ideology of *pativratya*, which literally means husband worship, provides legitimacy for the state of affairs described above. This ideology defines women's position as subordinate to their husbands. According to the tenets of this ideology a woman finds meaning and fulfillment in this life and salvation hereafter only in diligently serving her husband in any way he deems appropriate. The principle of subordination of women to men espoused by this ideology is applicable to all castes. As Allen and Mukherjee state,

> For the village men, that is the men of the world, women were substantively, though variously, valued; by the Brahmins as pure indices of high status, by the Kshatriya and Vaisya as fertile producers of progeny, and by the Sudra as sources of material and sensuous satisfaction. For the forest-dwelling seeker after *moksha*, that is, for this world-renouncer who has removed himself from the phenomenal world of social process, women were negatively viewed as without value. Controlling women, dominating them and using them for their own benefit by the men is considered proper and legitimate in all castes. (1982, p. 16)

The socialization experiences women go through in this ideological context is for dependence, which results in women devaluing themselves. The status of wives goes up as soon as they become mothers. Women as mothers exercise control over their daughters and daughters-in-law. The power women are accorded is to socialize their daughters and daughters-in-law to become pativratas. Essentially, women as mothers are coopted into the patriarchal family and become active participants in the reproduction of subordination of women through generations.

Certain assumptions and beliefs regarding the nature of men and women form the basis for this ideology. Men are believed to be ritually pure, physically strong, and emotionally mature. Women are believed to be ritually pollutable, physically weak, and lacking in will power. The philosophical underpinnings of this ideology are that male and female principles are different, but they need to come together to create and sustain life. The male principle represents consciousness and the female principle energy. The male provides the seed for creation and the female provides soil to nurture the seed. For an orderly life that is in keeping with nature, the man who provides the seed and the embodiment of consciousness should be in control of the woman with her pollutable body and undirected energy (Dhruvarajan, 1989). As Marchak points out, this ideology, just like any other dominant ideology,

> provides the ready references, the rules of thumb, the directives to the eyes and ears of its members. It is the glue that holds the institutions together, the medium that allows members of the population to interact, predict events, understand their roles, perform adequately, and—perhaps above all—strive to achieve the kinds of goals most appropriate to the maintenance of any particular social organization. (1975, p. 1)

Hindu conceptions of ideal womanhood are defined within this ideological context. An ideal woman is an ideal wife—a pativrata. Even those women in middle and upper-middle classes in urban areas, who have taken advantage of the educational and occupational opportunities, do not question this belief system. They try to accomplish their professional goals the best they can—if they can—by negotiating their way through the system as it exists. Many of these women, especially in lower, middle classes, perform double shift work because they cannot afford to refuse paid work and are unable to hire domestic help (Ramu 1989)....

As Daly (1973, p. 13) points out, "The belief system becomes hardened and objectified, seeming to have an unchangeable, independent existence and validity of its own. It resists social change that would rob it of its plausibility."

Possible Strategies for Change

It is obvious from the above discussion that subordination of women to men has political and economic advantages for those in positions of power and privilege. The unremunerated reproductive labor provided by women is the cheapest way of providing labor for society. Devaluation of women and their definition as dependents of men has provided conducive conditions for exploiting women as a cheap reserve labor force. Men who have been the beneficiaries of the subordination of women have become used to their position of centrality. As Goode (1982) points out, this state of affairs is a part of their taken-for-granted reality, and they find it very difficult to give it up.

The only way any changes are brought about is when women, the prospective beneficiaries of change, make demands. The political climate is favorable for such action since women's equality rights are enshrined in the constitution and to a certain extent in the laws of the land. But women's lives are circumscribed by the ideology of pativratya, which is built into the patriarchal family structure and dominates life in the private sphere. To prevent women from doing the bidding of the patriarchal family and to help them become advocates of their own rights, ways have to be found to discredit the androcentric ideology in favor of an egalitarian one. As Nemiroff writes,

> It is urgent for those people who strive for social change, for a society with equality between the sexes, to analyse the belief systems underlying these "strategies" for power and equality. Not only must ideology precede action and inform it with both consistency and meaning, but it is only through the discipline of a shared ideological base that the "Powerless" may become empowered to assume rightful control over their own lives. (1987, p. 531)

Several social institutions can aid in reaching this goal. Let us consider the possible roles of religion, education, the mass media, and women's groups.

Religion

To make gender equality a reality, active efforts have to be made to discredit the ideology of pativratya. The beliefs regarding the nature of the female body on which this ideology is based have to be questioned.

The various myths that dramatize the mystique of female sexuality—which is thought of as unbridled and insatiable—and the belief that women's bodies are susceptible to ritual pollution invoke fear and disgust. Such control myths magnify these emotions, making women develop a negative body- and self-image. As Lipman-Blumen (1984) has shown, control myths maintain and perpetuate the power imbalance between men and women. In contrast, as far back as 1926, Gandhi presented an equalitarian view on the issue of female purity, saying, "and why is there all this morbid anxiety about female purity? We hear nothing of women's anxiety about men's chastity. Why should men arrogate to themselves the right to regulate female purity?" (cited in Jayawardena, 1986, p. 96).

The rituals and symbolism that popularly signify women's transition from one stage of life to the other can be reinterpreted to emphasize the positive aspects. Such a tradition is prevalent even though not highlighted. For example, in my study in an Indian village (Dhruvarajan, 1989), the puberty rituals among *Vokkaligas* (a Sudra subcaste) highlighted aspects of fertility, youth, and awakening of sexuality, whereas among Brahmins, susceptibility to ritual pollution was highlighted. Clearly, the performance of puberty rituals can signify either of these aspects. Rituals during the marriage ceremony can emphasize the spirit of equality between spouses that is available in Hindu mythology (Upadhyaya, 1974, pp. 73–82). These efforts will help create conditions where women can develop a positive body/self-image.

Discussion of alternative goals for women's lives in addition to those of wife/mother, which are morally equivalent and considered legitimate by religion, can be of help in removing the rigid constraints imposed by pativratya on women's lives. Instead of fitting themselves into prescribed roles, women can then choose alternate paths for the achievement of self fulfillment. Even the wife/mother role can become one that is consciously chosen rather than ordained by destiny. Life in that context will allow various choices in ways desired by individual women.

During the Bhakti Era, many women saints rejected the ideology of pativratya by refusing to worship a husband as god. Instead they chose god as a husband and tried to find salvation for themselves (Kishwar & Vanita, 1989). Thus they defied conventions and carved a niche for themselves to suit their own individual needs. Such efforts should inspire women of today to fashion their lives to suit their own needs at the present time. Jayawardena (1986) has demonstrated that, even though not always recognized, there is a tradition of questioning the Hindu ideal of womanhood—the pativratya. As Mazumdar (1976) writes, Gandhi declared himself unable to subscribe to the doctrine of the infallibility of ancient lawgivers who had denied freedom to women and suppressed their development.

Thapar (1987) points out how particular images of women from the past have been chosen for projection and emulation. She demonstrates how, among many different types of images of Indian epic heroines, the docile, shy, and obedient images have been emphasized, even though other versions, where they were portrayed as confident, articulate, and assertive, were in fact available. This indicates the possibility that, through conscious deliberation, appropriate images that empower women can be chosen and portrayed for emulation.

Based on evidence from oral history, archaeological evidence, and religious practices, Liddle and Joshi (1986) argue that male dominance and female subordination were achieved after a struggle between native Dravidian belief in the superiority of the female power principle and the invading Aryan belief in the superiority of the male power principle. Even though eventually the invaders had their way, they could not completely obliterate the Dravidian belief system. The matrilineal traditions in some parts of India, especially in the state of Kerala, have managed to survive to a certain extent. This tradition has had effects on women in contemporary Kerala, as indicated by the fact that the status of women is highest there on almost all indices. In addition, it is this heritage that accounts for the fact that women's ability to achieve is not questioned among Hindus even today. Women are dominated and subjugated because of the fear of female power rather than contempt, as has been true in the West.

Hindu conceptions of femininity give much scope for new interpretations because of the ambiguity in beliefs regarding the nature of the female character and personality. Jacobson and Wadley (1977) point out that when women are conceptualized as mothers they are strong willed, self-directed, proud, and dignified, while as wives they are compliant and weak. The role of the mother is subsumed under the wife role, thereby leading to adoptation of mothers into the patriarchal family. But possibilities do exist for reinterpreting these roles in a creative way to facilitate the empowerment of women as mothers. Jacobson and Wadley (1977) illustrate how Indira Gandhi, the former prime minister of India, was accepted by Indians since she was conceptualized and portrayed as a "mother goddess." . . .

Conclusion

This paper argues that unless a new life plan informed by an ideology of gender equality is prepared and used to guide action programs, the position of Hindu women in India will continue to deteriorate. Unless women who will be the beneficiaries of changes toward gender equality demand it, changes will not be made. A concerted effort needs to be made by agencies such as religion, education, the media, and women's groups to raise women's awareness of their position so that they will become capable of demanding such changes. The difficulties in reaching women who are confined in the patriarchal family must be recognized, and even if these efforts are successful, the current generation of women may not benefit personally from this process of consciousness raising. However, if the current generation of women as mothers socialize their children to embrace the ideology of gender equality, the next generation of men and women will be better equipped to usher in an egalitarian society. The next generation of women, if they have been socialized for autonomy and self-reliance rather than dependence, will be in a better position to demand implementation of changes that are necessary in order to achieve gender equality.

References

Allen, M., & Mukherjee, S. N. (1982). *Women in India and Nepal.* Canberra, Australia: Australian National University.

Beteille, A. (1965). *Social change in modern India.* Berkeley: University of California Press.

Bookman, A., & Morgen, S. (1988). *Women and the politics of empowerment*. Philadelphia: Temple University Press.

Desai, N., & Krishnaraj, M. (1987). *Women and society in India*. Delhi: Ajanta.

Dhruvarajan, V. (1989). *Hindu women and the power of ideology*. Granby, MA: Bergin & Garvey.

Goode, W. J. (1982). Why men resist. In B. Thorne (Ed.), *Rethinking the family: Some Feminist questions*. New York: Longman.

Haksar, N. (1985). Women and public interest litigation: A decade of struggle. *Samya Shakri: A Journal of Women's Studies, 2*(1).

Hale, S. (1987). *The elusive promise*. Montreal: Centre for Developmental Studies.

Indian Council of Social Science Research (ICSSR). (1975). *Status of women report*. New Delhi: Allied.

Jacobson, D., & Wadley, S. S. (1977). *Women in India: Two perspectives*. New Delhi: Manohar.

Jayawardena, K. (1986). *Feminism and nationalism in the third world*. London: Zed.

Kishwar, M. (1984). Some aspects of bondage: The denial of fundamental rights to women. In M. Kishwar & R. Vanita (Eds.), *In search of answers: Indian women's voices from Manushi* (pp. 230–242). London: Zed.

Kishwar, M., & Vanita, R. (1989). Poison to nectar: The life and work of Mirabai. *Manushi*, No. 50–52, pp. 74–93.

Lebra, J., Poulson, J., & Everett, J. (Eds.), (1984). *Women and work in India: Continuity and change*. New Delhi: Promilla.

Liddle, J., & Joshi, R. (1986). *Daughters of independence: Gender, caste and class in India*. London: Zed.

Lipman-Blumen, J. (1984). *Gender roles and power*. Englewood Cliffs, NJ: Prentice Hall.

Marchak, P. M. (1975). *Ideological perspectives on Canada*. Toronto: McGraw-Hill Ryerson.

Mazumdar, V. (1976). The social reform movement in India—From Ranade to Nehru. In B. R. Nanda (Ed.), *Indian women*. New Delhi: Vikas.

Mies, M. (1980). *Indian women and patriarchy*. New Delhi: Concept.

Mies, M. (1986). *Patriarchy and accumulation of capital on a world scale: Women in the international division of labour*. London: Zed.

Mies, M., Bennholdt-Thomsen, V., & Werlhof, C. V. (1988). *Women: The last colony*. London: Zed.

Nemiroff, G. H. (Ed.). (1987). *Women and men: Interdisciplinary readings on gender*. Montreal: Fitzhenry & Whiteside.

Omvedt, G. (1975). Caste, class and women's liberation in India. *Bulletin of Concerned Asian Scholars, 7*.

Pathak, Z., Rajani, R. S. (1989). Shahbano. *Signs, 14*, 558–582.

Ramu, G. N. (1989). *Women, work and marriage in urban India*. New Delhi: Sage.

Reck, A. J. (Ed.). (1964). *Selected writings: George Herbert Mead*. Indianapolis: Bobbs-Merrill.

Srinivas, M. N. (1968). *Social change in modern India*. Berkeley: University of California Press.

Thapar, R. (1987). Traditions vs. misconceptions. *Manushi*, No. 42–43, pp. 2–14.

Upadhyaya, B. S. (1974). *Women in Rigveda*. Bombay: S. Chand.

Questions for Discussion

1. What is the relationship between female gender imagery and the status of "real" women in Hinduism? What factors can you point to that help explain this relationship?
   - What factors can you point to that help explain this relationship?
2. Does Hinduism provide women with resources to empower themselves in a patriarchal and sexist society, or does it simply legitimate and reinforce that society?
3. What impact has Hinduism had on development efforts for women?
4. What influence did British colonialism have on women's status in Hinduism?
5. Does the role of devadasi strengthen or weaken the moral agency and identity of the women involved?
   - What influence has devadasi reform had?
6. Would the status of women in Hinduism improve if more women were given roles of spiritual authority?
   - Do the readings make you optimistic or pessimistic about this possibility being realized in the future?

References and Materials for Further Study

Books and Articles

Babb, Lawrence. 1975. *The Divine Hierarchy: Popular Hinduism in Central India*. New York: Columbia University Press.

———. 1984. "Indigenous Feminism in a Modern Hindu Sect." *Signs: Journal of Women in Culture and Society* 9, 3: 399–416.

Cooke, Miriam. 2001. *Women Claim Islam: Creating Islamic Feminism Through Literature*. New York: Routledge.

Dhruvarajan, Vanaja. 1990. "Religious Ideology, Hindu Women, and Development in India." *Journal of Social Issues* 46, 3: 57–69.

Feldhaus, Anne. 1999. "Hinduism: Religious Rites and Practices," in Serinity Young, ed., *Encyclopedia of Women and World Religion*. New York: Macmillan Reference.

Findly, Ellison Banks. 1999. "Hinduism: An Overview," pp. 418–24 in Serinity Young, ed., *Encyclopedia of Women and World Religion*. New York: Macmillan Reference.

Hawley, John Stratton. 1994. "Hinduism: *Sati* and Its Defenders," in John Hawley, ed., *Fundamentalism and Gender*. New York: Oxford University Press.

Hawley, John Stratton, and Donna Wulff. 1996. *Devi: Goddess of India*. Berkeley: University of California Press.

Hopkins, Thomas. 1971. *The Hindu Religious Tradition*. Belmont, CA: Wadsworth Publishing Company.

Jacobson, Doranne, and Susan Wadley. 1977. *Women in India: Two Perspectives*. Columbia, MO: South Asia Books.

Johnsen, Linda. 1994. *Daughters of the Goddess: The Women Saints of India*. St. Paul, MN: Yes International Publishers.

Jordan, Kay. 1993. "Devadasi Reform: Driving the Priestesses or the Prostitutes Out of the Hindu Temples?" in Robert Baird, ed., *Religion and Law in Independent India*. New Delhi, India: Manohar Publishers.

Kalwant, Bhopal. 1998. "South Asian Women in East London: Religious Experience and Diversity." *Journal of Gender Studies* 7, 2: 143–56.

King, Karen, ed. 1997. *Women and Goddess Traditions: In Antiquity and Today*. Minneapolis, MN: Augsburg Fortress. Essays by Erndle, Humes, Wulff, and Gupta on Hindu women and goddesses.

Kinsley, David. 1986. *Hindu Goddesses: Visions of the Divine Feminine in the Hindu Tradition*. Berkeley: University of California Press.

Kumari, Ranjana. 1985. "Femaleness: The Hindu Perspective." *Religion and Society* 32, 2: 3-10.

Leslie, Julia, ed. 1991. *Roles and Rituals for Hindu Women*. Rutherford, NJ: Fairleigh Dickinson University Press.

———. 1989. *The Perfect Wife: The Orthodox Hindu Woman according to the Stridharmapaddhati of Tryambakayajvan*. Delhi, India: Oxford University South Asian Series.

———. 1983. "Essence and Existence: Women and Religion in Ancient Indian Texts," pp. 89–112 in Pat Holden, ed., *Women's Religious Lives*. London: Croom Helm.

Marglin, Frederique Affel. 1985. *Wives of the God-King: The Rituals of the Devadasis of Puri*. Oxford: Oxford University Press.

———. 1985. "Female Sexuality in the Hindu World," in Clarissa Atkinson, Constance Buchanan, and Margaret Miles, eds., *Immaculate and Powerful: The Female in Sacred Image and Social Reality*. Boston: Beacon Press.

Mitter, Sara. 1991. *Dharma's Daughters: Contemporary Indian Women and Hindu Culture*. New Brunswick, NJ: Rutgers University Press. Written by an American woman married to an Indian man. Part II deals with Sakti, Sridharma, the conflicting images and roles of women in Hinduism.

Narayaran, Vasudha. 1999. "Hinduism: In the West," in Serinity Young, ed., *Encyclopedia of Women and World Religion*. New York: Macmillan Reference.

———. 1990. "Hindu Perceptions of Auspiciousness and Sexuality," pp. 64–92 in Jeanne Becher, ed., *Women, Religion, and Sexuality*. Philadelphia: Trinity Press.

Orr, Leslie. 1999. "Recent Studies of Hindu Goddesses." *Religious Studies Review* 25, 3 (July): 239-446.

Pintchman, Tracy. 1994. *The Rise of the Goddess in the Hindu Tradition*. Albany: State University of New York Press.

Raheja, Gloria Goodwin, and Ann Grodzin Gold. 1994. *Listen to the Heron's Words: Reimagining Gender and Kinship in Northern India*. Berkeley: University of California Press.

Ratte, Lou. 1985. "Goddesses, Mothers, and Heroines: Hindu Women and the Feminine in the Early Nationalist Movement," in Yvonne Yasbeck Haddad and Ellison Banks-Findly, eds., *Women, Religion, and Social Change*. Albany: State University of New York Press.

Robinson, Catherine. 1999. *Tradition and Liberation: The Hindu Tradition in the Indian Women's Movement*. New York: St. Martin's Press.

Robinson, Sandra. 1985. "Hindu Paradigms of Women: Images and Values," in Yvonne Yazbeck Haddad and Ellison Banks Findly, eds., *Women, Religion, and Social Change*. Albany: State University of New York Press.

Seager, Joni. 1997. *The State of Women in the World Atlas* (new edition). London: Penguin Books Limited.

Thampuran, K.V.K. 1985. "Hinduism and Its Impact on Women," *Religion and Society* 32, 2: 11–19.

Thompson, Catherine. 1983. "Women, Fertility and the Worship of Gods in a Hindu Village," in Pat Holden, ed., *Women's Religious Lives*. London: Croom Helm.

Wadley, Susan. 1977. "Women and the Hindu Tradition," *Signs: Journal of Women in Culture and Society* 3: 113–25.

Wulff, Donna Marie. 1985. "Images and Roles of Women in Bengali Vaisnava *padavali kirtan*," pp. 219–45 in Yvonne Yazbeck Haddad and Ellison Banks Findly, eds., *Women, Religion, and Social Change*. Albany: State University of New York Press.

Young, Katherine. 1994. "Introduction," in Arvind Sharma, ed., *Today's Women in World Religions*. Albany: State University of New York.

———. 1994. "Women in Hinduism," in Arvind Sharma, ed., *Today's Woman in World Religions*. Albany: State University of New York Press.

Internet and Media References

The Committee on South Asian Women (COSAW):
  http://http.tamu.edu/~e305jj/cosaw.html.
Journal of South Asia Women Studies:
  http://www.asiatica.org/publications/jsaws/default.asp.
Offical Home Page of Ma Amrittanandamayi:
  http://www.ammachi.org/.
Sawnet: South Asian Women's Network:
  http://www.umiacs.umd.edu:80/users/sawweb/sawnet/.
South Asian Diaspora Women: A Bibliography:
  http://www.lib.berkeley.edu/SSEAL/SouthAsia/ women.html.
South Asian Women's Network:
  http://www.umiacs.umd.edu/users/sawweb/sawnet.

Women and Buddhism

Overview

As is the case with some of the other traditions we will meet later in this volume, especially Christianity and Islam, Buddhism is a "world religion." As such, it has evolved in significantly different ways in the cultures it has been introduced into, resulting in an incredible variety of different Buddhist schools and traditions. Buddhism began in India in the fifth or sixth century B.C.E. after Siddhartha Gautama attained "Enlightenment" or "liberation," became the "Buddha" (a Sanskrit word meaning "awakened one"), and began teaching the spiritual path (*dharma)* that he had discovered to others. Over the next few centuries, what later became the "Northern School" or Mahayana (the "Great Vehicle") Buddhism spread into China in the second century C.E., from China to Korea in the fourth century C.E. and in Japan by the sixth century, and from India to Tibet by the eighth. What became the "Old" or "Southern School" of Buddhism, referred to polemically by Mahayanists as Hinayana ("small" vehicle—in the sense of being inferior), of which now only the Theravada tradition (literally, "the tradition of the elders") remains, spread into Sri Lanka by the sixth century and then into the mainland countries of Thailand, Cambodia, Laos, and Vietnam between the ninth and thirteenth centuries. For a time, Buddhism was also practiced in what is now Central Eurasia and parts of the Middle East (present-day Iran, Iraq, and Turkey, the Uzbhek Republics, Mongolia, and surrounding regions) as well as parts of Indonesia. Buddhism died out in

India, the land of its birth and early development, somewhere around the twelfth century, the victim of too many invasions from the Mongols and other foreigners, as well as the rise of Hinduism and, later, Islam.

As Buddhism moved into new cultural contexts, it not only influenced the preexisting cultures and religions but was also transformed by them. For instance, in China (where Buddhism was introduced in the second century C.E.), Buddhist religion confronted the Confucian tradition, which was very pro-family and had no tradition of celibacy, one of the primary requirements for being a Buddhist monk. Buddhism in China today (more prominently in Taiwan and Hong Kong)[1] is practiced at the popular level together with aspects of Confucianism and Taoism as well as indigenous folk religions. The influence of folk traditions is also evident in Buddhist practices in Burma (the *Nat* cult), Nepal, and Tibet (the native Bon religion). In Japan, Buddhism and Shinto worship are sometimes integrated, and in Sri Lanka and Nepal, it is common to find temples with both Buddhist and Hindu elements.

Buddhism was first introduced into the West in the eighteenth century but did not become popular until the nineteenth century, when figures such as Ralph Waldo Emerson and Henry David Thoreau disseminated it through their writings to the larger culture. Waves of immigrants to North America from China and Japan during this time period also brought many Buddhist practitioners but had little evident influence on mainstream society. Then, after a period of relative disregard, interest in Buddhism arose again in the 1950s with the "Beat Generation." Writers and poets like Jack Kerouac and Alan Ginsberg discovered Buddhism; D.T. Suzuki became a well known Zen (a school of Japanese Buddhism) teacher and author and celebrities like the Beatles in the 1960s and 1970s introduced Buddhism (especially Zen) to the American counterculture.

The brutal takeover of Tibet by China in 1959, which destroyed hundreds of Buddhist monasteries and persecuted many thousands of Buddhist monks, causing them to flee the country or disrobe (renounce their Buddhist vows and return to lives as lay persons), had the ironic consequence of spreading Buddhist teaching and practices in the West. The exodus of Tibet's spiritual leader, His Holiness the Dalai Lama, and many other Tibetan Buddhist teachers and spiritual leaders *(Lamas* and *Rinpoches)* on the eve of China's takeover (or thereafter) has brought Tibetan Buddhist culture to centers throughout North America and Europe. All four of the main traditions of Tibetan Buddhism are represented in the United States, Canada, Australia, and other Western European countries. In addition, U.S. military stationed overseas during Vietnam, and Peace Corps volunteers stationed in Asian countries during the 1960s and 1970s, returned to the United States having learned Theravada forms of Buddhist practice, especially *Vipashyana* or "Insight Meditation." In sum, Buddhism has been transformed by the many cultural contexts it has encountered and continues to be reshaped and also to reshape the cultures where it is practiced.

There are tremendous variations among the different schools of Buddhism. The "Southern School" or Theravada traditions of South and Southeast Asia regard the *Pali Canon* (the oldest strata of Buddhist scriptures still extant) as authoritative and exhaustive of the Buddha's teachings. In contrast, the Mahayana (and its offspring, the "Vajrayana" or "the Diamond" or "Adamantine" vehicle, which is based on tantric ["esoteric"] teachings and is practiced in Tibet and parts of Mongolia, Bhutan, and Sikkhim) recognize a much wider range of texts as authoritatively Buddhist. Despite this tremendous variation, however, there are a few commonalities shared almost universally across the different Buddhist schools and traditions. One is acceptance of Siddhartha Gautoma, born in Lumbini India in the fifth or sixth century B.C.E., the son of a Ksatriya king, as having attained "Nirvana" or Enlightenment after years of spiritual searching and becoming the Buddha (sometimes called "Sakyamuni" or "King of the Sakyas"). This historical figure is also accepted by all Buddhists as the founder of the Buddhist religion (at least in this world system and time in history) and the expounder of at least some of the teachings which are practiced to this day.

According to the tradition, after hesitating for seven weeks after attaining Nirvana, the Buddha was convinced by the God Brahma to teach the Dharma. During his first sermon, he taught "the Middle Way," the path between the two extremes of sensual indulgence and self-torture. This Middle Way is contained in the "Four Noble Truths" and the "Eightfold Noble Path." In brief, the Four Noble Truths are the truth of suffering (as the inevitable condition of existence in this world, or *Samsara*); the cause of suffering (craving or attachment to what is impermanent because of wrongly perceiving it to be permanent); the cessation of suffering (through renunciation of attachment); and the path to the cessation of suffering (the Eightfold Noble Path).

This Path requires acting with

1. right view (understanding the Four Noble Truths)
2. right effort (acting skillfully)
3. right speech (refraining from lying, harsh, divisive, gossip)
4. right action (abstaining from killing, stealing, or sexual misconduct)
5. right livelihood (avoiding occupations which cause harm)
6. right effort (avoiding negative mental states and cultivating positive ones)
7. right mindfulness (of the body, feelings, mind-states, mental qualities)
8. right concentration (meditation).

The Buddha's second teaching was on the "Five Skandhas," the five constituents or aggregates of all persons (form, feeling, sensation, formations, and consciousness), and their character as bearing the "Three Marks of Existence," that is, being impermanent, having the quality of suffering, and having no intrinsic or ultimately real self or identity.

Buddhists everywhere, both lay and monastic, become and maintain their identity as Buddhists by taking "refuge vows" in the "Three Jewels"— the Buddha, the Dharma, and the Sangha (referred to variously as the official [male] monastic institution); the entire community of Buddhist practitioners, both law and monastic, or the assembly of *Bodhisattvas*—"Buddhas in training" or "Buddhas to be"; and the Five Precepts (vows not to harm, to misuse speech, have wrongful sex, take intoxicants, or steal). From these basic foundational teachings have arisen incredibly diverse and complex Buddhist traditions, which have somewhat similar understandings about the significance of gender and gender differences.

Relationship of Female-Gendered and Feminine Images and Symbols to "Real" Women

In general terms, earlier (Theravadan) texts tend to contain more negative images and symbols of women and the female, especially of women as sexual temptresses, who deliberately tempt (otherwise chaste and virtuous) men away from the spiritual path. Scholars have suggested that the negative images of women in many early Buddhist texts, especially as sexual temptresses, indicate that monks considered women's sexuality as a threat, not only to their pursuit of the spiritual path, but also to the stability of the monastic order as a whole, and even to the cycles of birth and death within *samsaric* existence as a whole (Sponberg 1992, 20; Lang 1986, 64; Paul 1985, 303; Falk 1974, 108). In contrast, Mahayana texts as a whole reflect a broader array of feminine images, ranging from the most misogynistic to the most elevated of spiritual doctrines.

The use of the female body as a symbol of attachment to the world of sensuality is a common theme throughout the Buddhist world, beginning with the story of the Buddha's renunciation of lay life, and his rejection of his new wife Yasodhara and newborn son Rahula. The Buddha's struggle under the Bodhi tree for Enlightenment years later involves rejecting the sensual enticements of Mara's "daughters" who have been sent to seduce him away from his spiritual goal. Women's identity is depicted in Buddhist scriptures as embodied and social, embedded in relationships with others, and dependent on things of this "world"—the world of *samsara* or suffering. Buddhist scriptures emphasize that women are attached to the material world of the senses and emotions, in contrast to men, who are more able to practice detachment, and, consequently, pursue the spiritual path (see, e.g., Murcott 1991; Rhys Davids and K.R. Norman 1989; Sponberg 1992, 20; Lang 1986, 64; Paul 1985, 303; Falk 1974, 108).

In popular Buddhist understanding, to be born a woman is itself the result of previous bad *karma* (the sum of actions in previous lives). In fact, many Buddhist scriptures state, among a number of derogatory and misogynistic comments, that a woman can only achieve Enlightenment after having been reborn as a male. But in order to obtain such a favorable rebirth, females must enhance their store of merit (virtue required to acquire good *karma* for this and future lives). However, the exclusion of women from the official male monastic establishment (the *Sangha*), discussed below, forecloses an important means of making merit which is accessible to males and contributes to the denigration of females in Buddhist cultures by providing "evidence" of their spiritual inferiority.

Mahayana texts include both negative and positive images of women. In some scriptures, women are argued to be inherently weak in intellect and virtue, traits which would certainly limit their capacity for Buddhahood (Schuster 1985, 102), and are in fact denied entrance to a Buddha land. In other scriptures, women are accepted as either lower-stage or advanced *Bodhisattvas* (Paul 1985, 169). In addition to these textual depictions of women and the feminine, however, the very highest qualities of Enlightenment are symbolized in female form. *Prajnaparamita*, the "Perfection of Wisdom," for example, is symbolized as a female goddess in India and Tibet.

In China, the Indian *bodhisattva Avolokiteshvara* was transformed into the female *Kuan Yin*, one of the most highly revered spiritual figures in Chinese popular religion. Similarly, Tibetan Vajrayana texts contain a multitude of female images, many of them quite positive. These include symbolic representations of the perfection of wisdom as the Goddess *Tara*, multitudes of *Dakinis* (a kind of female goddess or spirit who renders spiritual assistance to practitioners), and a number of female bodhisattvas and female "consorts" or partners of male Buddhas (see Campbell 1996; Gross 1993; Klein 1994; Shaw 1994; Havnevik 1990).

Women's Relationship to Buddhism

Women-Specific or Distinctive Aspects of Buddhism

Unlike some religions we will explore in this volume, including African, Hindu, and Goddess traditions, there is little that might be considered to be distinctively female practices or traditions in Buddhism. In general, it has been a male-dominated tradition throughout its history, and women have struggled just to be included. Indeed, one of the great ironies of the relationship between women and Buddhism is that women are (and evidence shows that they were in the very early period of the tradition as well) far greater supporters of Buddhist institutions and practices than men have been. For example, Tessa Bartholomeusz points out that women are the main participants at almsgiving ceremonies and in temple life and are also the majority of participants at the lay insight meditation centers that have emerged in recent decades in Thailand, Burma, and Sri Lanka (Bartholomeusz 1999, 125-126). Indeed, it is accurate to say that women are the main supporters and social reproducers of the Sangha, both as almsgivers and sustainers of the infrastructure of monastic and religious institutions. Without their support, it would be extremely difficult for the Sangha to sustain itself.

Yet, despite their disproportionately greater support for Buddhism, women seeking spiritual careers are not supported by Buddhist institutions. In Southeast Asian Buddhist countries, for example, the prevailing belief is that women fulfill their spiritual obligations through their domestic duties as wives and mothers and are not required to make additional efforts. This ideology makes it quite difficult for many women to renounce lay lives and the traditional gender role expectations that they will be wives and mothers. Frequently, they receive no social or familial support and live lives of near destitution as a result (see Bartholomeusz 1999, 124-25).

To the extent that there have been traditions and practices distinctively for women, they have tended to make women's lives more difficult, such as the eight *Gurudharma* ("Special Rules"), described below, and the *Vinaya* (the code of conduct or ethical rules for monastics) for ordained women, which includes a number of obligations and restrictions applicable to nuns that are not included in the *Vinaya* for monks.

Nonetheless, monastic institutions for women (for which we will use the Christian terms "convent" or "nunnery") have been one place where women have to some extent been able to develop a "separate sphere" away from male control and regulation. Many women have felt liberated by renouncing lay life for a spiritual existence with "sisters" who shared their spiritual aspirations. Freed from the obligations of domestic and childbearing and childcaring responsibilities, many Buddhist renunciants have written glowingly of their good fortune at having left lay life for a spiritual one. In China, women could join either a nunnery or a semi-monastic vegetarian society, which also enabled them to avoid marriage. Similar unofficial monastic or semi-monastic institutions for women are now emerging in countries like Thailand, Burma, and Sri Lanka.

Another aspect of some Buddhist cultures is to make available separate educational facilities for females, often providing opportunities that are not available in the wider society. This is true, for example, in Taiwan. The viability of Buddhist monastic and/or educational institutions for women are to a large degree dependent upon the financial and other support of lay women. Given the traditional belief that it is more meritorious to make *dana* donations to monks rather than nuns, however, it often has been difficult for nuns and other women seeking spiritual training to be adequately supported. One counterexample is Nepal, where a revival of Theravada Buddhism has been underway since the late nineteenth century. In that country, despite the lack of official ordination for women, female lay renunciants are supported to the same extent that male monks are and have equivalent authority.

Gender-Based Segregation and Inequalities

Some examples of gender-based inequalities in Buddhism have already been noted. In general, Buddhist cultures everywhere devalue women. In addition, females throughout the Buddhist world, whether monastic or lay, generally receive an inferior education to that of males, although there are significant variations among different countries (with Taiwan having one of the strongest systems of education for Buddhist women and Thailand, Sri Lanka, and Tibet having the weakest).

As Karme Lekshe Tsomo, an American woman ordained in the Tibetan Buddhist tradition, tells us in her essay "Mahāprajāpatī's Legacy," the traditional story of how women first became nuns is a troubling one. According to the tradition, the Buddha's aunt Mahāprajāpatī traveled across India with several hundred other women, barefoot and without resources, for weeks in order to request the Buddha to allow women to enter the Sangha (the official monastic establishment) and was refused on three separate occasions. Then, the legend goes, Mahāprajāpatī petitioned Ananda, the Buddha's faithful servant, who agreed to ask on her behalf. When the Buddha was unable to answer "no" to Ananda's questions regarding whether women lacked the capacity to attain Enlightenment, the Buddha relented and allowed women to enter the Sangha. However, the texts relate that as a condition for allowing women's ordination, the Buddha propounded the *Eight Gurudharma* ("Special Rules") that formalize the subordinate relationship of nuns to the male monks and establish the superiority of the male Sangha. One possible explanation for the Buddha's reluctance in admitting women to the Sangha is the sexism of the ancient India at the time of the Buddha, which made enabling women to lead independent, spiritual lives a radical act. Nonetheless, according to the tradition, the Buddha's acceptance of women's request for ordination as nuns was accompanied by the prophecy that as a result, the *Dharma* would flourish for five hundred years less time than otherwise.

Women's ordination was established in several Buddhist countries, including India (sometime during or before the fourth century C.E.), China (in 357), Korea (fourth century C.E.), Sri Lanka (434), and Japan (sixth century). The earliest nunnery or convent for which there is historical evidence was founded in 312 C.E. The female Sangha died out (undoubtedly at least in part because of the lack of support from the official male sanghas and laity in those countries) by about the eleventh century everywhere except countries that follow the Chinese *Vinaya* (the rules that govern members of the Sangha, of which there are several different versions).

In some countries, like Korea, the full ordination ceremony for the *Bhikshuni* Sangha has been reintroduced (in Korea, this happened only in 1982). In other countries, such as Thailand, a formal order of nuns was never established to begin with. Many Buddhist women in countries that do not now have an official ordination ceremony for the *Bhikshuni* order (this includes all Theravada communities of South Asia [India, Nepal, and Sri Lanka] and Southeast Asia [Thailand, Burma, Laos, Cambodia, Vietnam]) have renounced lay life nevertheless and have taken vows to uphold some portion of the hundreds of vows contained in the *Vinaya*.

A modern movement to reestablish ordination for women, led in part by the Buddhist women's organization *Sakyadhita* ("Sisters of the Buddha"), has encountered determined resistance from the official Sanghas in some countries, especially Thailand and Sri Lanka. However, many Buddhist women from traditions where ordination is not possible (including Tibet, Thailand, and Sri Lanka) have traveled to Korea or Taiwan and received their *Bhikshuni* vows there, even though ordination "outside of their tradition" is not officially recognized by the male monastic establishments of their homelands. Some Buddhist women object to the movement for women's ordination, however, on the grounds that formalizing women's status in the Sangha would resubject them to the control and authority of male monks. While they may be given less respect and fewer resources as "unauthorized" renunciant women, lay nuns and female monastics now have the freedom to practice the *Dharma* and organize their lives as they see fit.

Regardless of whether their status as nuns is officially sanctioned by the Sangha or not, however, female renunciants throughout the Buddhist world have a secondary status compared with that of male monastics. They are generally less respected and provided with fewer resources, in part because of the view prevalent throughout Buddhist countries that making donations (*dana*) to male monastics earns greater merit than making donations to females. (This is again ironic, given that the greatest support for the Sangha comes from lay women, who are most often the ones making food offerings to monks who make daily rounds to beg for alms.)[2]

In general, then, Buddhist women are not considered to be the equals of Buddhist men in either lay or monastic contexts. However, there is tremendous variation across cultures. In the West, for example, where equality between men and women has been established, at least as a formal, legal matter, there is far less overt discrimination. In countries like Thailand and Sri Lanka, however, the inequalities have been so entrenched for so long and in such institutionalized ways that it is difficult to imagine how much effort will have to be expended to eliminate them. Nevertheless, change is possible. In Japan, for example, Soto school nuns waged a determined campaign and were finally officially recognized by the school as formal equals to the monks (Levering 1999, 123). Similar campaigns are underway in other Buddhist countries.

Women's Access to Religious Training and Education and Opportunities for Leadership Roles

As Tsomo's essay shows, it was necessary for women to struggle to gain entrance into the official Sangha. Once the Buddha was required to admit that they were as spiritually capable as men, however, he gave them access to dharma teachings and provided them with opportunities for spiritual advancement. In general, however, throughout Buddhist history, it has been more difficult for women to obtain access to the Dharma, especially in regard to formal teachings in a monastic setting.

Especially since the *Bikkshuni* Sangha died out in several Buddhist countries, the opportunities for women to receive Dharma teachings and practices have been more limited than those available to men. There are marked differences in attitudes toward women's education and spiritual training, however. Whereas attitudes in Vietnam are fairly hostile and paternalistic, in Korea women have the same opportunities available that men have. In Japan, even though it was women who were responsible for the first Buddhist temple being built (in the sixth century), during the Heian period (794–1185), women were prohibited from entering the major Buddhist study and practice centers out of concern about sexual liaisons with the men there. This ostracism led to the view that women were spiritually inferior and defiling (Levering 1999, 123). Yet during the Kamakura period (1185–1333), women studied in the Zen school with the most respected male masters. Thus, views and attitudes toward women in different Buddhist cultures influence access to their opportunities for spiritual training and education.

At the very beginning of Buddhist history, Mahāprajāpatī demonstrated powerful leadership abilities, both in bringing 500 barefoot women across India with her to request that the Buddha admit women into the Sangha and in continually entreating the Buddha (and his attendant, the famous monk Ananda), until the Buddha agreed to do so. Since that time, however, there have been very few legendary women Buddhist leaders. This speaks more to the extreme androcentrism and sexism of the organized Sangha throughout the Asian Buddhist world, however, than it does to the lack of Buddhist women's leadership abilities.

As with their access to education and spiritual training, women over the centuries have had widely varied experience with respect to leadership opportunities, depending on historical and cultural particularities. There are numerous examples of female heads of abbeys, teachers, lamas, and adepts throughout the tradition. For example, the narratives that describe the establishment of Buddhism in Sri Lanka specify that both monks and nuns were responsible. In the Muromachi period in Japan, some women were received as *Dharma* heirs (Buddhist master teachers and leaders) and organized their major convents into a system paralleling that of the male monks. (Since then, however, nuns in Japan generally have not received much support or social recognition from the major Buddhist schools to which they belong [Levering 1999, 123]).

Today, there are a growing number of female Buddhist teachers and heads of monastic institutions, both in Asia and in the West. Within North America, for example, prominent Buddhist leaders who are women include Pema Chodron, the abbess of Gampo Abbey in Nova Scotia; Joan Halifax, the head of a Zen Peacemaker Order Center in Santa Fe, New Mexico; Sharon Salzberg, a nationally known Vipashyana teacher and author; Ruth Denison, Vipashyana teacher and founder of Dhamma Dena Meditation Center in the Mohave Desert; Joanna Macy, an engaged Buddhist leader and social activist; Khandro Rinpoche, a young Tibetan lama who directs Samten Tse monastery in Uttar Pradesh, India, and teaches extensively in Europe and North America; Karme Lekshe Tsomo, who established both the Tibetan Nuns Project and Sakhyadita, an organization founded to promote the interests of Buddhist nuns; and Jetsun Ma, originally from Brooklyn, New York, who was recognized by the head of the Nyingma lineage of Tibetan Buddhism as a "tulku" (a reincarnated person of great spiritual advancement) and heads Tibetan Buddhist Centers in Maryland and Arizona.

Given their greater involvement and participation in Buddhist practice, it is possible that as time goes on, women will dominate the leadership positions of Buddhist institutions, especially if women's ordination is reestablished in countries where it is now absent. In Korea today, for example, there are more than 6,000 nuns, many of whom play prominent roles in directing the affairs of the Sangha.

Well-Known and/or Influential Women in the Tradition

Within Buddhist scriptures, the most prominent women are the Buddha's aunt and stepmother, Mahāprajāpatī, who succeeded in gaining access to the Sangha for women, the Buddha's mother Maya, who died within a few days of his birth (but, like Jesus' mother Mary, conceived him "immaculately," here in a dream of a white elephant); and his wife, Yasodhara, whom Prince Siddhartha abandoned for his quest for Enlightenment soon after she had given birth to his son Rahula. Within each tradition of Buddhism are notable women, only a few examples of which can be noted here.

Stories of exemplary nuns in China are recorded in a seventh-century text called *Biqiunizhuan* ("Lives of Nuns") and the eighteenth-century *Shan nuren zhuan* ("Lives of Good Women"). In Taiwan, the nun Shig Hiu-wan founded an academic Buddhist studies program and a university. In Tibet, famous female Buddhist practitioners include Yeshe Tsogyal and Machig Labdron, who are featured in a set of hagiographical biographies by Tsultim Allione called *Women of Wisdom* (1984). Also see "Famous Women Who

Happen to Be Buddhist" and "Female Buddhas and Bodhisattvas According to Tibetan Buddhist Tradition," under Internet resources below.

Outside of North America, Buddhist women with international reputations include An San Suu Kyi, Nobel Peace Prize recipient and leader of the pro-democracy movement in Burma/Myanmar; Ayya Khema (who died several years ago), a German nun who started a women's retreat center on an island in Sri Lanka; Chatsumarn Khabilisingh, author of *Women in Thai Buddhism*, and a key leader in the movement to reestablish ordination for women in Thailand; and many meditation teachers in Burma and Thailand. The list is growing longer all the time as more opportunities for Buddhist women emerge.

Changes in the Status of Women

Historically

The status of women in Buddhism has varied widely in different time periods and in different cultures. We have already considered some of the changes that have occurred in the portrayals of women and the feminine as the Buddhist tradition developed from the Southern School traditions into the Mahayana and Vajrayana, as well as changes in the status of Buddhist nuns and other renunciant women over history. In some Buddhist countries, more opportunities have been opened to women in recent years to become Dharma teachers and meditation instructors, especially in Buddhist lay movements. The status of Buddhist women has improved markedly in some countries, such as Thailand, Burma, and Sri Lanka, and then declined again.

In China, for example, Buddhist schools such as T'ien-t'ai, Hua-yen, and Ch'an (Zen) all recognized that all beings, regardless of gender, have the same potential for Enlightenment. At the same time, however, they also perpetuated the idea from the earliest Buddhist scriptures that it is more difficult to gain Enlightenment in a female body than a male one. Nonetheless, Ch'an recognized women as equal in merit to male teachers and spiritual guides from its beginnings in the twelfth century (see Levering 1999, 121).

Future Prospects

At the present time, the status of Buddhist women in the West is generally much greater than in Asia. Recent issues of prominent Buddhist periodicals, for example, have focused on women and feminism (*Turning Wheel* 1999; *Shambhala Sun* 2000). International organizations of Buddhist women like Sakyadhita, as well as networking connections made possible through the Internet, have the potential to significantly alter the status of Asian Buddhist women in the future. As several commentators have noted, it is likely that Western Buddhists will continue to advocate for equality for women, both in Western as well as Asian institutions. The extent to which such efforts will result in tangible changes in the status of Buddhist women, especially female monastics in Asian countries, remains to be seen, however.

The readings for this chapter span almost two millenia, beginning with translations of a poem (*gathas*) written by an early Buddhist nun (*theris*) from Susan Murcott's *The First Buddhist Women*, and ending with an essay by Ouyporn Khuankaew, a contemporary Thai Buddhist nun. Her essay "Thai Buddhism: Women's Ordination or More Prostitution?" discusses how negative attitudes toward women in Thai Buddhist culture contribute both to their exclusion from full ordination as nuns as well as to their participation in the prostitution industry. Mediating these ancient and contemporary perspectives by Buddhist nuns is an essay by Karme Lekshe Tsomo, an American nun ordained in the Tibetan Buddhist tradition. Her essay "Mahāprajāpatī's Legacy: The Buddhist Women's Movement" provides an overview of the emergence and development of women's participation in Buddhism.

NOTES

1. Buddhism is not widely practiced in the People's Republic of China today since the Communist regime attempted to completely suppress religious practice from 1949 to 1980 and since then has continued to impose restrictions which prevent the free exercise of religion, as illustrated by its efforts to eliminate the Falung Gong "cult" in recent years, and to suppress Tibetan Buddhism.
2. Begging for alms is part of the earliest Buddhist tradition, still practiced by certain (non-Buddhist) asetics in India, and in most Southeast Asian Buddhist countries, of living only on the basis of what is provided by the generosity of others.

The First Buddhist Women: Translations and Commentaries on the *Therigatha*

Susan Murcott

Ambapali

Her origins were supernatural. According to legends, Ambapali came to birth spontaneously in the city of Vesali. She was discovered by a gardener at the foot of a mango tree—her name, Ambapali, means "mango protectress," or "mango guardian." She was so astonishingly beautiful that princes fought to possess her. The strife was settled by appointing her the chief courtesan of Vesali. Because of her, Vesali was said to have become very prosperous.

Among Ambapali's patrons was King Bimbisara. Like Padumavati, Ambapali also bore a son by Bimbisara who became a Buddhist monk. These sons seem to have become convincing proselytizers; Ambapali's son too was influential in his mother's decision to renounce the world.

Ambapali abandoned fame and money to become a devout Buddhist disciple. She had never heard the Buddha preach, though he was by now a man in his late sixties or early seventies, with a wide reputation and following. When Ambapali learned that Gautama was preaching in a nearby town, she went out to meet him and hear his sermon. She also invited him and his monks to eat with her the coming day. Gautama accepted, and though later that day he received a similar invitation from the powerful and prestigious Licchavis tribe, he postponed that lunch until the day after his lunch with Ambapali, in order to keep his promise to her.

When the next day dawned, the Buddha warned his monks to guard their passion and to be careful not to lose their heads over Ambapali. From Ambapali's point of view, the event was a great success. As a result, she built a hermitage on her land and gave it to the sangha. It was in that very place that the Buddha rested in his eightieth year, four months before he died.

Ambapali's poem, while not a formal meditation—as, for instance, the meditation on the thirty-two parts of the body—similarly seeks to bring the image of impermanence into focus. In this respect it is a serious poem. But it also strikes us, and probably struck the ancient Indians as well, as humorous. For this reason, it is the only poem in this collection which has been translated into rhyme, as rhyme seems befitting of its humor.

From Susan Murcott 1991. *The First Buddhist Women: Translations and Commentaries on the Therigatha*. Berkeley, CA: Parallax Press (excerpted). Reprinted with permission of Parallax Press.

It is interesting to note the striking parallels between Ambapali's poem and another ancient love poem, the bridegroom's poem in the *Song of Songs*. Both compare the beauty of a woman to the most resplendent things in nature. But whereas the bridegroom, King Solomon, in the *Old Testament* poem can see only the beauty, Ambapali's poem emphasizes the contrast between former beauty and the ugliness of old age. Here is an excerpt from the *Song of Songs:*

How beautiful you are, my love,
how beautiful you are!
Your eyes behind your veil
are doves;
your hair is like a flock of goats
frisking down the slopes of Gilead.
Your teeth are like a flock of shorn ewes
as they come up from the washing.
Each one has its twin,
not one unpaired with another.
Your lips are a scarlet thread
and your words enchanting.
Your cheeks, behind your veil,
are halves of pomegranate.
Your neck is the tower of David
built as a fortress,
hung round with a thousand bucklers,
and each the shield of a hero.
Your two breasts are two fawns,
twins of a gazelle,
that feed among the lilies.

While the bridegroom's song strikes us as lovely, Ambapali's poem evokes a mixture of humor and disgust. That Ambapali's poem succeeds so well in evoking disgust means that it has achieved its purpose. Such poetry was first and last religious, not aesthetic. Here the purpose was to jolt the listener into anxiety about her or his own transiency, hopefully stimulating in that person the desire to renounce the world and strive for enlightenment.

My hair was black and curly
the color of black bees.
Now that I am old
it is like the hemp of trees.
This is the teaching of one who speaks truth.

Fragrant as a scented oak
I wore flowers in my hair.
Now because of old age,
it smells like dog's hair.
This is the teaching of one who speaks truth.

It was thick as a grove
and I parted it with comb and pin.
Now because of old age,
it is thin, very thin.
This is the teaching of one who speaks truth.

I had fine braids
fastened with gold:
Now old age
has made me bald.
This is the teaching of one who speaks truth.

My eyebrows were crescents,
painted well.
Now they droop, and
are wrinkled as well.
This is the teaching of one who speaks truth.

My eyes flashed like jewels,
long, black.
Now they don't make
anyone look back.
This is the teaching of one who speaks truth.

My earlobes are beautiful
as bracelets, highly-crafted and bright.
Now they sag
and have wrinkles alright.
This is the teaching of one who speaks truth.

My teeth were beautiful
the color of plantain buds.
Now because of old age
they are broken and yellow.
This is the teaching of one who speaks truth.

I had a sweet voice
like a cuckoo moving in a thicket.

Now cracked and halting
you can hear my age in it.
This is the teaching of one who speaks truth.

My neck was beautiful
like a polished conch shell.
Now because of old age
it bends and bows.
This is the teaching of one who speaks truth.

My arms were beautiful
twin pillars, they hung free.
Now because of old age,
they are weak as the patali tree.
This is the teaching of one who speaks truth.

My hands were beautiful
set off by rings gold as the sun.
Now because of old age
they are radishes or onions.
This is the teaching of one who speaks truth.

My breasts were beautiful
high, close together and round.
Now like empty water bags,
they hang down.
This is the teaching of one who speaks truth.

My thighs were beautiful
like an elephant's trunk.
Now because of old age
They are like bamboo stalks.
This is the teaching of one who speaks truth.

My calves were beautiful
gold anklets I wore as jewelry,
Now these same calves
look like sticks of sesame.
This is the teaching of one who speaks truth.

My feet were beautiful
delicate as if filled with cotton.
Now because of old age

they are cracked and rotten.
This is the teaching of one who speaks truth.

This is how my body was.
Now it is dilapidated,
the place of pain,
an old house
with the plaster falling off.

Mahāprajāpatī's Legacy:
The Buddhist Women's Movement
An Introduction

Karma Lekshe Tsomo

Buddhist Women Face Their History

Several centuries before the Christian era began, an aristocratic woman by the name of Mahāprajāpatī began a spiritual and social revolution in northern India. After trudging several hundred miles barefoot across the dusty plains to make her point, she lobbied Śākyamuni Buddha, who was both her nephew and stepson, for an order of women renunciants.[1] Due to her courageous agitation for equal opportunity, the Buddha affirmed the equal potential of women to achieve spiritual enlightenment and recognized their right to wear the robes of a Buddhist mendicant. The Buddha was unable to ensure the total reformation of patriarchal Indian society, however. After the Buddha's death, earlier modes of gender relations gradually reasserted themselves. The positive attitude toward women evident among the early Buddhists seems to have declined sharply around the time written Buddhist literature began to appear. These texts contain contradictory statements on women, who are portrayed as capable of enlightenment on par with men and also as sirens luring men from the spiritual path. These ambivalent attitudes toward women persist today in the minds and institutions of Buddhist Asia.

As we read through studies on the interrelationship between Buddhism and political power in Asia over the past two and a half millennia, we are struck by the conspicuous lack of information on women. We encounter a few scattered references to prostitutes or beggars in the garb of nuns, yet women are rarely mentioned as playing a role in either religion or politics, two of society's most important spheres of activity. Ample attention is given to the monks' order, the Bhiksu Sangha, and its role in religion and politics. Clearly this sector of society is a force to be reckoned with in any analysis of the region. Throughout history, the support of the Sangha has been actively sought as a means of legitimation by those wishing to gain and maintain positions of political power in Buddhist countries.[2] When we look closely, however, we find that in certain Buddhist countries—Burma, Cambodia, Laos, Sri Lanka, and Thailand—women are categorically denied admission to the Sangha, Buddhism's most fundamental institution.

However egalitarian the Buddha's original teachings may have been, today preconceptions about the inferiority of women prevail in Buddhist cultures. Although these attitudes may trace to patriarchal social mores with no verifiable connection to Buddhist tenets, women have consistently been excluded from religious structures. They certainly are not barred from commerce or agriculture—where there is profit to be gained from her endeavors, a woman is given free rein. In many cultures, she is in control of affairs within the family, such as the keys, the finances, the children, and decisions of major importance. In the realm of the unseen or transcendent, however, she is thwarted, as if the spiritual potential within and among women posed a threat greater than financial control. This suggests that the issue of gender in religion is an issue of power politics at a very fundamental level.

The history of women in Buddhism dates to even before the Buddha's enlightenment.[3] After realizing that physical austerities do not lead to liberation, Siddhartha Gautama is said to have accepted an offering of rice pudding from a village woman named Sujātā and regained strength to become enlightened. Thus, since the very earliest days, women have been credited as nurturers and supporters of the tradition, symbolized by Sujātā reviving Siddhartha's physical strength at a juncture critical to his ultimate achievement. Although his cohorts mocked him for this perceived weakness, the Buddha continued to instruct and counsel women throughout his fifty-year-long teaching career. With Siddhartha's stepmother Mahāprajāpatī in the vanguard, women began to create their own communities and the order of women renunciants, the Bhiksunī Sangha, has continued to thrive up to the present day. Women throughout India and later abroad became renowned for their spiritual achievements—the depth of their realizations, their talent as teachers, and their miraculous powers. This spiritual legacy has inspired women for centuries.

The Buddha allegedly hesitated to admit women to the Sangha, and several theories have been put forward to explain why. First, it is obvious that close proximity between an order of celibate women and an order of celibate men could lead to sexual temptations. There are statements attributed to the Buddha warning monks to be wary of contact with women as a distraction from spiritual pursuits. There are no records to prove it, but the Buddha may have similarly warned nuns against close contact with men. Human beings do not necessarily eradicate desire by living a celibate lifestyle; close relations between ordained men and women can easily lead to infatuations and eventually to disrobing. A second theory about the Buddha's hesitation to admit women to the Sangha attributes it to the Indian cultural context. In ancient Indian society, women's ideal role was in the family. Allowing a woman to leave her family and roam about unprotected was considered both dangerous for women and a threat to family life, the bedrock of society.

A third theory about the Buddha's hesitation to admit women to the Sangha concerns the organizational difficulties that might arise in monastic institutions that include members of both genders. The *bhiksus* and *bhiksunīs* had to develop systems for effectively organizing practical matters, such as housing, seating, ritual activities, and communications. The systems that evolved are evident in the regulatory monastic codes of the two orders. With parallel orders of women and men, the Sangha could potentially double in size. The difficulty of ensuring the smooth functioning of such a large monastic institution may have been another consideration in the Buddha's hesitation.

A fourth theory, which is whispered but rarely articulated, claims that monks saw nuns as unwanted competition, both for limited material resources and for spiritual achievement. The two are interrelated, since spiritual prowess attracts donations from the laity. If nuns were perceived as competition and a threat to the material welfare of the monks, and it was monks who transcribed the scriptures, this could explain certain misogynist statements that appear in the texts, including certain discriminatory statements attributed to the Buddha.

In some cases, negative stereotypes of women prevalent in Buddhist societies actually derive from Brahmanical, Confucian, or other sources, yet some are also found in both Theravāda and Mahāyāna texts. Whether these passages are the authentic words of the Buddha and his disciples or not, they are often used to legitimize negative typecasting of women. Interpretations of these passages vary, but they are difficult to justify or ignore. To repudiate the canonical texts altogether is problematic for Buddhists. Not only is it an affront to the sensibilities of orthodox adherents, but it also calls into question the validity of the texts as a whole. Even a revisionist view ruffles feathers among the orthodox, yet a reevaluation of the texts is essential if women in Buddhism are to meaningfully apply and actualize the teachings the texts contain.

In the earliest stratum of *sūtras*, the Buddha affirms women's capacity to achieve liberation and, from among the thousands of women who achieved *nirvāna* at that time, names many individually for their exceptional qualities. The Mahāyāna *sūtras*, which appeared several hundred years later, symbolize wisdom as female and inclusively address the "sons and daughters of good family." Along with accounts of the virtuous lives and spiritual achievements of women, however, we encounter repeated warnings against the temptations of women and a prophecy (as yet unfulfilled) warning that women's admission to the order would shorten the life of the Dharma.[4] The images of women are thus equivocal and often confusing.[5] An extreme example occurs in the *Upāyakauśalya Sūtra*, where the girl Daksinottarā sets herself on fire out of frustrated desire for the bodhisattva Priyamkara and achieves the fortunate result of birth as a male in paradise surrounded by fourteen thousand celestial females.[6] Even though the girl compounds lust with a horrifying suicide, her meritorious act of generosity to a (male) bodhisattva results in a heavenly (male) rebirth. Another perplexing example is the *Tathāgataguhya Sūtra*, where innumerable beings are cured of all diseases and afflictions by consummating union with the bodhisattva Vaidyarāja manifesting the form of a girl.[7] In the early Mahāyāna *sūtras*, a woman transforms herself into a male body upon enlightenment; in others, she achieves enlightenment in a female body. All these conflicting images make the study of women in Buddhism complex and intriguing; there are problems both in authenticating allusions to women in the texts and in discounting the texts altogether.

Throughout most of Buddhist history, the socially approved roles available to women were those of wife and mother. In these roles, laywomen accumulated merit by tending to the family shrine, making offerings to the Sangha, giving charity to the needy, transmitting the Buddhist teachings to children, keeping precepts, promoting ethical principles in the household, chanting the *sūtras*, and meditating. The most famous laywoman in the Buddha's day was Visākhā, who regularly fed two thousand monks at her home and was often called upon to mediate disputes.[8] The spiritual achievements of laywomen are described in a number of texts, such as the *Saddharma Ratnāvaliya*, where Subhadra and her younger sister achieve the state of a Stream-enterer (*sotāpanna*) and Sumanā attains the stage of a Once-Returner (*sakadāgāmī*).[9] Laywomen are portrayed as having more flexibility in Buddhist societies than previously; women had the right to divorce, remarry, inherit, and the freedom to practice religion without depending on men. Women gain inspiration from the Buddhist teachings on loving kindness and compassion, which use as their primary example the tremendous kindness and compassion that mothers have for their children. The central role of the mother in ensuring the happiness and harmony of the family is a common theme.

To exploit physical beauty and lead the life of a courtesan was one alternative lifestyle for women, and to renounce physical beauty and lead the life of a nun was another. For a woman, to renounce the pleasures of worldly life and become a nun represented the most radical departure from social expectations. In the *Therīgāthā*, we have the stories of dozens of women who achieved the final stage of liberation and became *arhats*. A number of these women, such as Kisāgotamī[10] and Vāsittī,[11] turned to intensive spiritual practice due to intense grief at the loss of a child. The story of Patācārā,[12] who became deranged after her husband died of snake bite and her two children were carried off by wild animals, is particularly poignant. After recovering her sanity, she became an *arhat* and, by explaining the sufferings of birth and death, became a source of consolation and inspiration to other women. Bhaddā Kundalakesā rejected lay life after being duped and almost killed by a lover she saved from execution, then went on to become the *bhiksunī* most skilled in philosophical debate. The decision to shave the head and don shapeless robes powerfully symbolized a rejection of the expected reproductive and familial roles, and asserted a new, independent identity as a full-time religious practitioner.

Religious leadership in Buddhist countries is traditionally in the hands of fully ordained monks (Sanskrit: *bhiksu*, Pāli: *bhikkhu*).[13] The monks are revered as the ideal model for human development and are financially supported by devout members of the lay community, primarily women. Around the eleventh century, the Bhiksunī Sangha died out in India and Sri Lanka,[14] and as far as is known, was never officially established in Cambodia, Japan, Laos, Mongolia, Thailand, or Tibet. In the fifth century C.E., the lineage of fully ordained nuns was transmitted from Sri Lanka to China[15] and subsequently to Korea and Vietnam. The lineage of full ordination for women has flourished in these countries uninterruptedly to the present day.

The status of nuns within the Buddhist traditions seems to correlate with ordination status. Coincidentally or not, where full ordination as a *bhiksunī* is available, the nuns' level of education and status within the society also tend to be high. Where novice ordination as a *śrāmanerikā* is available to nuns, women are recognized as members of the Sangha (the monastic order), even though they are not afforded equal treatment. Without access to full ordination or even novice ordination, women in such Theravādin countries as Burma, Cambodia, Laos, Sri Lanka, and Thailand are in a secondary and often subservient role, relative to the monks, in the religious sphere. The subordinate position of women in Buddhism does not derive solely from the lack of higher ordination, however, for even those women who have access to some level of ordination are sometimes marginalized and their needs ignored. For example, although women in the Chinese, Korean, and Vietnamese traditions enjoy parity in being fully ordained, they hold a clearly subordinate position in the religious power structures of their traditions. Certain wealthy women have exerted influence from behind the scenes, but most women over the centuries have typically lacked both a voice and power in Buddhist institutions. Today they are gaining courage and beginning to speak out....

A Tragic Case: Tibet

Throughout centuries of Tibetan Buddhist history, women have distinguished themselves in spiritual practice time and again. The Vajrayāna or Secret Mantra teachings, which thrive in the Tibetan milieu, guarantee women the possibility of enlightenment "in this very life, in this very body."[16] Although the lineage of full ordination for women apparently was not transmitted from India to Tibet, both laywomen and nuns became famous for their spiritual achievements.[17] Among those who availed themselves of this precious opportunity, perhaps the most famous is Machig Labdronma (1055–1149 C.E.), whose heroic example has inspired generations of Tibetan women. The twentieth century has also produced exemplars, such as Samding Dorje Palmo and Shungseb Jetsun Lochen Rinpoche, both of whom are said to have reached high levels of spiritual realization.[18]

Unfortunately, social and political factors have intruded and perforce compromised many ordinary women's spiritual potential. Mundane realities have mitigated against large numbers of women being recognized for their religious attainments: for example, societal expectations of women's roles, the time-consuming duties of family life, and in recent years, the takeover of the Tibetan homeland by an uncompromising Communist regime. The potential to manifest enlightened female meditational deities such as Tārā, Vajrayoginī, Saraswatī, and Prajñāpāramitā is ever present; the mystique of legendary female spiritual masters such as Gelongma Palmo, Yeshe Tsogyal, Mandarava, Niguma, and others, remains to inspire women on the path. In actual fact, however, most Tibetan women see their chances for immanent enlightenment as somewhat remote. Many are content to simply pray to be reborn as a male and indeed, for most, Buddhist practice consists of doing their best in everyday life situations.

Still, there are improvements that would enhance Tibetan women's spiritual well-being. Fundamental ones are greater literacy, greater educational opportunities at all levels, both secular and religious, and better facilities for religious study and practice for both lay and ordained women. Most crucial to the process of improving women's spiritual well-being is an improved image of the feminine—a bridging of the gap between theoretical possibilities and limited everyday realities....

Buddhist Women as Leaders in Social Transformation

The Buddhist women's movement is a vital aspect of the current cross-fertilization of cultures that is occurring as Buddhism assumes global significance. Another is the new emphasis on social action projects, in what is known as "socially engaged Buddhism." These two developments are integrally linked. Although Buddhist organizations in Asia have been slow to see women as logical beneficiaries of their efforts, individual women working independently, such as Bhiksunī Zhengyan in Taiwan and Maeji Khunying Kanitha Wichiencharoen in Thailand, have been exemplary agents of social change.[19] Social welfare programs directed by Buddhist women are having immediate constructive results for women in developing countries, including institutions for educating and training women, refugee relief projects, women's shelters, health care projects, counseling centers, economic development projects, and meditation retreat centers. As important as compassionate social service is, however, it would be unfair to promote the idea that women do social work while men meditate—it is not necessary to make a choice between meditation and service to humanity.

The Buddhist women's movement emphasizes women's social problems along with the traditional agenda of spiritual liberation. It is inspired by both the awakening social awareness of practicing Buddhists and the awakening spiritual consciousness of women discovering, individually and collectively, their own history of neglect and oppression, a history that must be reversed in order to ensure that women are optimally engaged in the continually challenging process of social renewal. Women's increasingly active engagement in social and spiritual renewal may yield quite a revolutionary outcome.

The Buddhist worldview recognizes change as intrinsic to human experience and essential for transforming both our inner life and the outer world. Buddhist agents of social change in recent history include B. R. Ambedkar in India,[20] Aung San Suu Kyi in Burma, Bhiksu Mahagoshananda in Cambodia, A. T. Ariyaratne in Sri Lanka, Bhiksu Buddhadasa in Thailand, Bhiksu Thich Nhat Hahn in Vietnam, Bhiksunī Zhengyan in Taiwan, and Bhiksu Tenzin Gyatso, the fourteenth Dalai Lama of Tibet. The term "engaged Buddhism," coined by Thich Nhat Hahn,[21] describes the active application of Buddhist principles toward social transformation. The concept which has spawned an entire literature.[22]

Socially engaged Buddhists need to recognize that Buddhist women are among the poorest, least educated, and most neglected sectors of society, often concentrating on religious practice at the expense of their own social welfare. It is common t0 hear both nuns and laywomen state: "I don't care about equality. I only care about *nirvāna*," or "What is the point of my getting an education? It is enough for me just to recite prayers." Lacking confidence in their own abilities, many women concentrate on merit-making through reciting prayers and making offerings to monks. It is common for Buddhist women to denigrate their own potential and abdicate responsibility for their spiritual life to men, praying for rebirth as a man in the next life. A major revaluing of women in the tradition is crucial—both a renewed affirmation of women's spiritual worth and an increased appreciation of women's spiritual practice.

In the Buddhist worldview, spiritual practice and helping living beings are accorded the highest value, but it is unrealistic to expect women to serve others if their own basic needs are not being met. While literacy is not essential to human happiness, for many women literacy is a major step toward empowerment, allowing women access to improved livelihood, to information on health and hygiene, to upward social mobility, to personal development and greater self-confidence, to greater educational options for their children, and to the texts that encode their spiritual heritage. It does not take vast resources or government initiatives to set up adult literacy programs: once one generation is literate, women can continue these programs themselves.

Progressive Buddhists may place their hopes in a future generation of socially enlightened young monks, but this is still only a dream. Even if open-minded monks gain access to positions of power, this does not ensure changes that would benefit women. Those in positions of power rarely relinquish their privileged positions with grace. Therefore, Buddhist women must work for their own social and spiritual liberation. Once women fully acknowledge their own spiritual potential and support women's spiritual practice, a profound social and spiritual transformation is possible. The effective mobilization of some 300 million Buddhist women for the good of the world is not to be underestimated.

The dialogue between Buddhism and feminism is a confluence of rich narratives. Just as Buddhist perspectives on personal development, nonviolence, and ethics can contribute toward social regeneration in Western countries, feminist perspectives can contribute to social renewal in Buddhist countries. Women's experiences are being articulated and analyzed in ways that may contribute to a rethinking and revitalization of Buddhist thought and culture. Rather than investing in gold statues and temples, for example, women are interested in creating more childcare programs, literacy programs, meditation courses, leadership programs, health care training, Buddhist hospice programs, rehabilitation centers, disaster relief programs, and creative expressions of spiritual practice. As the marginalized enter the stream, they inevitably change the stream. Women can move freely across sectarian and ethnic boundaries and pool their energies as never before. New dimensions of understanding and benefit will surely open up as women in the Dharma find their own unique and individual voices, for virtually the first time in 2,500 years of Buddhist history....

Notes

1. Her story is recounted in C. A. F. Rhys Davids' *Poems of Early Buddhist Nuns* (*Therīgāthā*) (Oxford: Pali Text Society, 1989), pp. 4–5, 71–73.
2. See, for example, E. Michael Mendelson, *Sangha and State in Burma: A Study of Monastic Sectarianism and Leadership* (Ithaca, N.Y.: Cornell University Press, 1975), and four books edited by Bardwell L. Smith: *Religion and Legitimation of Power in South Asia* (Leiden: Brill, 1978), *Religion and Legitimation of Power in Sri Lanka* (Chambersburg, Pa.: Anima Books, 1978), *Religion and Legitimation of Power in Thailand, Laos, and Burma* (Chambersburg, Pa.: Anima Books, 1978), and *The Two Wheels of Dhamma: Essays on the Theravada Tradition in India and Ceylon* (Chambersburg, Pa.: American Academy of Religion, 1972).
3. The best overall treatment of this history is probably still I. B. Horner's *Women under Primitive Buddhism: Laywomen and Almswomen* (Delhi: Motilal Banarsidass, 1930).
4. This story appears in several places in the Pāli canon and also in the literature of other early schools. See Jan Nattier, *Once upon a Future Time: Studies in a Buddhist Prophecy of Decline* (Berkeley: Asian Humanities Press, 1991), pp. 28–33. She notes that the *Mahāvibhāsā* offers a second interpretation: "According to other teachers, what the Buddha meant was that if women were allowed to enter the monastic order but did not obey the eight additional rules (*gurudharma*) imposed upon them—rules clearly designed to keep them in subordinate positions with respect to men—the *saddharma* [pure Dharma] would have lasted for only five hundred years. Since these rules were implemented, however, the *saddharma* will remain in the world for a full 1,000 years." Ibid., p. 44.
5. A compendium of unflattering portrayals of women in Buddhist literature appears in Liz Wilson's book. *Charming Cadavers: Horrific Figurations of the Feminine in Indian Buddhist Hagiographic Literature* (Chicago: University of Chicago Press, 1996).
6. Mark Tatz, *The Skill in Means (Upāyakauśalya) Sūtra* (Delhi: Motilal Banarsidass, 1994), pp. 39–45.
7. Related in Cecil Bendall and W. H. D. Rouse's tradition of Śāntideva's *Śikṣāsamuccaya: A Compendium of Buddhist Doctrine* (Delhi: Motilal Banarsidass, 1990), pp. 157–58.
8. Bimala Churn Law, *Women in Buddhist Literature* (Varanasi: Indological Book House, 1981), pp. 93–97.
9. Dharmasēna Thera (trans. Ranjini Obeyesekere), *Jewels of the Doctrine: Stories of the Saddharma Ratnāvaliya* (Albany: State University of New York Press, 1991), pp. 224–25. In this text, the Buddha describes Sumanaā, the youngest daughter, as senior in goodness to her father, because of her superior spiritual attainment.
10. Rhys Davids, *Poems*, pp. 88–91.
11. Ibid., pp. 64–66.
12. Ibid., pp. 55–59.
13. See note 3.
14. See Nancy Falk, "The Case of the Vanishing Nuns: The Fruits of Ambivalence in Ancient Indian Buddhism," *Unspoken Worlds: Women's Religious Lives in Non-Western Culture*, ed. Nancy Falk and Rita Gross (San Francisco: Harper & Row, 1979), pp. 207–24.
15. See Kathryn Ann Tsai, *Lives of the Nuns: Biographies of Chinese Buddhist Nuns from the Fourth to Sixth Centuries* (Honolulu: University of Hawaii Press, 1994), pp. 37–38, 53–54, 62–63.

16. Miranda Shaw presents a thorough study of women in Tantric Buddhism in *Passionate Enlightenment: Women in Tantric Buddhism* (Princeton: Princeton University Press, 1994). A feminist critique of women's role within this tradition is found in June Campbell, *Traveller in Space: In Search of Female Identity in Tibetan Buddhism* (New York: George Braziller, 1996).

17. See Reginald Ray's "Accomplished Women in Tantric Buddhism of Medieval India and Tibet," in *Unspoken Worlds: Women's Religious Lives in Non-Western Cultures,* ed. Nancy Falk and Rita Gross (San Francisco: Harper and Row, 1979), pp. 227–42.

18. See Janice D. Willis, *Feminine Ground: Essays on Women and Tibet* (Ithaca: Snow Lion Publication, 1989).

19. Bhiksunī Zhengyan, founder of Ciji Foundation, received the Magasasay Award in 1992. (See *Sakyadhita: International Association of Buddhist Women* 5.2, [Summer 1994]: 12–13.) Maeji Khunying Kanitha Wichiencharoen, director of the Thai government's Commission for the Promotion of the Status of Women, has founded a shelter which serves as a haven for battered women, unwed mothers, and pregnant women who are HIV positive. She was ordained as an eight-precept nun following the Third Sakyadhita Conference in Sri Lanka in 1993.

20. The life of Dr. Ambedkar and the movement he inspired are described in two recent articles: Christopher S. Queen's "Dr. Ambedkar and the Hermeneutics of Buddhist Liberation" and Alan Sponberg's "TMBSG: A Dhamma Revolution in Contemporary India," in *Engaged Buddhism: Buddhist Liberation Movements in Asia,* ed. Christopher S. Queen and Sallie B. King (Albany: State University of New York Press, 1996), pp. 45–71, 73–120. Also see Hilary Blakiston's book, *But Little Dust: Life amongst the Ex-Untouchables of Maharashtra* (Cambridge, U.K.: Allborough Press, 1990).

21. Queen and King, *Engaged Buddhism,* pp. 2, 34n.

22. For example, see Fred Eppsteiner, *The Path of Compassion: Writings on Socially Engaged Buddhism* (Berkeley, Calif.: Parallax Publications, 1988); Ken Jones, *The Social Face of Buddhism: An Approach to Political and Social Activism* (London: Wisdom Publications, 1989); Dhananjay Keer, *Dr. Ambedkar: Life and Mission* (Bombay: Popular Prakashan, 1990); Sulak Sivaraksa, *Seeds of Peace: A Buddhist Vision for Renewing Society* (Berkeley, Calif.: Parallax Press, 1992); Chan Khong, *Learning True Love: How I Learned and Practiced Social Change in Vietnam* (Berkeley, Calif.: Parallax Press, 1993); Ken Jones, *Beyond Optimism: A Buddhist Political Ecology* (Oxford: Jon Carpenter, 1993); Thich Nhat Hahn, *Love in Action: Writings on Nonviolent Social Change* (Berkeley, Calif.: Parallax Press, 1993); Christopher Queen and Sallie B. King, *Buddhist Liberation Movements in Asia* (Albany: State University of New York Press, 1996).

Thai Buddhism: Women's Ordination or More Prostitution?

Ouyporn Khuankaew

There are about 7,000 nuns registered under the Thai Nuns Institute, but the real figures are estimated to be over 10,000. More than 30 years ago the Thai Nuns Institute was established with the aim of helping to provide support for nuns, but because the nuns are not legally registered as ordained persons there was no budget allocated from any governmental agency to help the Thai Nuns Institute to execute its missions. Thus, the main support that the Thai Nuns Institute can offer is to organize a one-day annual meeting for its members. Even on this occasion most of the nuns from rural areas cannot afford to attend because they do not have money to pay for the transportation costs to come to the capital city.

The nuns have been neglected not only by government agencies but, also, by non-governmental organizations (NGOs). Among the many hundreds of NGOs working on women's issues, so far only one is working for the nuns. The Thai Inter-Religious Commission for Development (TICD) has been collaborating with the Thai Nun Institute to support the nuns for over ten years. Over the past 8 years this nunnery has been offering food, education and shelter to a few hundred young girls who are mostly from poor rural communities.

The TICD nuns project was at a halt for several years because its only staff member working for the nuns has been terminally ill since 1994. In 1997 TICD found a new staff person whose main task is accounting but is willing to overwork in order to support the nuns. Thus, with the addition of this staff member, TICD has been working closely with the Spirit in Education Movement (SEM) by including the nuns in various SEM training courses that were previously only offered to NGO staff and monks. The training courses offered include leadership and community building, conflict resolution, and training for social action trainers. Over the past three years, TICD has helped facilitate the inclusion of two nuns as members of the Sekhiyadhamma committee, a committee that represents a group of monks involved in various social works for many years. TICD has also cooperated with the Women and Gender Program of the International Network of Engaged Buddhists (INEB) to create opportunities for Buddhist nuns from different traditions in South and Southeast Asia to come and share their life experiences.

Reprinted from *Seeds of Peace*, Vol. 16, No. 1 (Jan.–Apr. 2543 [2000]), pp. 13–17, with the permission of Ouyporn Khuankaew.

As coordinator for the INEB Women and Gender Program, I have had a great deal of direct experience in facilitating the meeting and interactions of the nuns from the region. Initially, our main reason for working with the nuns was to empower them with more skills and encouragement. Additionally, we focus on helping nuns learn about structural violence in Thai society that is causing so much suffering to the environment and to various groups of people, especially women. After the nuns attended the training, we supported them in carrying out the social work in which they were already involved or in initiating new projects of interest to them. Our belief is that as the nuns' work become more visible society will recognize them and eventually their status will be improved. Our strategy also includes trying to work with the leaders of the Institute, knowing that working from the bottom up only is not enough to change the structure. This is very difficult; we managed only once to have a few of the nun leaders attend our team building workshop. At the workshop we helped them build alliances by organizing the workshop so that monks and nuns could learn from each other. In these workshops we created opportunities for the nuns to speak directly to the monks without fear and intimidation. The monks learned to listen to the nuns and were able to see that the nuns have potential and wisdom and strongly need the monks' support and respect. In addition to organizing the workshops for monks and nuns together, we have also attempted to encourage progressive feminist NGOs to include nuns as one of their target groups. This is a continuing challenge because of the obstacles from both TICD and the feminist groups.

After 3 years of learning and sometimes feeling like giving up we realized that working at the institutional level is not enough. The nuns are suppressed by the patriarchal system that pervades all spheres of their lives. The nuns with whom we have worked within the past three years have reported that, once they came out of the invisible zone and exposed themselves to different views and experiences provided by TICD, when they went back to their communities it became more difficult to turn a blind eye and continue living within that suppressive environment. Because many of them do not receive or want to receive financial support from their families, their only support resides with the temple abbot or the chief nuns who in turn often control their lives and work. Knowledge and skills the nuns have learned from the training courses, such as collective decision making, working as a team, being assertive, and especially the participatory Dhamma teaching methods, tend to be discouraged and may be considered taboo in their local nunneries. One of the nuns said *"that even my fellow nuns said to me that I became a communist after I came to be involved with TICD"*. Therefore some of the chief nuns have not been willing to send their nuns to attend our training courses because they are afraid that the nuns would learn things that are against the rules and regulation set by the Institute. There is a concern that the nuns will bring harm to the organization and the image of the nuns as a whole if they do not submit to the oppressive structures and practices that directly contribute to their low status.

When these nuns decided to leave their temple or nunnery and move to a new community in order to live a different life and do social work, it is very difficult because of the patriarchal system that blocks them from doing their work. If they relocate to a new community just to live and do cooking and cleaning for the monks, the community will most likely welcome them. When a nun enters any community it is common that she will not receive shelter, money, food, respect and moral support as monks do. Also, if the abbot of any community within which a nun may live does not support her, it will be impossible for her to do any social work. Further, when a monk decides to support a nun in the community it means that, in all likelihood, she will be controlled by the monk in return. A nun from Kanchanaburi said,

At the beginning three of us worked very hard to improve the situation of the kindergarten situated in a village close to the Burma border. The abbot asked us to work there because he said he himself did not know how to handle small kids. He supported us with everything and the school has improved a lot and the villagers were very pleased with our work. In the morning and evening three of us would go with a truck to pick up and send back the kids and by doing that we knew every kids' parents and their community. Later on the abbot was not so happy because the community started to be increasingly connected and they showed their appreciation of our work and dedication. Finally he said that he wanted the school back and will run it the way he used to do and we had to leave.

Another nun who just finished three months work with a hill tribe community in the North said,

I was invited to go there because the monk in that village was impressed with the participatory Dhamma teaching method that I used with the students from Chiang Mai University. When we went there the villagers, especially the temple committee, who are all male, did not like our style of teaching Dhamma. They wanted us to live like the abbot whose main duty was to perform ceremonies in Pali and the rest of his time was spent on watching TV. Although our work went well and was responded to by the kids, who were surprised to know that there were other ways of teaching Dhamma and by the group of housewives, the main supporters of our work, we finally had to leave the community because the power of the temple committee and the abbot was so strong.

During November 2–6 this year we organized a five-day community-building training course for 20 nuns. More than half of the nuns are living independently from the monks. This is the first time that we have been able to involve the rural nuns, most of whom were not part of the Thai Nuns Institute. The nuns came from various nunneries and temples in the South, North, Northeast and central part of Thailand.

The top priority expressed by the nuns was to learn how to work and live harmoniously in the ordained community. They wanted to know what society thinks of them and expects from them and about approaches and strategies for working with community. Another one of their main goals was to learn and share their life stories with other nuns.

The five-day training course was designed to address the topics of working as a team, knowing oneself and others, self-empowerment, power and leadership, gender, and sharing life stories. The learning was accomplished through various experiential activities such as games, role-play, drawing, asking and listening to each other and sharing stories. Following is a discussion of the important topics and issues covered during the workshop.

Why We Became Nuns?

One chief nun from the North said,

> I realized that worldly life was not my path while I was in the highest peak of business success. After living in the temple for three months as Upasika my partner came to visit. He kneeled to beg me to go back home to take care of the children and our business. I decided that day to have my head shaved and become a nun because otherwise he would have hope that I will one day go back. The most painful experience for me was the rejection I encountered from my children. For many years they refused to see me.

Another chief nun from a village in the northeastern province said,

> I became a nun because I experienced so much suffering from not being able to fulfill the endless desires in worldly life. The day I had my head shaved and wore the white robe I felt a very strong and deep transformation inside of me. The words that came out clearly at that moment was hearing myself saying that I will take the triple gems to give to my mother.

For most of the workshop participants, young or old, what motivated them to become nuns was the desire to follow the Buddha's path, not the quest to escape from their heart-broken, jobless, or aimless lives. The nuns were shocked when they realized that inside the temple and nunnery there were many problems such as conflict and the abuse of power and control both by their leaders and among the community members themselves. Many of them expressed that they experienced so many difficulties that they became confused about Sila, Samadhi and Panya, the core principles to be practiced within the ordained community. This was especially challenging for many of them because they became nuns in order to take refuge in the triple gems, to be able to cultivate peace and inner strength to cope with their suffering.

The workshop participants reported that they also realized that other nuns come to live in the community for various reasons. Some of the nuns are trauma survivors. Many became nuns because they were old or sick and their families did not want to take care of them. Many young nuns said they entered the nunhood because their parents could not afford to send them to pursue higher education. At the same time, their parents did not want them to get involved with drugs or to get pregnant like their friends. They themselves did not want to end up in a factory or a brothel.

What Prevents Us from Disrobing?

Because Thai society does not have an ordination for women, there has been no training or financial support for the nuns for their Dhamma education and living once their heads were shaved and their clothes changed to white robes. The situation is more difficult for the nuns who live in the temple where there are both monks and nuns live together although they live in separate sections.

The nuns said it was difficult to become a nun, to stay in the nunhood and to leave the nunhood. Most of the nuns who took the path because of their faith in the Buddha's teaching had to go through many challenges because their families often do not support their choice. Some nuns said that their family members, especially the parents, used different strategies to force them to disrobe. These tactics included not talking to them, not giving them financial support, telling them that they bring shame to the family, coming to visit every month or two to ask them to go back home, or saying that they have no gratitude to parents because they do not take care of them like other children. One of the nuns said,

> the general public and government agencies do not support us because we do not belong to any categorized groups of women, either the lay or ordained ones. Being a nun, then, is worse than being a lay woman because we are not even marginalized; our beings are not perceived at all.

For many of the nuns, these obstacles become the challenge that they used to prove their strength and determination to their families and to society. For them, leaving the nunhood would be their failure. Of course, for many nuns, once they receive support and are able to learn, practice and enjoy the fruits of Dhamma, this becomes a main reason for them to stay on.

One nun who stayed in the robe for 16 years had already decided to leave the nunhood once she finished the training. On the final day she admitted to the group,

> Originally, I just came to accompany my friend and did not intend to participate in the training. After the first day, I realized this was different than other training courses I ever attended before. Those training courses usually had a hundred nuns sitting in a row listening to one monk or two who do the talking. Sometimes there were Buddhist scholars who came to give a long lecture about Dhamma or other secular subjects. After sitting in a circle and sharing our stories like this, I felt very happy and empowered and this experience changed my mind. I will not disrobe. Yesterday evening I called the abbot and told him my feelings, which I had never told him before. I told him how I felt in our work having him sitting on a high alter telling everybody in the community what to do, even though I knew he meant well. I told him that I had changed my mind not to disrobe and he asked me what TICD training did to you that made you change your mind. I told him that here we learn how to listen and respect each other's feelings and ideas. He then told me that he realized that he himself has been putting himself far above from everybody. He said from now on he will come down half way and asked me and other community members to come up the other half way so that we can really work together.

But Where Do We Go from Here?

The nuns expressed a strong desire to get to know other nuns and share their struggle using the same learning style they experienced from the workshop. A 75-year-old nun from the South said,

> after being a nun for more than 10 years this was the first time I ever come to the training that was organized mainly for the nuns. (With tears streaming down her eyes she said) This might be an answer to my prayer that I finally was able to meet and share my stories with other fellow nuns. Before coming here I had always been worried about the future of Buddhism seeing the lack of women participation in it. Now having listened to the voices of commitment of the younger nuns I felt very hopeful for Buddhism. I think this should be the way for us nuns to live and practice Dhamma together.

The nuns who are not yet involved in social work said that they wanted to concentrate on both secular and Dhamma education. Because the public already has little or no respect for nuns it is important that they are well equipped with knowledge and confidence before they go out to help other people. An 18-year-old nun said, "at the moment I could hardly help myself, how can I help other people?"

Many nuns reported that if they had known about TICD earlier there would be much difference in their lives and especially in the lives of those young nuns in rural areas who had already disrobed as a result of seeing no future in the nunhood. They asked TICD to continue supporting them and extending its work to the nuns in the rural areas who are not reached by the Thai Nuns Institute. They indicated that there is a strong need to keep nurturing the friendship and network among them and to link the group to the existing network of nuns that has already been established through TICD over the past four years. The nuns expressed that, for them, it is important to build trust, friendship and respect for each other among the nuns' group. Many of them said, "even among the nuns we do not respect each other, we always look up to monks for our spiritual teaching and support. We have to change our attitude because if we look down at ourselves how can we expect society to look up to us?"

Thai Society: Women Ordination or More Prostitution?

There are about 200,000 monks in Thailand. The number of prostitutes in Thailand may be less or more than the number of monks depending on whose data we want to believe. The relatively equal number of monks and women prostitutes in Thailand suggests that monkhood and female prostitution may be closely related. We know that in every village or rural community temple is one, if not the primary, institution with extensive resources in its hand. We know that most monks are from rural areas and that many enter the monkhood in order to climb the social ladder or for other reasons than to learn and practice the Buddha's teachings or to help ease the suffering of sentient beings. Thus, Thai society has to tolerate endless corruption and scandals created by monks using the robes and the patriarchal system to consume the community's existing resources for their own power and comfort. This leads Thai Buddhism each day into a dark age where a glimpse of hope is almost impossible.

Most women who enter prostitution come from the same background as monks. Because they do not have another free choice like their fellow men they often only have a choice between a factory or a brothel. The feminist movement in Thailand has done an impressive job of helping to improve the status and the rights of rural women. But one of the core causes of violence against women has not yet been touched upon—the beliefs, attitudes, traditions and values that come out of a patriarchal society influenced by Buddhism itself.

Let us examine prostitution alone. For a few years, feminist organizations have not only had to deal with that problem in Thailand, but increasingly with the problem of trafficking women from our neighboring countries such as Burma, Laos, and Cambodia, all Buddhist countries. Why is that? Maybe this has something to do with the way Buddhism functions in this part of the region. Most of the time in the discussion of the local, national and international meetings of women organizations the root causes of prostitution have always been poverty, western mode of development and modernization, or the latest hit, consumerism. Hardly mentioned as a cause of prostitution is the lack of leading roles for women in Buddhism.

Before the Beijing Women's meeting in 1995, we were contacted to give a talk on women and religion because the feminist groups did not know how to deal with the issue. One reason the feminist movement did not see the role of Buddhism as one of the root causes of violence against women (e.g. prostitution) was because many of us in the movement rejected institutionalized Buddhism as our own spiritual guide. We realized that Buddhism was monopolized by our fellow men and betrayed us by suppressing us instead of liberating us. We could hardly find a monk who could really guide us in our spiritual development. If we did find one it was still difficult to relate to them because of the strict rules of our tradition toward the relationship between women and monks. We had heard of female Buddhist teachers but there are far too few, and thus, they are not really accessible to us. Because most of us have not seen nuns as our spiritual guides we have no one and no where to turn to for our spiritual exploration and liberation.

Why There Is a Need for Women's Ordination in Thailand

For a moment, let us just envision that women can be ordained legally, have their own temple with the support from the public and the government. What would happen? For the poor young rural women this would become another choice in their lives for making their parents happy. They could decide on something other than being a wife and a mother or going to a factory or a brothel to earn money for the family. They could see that living an ordained life is another way to pay gratitude to their families and their community. Women who have experienced traumas such as rapes or domestic violence could have the spiritual support that they do not tend to receive from the monks. If men bowed to women and held them up as spiritual guides, perhaps they would realize that women are not just sexual objects or the only ones to raise the children and do the housework.

How This Vision Can Be Materialized?

Working with nuns, the general public and the feminist groups is not enough to build a movement for women's ordination in Thai society because the group that holds the most power in Buddhism is the monks. To say that the failure of Thai Buddhism resulted from the control of the state and consumerism is not yet a holistic analysis. The big scandal that has been in the headlines of Thai newspapers since January of last year has caused a small movement of NGOs, Buddhist scholars and progressive monks to work on a process for a reform of the Monk Act. Many believe this act is the core of the contemporary problem of abuses within Thai Buddhism. However, it is not enough to fix Thai Buddhism.

We know that monks and temples cannot survive without community support and that the main support has always been from women. If women's ordination is included in the movement half of the effort will be needed to improve the monk sangha alone. The movement to revive the Bhikkuni ordination in Sri Lanka, another Theravada tradition, was much influenced by the support of the monks. We have to remember that in a monopoly system changing the ones who monopolize the system is not enough. Any social movement needs to look for and create other alternatives in society while looking for ways to repair the flaws within the existing system. Sometimes, it is more worthwhile to focus on creating alternatives than spending limited resources trying to fix the unfixable system. For example, in the successful movement to reduce chemical agricultural practices in the past ten years, the Thai NGOs did not focus their energy on stopping the government or the private sectors from promoting the use of toxic products. Their main work has always been to create and support various alternatives to compete with the mainstream.

It will not be easy for Thai monks to think or even to speak in public about the ordination of women. The main reason has always been that we have never had such a tradition in Thailand. If we look around at our society today there are hundreds of things that did not exist until the recent past. One of the great teachings of Buddhism is impermanence: that things always change according to causes and factors. Since our society has changed a great deal, it is likely that Thai Buddhism cannot survive and manifest the real essence of the Buddha's teachings if there is no movement to make Buddhism relevant to the realities of the present society. This movement will not be materialized if monks and progressive Buddhist male scholars are not aware of their own power, and are not willing to share their power by including women in the Sangha.

✦

Questions for Discussion

1. What is the relationship between female gender imagery and the status of "real" women in Buddhism? What factors can you point to that help explain this relationship?
2. Does the monastic, or "10 vow," option provide Buddhist women with resources to empower themselves in a patriarchal and sexist society, or does it legitimize and reinforce their secondary status by making them subject to the regulation of the male Sangha?
3. Are the poems of the *Therigatha* likely to be liberating or empowering for women today? Why or why not?
4. Would the status of Buddhist women be likely to improve if women were given greater roles in spiritual authority, such as monastic leaders, teachers, or gurus?
5. Do the readings make you optimistic or pessimistic about these possibilities being realized in the future?

References and Materials for Further Study

Books and Articles

Allione, Tsultrim. 1984. *Women of Wisdom*. London: Routledge & Kegan Paul.

Barholomeusz, Tessa. 1994. *Women under the Bo Tree*. Cambridge: Cambridge University Press.

———, 1999. "Southeast Asian Buddhism," in Serinity Young, ed., *Encyclopedia of Women and World Religion*. New York: Macmillan Reference.

Barnes, Nancy. 1994. "Women in Buddhism," in Arvind Sharma, ed., *Today's Woman in World Religions*, Albany: State University of New York Press.

Batchelor, Martine. 1996. *Walking on Lotus Flowers: Buddhist Women Working, Loving, and Meditating*. New York: Harper Collins.

———. 1995–1996. "Buddhist Nuns in Korea." *Karuna* (Winter): 16-18.

Blackstone, Kathryn. 1998. *Women in the Footsteps of the Buddha: Struggle for Liberation in the Therigatha*. Honolulu: Curzon Press.

Boucher, Sandy. 1997. *Opening the Lotus: What Women Want to Know About Buddhism*. Boston: Beacon Press.

———. 1993. *Turning the Wheel: American Women Creating the New Buddhism*. Boston: Beacon.

Campbell, June. 1996. *Traveller in Space: In Search of Female Identity in Tibetan Buddhism*. New York: George Braziller.

Dresser, Marianne, ed. 1996. *Buddhist Women on the Edge*. Berkeley, CA: North Atlantic Books.

Falk, Nancy. 1980. "The Case of the Vanishing Nuns: The Fruits of Ambivalence in Ancient Indian Buddhism," in Nancy Falk and Rita Gross, eds., *Unspoken Worlds: Women's Religious Lives in Non-Western Cultures*. San Francisco: Harper & Row.

———. 1974. "An Image of Woman in Old Buddhist Literature: The Daughters of Mara," in Judith Plaskow and Joan Arnold Romero, eds., *Women and Religion*. Missoula, MO: Scholars' Press.

Findly, Ellison Banks. 2000. *Buddhism's Women, Women's Buddhism: Tradition, Revision, Renewal*. Boston: Wisdom Publications.

———. 1999. "Women and the *Arahant* Issue in Early Pali Literature." *Journal of Feminist Studies in Religion* 15, 1 (Spring), pp. 58-76.

Friedman, Lenore. 1987. *Meetings with Remarkable Women: Buddhist Teachers in America*. Boston: Shambhala.

Friedman, Lenore, and Susan Moon, eds. 1997. *Being Bodies: Buddhist Women on the Paradox of Embodiment*. Boston: Shambhala Publications.

Gross, Rita. 1992. *Buddhism after Patriarchy*. New York: State University of New York Press. On the relationship of Western women to Buddhism.

Havnevik, Hanna. 1990. *Tibetan Buddhist Nuns: History, Cultural Norms and Social Reality*. Oxford, UK: Oxford University Press.

Hopkinson, Deborah, et al, eds. 1986. *Not Mixing Up Buddhism: Essays on Women and Buddhist Practice*. Fredonia, NY: White Pine Press.

Horner, I. B. 1975 [1930]. *Women Under Primitive Buddhism*. London: Routledge & Kegan Paul.

Kabilsingh, Chatsumarn. 1991. *Thai Women in Buddhism*. Berkeley, CA: Parallax Press.

Khuankaew, Ouyporn. 2000. "Thai Buddhism: Women's Ordination or More Prostitution?" *Seeds of Peace* 16, 1 (January-April): 13-17.

Klein, Anne. 1994. *Meeting The Great Bliss Queen: Feminism, Buddhism, and the Art of the Self*. Boston: Beacon Press.

———. 1985. "Primordial Purity and Everyday Life: Exalted Female Symbols and the Women of Tibet," in Clarissa W. Atkinson et al., eds., *Immaculate and Powerful: The Female in Sacred Image and Social Reality*. Boston: Beacon Press.

Lang, Karen. 1986. "Lord Death's Snare: Gender-Related Imagery in the Theragatha and the Therigatha," *Journal of Feminist Studies in Religion*, 2, 1, 63-79.

Levering, Miriam. 1999. "East Asian Buddhism," in Serinity Young, ed., *Encyclopedia of Women and World Religion*, New York: Macmillan Reference.

Minamoto, Junko. 1990. "Buddhist Attitudes: A Woman's Perspective," in Jeanne Becher, ed., *Women, Religion, and Sexuality*. Philadelphia: Trinity Press.

Murcott, Susan. 1991. *The First Buddhist Women: Translations and Commentaries on the Therigatha*. Berkeley, CA: Parallax Press.

Nakamura, Kyoko. 1983. "Women and Religion in Japan." Special issue of *Japanese Journal of Religious Studies*, 10: 2-3.

Nefsky, Marilyn. 1995. "Liberator or Pacifier: Religion and Women in Japan," in Ursala King, ed., *Religion and Gender*. Oxford, UK: Oxford University Press.

Paul, Diana. 1985. *Women in Buddhism: Images of the Feminine in Mahayana Tradition*, rev. ed. Berkeley: University of California Press.

Rhys Davids, C.A.F., and K.R. Norman, trans. 1989. *Poems of Early Buddhist Nuns*. Oxford, UK: Pali Text Society.

Schuster, Nancy Barnes. 1985. "Striking a Balance: Women and Images of Women in Early Chinese Buddhism," in Yvonne Yazbeck Haddad and Ellison Banks Findly, eds., *Women, Religion, and Social Change*. Albany: State University of New York Press.

Shambhala Sun. July 2000. Special Issue on "The Unprecedented Role of Women Dharma Teachers in American Buddhism."

Shaw, Miranda. 1994. *Passionate Enlightenment: Women in Tantric Buddhism*. Princeton, NJ: Princeton University Press.

Sponberg, Alan. 1992. "Attitudes toward Women and the Feminine in Early Buddhism," in Jose Cabezon, ed., *Buddhism, Sexuality, and Gender*. Albany: State University of New York Press.

Taring, [Mary] Dolma. 1987. *Daughter of Tibet*. Boston: Wisdom Publications.

Thitsa, Khin. 1987. "Nuns, Mediums and Prostitutes in Chiengmai: A Study of Some Marginal Categories of Women," in Centre of South-East Asian Studies, *Women and Development in South-East Asia I*. Canterbury, UK: University of Canterbury.

Turning Wheel. Spring 1999. Special issue on "Buddhist Feminism."

Tsomo, Karme Lekshe. 1999. "Mahāprajāpatī's Legacy: The Buddhist Women's Movement: An Introduction," in Karme Lekshe Tsomo, ed., *Buddhist Women Across Cultures: Realizations*. Albany: State University of New York Press.

———. 1995. *Buddhism Through American Women's Eyes*, Ithaca, NY: Snow Lion Publications.

———. 1989. "Living as a Nun in the West," in Karme Lekshe Tsomo, ed., *Sakyadhita: Daughters of the Buddha*. Ithaca, NY: Snow Lion Publications.

Uchino, Kumiko. 1989. "The Status Elevation Process of Soto Sect Nuns in Modern Japan." *Japanese Journal of Religious Studies*, 10 2-3: 177-194.

Willis, Janice D. 1985. "Nuns and Benefactresses: The Role of Women in the Development of Buddhism," in Yvonne Yazbeck Haddad and Ellison Banks Findly, eds., *Women, Religion, and Social Change*. Albany: State University of New York Press.

Willis, Janice D., ed. 1989. *Feminine Ground: Essays on Women and Tibet*. Ithaca, NY: Snow Lion Publications.

Internet Resources

A Bibliography in Buddhism for Feminist Web Site:
http://www.loudzen.com/skydancer/biblio.

GASSHO: Electronic Journal of DharmaNet International and the Global Online Sangha Web Site:
http://www.etext.org:80/Religious.Texts/DharmaNet/Journals/Gassho/gass0105.nws.

Lycos Internet site:
http://dir.lycos.com/Society/Religion_and_Spirituality/Buddhism/Sex_and_Gender/Women.

Sakyadhita, the International Association of Buddhist Women, Web Site:
http://www2.hawaii. edu/~tsomo.

SkyDancer: A Bibliography in Buddhism for Feminists Web Site:
http://www.loudzen.com/ skydancer/biblio/index.html.

Women Active in Buddhism (WAIB) Web Site:
http://members.tripod.com/ ~Lhamo.
Pages on "Famous Women Who Happen to Be Buddhist," "Female Buddhas and Bodhisattvas According to Tibetan Buddhist Tradition," "Resources on Women's Ordination."

Zen, Women, and Buddhism Web Site:
http://www.geocities.com/zennun12_8/index.htm.

Media Resources

Choice for a Chinese Woman: Enlightenment in a Buddhist Convent. Films for the Humanities, Inc., 1993.

Satya, a Prayer for the Enemy. Video, 28 min. Film Library, 1993. Focuses on personal testimonies of Tibetan Buddhist nuns who have taken the lead in the resistance against Chinese occupation of Tibet by fearlessly staging courageous demonstrations for religious freedom and independence.

We Will Meet Again in the Land of the Dakini, Video. Mystic Fire Video, 1998. About the life of the late Mongolian lama and Chöd yogini Doljin Kandro Suren, who practiced and taught the Dharma in Communist Mongolia when it was still illegal to do so.

Women and Other Asian Religious Traditions

Overview

There are many, many religious traditions throughout Asia in addition to the "world religions" of Hinduism and Buddhism we have already discussed. This introduction will provide an overview of several of these, but space permits selections covering only a few of these (Taoist, Confucian, and Shinto). Asian religions that have been especially important and meaningful in the lives of Asian women include shamanistic cults, folk or spirit religions, and the so-called "new religions" prominent in Japan. Some of these may be described as "women's religions," as they were either founded by women, or function through the leadership of women, or involve women as the main or exclusive participants.

Because "Asia" encompasses such a vast territory, for purposes of this introduction, the religions discussed here will be grouped according to whether they are more prominent in the East Asian or South Asian region. The first section below will provide an overview of the religions most prominent in East Asian countries—Taoism, Confucianism, Shinto, Korean Shamanic religions, and Japanese new religions. The second section will introduce the religions more prominent in South Asian countries—Jainism and Burmese spirit cults. Although the religions will be presented separately here, in lived reality, they are often combined together in a variety of ways to form "syncretic" or popular religions. For example, popular religious practice among many Chinese people combines elements of Buddhism, Confucianism, and Taoism. Folk religions are often part of the mix in Asian religious practice. We will see one example of such practice in the "*Nat* cults" in predominantly Buddhist Burma, for example. In Japan, Buddhism and Shinto are also often combined in actual practice, both with one another, and with elements of Christianity and/or indigenous religious traditions.

East Asian Traditions

Many East Asian religious traditions are based on rituals of worship to ancestors and household deities. The small farm in traditional Asian society was treated as a ritual unit, with different gods or deities inhabiting different parts of the household.

Confucianism Similar to the term "Hinduism," Confucianism is a Western term applied to a set of religious phenomena so as to render it intelligible as a single, coherent system of thought emerging from a single leader. In fact, the Chinese words for this collection of religious phenomena, *Rujiao* and *Rujia*, both based on the term *Ru*, makes the term "Literati Tradition" more consistent with the original. Nonetheless, in order to retain consistency with the familiar Western terminology, the words Confucian and Confucianism will continue to be applied here.

Confucianism is not a "living tradition" of religion in the sense of having a population of adherents who consider themselves to be "Confucianists." However, there are strains of Confucian thought and practice still evident throughout East Asian countries, as well as schools of "neo-Confucian" ideas, including Western academia, which keep aspects of Confucianism alive today. Confucianism first emerged during the late Zhou period in China (1050–256 B.C.E.) and is attributed to the thought of Kong Zi ("Master Kong"), whom the Jesuits named "Confucius."

As Kong Zi's dates (551–479 B.C.E.) indicate, he was roughly a Chinese contemporary of the Buddha. The famous *Analects* text is attributable to him. The Confucian tradition really became widespread only in the later Han dynasty (206 B.C.E. to 220 C.E.), however, as members of the Literati gained favor with the imperial government and insinuated themselves and their texts into official government activities. The second sage of the Literati tradition was Mencius.

The primary texts of Confucianism are called *The Five Classics*. Generally speaking, the Confucian religion is based on ancestor worship and the cult of the family. Compared with other religions, Confucianism is centered in the human realm rather than the god realm. That is, its concerns are more oriented to human beings in "this" world than to those of deities in a transcendent realm. Thus, its system of ethics and values stress "filial piety," or the obligations to elders, ancestors, and other superiors (for women, these superiors include men).

The transcendent realm is not ignored, however. Confucian texts stress correspondences between heaven and earth, and the need to maintain a harmonious balance between them. This harmony could be accomplished, Confucian texts state, by humans replicating the cosmic order in its hierarchical structure and complementary relationships of *yin* (associated symbolically with low, earth, and female) and *yang* (associated with high, heaven, and male) (see Jochim 1999, 196).

Keeping the mandate of heaven required secular leaders to adhere to ethical and ritual codes of propriety, and subjects to maintain the "Doctrine of the Three Bonds," which explicitly made subjects subservient to rulers, sons to fathers, and wives to husbands. Already we can discern in Confucianism a highly male-dominated, patriarchal religion in which women's roles are necessarily "lesser" than those of men. Literati of the Han disseminated texts defining women's roles, which became models for later texts. Because of its patriarchy and androcentrism, Confucianism provides perhaps the greatest contrast with the folk religions described here which elevated the female role to a revered spiritual status.

The four main rituals in Confucianism revolve around the life cycle and the family: coming of age, weddings, funerals, and ancestral sacrifices. Women's power and authority are based on their roles as wives and mothers. Although limiting from a Western perspective, because Confucianism conceptualized the family as a microcosm of the state and also as a sacred community, those roles have sometimes carried considerable authority. Because political authority in China was passed through a family lineage, women sometimes have held power by virtue of their status within the family structure, although seldom as leaders in their own right.

Although the Literati tradition continued to have an influence in China following the Han period, it was in competition with Taoism and the influx of Buddhism. During the Tang period (618–907), these three religions, known as the "three teachings," were generally accepted by the Literati as coexisting harmoniously. During the Sung dynasty (989–1279), however, orthodox disapproval of the "three teachings" led to a renaissance of the Literati tradition, referred to by scholars today as the neo-Confucian movement (see Jochim 1999, 197).

Confucianism spread to Korea and Japan around the third century C.E. but did not have a major impact there and in Vietnam until the Sung dynasty and thereafter. Its ideology of patriarchy and the relationship between virtuosity in the home and the state were well established in these countries by the seventh century and continued to hold sway until the modern period. By the nineteenth century in Japan and the early twentieth century in China, Vietnam, and Korea, the ruling regimes which had supported Confucian ideas and values ended and the Confucian tradition entered an identity crisis. Neo-Confucian scholars of the twentieth century, who have defended Confucian values against the criticisms leveled against it (e.g., as antithetical to social and economic progress), have not addressed the tradition's deep-seated patriarchy and sexism, however.

Taoism The term "Tao" means "road" or "way," and, by extension, also terms such as "principle," "method," "order," and "morality." In Taoist writings, the term is used mainly to refer to the ineffable and ultimate reality underlying all phenomena in the universe. The Tao is associated with nature, which is peaceful, harmonious, and good, and which has been disrupted by human consciousness. Somewhat more recent than Confucianism, Taoism originated in ancient China and emerged out of a variety of archaic religious practices from different regions and time periods. Although women were prominent in the early eras of Taoism, they were marginalized as time went on. Taoism is usually classified into three time periods: Classical (fourth to second century B.C.E.), Traditional (second to tenth centuries C.E.), and "New" (tenth century to the present).

Classical Taoism is based on practices of cultivating life-force energy called *qi* (*ch'i*) which were detailed in a text called the *Neiye* (fourth century B.C.E.) and are mentioned in two well-known books of Taoism, the *Laozi* and *Zhuangzi*. The latter text is based on the expanded and edited thoughts of Zhuang Zhou, a fourth-century B.C.E. philosopher. The practice of cultivating *qi* was accessible to both men and women, although the sparse ancient texts that remain do not specifically mention any female practitioners. The most famous text of classical Taoism is the *Daode jing*, attributed to a man named "Laozi" (Laotzu) but actually compiled by an unknown writer who brought it from the region of his elders (*laozi/laotzu*), a Southern nation called Chu (Ch'u), to the northern cities. Based on oral teachings that people should return to "feminine behaviors" of quiet selfless beneficence, the texts came to compete with Confucianism and other prevalent ideas of the time.

In Traditional Taoism, after a period in which the community that produced the *Neiye* had died out, the cultivation of *qi* reemerged in the second century C.E. in a text called the *Taiping jing*, which envisioned a utopian society based on harmonious relations. In one of the popular movements inspired by this text called Tianshi, women held an explicitly equal relationship in the priesthood and could hold highest offices, even if married. Revelation from a female priest named Wei Haucun (Wei Hua-ts'un, 251–334) was the basis for a fourth-century movement called Shangqing Taoism, which taught how mortals could purify themselves through visualized meditation, including the projection of one's own *qi* energy into a visualized goddess.

From about the fourth to ninth centuries C.E., male and female priests (*daoshi/tao-shih*) lived a spiritual life in monastic environments, engaging in self-cultivation and liturgy. They had the support of the Chinese imperial leaders and the cultural elite. Unlike some other world religions, when Taoism unified, women clerics generally held the same titles as men, rather than being relegated to a secondary status in the wake of increasing bureaucratization and institutionalization. However, there were fewer women participants. Based on the numbers of abbeys and monasteries that reportedly were in existence in 739, there were 550 abbeys for women, in contrast with 1,137 monasteries for men (Kirkland 1999, 961). In addition, women may have been mentioned less often because of the Taoist valorization of the unknown sage whose beneficial influence is attributed to the course of nature as well as the perceptions of the dominant Confucian societies that many Taoist women practitioners lived in (Cleary 198,; 6-7).

During the high Tang dynasty (c. 700), imperial princesses became ordained as priestesses. The goddess Xiwangmu (Hsi Wang Mu), "the Queen Mother of the West," also called "the Golden Mother" and "the Golden Mother of the Tortoise Petal," was viewed as the deity who controlled access to transcendence. Although she was revered by both men and women, she held special appeal to the latter as the patron of women who renounced traditional female roles as wife and mother for spiritual life. All women who attain the Tao are considered to be her successors.

During this period, many women felt free to renounce their assigned gender roles and become Buddhist nuns or Taoist priestesses (see Kirkland 1999, 961). But, as we saw with Confucianism, the status of women declined, beginning in the Sung dynasty.

"New Taoism" is a label for several different movements that arose beginning around the tenth century C.E. One of the two main movements that arose was Qingwei Taoism, founded by a young woman, Zu Shu (Tsu Shu) around 900. Its main practice was "thunder rites" that empowered priests to heal, banish evil spirits, and bless children (see Kirkland 1999; 961). The other main movement to emerge from this third period of Taoism resulted from the invasion of Mongol emperors. Called Zhengyi (Cheny-i), it purported to be a renewal of the earlier Tianshi form of the religion. Zhengyi priests were all male. Women were banned from the sacred space that the priest created and played a marginal role in this form of Taoism. In fact, the participation of women in Taoism declined sharply during this period. By 1077, for example, there were only 700 ordained women, in contrast to 18,500 men.

Other new movements that arose during this third wave of Taoism stressed the self-cultivation and perfection of the classical and traditional forms of Taoism (especially through morality, meditation, and insight), and the harmony of Taoism, Buddhism, and Confucianism. Although little known in the West, one of these movements, Quanzhen, included a woman named Sun Buer (Sun Pu erh) among its twelfth-century founder Wang Zhe/ Wang Che's main disciples. This form of Taoism is still practiced in northern China and women are among its practitioners.

Shintoism Shinto, or "the way of the Gods" (called *kami*), is an indigenous Japanese religion that began in the prehistorical period. It is based on rituals for respecting the gods of the natural world, the state, and the home and enshrined in myths that were compiled in written form in the eighth century C.E. There are a number of important female *kami*, including the most important of all the *kami*, the goddess Amaterasu. Amaterasu began as a local clan deity and grew to national prominence as the protective deity of the state in the sixth and seventh centuries.

As the selection on "Women and Shinto" by Karen Smyers explains, women held very powerful roles in the earliest period of Shinto in Japan, including roles as empresses and compilers of spiritual texts. In addition, they frequently held roles as shamanesses, who mediated between the human realm and the realm of the *kami*. And as with many of the other religious traditions discussed in this chapter, the strength of Shinto, as well as the authority of and respect for women, especially in religious roles, began to wane, at least publicly, with the introduction of Confucianism and Buddhism to Japan. Part of what contributed to the waning of women's status in Shinto, as in Japanese society more widely, were increasingly repressive notions of women's purity and the pollution of menstruation, sex, and childbirth.

Japanese New Religions The so-called "new religions" in Japan are largely a product of the post–World War era, although the earliest of the so-called "new religions" arose in the nineteenth century. They are tremendously popular, drawing approximately one-quarter of the Japanese population into some kind of association with them. They reflect the process of religious change, incorporating elements of the "older" Buddhist and Shinto religions with responses to modernity. They tend to share several characteristics in common: they are based on charismatic leadership; have a "this worldly" orientation offering concrete benefits (such as cures, wealth, solutions to problems, etc.) rather than a transcendental or "other worldly" perspective; take a critical stance toward the traditional Buddhist and Shinto religions; and are especially attractive to, and populated by, women. In keeping with the values of feminist "care ethics," the new religions conceptualize persons not as autonomous individuals whose salvation is dependent upon the will of a single, creator God, but as relational beings whose goal is to live in harmony with others through the perfection of virtue (Hardacre 1992, 299).

Contemporary Japanese women are drawn to the new religions in far greater numbers than to traditional religions, and the majority membership of new religious groups is female. Indeed, many new religions were founded by women, and women have held many prominent roles in these religions, as well as being mainly responsible for their daily operations. Several of the new religions were founded by women whose followers consider them to be living *kami*, thus suggesting the continuity of the "new" religions with Shinto.

Helen Hardacre suggests that "women's phenomenal participation" in Japanese new religions reflects a change in religious attitudes, especially toward women (Hardacre 1992; 298). Among these changes is the belief that salvation is imminent, as opposed to a distant goal as in Buddhism and shrine Shinto, especially for those unfortunate enough to be born with a female form. Beliefs about women's pollution do not inhibit women from leadership roles or from the rewards of dedicated religious practice.

These modern traditions have provided one of the few means for Japanese women to exercise positions of public prominence and have continued significant premodern roles for women as shamanesses, priestesses, diviners, and healers from folk or popular religious traditions. At the same time, some of these new religions represent a paradox. Certain fundamentalist strands teach that women should return to being primarily wives and mothers and give up choices they have gained regarding reproduction, marriage, and divorce in favor of traditional roles of subservience and deference to their husbands (see Hardacre 1992, 300-09).

Folk Religion In general, folk religions are based at the local or community level, often around a centralized temple for the community. They are typically based on rituals and supplications to local spirits and deities to protect the environment and the people living in it from misfortunes, such as droughts, floods, and so on, to preserve the harmony and well-being of the community, and for healing. Within Chinese folk religions, ritual tasks are gendered, with men worshiping the household gods (especially the Kitchen God on New Year's) and women performing rituals for the ancestors (Kendall 1999, 282).

The Korean folk religion (Korean "Shamanism" or "household religion") has been the most prominent religious tradition in Korea throughout its history, despite the imposition of Buddhism, Confucianism, and Christianity at various points along the way. Even today, in spite of urbanization, industrialization, and other forms of modernization, folk religion remains far more popular than Buddhism and Christianity, the two main world religions active in the country. However, there are not sharply demarcated lines separating the different religious traditions in Korea. Because Buddhism does not demand any exclusive allegiance, many Buddhists also draw upon shamanesses and Christian churches, participating in rituals and ceremonies of all three traditions.

Contrary to the male domination of these other religions, in Korean folk religion, the female shaman (shamanness) has had great authority, and her services have been highly sought after. Shamanesses perform rituals to the gods in the larger context of the community, whereas "senior housewives" perform such rituals at home. Shamanesses' services as ritual specialists have been especially important for women, enabling them to bargain with gods, spirits, and ancestors responsible for their current misfortunes. At elaborate rituals, the shamaness seeks out and is then possessed by a succession of ancestors and gods (see Sered 1994, 18).

Requests for the shamaness' services range from help with success in childbirth, curing illnesses, to the economic and psychic well-being of the family and the larger community. Thus, women have had a major role to play in mediating relations between humans in "this world" and humans and other beings in other realms of existence.

Although perhaps not quite accurately characterized as a "folk religion," the *kami-sama* religion described in the selection from *Women of the Sacred Groves* by Susan Sered also involves women in prominent roles, including that of taking on the being of the *kami* (gods) themselves. Perhaps more than any of the other religious traditions described in this chapter, the *kami-sama* religion of Okinawa can be considered a "woman's religion," as women comprise the vast majority of the leaders as well as the participants in the religious rituals and other aspects of religious life. Sered's essay suggests that religions dominated by women tend to be characterized as less hierarchical and insistent upon a gendered division of labor. Sered's essay provides an excellent introduction to thinking about the relationship between gender and religion, how religion legitimates and perpetuates gender differentiations and hierarchies, and how these inequalities are maintained through gender ideology. In these respects, Sered's essay is useful, not only for thinking about women in Asian religious traditions, but also for thinking about women in religions generally.

South Asian Traditions

In addition to Hinduism, Buddhism, and Islam, which are the dominant religious traditions in the South Asian region, there are a number of other, smaller traditions which deserve note. The following discussion will focus on Jainism and Burmese Spirit Cults, two of the most prominent of these traditions.

Jainism Jainism is one of the world's oldest religions, being established in India around the fifth or sixth century B.C.E., based on the teachings of Mahavira, who was roughly a contemporary of the Buddha. Most of the approximately three and one-half million Jains live in India or in countries to which Indians have migrated. Jainism is basically atheistic. Its mythology centers around the 24 "Tirthamkaras" or "Jinas," called "ford builders." These are beings who have passed through different realms of existence (e.g., God, animals, humans), and who are reborn as human beings in their last lifetime. Mahavira is regarded as the twenty-fourth of 24 Jinas. In their last incarnation, they devote themselves to renouncing worldly existence for the practice of asceticism, which results in perfect knowledge and, finally, Emancipation (Balbir 1999, 521-22).

Contrary to both Buddhism and Hinduism, Jain women play central roles in religious life, both as lay persons and as nuns. Contrary to Buddhism, there is no record of the establishment of the order of nuns being problematic, and even today, there are more nuns than male monks. The names of prominent women are included in the early narrative texts, which was unusual for Indian society.

Similar to Buddhism, however, the regulations governing the lives of nuns are more strict than those for monks, reflecting the stereotypical view that women's natures are unsteady and need greater control. Similar to Buddhism's "Eight Special Rules," the specific regulations governing nuns subordinate them to the monks. While some sects allow both nuns and monks access to all the texts, others claim that women are of lesser ability and thus restrict their access to certain advanced texts, especially those relating to the monastic code. Other sects, by contrast, stress the importance of education for girls and women. Although nuns are allowed to give public sermons, not many do (Balbir 1999, 520).

Lay women play important roles in Jain religious life. Food and ritual are central aspects of Jain religious life, and women are largely in control of these domains. Women offer alms of food to begging mendicants. They prepare the family's meals, which requires attention to ritual specifications. (Ironically, women gain virtue and a reputation for religiosity by fasting.) They are also the authorities regarding the conduct and performance of ritual.

Lay women are also in charge of reproducing family life. They pass on religious beliefs and moral values to the next generation, largely through religious narratives, and arrange marriages for their offspring. They are also renowned for their proficiency for singing hymns, chanting, and reciting. Sects differ, however, regarding the extent to which women are allowed to worship images, with the anti-idolatry sects that are focused on inner cultivation being more egalitarian (see Balbir 1999, 521). A fundamental split between the two main sects, the Digambaras ("Sky-clad") and the Svetambaras ("White-clad"), has existed for centuries regarding the issue of whether women are capable of full emancipation. The former believe that nudity is essential for full emancipation, and since it is inappropriate for women to be naked, they must be reborn in a male body before being capable of attaining the highest state. The Svetambaras, on the other hand, do not believe in any such impediment, since what matters is moral cultivation of the self, not one's outward appearance. The Svetambaras and Digambaras disagree regarding whether one of the 24 Jinas, a person named Malli, was female.

Burmese Spirit Cults   Although Buddhism is the state religion of Burma (now Myanmar) and is considered to be the more powerful religion, existing closely alongside are earlier, indigenous spirit religions or cults devoted to appeasing spirits called *nats*. *Nats* are believed to have control over creating and curing illnesses. Unlike Buddhism, which is male dominated, the *nat* spirit cults are dominated by women. Women tend the village *nat* shrines, perform and attend the ceremonies to the *nats,* and become the shamans, who are possessed by *nats.* Each household makes offerings to a *nat*, which is usually descended from the mother's side. Whereas men are more closely identified with Buddhism, women are more identified with the *nat* religion. Nonetheless, the two religions are closely intertwined, with some rituals and shrines occurring in close proximity to one another.

In some respects, the *nat* religion can be seen as an expression of opposition to the dominance of Buddhism. For example, *nat* myths often convey anti-Buddhist sentiments, opposing the monastic life, for instance, or honoring sexuality (with which women are more closely identified in Buddhist cultures generally). (Indeed, the method of becoming a *nat* shaman is through having sexual intercourse with a *nat* [Sered 1994, 17.]) Whereas Buddhism is focused on adherence to moral precepts and eliminating craving to the things of "this world," *nat* worship ignores morality, broadly defined, and is focused on acquiring "this worldly" benefits like good health and livelihood. And even though Buddhism is considered to be more powerful than the *nat* religion, so that a devoted Buddhist practitioner would have no need to propitiate the *nats*, the spirit cults devoted to *nats* have continued to flourish. Susan Sered speculates that this may be precisely because the *nat* religion accords a central role to women, whereas Buddhism only affords them secondary status (Sered 1994, 17).

Relationship of Female-Gendered and Feminine Images and Symbols to "Real" Women

Chinese Traditions

Ancient Chinese folk religious practice involved several female deities, usually related to fertility. The most prominent of these goddesses was the dragon, who was called upon for rain. Early Taoist texts described the goddess "Queen Mother of the West" and her significance in the mythology that supported rulership (Cass 1999, 279). One of the most revered goddesses in China is Kuan Yin (Guan Yin), who is an amalgam of a Buddhist bodhisattva (as noted in Chapter 3 on Buddhism, the Indian male bodhisattva of compassion Avolokitesvara was transformed into the female Kuan Yin in China), and two local Chinese religious goddesses. The first of these is Mazu, a cult which was originally centered around a pious daughter who rescued her brother and father at sea. The second is Miashan, another filial daughter who sacrificed her eyes and arms to heal her father when he became ill. Both of these local goddesses were absorbed into Kuan Yin and are thought to have been an influence in the spread of Buddhism in China (Cass 1999, 281).

As already noted, gender symbolism enters into the very foundations of Confucianism. Male imagery is prominent in the notion of the father as the ultimate source of all life. Gender imagery is also pronounced in the concept of *yin*, the weak, female principle complementing the strong male principle *yang*, and the "natural hierarchy" of male heaven over female earth, with its social corollary of the relationship between husband and wife. It was not until the Sung dynasty (960–1279), however, that "neo-Confucian" ideas of feminine sanctity had wide circulation in Korea and Japan. Perhaps because Confucianism is a religion focused mainly on "this worldly concerns," there is a direct correlation between the ideal characteristics of females promulgated in Confucian gender ideology and the social prescriptions for women's conduct. Contrary to some religious traditions, where the images of women and/or the feminine are in stark contrast to the views of actual women, here the correlation seems to be accurate and precise.

Whereas the elevated gender symbols in Confucianism are male, those in Taoism are predominantly female. Feminine imagery, especially of the maternal, has often been used to describe the Tao, even though it is understood to be beyond concepts and description. For example, Lao Tze refers to the Tao as "the mother of all things" or "the mother of the world" (see Chen 1974, 51). He encouraged both men and women to cultivate the *yin* or female principle. Reflecting the symbolic association of valleys as *yin*, Lao Tze directs, "Know the masculine, but practice the feminine: be the valley stream of the world" (see Young 1999, 963). The *Chuang Tzu* describes a prehistoric matriarchal society in which people knew their mothers but not their fathers, and in which universal peace reigned until the human consciousness and morals developed (see Chen 1974, 61). In Traditional Taoism, as noted above, there were a number of female divinities, including women who had attained the highest state of transcendence. The gender imagery of females appears to have had a straightforward correspondence with "real women," as opposed to the antithetical imagery that we have seen operating in aspects of Hinduism and Buddhism.

Jainism Like other Indian traditions, Jainism reflects a tension between symbolic images of women and the actual status of "real" women. Among the prominent Jain divinities are the female attendants of the main Jinas. Several of these figures, such as Cakresvari, Padmavati, and Ambika, have attained independent significance and are worshiped in their own right for the protective power they are believed to offer. In addition, knowledge, which is revered in Jainism, is always represented by feminine imagery (similar to Prajnaparamita, the perfection of wisdom, in Mahayana Buddhism). These female deities are considered to be closer to the human world and its problems than the more distant Jinas.

Whereas much of the imagery of women is basically negative—and similar to Buddhism in denigrating women as hindrances to male spiritual progress—some women are revered for their spiritual attainments or as representing protective, maternal entities. For example, there is a fairly ancient cult devoted to worship of the mothers of the Jinas. Especially prominent is Marudevi, the mother of the first Jina, who is known as the first emancipated soul (Balbir 1999, 522).

Women's Relationship to Asian Religions

Women-Specific or Distinctive Aspects of Asian Religions

Confucianism As Kelleher's essay describes, Confucianism provides a number of prescriptions for how women are to behave and act in order to be "womanly." These prescriptions generally revolve around women's roles as wives, which was regarded by the Literati tradition as their primary role in life. Within the Six Dynasties period in China (222–589 C.E.), women held a variety of different roles within the monastic environment: as priestesses, visionaries, spirit mediums, teachers, clerics, nuns, adepts, recluses, and healers. Some women also held the unusual status of being "living auspicious omens" who were allied with the legitimacy of the ruling dynasty. These roles gave women iconic status as charismatic community leaders. Some women also took on roles as warriors and millenarian rebels (Cass 1999, 279).

The syncretic religions that developed as a result of the incorporation of Buddhist and Taoist elements into Confucianism during the Sung, Yuan (1279–1368), and Ming (1368–1644) dynasties provided women with non-domestic spiritual roles and even some opportunities for leadership positions (see Jochim 1999, 197).

Although texts such as *Biographies of Exemplary Women* present women as being the foundations of social morality, other texts, such as the Confucian *Five Classics* discussed in the Kelleher reading, describe women as inferior by nature, ruled by emotion, and lacking in intellect. Similar to early Buddhist views, these Confucian Literati texts also view women's beauty as lures to trap men, to their ruin. The "three followings" or "three obediences"—which have been tremendously influential in shaping gender ideology about Chinese women ever since—prescribe that females should follow their fathers in their youth, their husbands after marriage, and their sons in their widowhood (see Jochim 1999, 197). This prescription leaves women with no opportunities to pursue scholarly or political pursuits, only domestic ones as servants to the males in their lives.

Based on the centrality of the family and filial piety, the "cult of the martyred (or chaste) woman" in Confucianism elevated the status of women who sacrificed themselves within the domestic sphere. Mothers and wives who train their sons and husbands in virtue were depicted as the ideal women. Sacrificial acts such as self-mutilation to heal an ill relative, suicide or withdrawal into a life of mourning upon the death of a spouse, were highly regarded and result in elevation of the female martyr's status to that of a local divinity capable of protecting the community from natural disasters. The ideal of the "pious daughter" is prominent not only in Confucianism, but also in Buddhism, Taoism, and folk religions as well (Cass 1999, 280).

Why have women been so willing to maintain and perpetuate oppressive social roles in Chinese society? Perhaps one of the most important reasons is the Confucian cosmology, which makes women's subordination to men a natural part of the cosmic order. Similar to the concept of *Dharmashastra* in Hinduism, when one believes that one's status in life has been divinely ordained, it is far more difficult to resist or challenge it as unjust. Further, because women's roles in Confucianism revolve around the family as a sacred order, this has been taught to women as the entire sphere for their devotion. In contrast to Buddhism and Taoism, which maintained opportunities for women to pursue monastic lifestyles, this option has not been available to Chinese women under Confucianism. In addition, rather than directly challenging oppressive gender role prescriptions and values, women in Confucian society have found some modicum of power using more subtle and indirect methods.

Taoism In general, Taoist practices are not gender specific or gender segregated in any respect. As mentioned earlier, women as well as men can become monastics or priests and are not restricted to lay, domestic roles.

Nat Spirit Cults According to the 31 realms of existence of Buddhism, *nats* occupy a place between women, who are lower, and men, who are higher. For this reason, women bow to *nats* whereas men do not. Women are also thought to be more vulnerable to being attacked by *nats* than men are and tend to believe in *nats* more than men do.

Well-Known and/or Influential Women in the Tradition

Confucianism The reading by Kelleher describes several Confucian women who wrote treatises for women which had a widespread impact, including Pan Chao, the author of the Han dynasty treatise *Instructions for Women*, Ms. Ch'eng, who wrote the *Classic of Filial Piety for Women;* and Sung Jo-chao, who wrote the *Analects for Women*. Again, during the neo-Confucian period, Empress Hsu, the second empress of the Ming dynasty, wrote *Instructions of the Inner Quarters*. These examples represent one of the anomalies of some women in religion: Highly accomplished and relatively independent themselves, they devoted their life's work to disseminating their religion's gender ideology on the subordination of the female gender by teaching other women how to be properly deferent and obedient to men. They might be compared to Phyllis Shafley of the Eagle Forum and fundamentalist Anita Bryant as modern examples of this phenomenon in American culture. One distinction between these texts is that Empress Hsu's later neo-Confucian text exhorts women to strive for sagehood, in keeping with the influence of Buddhist conceptions of self-cultivation on this later strand of Confucianism.

Kelleher tells us that the most celebrated mother in Chinese history is the widowed mother of the famous philosopher Mencius.

Shinto and Japanese New Religions As Smyers' essay describes, in response to her survey, the overwhelming majority of respondents identified Ameratsu Omikami, the Kami Goddess, as the "most important woman in Japanese history," signifying a marked absence of strong differentiation between female deities and women. This parallels Sered's discoveries about the female Omi-kami priests in the Okinawa folk religion.

The presence of so many female leaders and shamanesses among the Japanese folk and "new" religions suggests that the Japanese have retained a fondness for strong female religious leaders since the earliest days of Shinto, even though women have been "demoted" from the mainstream and state-sanctioned religions of Buddhism and Confucianism.

Gender-Based Segregation and Inequalities

In general, it seems apparent that women have fared better in Asian religions that remained independent of the state than in those that have been linked to state power and authority. In Korea, for example, from the Koryo period (918–1392), women were respected as shamanesses, had the right to perform family rituals, inherit property equally with sons, could succeed to the family line, and widows were allowed to divorce. During the Choson dynasty (1392–1910), the educated class attempted to turn Korea into a Confucian state. With the rise of neo-Confucianism, women's status declined (Cass 1999, 280).

In Chinese folk religion, menstruation and birthing were considered impure and polluting and associated women with unclean spirits, the dead, and "little low goddeses," who were associated with childbirth. Such beliefs rationalized women's subordinate positions and signified the danger that women (through their association with birth, death, and menstruation) were thought to pose to the integrity and security of the family. Because family lineages are traced through the male line, and women went to live with their husbands' families upon marriage, women's ritual impurity and pollution were more specifically associated with wives than with women generally (Kendall 1999, 283).

During the Sung period in China, when Buddhist ideas of ascetic self-denial became incorporated in the Literati tradition, the denigration of women increased, and earlier Confucian valorization of characteristics associated with women—such as the emotions, the human body, and the natural world—were rejected. During this time, social practices oppressive to women such as foot binding and female seclusion were also established in China (see Jochim 1999, 197). Since it was the Confucianism of this time period that had the largest impact on changing Korean, Vietnamese, and Japanese religious practices and social values, such negative attitudes toward women became prevalent there as well. These societies, which had been relatively non-patriarchal prior to the infusion of the Literati tradition, adopted Confucian values of hierarchy, divine rulership, sexism, and rigid gender roles.

Because of China's direct influence on Korea, it is not surprising that Chinese religious views of women and families are similar in Korean religious traditions. It is thus unusual to find a reversal of gender roles in Korean ritual, where men perform the rituals associated with ancestors, and women those relating to the household deities. Although wives and daughters-in-law prepare the food used in the ancestor rituals, men are the actual ritual performers except in cases of widows who do not have sons. Women still have some relationship to death in Korea, though, including administering "meals" to the newly dead, performing simple exorcism rituals, and sponsoring elaborate ones.

But the central ritual obligations for Korean women are to the household gods. The main responsibility for performing these rituals—which include offerings to the gods at harvest time and other occasions of boons and misfortunes—falls to the "senior housewife" and is taken over by the daughter-in-law when she retires. Menstruation and childbirth are considered to make women temporarily polluted and unfit to perform the household rituals (or to visit temples or sacred mountains).

In Japan, women provide ritual food offerings to both the ancestors and the household gods in the course of preparing food for the rest of the family. There is no strict gender division between serving the household gods (*kami*) and the ancestors, because the latter are eventually adopted into the pantheon of the former, so no strict division is maintained.

It should be noted that in contemporary Asian countries, many of these domestic rituals have been abandoned, since many were tied to the agricultural calendar, and many people have left rural areas for urban ones. In addition, housewives who live away from their mothers-in-law sometimes rely on ritual specialists to perform ceremonies that were once the common knowledge of all wives (see Kendall 1999, 284).

As we have seen in several other religions, women's once-prominent position in the Shinto tradition appears to have eroded over time. As Smyers describes in the selection on women in Shinto, whereas spirit possession was only accepted as a possibility for all women, as time went on only virgins were seen as having the capacity for being possessed by spirits.

Women's Access to Religious Training and Education and Opportunities for Leadership Roles

Throughout the history of East Asian religions, women have often had prominent leadership roles. They are viewed as "divine intermediaries" between "this world" and the divine realm, However, women's status as intermediaries has varied among the different religious traditions. Viewed along a continuum, women's roles as divine intermediaries have been most prominent in local, folk religions and least so in Buddhism (Cass 1999, 278).

In East Asian religions, the female intermediary is called a shamaness. The shamaness is present in religious texts as far back as earliest recorded history in ancient China. Early shamanesses were called upon to perform rituals to influence the course of the natural world, such as to bring fertility or rain, or purify the environment. The status of the shamaness in China declined after the end of the Zhou dynasty (1027–221 B.C.E.) and was actively denigrated by the Ming and Qing imperial dynasties.

The situation in Korea is parallel. The shamaness (*mudang*) was highly respected and active until the Choson period in the fourteenth century, when neo-Confucianism, with its patriarchal and sexist ideology, gained ascendency. However, during the Six Dynasties period in China, Taoist women were recognized as religious leaders. Though the shamaness was banished from elite religion, Victoria Cass informs us that the shamaness became transformed into the Taoist adept and cleric (Cass 1999, 280). There are still shamanesses active in Korea. Although Buddhist monks and nuns distance themselves from these women, they have nonetheless incorporated certain elements of Buddhism into their practices. The role of shamaness in Korean society, like that of the Buddhist nun, provides a means for women to gain independence from men and to escape the socially accepted roles of wife and mother for freedom from familial obligations. In addition, shamanesses concern themselves with the needs of women and serve both as their healers and counselors (see Watt 1999, 286).

In Japan, the shamaness role in Shinto never diminished as it did in China and Japan (perhaps because of the lesser significance of Confucianism in Japanese culture and society?) and continues to be important in folk Shinto practices to the present day (Cass 1999, 279).

In the *Nat* Spirit cult in Burma/Myanmar, which mixes with Buddhism, a clearly male-dominated tradition, women are considered authoritative (Bartholomeuz 1999, 126; Sered 1994, 17).

Changes in the Status of Women

As the preceding discussion suggests, the status of women in Asian religions has varied significantly, depending upon the specific religion, geographical location, and time period involved. In some instances, such as in the Classic period of Taoism, the *nat* cults of Burma, and Korean shamanic cults, women have been held in high esteem. In others, the same biases toward women that we have seen in Buddhism and Hinduism are conspicuously present. To some extent, the difference has seemed to rest on whether the religious practices were important to men or not (as with the *nat* cults).

With increasing globalization and modernization, there will no doubt be further significant changes in women's roles and status in Asian religions. If women's status in a religion does in fact rest upon some correlation with the degree of men's interest, then increasing secularization of society would serve to enhance women's opportunities for participation and leadership roles in these religions.

Women and Shinto: The Relation Between Purity and Pollution

Karen A. Smyers

Introduction

It is in the earliest period of Japanese history, before the word "Shinto" even existed, that most of the fundamental contributions by women to Shinto occurred. Japan was called the "Queen Country" in third century Chinese histories, because of the frequency of female rulers. The legendary Himiko was such a shamanic queen, who ruled from 180 to 248. The Empress Jingū (actually Regent: she never officially ascended the throne) was an extremely successful ruler "who first brought Japan as a more or less centralized state into contact with the Asiatic mainland, and thus prepared a way for the inflow of continental culture during the fifth century and onwards."[1] During the period from 592 until 770 there were six empresses, and in fact the first time the word *tennō* was used as the imperial title was during the reign of the Empress Suiko (592–628).[2] Empress Gemmel (707–715) had the first permanent capital

From 1983. *Japanese Religions* 12; 1, 17–18, Reprinted with permission of Karen Smyers.

built at Nara, and ordered completion of the *Kojiki*, Japan's first written chronicle.

The word used for "empress" was *nakatsu-sumera-mikoto*, which can be translated in two ways, "the one who carries on the imperial duty between the death of her husband and the accession of the next emperor," or "the august medium who transmits the *mi-koto* (divine word) of the heavenly *kami*."[3] These interpretations show her function as an intermediary in both a political and spiritual sense.

The compiler of the *Kojiki* is also thought to be a woman. In 682, Emperor Temmu requested that Hieda no Are memorize the oral traditions and dictate them to a scribe. Long thought to have been a man, scholarship beginning in the Edo period asserts that Hieda was the surname of a matriarchal line of shrine maidens, and that Are means "to act as medium for a god."[4]

There are many other hints of the important role of women in the society of this time. Descent was traced through the female line in some families. In the *Kojiki* it states: "Again the emperor said to his empress: 'It is usual for the names of children to be given by the mother. What name shall be given to this child?'"[5] A third-century Chinese chronicle relates that: "... Father and mother, elder and younger brothers and sisters live separately, but at meetings there is no distinction on account of sex."[6]

This central position held by women in the formative period of Japanese history, although eroded by continental influences, has remained an important element in the Japanese consciousness, most clearly symbolized in Amaterasu, the Sun Goddess from whom the Japanese believe themselves to have descended. "The ascription of the female sex to the most prominent among the Shinto Gods is not owing merely to caprice. Myth makers have often more substantial reasons for their fancies than might be supposed."[7]

The Paradox of Purity and Pollution

The concept of taboo includes two seemingly contrary feelings: extreme reverence and extreme horror. That is, a thing may be taboo because it is perceived as holy, other, or numinous, or because it is unclean or polluted. At first, these two ideas were not differentiated, and were seen as equally dangerous conditions. In most cultures, menstruation, childbirth, and the consummation of marriage were taboo states, certainly because of the appearance of blood, but also because they were seen as the source of women's magic powers.[8]

In early Shinto, fertility was at the core of all beliefs, and purity was at the core of all ritual.[9] Because fertility was as important as purity, because women had a very important role in society, and because the two aspects of taboo were still undifferentiated, the conditions of women's sexuality were not seen as merely polluting. Philippi explains a song in the *Kojiki* thus:

Women may have been considered polluted during the menstrual period, as in later centuries in Japan; or they may have been considered sacred to the gods and therefore unapproachable during this time. In the latter case, menstrual blood, far from being a defilement, would be a sign of religious consecration, and this song merely a light and roundabout expression of disappointment that ritual considerations prevent immediate sexual union.[10]

Further weight can be given to this interpretation by noting that the Ainu consider menstrual blood a talisman. "When a man sees some on the floor of a hut, he rubs it over his breast believing he will thereby secure success."[11] There is an old Japanese saying that "When a woman is menstruating she is purified, becoming the wife of the *kami*." (*Gessui no aru aida wa junsui ni "kami no tsuma" to naru*.). This too hints at a sacred status for menstruating women.

Not only were women not seen at this time as inherently polluted beings, they may have even had the power to remove pollution. It is a curious fact that in the *Obaraekotoba*, the ritual prayer for the very solemn semiannual purification of the Japanese nation, the four kami who are invoked are all female.[12]

In the early days of Shinto, the sacred and the sexual were more closely integrated, and, in contrast to later days when virginity became a requirement for a woman to be possessed by *kami* (divinity), we see that even pregnant women were possessed. In Chapter 93 of the *Kojiki*, the EmpressJingū is possessed and told that the child in her womb is a boy and that he will conquer Korea.

Purity was of course necessary at this time for the rituals involving the *kami*, but what is important is that this purity was spiritual or psychological, as opposed to an actual physical condition (i.e. virginity). We are apt today to construe the word "virgin" too narrowly. In the ancient Great Mother cults of many lands, the word "virgin" was used to describe the mother. In this case "virgin" is the opposite of "married," in the sense that a married woman was merely the property of her husband.

> She is essentially one-in-herself.... Her divine power does not depend on her relation to a husband god, and thus her actions are not dependent on the need to conciliate such a one or to accord with his qualities and attitudes. For she bears divinity in her own right.[13]

Certainly this "virginal" power can be seen in the Empress Jingū who prophesies for the *kami* even though her husband becomes angry and refuses to believe the divine words.[14]

Blacker points out the double sense of possession in divine marriage legends in which a woman is possessed both spiritually and sexually.[15] The term *Tamayori-hime* occurs three times in the classics, and is not a proper name, but means a woman (*hime*) possessed (*yori*) by a spirit (*tama*), and refers to the belief in early Japan "that a *kami* might possess a pure and holy virgin and that she might become aware of this divine power and give birth to a child of the *kami*...."[16] It was further believed that virginity could be restored after a certain period of continence.[17]

Thus it is important to note that in this early period, there are no absolute rules determining purity, and that purity was not seen as the absence of sexuality. In contrast to Siberian shamanism, in which the shaman travels to the other world, in Japan the shamaness draws the *kami* to her; her body is a vessel for the presence of the sacred.[18] In fact, one of the local names for "shamaness" is *o-kami-sama*, which shows the confusion between the shamaness and the kami possessing her.[19]

The Polarity of Purity and Pollution

The "golden age" of women's position in Japanese society reflected in the mythology and early chronicles begins to decline with the introduction of Buddhism and Confucianism from China and with the growing centralization and bureaucratization of the Japanese state. The clan system and its inherent matriarchal organization were abolished by the Taihō Code of 702 and the Yōrō Code of 718. "They established a patriarchal system, called for the subjugation of women in the Confucian manner, and discriminated against women in matters of property, marriage, and divorce."[21] The Buddhism which came to Japan contained antifeminine elements which it had acquired in China, and emphasized the psychological and biological uncleanliness of women.

> While Buddhism had not generally held that women were excluded from salvation, the strict Tendai and Shingon sects taught that women suffered from oriental sin as well as *Goshō,* the Five Obstructions, which prevented them from obtaining any of the five states of spiritual awareness which men were capable of attaining. A woman's only hope for salvation lay in the possibility of being reborn as a man.[21]

With the increasing centralization of the government came the corresponding institutionalization of religious practices in the seventh and eighth centuries. The unpredictable charismatic structures of both religious and political authority, in which women played such a key role, gave way to stable, patriarchal, bureaucratic structures, from which women were increasingly excluded. "At the turn of the eight century a department of Shinto affairs was established side by side with the great council of state. Chieftans of the hereditary Shinto priestly families thus became bureaucratic government officials with graded rank and prescribed duties."[22]

Thus, through Buddhism's emphasis on her uncleanliness, woman lost her spiritual powers, through Confucianism's emphasis on her status only in relation to men (her father, husband, and son), woman lost her independence, and through the development of a rigid bureaucracy, woman lost her charismatic political authority.

The concept of purity at this time became extremely literal, and was antithetical to sexuality. Women were thought to be pure if they were pre-pubescent virgins—in other words, not yet women. The same things which previously gave women their numinosity were now considered unclean: menstruation, sex, and childbirth.

The quintessence of the Shinto priestess at this time exemplified by the Saiō of Ise. Saō? literally means "abstinence princess" or "consecrated princess" and may also be read *itsuki no miko*. This office is very ancient and the mythological prototype is Yamato-hime, the daughter of Emperor Suinin and founder of the shrine for Amaterasu in Ise. The role of Saiō was especially important from 677 to 1336 (when the last Saiō retired to become a Buddhist nun).[23]

The girl chosen (by divination) to be Saiō was a relative of the emperor, a virgin, and often only a child (one was five years old). She spent two full years in seclusion to prepare for living in the Saigū (Abstinence Palace) in Ise. There was no spiritual requirement for this position; it was basically political. The ritual calendar she followed was not that of Ise, but rather that of the court. She was a symbol of the emperor, and was also called *mitsueshiro*, "staff substitute." The ancient priestess holding a staff by which the kami entered and possessed her has now herself become a representative of the emperor's staff, or his symbol of power.

> The Saiō as the Emperor's *mitsueshiro* is the Heian court as it would like to be seen by the great primordial ancestral kami of the Imperial House, as pristinely pure as a young maiden, without a hint of the pollution of blood or death or sin or of the alien Buddhist language.[24]

Although the *miko* of Ise gave "inspired utterances" induced by the sprinkling of boiling water,[25] and there was still a kind of divination (*miura*) in which the *kamagi* (a kind of high-ranking *miko* at Ise) participated, for the most part, these kinds of functions were excluded from official Shinto. The women within the shrines were required to be pure and performed such tasks as the sacred dance (*kagura*) and preparing sacred offerings for the *kami*. But it is an indication of the power and tenacity of the older forms that they did not disappear.

> The mantic power with which the ancient sibyl was endowed passed from the large shrines to the level of what Robert Redfield called the "little tradition," the largely unrecorded, orally transmitted folk reli-

gion of the villages. The mantic gift of the ancient miko survived in a variety of humbler folk—in the traveling bands of women such as the Kumano *bikuni*, who like strolling minstrels walked the countryside offering their gifts of prophesy and divination, and in the blind women of the north who, without the music and dance so essentially a part of the older miko's shamanic performance, transmit the utterances of numina and dead spirits.[26]

At this time there also grew up a body of rules governing the attendance of people worshipping at a shrine. In the *Korō kujitsuden* from 811, the following prohibitions are listed. A man may not stay in the same house as a woman on the night before going to a shrine. Menstruating women may not go; they must wait seven days, clean their body for three days, and may go to a shrine on the eleventh day after their menstrual period has ended. Women who give birth may not attend a shrine for ninety days after the flow of blood stops and may not use the same cooking fire as men for one-hundred days.[27]

These kind of rules make it very clear that menstruation and childbirth were now viewed in a negative way, as things inappropiate at a shrine and displeasing to the *kami*.

The Proscription of Purity and Pollution

After the Meiji Restoration of 1868, a number of directives were issued concerning women and Shinto in an effort to promote the enlightenment of the country by purging Shinto of all Buddhist and superstitious elements.[28] In 1873, and again in 1874, the practices of the *miko* who worked as mediums (mostly outside shrine Shinto) were outlawed. Women could now climb Mount Fuji, previously thought too holy for the possible pollution from women. The office of the Saiō at Ise, which ended in 1336, was restored in a modified way in the person of the Saishu, again filled by the daughter of the emperor. The effect of the first two rules was a devaluation of both of women's sacred aspects, her mantic gift and her "pollution," by declaring them merely superstitions. The restoration of the office of Saishu was in some ways symbolic of the previous high position of women in Shinto, although the role of the Saishu was narrowly construed.

During and after the Second World War, due to the lack of Shinto priests (*kannushi*), the Jinja Honchō, the official organization of Shinto shrines, recognized women as priests. The number of women priests has grown steadily since then, and in 1981 there were 1,100 women, five percent of the total number of Shinto priests in Japan.[29] Many of these women work in small rural shrines as part of a husband-wife team, or have taken over their husband's job upon his death. Women priests are somewhat less visible in the larger shrines.

In an effort to facilitate the participation of women priests, the Jinja Honchō told them not to be concerned about pollution (*"kegare to sezu"*). This meant that women could now be priests by stepping into a male role, and were to disregard the conditions which had once defined their sacredness. At a roundtable discussion in 1981, some women priests (especially the older ones), expressed dissatisfaction with this simplistic dismissal of a complex issue. Some women felt that menstruation was a gift from *kami* because it allowed them to have children and to perpetuate the Japanese race. Further, they felt it was a barometer of health rather than of sickness. But although they expressed these positive aspects, they also carried purifying charms such as salt, *sakaki* (sacred evergreen), and matches with them, if they approached the *kami* while they were menstruating. Although some of these women perceived menstruation as simultaneously sacred and impure, others (younger women) tended not to pay it much attention in either aspect.[30]

In order to determine the current feelings of Shinto priests and *miko* about the role of women in Shinto, the members of Yasaka Jinja in Kyoto responded to a questionnaire with the following results.[31]

People felt strongly that women do not have more pollution (*kegare*) than men, but they felt equally strongly that women priests should restrict their activities relating to the *kami* while they are menstruating. This seems inconsistent, but may be explained by a somewhat new interpretation about *kegare*. Shinto respects life and the continuation of life and therefore menstruation and childbirth are not considered pollution in themselves. Rather, the loss of blood involved implies a loss of vitality, and it is that which is *kegare*. Although this interpretation explains the problem, it does not resolve it, and it is usually said that this is a "spiritual" problem to be resolved by each individual woman priest as she sees fit.

As to whether a *miko* could be married and the necessity of women priests opinion was divided. Surprisingly, it seems to be the younger people who feel *miko* must be unmarried and that there is no need for female Shinto priests. This may not bode well for the future of women in Shinto, unless we assume that a certain mellowing of attitude will take place over time.

Amaterasu Ōmikami was overwhelmingly thought to be the "most important woman in Japanese history" by all of the female respondents and about half of the males. Other responses included Himiko, the Empress Jingū, Kushi-inada Hime (the wife of Susano-o-no-mikoto, the *kami* worshipped at Yasaka Jinja), and "my mother."

That there is still even today a strong positive feeling in the Japanese consciousness for religious leaders such as the ancient shamanesses can be seen in the popularity of the female founders of several of the new religions under the heading of "sectarian Shinto." Tenrikyō, Ōmoto, Reiyūkai, Risshō

Kōsei Kai, Tenshō Kōton Jingūkyō, and Jiu were all founded by shamanic women whose followers consider them to be *ikigami*, or living *kami*.[32]

> For those within [the gates of the headquarters], the primary allegiance is paid not to the Emperor, nor to any government, nor to any set of abstract principles, but to the figure of the living goddess in their midst, whose clairvoyant eyes penetrate to their very souls, and whose utterances, coming straight from the divinity within her, give meaning and hope and purpose to their lives.[33]

Conclusion: Women and Shinto

The history of women in Shinto shows the very important role woman played in ancient times and the corresponding numinosity of her physiological functions. This gave way to a carefully defined role for women within the organized religious structures along with the polarization of the concepts of purity and pollution. In modern times, women's role in Shinto is viewed simultaneously from rational and traditional viewpoints. The result is ambiguity, confusion, and some rather strained explanations of inconsistencies.

In the red color of the miko's *hakama* (divided skirt) is expressed the paradox of the position of women in Shinto. Red is the color of pollution, of the mysterious blood associated with menstruation and childbirth. But red also represents health, happiness, and perhaps surprisingly, purity. When all of these elements are in balance, this perhaps approximates the original constellation of symbols associated with women in Shinto.

Notes

1. G.B. Sansom, *Japan: A Short Cultural History* (Tokyo: Charles F. Tuttle Co., Inc.), p. 33.
2. Cornelius J. Kiley, "State and Dynasty in Archaic Yamato." *Journal of Asian Studies*, Vol. XXXIII, No. 1, Nov, 1973, p. 48.
3. Joseph M. Kitagawa, *Religion in Japanese History* (New York: Columbia University Press, 1966). p. 22.
4. Yoshiko Wada, "Woman and Her Power in the Japanese Emperor System," *Feminist*, Vol. I. No. 4, Feb. 1978. p. 15.
5. *Kojiki*, translated by Donald L. Philippi (Tokyo: University of Tokyo Press, 1968). p. 217 (Ch. 72).
6. Sansom, pp. 29-30.
7. W.G. Aston, *Shinto, The Way of the Gods* (London: Longmans, Green, and Co., 1905), p. 133. The sun deity being seen as female in Japan is especially interesting because in many cultures, including China, the sun was seen as male. Further, there is evidence that in ancient Japan the earliest solar cult deity was actually male and was worshipped by shamanic priestesses. See Matsumae Takeshi, "Origin and Growth of Amaterasu," *Asian Folk Studies*. Vol. 37, No. 1,

1978, pp. 1-11, and Waida Manabu, "Sacred Kingship in Early Japan: A Historical Introduction." *History of Religions*. Vol. 15, No. 4, May 1976, pp. 319–342.

8. Robert Briffault. *The Mothers* (New York: Atheneum, 1977), p. 285.
9. Samson, p. 53.
10. *Kojiki*, p. 245 (Ch. 85).
11. Briffault, p. 246.
12. Suzuki Giichi, "Joshi hōshisha no 'kegare' ni tsuite," *Reiten*, (Kokugakun Daigakul, No. 18, July 1981, p. 47.
13. M. Esther Harding. *Woman's Mysteries: Ancient and Modern* (New York Harper and Row, 1971), p. 125.
14. *Kojiki*, pp. 257–8 (Ch. 92).
15. Carmen Blacker, *The Catalpa Bow: A Study of Shamanistic Practices in Japan*, edited by Joyce Lebra, et. al. (Stanford: Stanford University Press.
16. Hori Ichiro, "Shamanism in Japan." *Japanese Journal of Religious Studies*, Vol. 2. No. 4, Dec. 1975, p. 233.
17. Okano Haruko, *Die Stellung der Frau im Shinto* (Wieshaden: Otto Harrassowitz, 1976). p. 210.
18. Blacker, p. 108.
19. Hori Ichir?, *Folk Religion in Japan*, (Chicago, 1958). p. 201.
20. Joy Paulson, "Evolution of the Feminine Ideal," in *Women in Changing Japan*, edited by Joyce Lehra *et al.* (Stanford: Stanford University Press 1976). It is important to note that because the status of women was so high, it took centuries for this type of proclamation to have a deep effect. Some changes were, of course, obvious, such as the prohibition of women as emperor from the eighth century, but Sansom notes that even in the early stages of feudalism feminine influence was strong and there was no indication of the definite subordination of women. But by the Muromachi Period, daughters could no longer inherit property, and it was then that the true subjugation of women began. See Sansom, p. 304 and 365.
21. Paulson, p. 9.
22. Kitagawa, pp. 32, 33.
23. Robert S. Ellwood, "The Saigū: Princess and Priestess," *History of Religions*. Vol 7, No. 1, Aug. 1976, p. 40. There was a similar office at the Kamo Shrine in Kyoto from the Heian Period called *Saiin*. There is still a symbolic enactment of the riverside purification of the Saiin during the Ani Matsuri today.
24. *Ibid*. p. 44.
25. Aston, p. 357.
26. Blacker, p. 30.
27. Suzuki, p. 43.
28. Blacker, p. 127.
29. Takazawa Shinichirō, "Joshi shinshoku ni tsuite no tokushugō o okuru," *Reiten*, No. 18, Forward.
30. "Joshi shinshoku no kegare no ishiki," Discussion in *Reiten*, No. 18, pp. 3–15.
31. This is not a scientific sampling, but is rather the opinions of the group of people working at a Shinto shrine. Twenty-three people filled out the questionnaire: 20 priests (including 3 women), 2 miko, and one office worker. Ages ranged from 19 to 73.
32. Agency for Cultural Affairs, *Japanese Religions* (Tokyo: Kodansha International Ltd.), p. 97.
33. Blacker, p. 138.

Women of the Sacred Groves: Divine Priestesses of Okinawa

Susan Sered

Introduction

Eight middle-aged and elderly women enter the *kami-ya* (village shrine). They sit on tatami mats on the floor and chat. Gradually, the conversation ceases. One of the women instructs a male assistant to light incense and place it on the altar. This woman, flanked on either side by her associates, turns toward the set of three rocks arranged on the altar and pours sake (rice wine) over the rocks. All of the women kneel, press their hands together, and quietly murmur prayers. The eight women then file outside, where a bus provided by the town hall drives them to the beginning of a trail that leads into the jungle. They begin their ascent, single file, the male assistant walking in front in order to clear away vines and look out for poisonous *habu* snakes. After fifteen minutes of steady climbing, they pause at a clearing. The male assistant walks on. The women take out five-piece white robes from the bags they have been carrying and quietly don the robes. *The eight kami-sama* continue their trek into the increasingly dark jungle, finally reaching the sacred grove. There are two stone benches where they sit and weave crowns of leaves and vines to put on their heads. One of the kami-sama goes further into the sacred grove, stopping at a small stone altar on which rest six conch shells. She squats in front of the shells, prays briefly, and "feeds" rice and sake into the opening of each shell. She then joins her fellow kami-sama at the benches, taking her place on the center seat. The male assistant pours sake for each kami-sama; they pray briefly and quietly. The eight kami-sama rise and begin their journey back to the bus. The bus driver takes them to the edge of the village, and the kami-sama walk to the village square, where they are met by clan members and by the village headman, who bows and pours sake for each kami-sama. Clanswomen provide food and drink for the kami-sama. After a small meal the kami-sama rise, take off the white robes and hang the crowns of leaves on special nails in the village square.* Eight middle-aged and elderly women then

---

* The Japanese word *kami* is usually translated as 'god'. However, since *kami* encompasses a much larger range of meanings than does the English 'god', I prefer to translate it loosely as 'divinity' or 'spiritual energy' (cf. Kitagawa 1987: 44–45). *Sama* is an honorary suffix added to names or titles.

From Susan Sered 1999 *Women of the Sacred Groves: Divine Priestesses of Okinawa*. New York: Oxford University Press. Reprinted with permission of Oxford University Press.

walk home to prepare food for their families, to weed their vegetable gardens, and to do their housework.

The power of patriarchy—or of any other strongly embedded hierarchical form of cultural organization—lies less in specific expressions of inequality than in the taken-for-grantedness of that inequality. Patriarchy, as feminist scholars such as Mary Daly (1978) have explained, takes hold of consciousness, of thought patterns; it persuasively presents an oppressive status quo as natural, universal, biologically ordained, and inevitable. In the presentation of patriarchy as inescapable—as essentially good and right—religion has a crucial role. Religion, through emotionally compelling rituals and stories, constructs a view of reality from which it is nearly impossible to fully escape.

As an anthropologist who lives with and studies non-European societies, my own research efforts have been aimed at exploring religious cultures in which women are the leaders—the paradigm-builders and maintainers. Although most historical and contemporary religions are indeed governed by men, there are, scattered throughout the world, a small number of well-documented religions that are led by women. Examples include *zar* possession religion in Africa; matrilineal spirit religion of northern Thailand; *nat* religion in Myanmar (cited as Burma in the literature); shamanism in Korea; Sande secret societies in west Africa; ancestor religion among the Garifuna of Belize; Candomble and Macumba in Brazil; Christian Science, Shakers, and Spiritualism in the United States, Mexico, and Great Britain; the contemporary Feminist Spirituality movement; and the indigenous religion of Okinawa (Ryukyu Islands). These religions are dominated by women in the sense that the majority of members and leaders are women and that they are independent of any kind of overarching male-dominated institutional framework.

Few if any traits are shared by all of these religions: leadership by women does not automatically lead to particular kinds of religious beliefs or rituals. As I argued in *Priestess, Mother, Sacred Sister: Religions Dominated by Women* (1994), this finding is consistent with the feminist and the social scientific understanding that gender patterns are culturally constructed and therefore vary from society to society. There is no reason to assume that women cross-culturally, any more than men cross-culturally, are attracted to certain religious modes as a function of their biological sex.

There is, however, a structural position shared by all but one of these women's religions. With the exception of the indigenous religion of Okinawa (Ryukyu Islands), all known religions led by women are comprised only of women and/or are considered marginal, subordinate, or secondary in the societies in which they are located. Only on the Ryukyu Islands do women lead the official mainstream religion—Okinawan women are the acknowledged and respected leaders of the publicly supported and publicly funded indigenous religion in which both men and women participate. Okinawa is the only known society in which women's religious endeavors are neither reactive to nor a consequence of those of men; men do not oversee, define, circumscribe, or persecute women's religious leadership in Okinawa. For this reason, Okinawan ethnography is an especially intriguing case study of the intersection of gender and religion.

This book looks in depth at one Okinawan village, Henza, in an effort to understand the links among religious beliefs, gender roles, and other aspects of community life. I make no claim that Henza is a 'typical' Okinawan village. Indeed, villagers enjoy talking about the ways in which Henza is different from other Okinawan villages—most particularly in terms of Henza's scant and meager supply of land and the resulting dependence upon the ocean for subsistence. Despite this disclaimer, in many (but not all) matters, my findings are consistent with those of anthropologists who have studied other Okinawan villages.

In Okinawan villages such as Henza, priestesses (*noro* and *kaminchu*) perform rituals on behalf of the community. Some of these rituals take place in the jungle, in the sacred grove, where villagers cannot see. Other rituals take place at the village square, in full sight of the community, and with the assistance of the village headman. Each clan has several priestesses who pray for the clan at public and private ceremonies. Within the household, the senior woman is responsible for rites directed toward the household kami-sama. In addition, a variety of independent practitioners—*ogami* (prayer) people and *yuta* (shaman-type practitioners)—communicate with kami-sama and ancestors on behalf of village families. These practitioners, almost all of whom are women, include both unpaid lay grandmothers and well-paid professionals.

Over the centuries, women's religious preeminence in Okinawa has endured through a range of political structrues and political changes: decentralized villages, warring feudal chiefdoms, a centralized monarchy, occupation by a foreign power, and annexation by another foreign power. It has survived extensive culture contact with Buddhist, Shinto, and Christian missionaries. And it has coexisted with Chinese ancestor worship, American cinemas, and Japanese schools (see Kerr 1958; Haring 1964). There does not seem to be one unique social or historical backdrop to women's religious leadership in Okinawa (or anywhere else).

Okinawan women's religious preeminence should not be treated as an unsullied bubble that hovers over shifting political and economic realities, however. Gendered religious roles can only be understood in the context of a variety of social and cultural patterns that compose a constantly changing, lived reality. My approach in this book is a three-pronged one: I treat rituals and ritual roles as constituted and shaped by long-standing cultural themes and patterns, by specific historically discernable social forces, and by the individual personalities of the particular people who perform the rituals and fill the roles at any given time (cf. Geertz 1973).

What elements of Okinawan social arrangements support, sustain, give form to, preserve, and inspire women's religious activity? How do Okinawan religion and other aspects of Okinawan social arrangements enhance, reflect, and conflict with one another? What other cultural or social elements have tended to cluster with women's religious preeminence? As we shall see in the chapters that follow, in Henza this cultural cluster includes village endogamy, extended male absence, a central role for women in subsistence work and commerce, lack of substantial inheritable property, marriage and childbirth patterns that enhance women's longevity, weak political structures, aversion to hierarchy and rules, and strong social integration among women. It is crucial, however, to clarify that other East and Southeast Asian societies are characterized by some or many of these same features (including significant religious roles for women; cf. Karim 1995; Errington 1990), and thus the presence of a religion led by women should not be seen as an automatic corollary to any specific social structural arrangement but rather as one part of a complex, multilayered, and nonstatic cultural configuration.

Henza cultural thinking and activity tend to mitigate against the reification of social and cosmological categories. Although certain rituals seem to play with the idea of construction and deconstruction of shifting dualistic structures, in village ideology male and female, death and life, leader and laity, good and bad, and human and kami-sama are not understood as natural or essential polarities. Divinity is not perceived as a discrete entity situated outside of everyday reality, but rather as a vague spiritual force potentially present anywhere. Divinity can be summoned into immediacy through ritual, and Henza culture includes a wide variety of old and new, communal and personal, formal and idiosyncratic rituals. In Henza, humans can be kami-sama, and human kami-sama can be plain old housewives; there is no ontological distinction between divine and human. The (Japanese) word which can be roughly translated as god (kami-sama) is neither masculine nor feminine, neither singular nor plural, and nothing in Henza liturgy or material culture serves to portray kami-sama as one or the other.

Despite its small population (approximately 1800), Henza is home to a large number of ritual leaders and experts, almost all women, whose various spheres of expertise and authority are not regulated or clearly delineated. In general, in Henza rules of social behavior are not codified or reified, and divergence—as long as it is not aggressive—is barely noticed. The notion of cosmic prohibition does not exist: When I naively tried to elicit a list of taboo foods from villagers, the closest they could come up with was "maybe poison."

Although Henza men and women tend to engage in different activities, villagers do not describe this arrangement as existentially meaningful, universal, or absolute. Men who wear women's clothing at rituals elicit no social response, nor do women who take on roles that are usually filled by men. In Henza, the reality of women's religious leadership demands no explanation, interpretation, excuse, or mystification. Concurrently, although most political leadership is in the hands of men, the reality of men's political leadership is not bolstered or justified via gender beliefs or rules.

Nonhierarchical complementarity—including gender complementarity—is a pervasive pattern in Henza ritual, social life, and cosmology. In a variety of contexts, villagers explain that the living help their ancestors and the ancestors help the living, that men go to sea and women work on the farms and that both are necessary, and that there are both male and female kami-sama just as there are male and female people. Many Henza rituals strive toward social and cosmic harmony, toward smoothing out or clearing up rough spots, and toward dramatizing themes of complementarity and balance.

Doing Gender

Feminist scholarship has devoted a great deal of attention to deconstructing sex and gender as natural or universally constituted categories. Although this literature is, by now, familiar to most anthropologists, I wish to clarify how I use the term 'gender' throughout this book. Gender is not an immutable fact of life or state of being, but rather an expression of social processes. What Judith Lorber (1994) and Sherry Ortner (1996) call "doing gender" or "making gender" begins with the cultural construction and acknowledgment of conceptualizations that designate essential differences. These differences are most often thought to be biological (what we call sex) and tend to be perceived as dichotomous (Harding 1986). Perceived essential differences are potentially gravitational, drawing to themselves—gendering—other sorts of cultural material. This process can be thought of as the naturalization of gender through reference to supposedly immutable biological characteristics. To take a somewhat extreme example of doing gender, Maurice Godelier explains that among the New Guinea Baruya:

> The differences of form, substance, and bodily function, the anatomical and physiological differences that arise from the different functions of the sexes in the process of the reproduction of life—supplies a steady stream of material from which are fashioned the messages and explanations that serve to interpret and justify the social inequalities between men and women. It is as if sexuality were constantly being solicited to occupy every nook and cranny of society, to act as a language to express, and as a reason to legitimize, the facts of a (mainly) different order. (1986: xii)

The amount and content of gendered material varies from culture to culture. In some cultures (such as Okinawa), very few traits are recognized as gendered; only external genitalia or pregnancy are perceived and acknowledged as essential differences, whereas other attributes and roles, even if they sometimes tend to be associated with men or with women, are understood to be temporal or local rather than essential. In other cultures (like the Baruya of New Guinea), many traits are gendered—are associated with or assimilated into a perceived core of essential and dichotomous difference. A well-known expression of the latter pattern is found among the East Asian cultures that elaborate upon and find meaning in the yin-yang dichotomy. In these cultures, categories of perceived essential differences seem to have the power to attract myriad symbols, attributes, and roles, making them look as if they are biological, inherently meaningful, and dichotomous.

Differences that are envisioned as being absolute (for example, black and white or good and bad) are particularly compelling; binary distinctions leave no gray area, no room for doubt, and no room to negotiate. The construction of two and only two sexes or genders leads to cultural understandings in which men and women are not only essentially different but also antithetical and mutually exclusive types of beings. A popular form of this kind of thinking is represented in contemporary American culture by books like *Men Are from Mars, Women Are from Venus* (Gray 1992) in which men and women are characterized as species from different planets who need an interpreter in order to learn how to communicate with one another.

The perception and acknowledgment of differences that are believed to be rooted in nature (naturalized differences) are a precondition for hierarchy—for systematic, permanent distinctions in access to power and prestige. If everyone is the same, there is no basis out of which hierarchy can develop or be sustained. The more that differences are perceived to be absolute and natural, the more forceful and self-sustaining the hierarchy. As Elizabeth Colson explains, "Hierarchy implies something institutionalized which governs relationships *over time* between individuals who *consistently* accept placement in a system of ranking ... it involves *legitimation* as well as pecking order" (1993: xv–xvi; my emphases).

In the case of gender hierarchies, gender ideology provides that legitimation. Peggy Reeves Sanday defines gender ideology in this way:

> Ideology refers both to a system of thought that guides and legitimates social action and to attempts to create a transcendental order by legitimating the power of that order.... Viewed in these terms, gender ideology can be defined as (1) the system of thought that legitimates sex roles and customary behavior of the sexes, and (2) the deployment of gender categories as metaphors in the production of conceptions of an enduring, eternal social order. (1990: 6)

Gender ideologies are ideologies of difference that elaborate and legitimate the attribution of a range of traits, roles, and statuses either to men or to women. Gender ideologies are how societies establish and justify the links between bodies, laws, emotions, customs, and behaviors; between sex and gender. We can ask how strong, how compelling, how total, and how persuasive the ideological links are in specific societies. In the late-nineteenth- and early-twentieth-century United States, for example, the thick link between sex and gender was reflected in medical, political, and religious discourses that claimed that voting and higher education are "naturally" male activities and liable to cause gynecological malfunction in women. Women who did not adapt to contemporary gender patterns ran the risk of being subjected to gynecological surgery intended to correct their "abnormal" bodies (Ehrenreich and English 1979). In Okinawa, as I shall show in this book, the ideological bonds linking gender to sex are exceptionally thin.

Cross-culturally, people and groups of people tend to be ranked according to intangible social or religious values (like purity or sacredness) that transcend, encompass, and outlast day-to-day and tangible political or economic realities (Dumont 1970). Drawing upon the ideas of Louis Dumont, Sherry Ortner argues that gender is first and foremost a prestige system—a system that is, by its very nature, hierarchical and encompassing vis-à-vis other principles of social organization. According to Ortner, "Gender is ... a system of discourses and practices that constructs male and female not only in terms of differential roles and meanings but also in terms of differential *value*, differential 'prestige'" (1996: 143).

Because strong and long-lasting gender hierarchies are prestige systems that rest upon persuasive ideologies, we can easily understand why so many cultures augment naturalizing gender ideologies with religious beliefs in the gendered order of the cosmos, beliefs in gendered creation, beliefs in divine decree regarding sexuality and sex roles, and beliefs that define purity and pollution, good and evil, and sacred and profane in gendered terms. Cross-culturally, gender is likely to be reified both through reference to immutable biological characteristics and through reference to cosmically ordained religious ideologies. The "natural" and the "supernatural" serve as complementary tools for naturalizing and sanctifying difference, prestige, and hierarchy.

Okinawan religion is unusual in that it does not embrace or advance an elaborated gender ideology. Male-dominated religions typically devote a great deal of effort to idealizing men's superiority and women's religious subordination: Women are less rational (Islam), women are more tied to this world because of their role as mothers (Buddhism), women are the cause of original sin (Christianity), women are polluted because of menstruation and childbirth (Hinduism and some Japanese religions), and women are by definition private rather than public beings (Judaism). These ideological efforts, one could argue, are necessary to counteract the empirically observable reality that women and men are far more similar than different and to rationalize the truly irrational male dominance of social institutions. These ideologies play key roles in creating and upholding the prestige systems that we call gender.

Women-led religions also tend to devote a great deal of energy to idealizing women's religious leadership: The northern Thai believe that women have softer souls that are easier for the spirits to penetrate (Tanabe 1991), members of Afro-Brazilian religions surmise that men's involvement with money and alcohol interferes with their spiritual prowess (Lerch 1982), and Spiritualists interpret women's suffering as making them more sensitive to spiritual forces (Moore 1977: 121). Attention to gender ideology, to explaining why women can be religiously dominant, is a crucial reactive task in cultural situations in which the official and normative religion is dominated by men (as it is in Brazil, Thailand, and so forth). This task is unnecessary in Okinawa, and Henza villagers are surprised—sometimes to the point of disbelief that such gender differentiation exists—when asked why all their religious leaders are women. Villagers offer no ideology to promote or enforce gendered social roles. *Kami-sama* are not called upon as arbiters of gender arrangements.

Judith Lorber has astutely argued that the paradox of gender is its ubiquitousness; it is hard to find a society that does not create gender as a cultural category and infuse it with singular potency. Societies seem to need to work hard *not* to reify gender. As I show throughout this book, a noteworthy pattern in Henza culture is the ritual construction followed by the ritual deconstruction of dualities. In a variety of settings, binary categories—like male and female—are very obviously and artificially created, only to be shattered. That villagers repeatedly see dualities publicly constructed and deconstructed seems to serve as a kind of prophylactic against the naturalization of hierarchical differences that occurs in so many other cultures.

The ritual described at the beginning of this introduction is a key example: Before the eyes of villagers, women both become and unbecome *kami-sama*, a ritual process that deconstructs any notion that there may be ontological differences between human and divine. To take another example, ... the village that for other purposes is divided into five hamlets temporarily divides itself into a male half and a female half, a division that has no relevance in any sphere of life except the tug-of-war (for example, there are no marriage rules regarding parts of the village, no subsistence patterns or stereotypical personality traits regarding halves of the village, and so forth). One rope is supposedly male and one is supposedly female, but the difference is far from obvious—the "female" rope has a slightly larger loop at the end. Henza villagers explain the success of the winning team in terms of how many people on each team came to pull in a particular year, rather than in terms of any sort of biological or cosmological factor. I see these and other rituals as devices for playing with categories such as gender: for putting gender on and taking it off, and thus mitigating against its naturalization. These rituals defuse the pull of sex-gender gravity.

In a broader sense, I suspect that Henza villagers are intrigued not only by the making and unmaking of gender but also by other manifestations of order and disorder. A variety of rituals express some sort of concern with situations characterized by too much structure; these rituals experiment with and ultimately deconstruct order, categories, and structure. Concurrently, disordered situations seem to be experienced both as problematic and in need of ritual treatment and as spaces in which growth and transformation—and especially spiritual growth and transformation—are possible. The embrace of disorder as a socially and cosmically positive state nourishes the absence of reified social categories in Henza.

References

Colson, Elizabeth. 1993. A Note on the Discussions at Mijas. In *Sex and Gender Hierarchies*, ed. Barbara Diane Miller, xv–xix. Cambridge: Cambridge University Press.

Daly, Mary. 1978. *Gyn/Ecology: The Metaethics of Radical Feminism*. Boston: Beacon.

Dumont, Louis. 1970. *Homo Hierarchicus: The Caste System and Its Implications*. Trans. Mark Sainsbury. Chicago: University of Chicago Press.

Ehrenreich, Barbara, and Deidre English. 1979. *For Her Own Good: 150 Years of the Experts Advice to Women*. Garden City, New York: Anchor Press/Doubleday.

Errington, Shelly. 1990. Recasting Sex, Gender, and Power: A Theoretical and Regional Overview. In *Power and Difference: Gender in Island Southeast Asia*, ed. Jane Monnig Atkinson and Shelley Errington, 1–58. Stanford: Stanford University Press.

Geertz, Clifford. 1969. Religion as a Cultural System. In *Anthropological Approaches to the Study of Religion*, ed. Michael Banton. London: Tavistock Publications.

Godelier, Maurice. 1986 [1982]. *The Making of Great Men: Male Domination and Power Among the New Guinea Baruya*. Trans. Rupert Swyer. Cambridge: Cambridge University Press and Editions de la Maison des Sciences de l'Homme.

Gray, John. 1992. *Men Are from Mars, Women Are from Venus: A Practical Guide for Improving Communication and Getting What You Want in Your Relationship*. New York: HarperCollins.

Harding, Sandra. 1986. *The Science Question in Feminism*. New York: Cornell University Press.

Haring, Douglas G. 1964. Chinese and Japanese Influences. In *Ryukyuan Culture and Society*, ed. Allan H. Smith, 39–55. Honolulu: University of Hawaii Press.

Karim, Wazir Jahan. 1995. Introduction: Genderising Anthropology in Southeast Asia. In *"Male" and "Female" in Developing Southeast Asia*, ed. Wazir Jahan Karim, 11–43. Cross-Cultural Perspectives on Women. Oxford: Berg.

Kerr, George H. 1958. *Okinawa: The History of an Island People*. Rutland, Vermont: Charles E. Tuttle Company.

Kitagawa, Joseph M. 1987. *On Understanding Japanese Religion*. Princeton: Princeton University Press.

Lerch, Patricia. 1982. An Explanation for the Predominance of Women in the Umbanda Cults of Porto Alegre, Brazil. *Urban Anthropology* 11(2):237–261.

Lorber, Judith. 1994. *Paradoxes of Gender*. New Haven: Yale University Press.

Moore, R. Laurence. 1977. *In Search of White Crows: Spiritualism, Parapsychology, and American Culture*. New York: Oxford University Press.

Ortner, Sherry. 1996. *Making Gender: The Politics and Erotics of Culture.* Boston: Beacon Press.

Sanday, Peggy Reeves, and Ruth Gallagher Goodenough, eds. 1990. Introduction. In *Beyond the Second Sex: New Directions in the Anthropology of Gender. Philadelphia: University of Pennsylvania Press.*

Sered, Susan Starr. 1994. *Priestess, Mother, Sacred Sister: Religions Dominated by Women.* New York Oxford University Press.

Tanabe, Shigeharu. 1991. Spirits, Power, and the Discourse of Female Gender: The Phi Meng Cult in Northern Thailand. In *Thai Constructions of Knowledge*, ed. Manas Chitakasem and Andrew Turton, 183–212. London: School of Oriental and African Studies.

Confucianism

Theresa Kelleher

This chapter will examine the position of women in Confucianism, focusing primarily on the classical period and to a lesser extent on its later phase, Neo-Confucianism. As I shall show, women played a central role in Confucianism by virtue of their place in both the cosmic order and in the family. Nevertheless, since Confucianism was a patriarchal religious tradition, its estimation of women's nature was by and large a low one. Richard Guisso has summed up the negative attitudes toward women which appear in the canonical texts of early Confucianism, the Five Classics, as follows: "The female was inferior by nature she was dark as the moon and changeable as water, jealous, narrow-minded, and insinuating. She was indiscreet, unintelligent, and dominated by emotion. Her beauty was a snare for the unwary male, the ruination of states" (Guisso 1981, 59).

I have chosen not to dwell so much on these negative attitudes as on the actual religious path set forth for women in the tradition. I will give particu-

From Arvind Sharma, ed. 1987. *Women in World Religions.* Albany: SUNY Press, pp. 135–60, 154–59. Reprinted with permission of SUNY Press.

lar attention to the types of attitudes and behavior considered desirable for a good Confucian woman and the models put forth for women to emulate. To do so, I will draw on various instructions for women found in the classical ritual texts and in pieces written by women for women, as well as biographies of exemplary women.

There are, of course, limitations in the use of these sources. They were all in support of the dominant male teachers and were addressed to an elite group in society. Social historians have pointed out the cruel use to which some of these teachings were put at different periods of Chinese history to make the lot of women difficult. Although there were surely discrepancies between the ideals articulated in the texts and the realities of women's lives in Chinese history, we have evidence that many women did take these teachings seriously, fervently believed in them, and were even willing to die to honor them. For this reason, though other readings of the texts are possible (and even necessary) to fully understand the position of women in Confucianism, I will keep to a fairly straight-forward description of the texts and their teachings, supplying occasional critical commentary.

Since the basic religious orientation of Confucianism may not be well understood by many and since such an understanding is necessary if one is to appreciate the part women played in the tradition, I will begin with a brief overview of basic Confucian teachings. I will do so in terms of the cosmic order of Heaven and earth, the human order, which parallels the cosmic order with its roots in the family and its fullest expression in the state, and lastly, the proper response of humans to these two orders.

The cosmic order in its fullest sense is seen as comprised of the triad of Heaven, earth, and the human. Humans are intimately linked to Heaven and earth, but not in the same way as they are related to the divine in the West. The call of the human community is not to worship Heaven and earth, but to learn from them, imitate their behavior, and thus form a human order modeled upon the cosmic order. Three aspects of the cosmic order especially impressed the Confucians as lessons worth learning in the human order.

First, Heaven and earth were seen as fundamentally life-giving; they continually bring new life into being, nurture and sustain it, and bring it to its completion. The fundamental optimism of Confucianism that life is good—indeed, that life is the most precious gift of all—comes from this sense of the universe as being fundamentally oriented toward the production and promotion of life.

The second aspect of the cosmic order valued by the Confucians was that everything in life is relational. Nothing comes into being in isolation, and nothing survives in isolation. Both the creative and the nurturing process depend on the coming together of two different elements in a relationship. Now the relationship between Heaven and earth is the most primal and most creative one in the universe. But these bodies do not function as equals; rather, they observe a hierarchy, with Heaven as the superior, creative element, positioned high above, and earth as the inferior, receptive element, positioned down below. What mattered was the overall effectiveness of the relationship rather than which was superior or inferior.

The third aspect of the cosmic order which impressed the Confucians was the orderly fashion in which it worked, with harmony rather than conflict prevailing among its parts. Each part seemed patterned to work for the good of the whole and yet at the same time to realize its own nature. It appeared to the Confucians that the parts observed a type of deference, or "polite form," with each other. For example, the sun dominates the day but yields its place to the moon at night with an absence of strife. Each of the four seasons gets its turn to dominate part of the year, but then gives way, or defers, to the season that follows.

In sum, the cosmic order was seen as life-giving, relational, and harmonious in the interaction of its parts. All these concepts formed the cornerstone of the Confucian ordering of human society.

The capacity of humans to be life-giving, for human life to be passed down from generation to generation in an unbroken chain was an awesome thing for Confucians. The most direct and profound experience of this for any human was the gift of life at birth from one's parents. Birth brought one into this continuum of life, which was much larger than any one individual life. One felt oneself caught up in a flow of life which connected one to countless generations before and many more to come. A worshipful attitude was thus directed toward the progenitors of life: in the most concrete sense one's own parents, but also their parents and their parents' parents. This reverence and gratitude for life formed the basis of ancestor worship.

The family, as the nexus of this life-giving activity and the custodian of the chain of life, thus came to be enshrined as a sacred community and was reverenced in a way that few religious traditions of the world have reverenced it. All other social groupings, including the state, had their basis in the family, and indeed, were often seen in terms of the family metaphor. Since Confucianism had no priesthood or special houses of worship, the roles of husband and wife took on a sacerdotal character. Marriage was a vocation to which all were called. Just as one received life at birth, one was to pass on that life to the next generation. Not to do so was a serious offense. As the philosopher Mencius said, "There are three things which are unfilial, and to have no posterity is the greatest of them" (Mencius 4A:26, Legge 1966, 725). As we shall see, this sense of the primacy of marriage and the sacredness of the family had an immense impact on the lives of women in Confucianism.

The second lesson that Confucians learned from the cosmic order was the relational aspect of things. All humans exist in relationships; there are no solitary individuals. These relationships are not just any relationships, but five very specific ones, known as the "Five Cardinal Relationships." The family generates three of them, and society generates the other two. Man and woman come together as husband and wife. They produce children, thus establishing the parent-child relationship was well as the older-younger sibling relationship. These bonds form the basis of the political relationship of ruler and subject and the social one of friend and friend.

For the Confucians, these relationships were not just biological or social; more importantly, they were moral. Since humans are not like plants and animals, they need more than food and shelter to sustain themselves—they need the empathetic response and support of other humans. Confucians had a profound awareness of the capacity of humans to nurture (be life-giving) or tear down (be life-destroying) in their interactions with others. Confucius thus made as the focus of his teachings in the Analects the virtue of *jen*, variously translated as "benevolence," "humaneness," "humanity," "love," or even just "virtue." The Chinese character for jen is composed of two elements: a human being on the left and the word for 'two' on the right. The implication is that humans are structured to be in relationship, that our fundamental being is wrapped up in the existence of others. We are called upon to be as responsible and as empathetic as possible, both for the sake of the other and for our own good. One of the descriptions of jen given by Confucius explains it thus:

> Now the man of perfect virtue, wishing to be established himself, seeks also to establish others; wishing to be enlarged himself, he seeks also to enlarge others. To be able to judge of others by what is nigh in ourselves: this may be called the art of virtue. (Analects 6:28, Legge 1966, 77)

Thus the Confucians were puzzled and disturbed when Buddhism made its way to China with its monastic system, which called for males to leave home and lead a celibate existence away from any family or social context.

The actual practice of jen in the Five Cardinal Relationships varied because of the hierarchical nature of these relationships. The same sense of hierarchy that exists in the cosmic order was seen as existing in the human order. Except for the friend-friend relation, all the others were conceived of as hierarchical in nature, with one party in the superior position and the other in the inferior position. This hierarchy was seen as necessary if the relationships were to work. Those who occupied the superior positions were parents, rulers, husbands, and older siblings; those in the inferior positions were children, subjects, wives, and younger siblings. Children were exhorted to be filial to their parents, subjects loyal to their rulers, wives submissive to their husbands, and younger siblings respectful to their older siblings. While most moral teachings in Confucianism were directed to those in the inferior positions, persons in the superior positions were obliged to use their superior status for the well-being of the other.

The third aspect of the cosmic order which impressed Confucians was the order and harmony which prevailed among the various elements, the correct positioning of each part in relation to the whole. Desirous of establishing the same order and harmony in the human community, from the family up to the state, Confucians attempted to choreograph the gestures, speech, and behavior of human beings with ritual. Here ritual included not just the more overtly religious ceremonials associated with coming-of-age ceremonies, weddings, funerals, and ancestral sacrifices (the four major rituals in Confucianism), but also what Westerners would put in the category of comportment and good manners. The classical ritual texts (notably, the Book of Rites, the Book of Etiquette and Ceremonial, the Rites of Chou) are filled with directives on the correct and proper behavior for every conceivable human interaction. The range extends from details for children to follow in serving their parents on a day-to-day basis in the household to the correct protocol for officials at court. While Confucius was all too aware of the dangers of formalism to which such a heavy emphasis on ritual could lead, nevertheless, he feared leaving the carrying out of virtue to chance. How was a child to be filial? Did he have to figure that duty out anew each day? Though one's understanding of filial piety should deepen over one's lifetime, one must begin with patterns to follow, both to ensure the smooth running of the household and also to initiate a person into a sense of what filial piety consists. Similar directions could be applied to the other relationships, including that of husband and wife.

From this brief presentation of the basic teachings of Confucianism, we see that the cosmic order is the primary source of divine revelation and the model for the human order, that the family is perceived as the nexus of the sacred community, and that all humans, both male and female, operate in a highly contextual, hierarchical, and choreographed setting. Relationships and the behavior considered appropriate to them are spelled out in quite specific terms. The religious pursuit for a Confucian is not to leave the world, but to realize the fullness of his or her humanity by a total immersion in human life, beginning with the family and extending outward to society through public service. By so doing, one achieves a mystic identification with the cosmic order, and one is "able to assist in the transforming and nourishing powers of Heaven and earth" (Doctrine of the Mean, ch. 22, Legge, 1966, 399).

This, then, is the context in terms of which I will base my discussion of the role of women in Confucianism. I will show how that role was said to mirror the cosmic order, how women were identified in terms of their roles in the network of human relationships rather than as individuals, and how their behavior was informed by the elaborate ritual code.

In the cosmic order of things, the feminine as yin constitutes one of the two primary modes of being. This feminine force is identified with the earth, with all things lowly and inferior. It is characterized as yielding, receptive, and devoted, and it furthers itself through its sense of perseverence (Book of Changes, *k'un* hexagram, Wilhelm, 1967, 386–88). Though inferior to the masculine yang principle, the yin principle is nevertheless crucial and indispensable to the proper workings of the universe. From this cosmic pattern it was deduced that the position of women in the human order should be lowly and inferior like the earth and that the proper behavior for a woman was to be yielding, weak, passive, and still like the earth. It was left for men to be active and strong, to be initiators like Heaven. Though men were considered superior, they could not do without women as their complementary opposites.

In the human order, women were seen only in the context of the family, while men were seen in the wider social-political order. And within the family, a woman was subject to the "three obediences": as a daughter she was subject to her father; as a wife, to her husband; and when older, to her son. If the Confucian calling for men was "the way of the sages" (*sheng-tao*), for women it was "the wifely way" (*fu-tao*). The Chinese word for 'wife' shows a woman with a broom, signifying the domestic sphere as her proper place. Marriage was indeed the focal point of a woman's life, and she was identified in terms of her role as wife, along with her two related roles as daughter-in-law and mother. In theory, females as step-daughters did not have much status within their natal families because, destined as they were to join the ranks of another family at marriage, they would never be official members of their natural families (no tablet would ever stand for them on the family's ancestral altar).

All childhood education for females was solely to prepare them for their future roles as wives and mothers. In contrast to boys, who went out of the house at age 10 for their education in history and the Classics girls remained at home, sequestered in the female quarters and under the guidance of a governess. They learned good manners and domestic skills like sewing and weaving.

> A girl at the age of ten ceased to go out [from the women's apartments]. Her governess taught her [the arts of] pleasing speech and manners, to be docile and obedient, to handle the hemper fibres, to learn [all] woman's work, how to furnish garments, to watch the sacrifices, to supply the liquors and sauces, to fill the various stands and dishes with pickles and brine, and to assist in setting forth the appurtenances for the ceremonies. (Book of Rites, ch. 12, Legge 1967, 1:479)

At age 15, according to this chronology, a girl would receive the hair pin in a coming-of-age ceremony. At 20 she was to marry. Three months before her marriage, a young woman was to be instructed in the four aspects of womanly character: virtue, speech, comportment, and work (Book of Rites, ch. 44).

Both for the woman and the families, marriage and the wedding ceremony were extremely important events. As mentioned earlier, marriage marked the formation of a new link in the family chain of life, the sacred passing on of one generation to the next. The emphasis was on this sense of linkage or continuity rather than on any sense that marriage was the start of something new; that is why the Book of Rites says that no one congratulates anyone at the time of marriage (Legge 1967, 1:442). In addition, the Book of Rites comments on marriage as follows:

> The ceremony of marriage was intended to be a bond of love between two [families of different] surnames, with a view, in its retrospective character, to secure the services in the ancestral temple, and in its prospective character, to secure the continuance of the family line. Therefore, the superior men (the ancient rulers), set a great value upon it. (Book of Rites, ch. 44, Legge 1967, 2: 428).

Because the event had repercussions not just in the existing human order but also in the cosmic order and with the ancestors, the ceremony had to be done with careful attention to detail so that it would have its proper effect. Below are several of the most important details.

When the groom is about to set forth to fetch his bride, he receives the following command from his father: "Go meet your helpmeet, and so enable me to fulfill my duties in the ancestral temple. Be diligent in taking the lead as husband, but with respectful consideration, for she is the successor of your mother. Thus will the duties of the women in our family show no signs of decay" (I-li, or Book of Etiquette and Ceremonial, 4B, Steele 1966, 38). The groom then sets forth to the home of his bride. It is important that he take the initiative in this matter to remind all the parties that as husband, he is to be the active agent like Heaven, while the wife is to be passive agent like earth.

When the groom arrives at her house, the bride receives the following command from her father: "Be careful and reverent. Day in and day out disobey no command of your new parents." Her mother also repeats this exhortation, modifying the last line to "Disobey no rule of the household" (I-li 4B, Steele, 1966, 39). Once she leaves with the groom, the bride is no longer a member of her natural family.

When the bride and groom arrive back at the groom's family, there is great feasting with food and wine. "They ate together of the same animal, and joined in supping from the cups made of the same melon; thus showing that they now formed one body, were of equal rank, and pledged to mutual affection" (Book of Rites, ch. 44, Legge, 1967, 2:429–30). The following day the bride is formally presented to her parents-in-law, to whom she now owes perfect obedience as well as care in their old age and mourning for them when dead. On the third day, the parents-in-law fete the new bride in a ceremony which indicates that she is now the primary childbearing woman in the household, replacing the mother of the groom (ibid. 2:431). After the third month, the new bride is formally presented to the ancestors as a new member of the family, and from thereon she has a place on some ancestral line, something she never had in her natal family.

Several points are worth noting about this ceremony. First, the idea of marriage is different for men and women, as can be seen both in the marriage ceremony itself and in the Chinese terms for marriage. The verb for a woman to marry is *kuei*, "to return home," implying that her rightful place is wherever her husband's family is, not her own natural family. In contrast, the word for a man to marry is *ch'u*, "to go out and fetch" someone. The second point is that the entering of marriage is more for the good of the overall family, past, present, and future, than for the personal happiness of the couple. In terms of the past, the wife and the husband must ensure the continuation of the periodic sacrifices to the ancestors; in terms of the present, the wife must dedicate herself to serve her parents-in-law; and in terms of the future, she must provide male heirs who will someday be able to carry on the family sacrifices. Third, while the new bride is deserving of respect for the crucial role she is about to play in the overall family structure, her immediate role in the hierarchy is not a very high one, so she is cautioned by her parents to be especially careful and obedient.

After the wedding ceremony, the couple was to observe a certain amount of sexual segregation in the household. They were not to mix freely, but rather to keep to separate quarters, except when sleeping.

> The observances of propriety commenced with a careful attention to the relations between husband and wife. They built the mansion and its apartments, distinguishing between the exterior and interior parts. The men occupied the exterior; the women the interior.... Males and females did not use the same stand or rack for their clothes. The wife did not presume to hang up anything on the pegs or stand of her husband; nor to put anything in his boxes or satchels; nor to share his bathing house. (Book of Rites, ch. 12, Legge 1967, 1:470)

However, this separation of the sexes was never observed to the degree and level of strictness as the Islamic *purdah*.

Though they were to observe this type of separation, both husband and wife had to share in attending upon his parents and carrying out their orders. For example, upon rising in the morning and dressing, the couple were to proceed immediately to their parent's quarters.

> On getting to where they are, with bated breath and gentle voice, they should ask if their clothes are too warm or too cold, whether they are ill or pained, or uncomfortable in any part; help and support their parents in quitting or entering the apartment. They will ask whether they want anything and then respectfully bring it. All this they will do with an appearance of pleasure to make their parents feel at ease. (ibid. 450–1)

The ritual texts also stipulate that neither the son nor his wife should own any private goods, and any gifts to them should be offered to their parents and not kept for themselves.

Marriage was regarded as such a sacred event, registered in the cosmic order and with the ancestral line, that it could not be dissolved. However, if a wife was guilty of certain behavior, she might be divorced by her husband and sent back to her family. The seven traditional grounds for divorce (literally, *ch'i-ch'u*, "seven reasons for sending out of the house") were disobedience to his parents, failure to bear a male child, promiscuity, jealousy, having an incurable disease, talking too much, and stealing. Three extenuating circumstances, however, prevented a husband from divorcing his wife. They were that her parents were dead and she had no home to which to return, she had already carried out the mourning rites for one of his parents, and he began the marriage a poor man but upon achieving riches wished to get rid of her (K'ung-tzu chia-yü 6:6a).

The wife never had any grounds for initiating a divorce against her husband. Even after the death of her husband, she was supposed to remain faithful to him and never remarry.

> Faithfulness is requisite in all service of others, and faithfulness is specially the virtue of a wife. Once mated with her husband, all her life she will not change her feeling of duty to him, and hence, when the husband dies, she will not marry again. (Book of Rites, ch. 11, Legge 1967, 1:439)

A good deal of the reason for this was that a woman's bond in marriage was not just with her husband, but also with his family. Thus, even with his death, she had duties to his living relations and his ancestors. Though women were encouraged not to remarry, the social sanctions against those who did, in classical and medieval Chinese history, were not nearly as heavy as they were to become in later Chinese history under the influence of Neo-Confucianism.

Such was the wifely way as outlined in the ritual texts of classical Confucianism. During the Han dynasty (206 B.C.E.–220 C.E.) when Confucianism was first made a state orthodoxy, there was a more conscious attempt to bring women into the mainstream of the tradition and to give them more specialized instructional writings and biographies of women to emulate. Specifically, we have in the Han dynasty two pieces, Instructions for Women (Nü-chieh) by Pan Chao, and Biographies of Exemplary Women (Lieh-nü chuan) by Liu Hsiang.

Pan Chao (?–116 C.E.), author of Instructions for Women, was a highly educated woman who was publicly recognized for her scholarship and intellect. She was called to court to tutor the women of the imperial family, and also was instrumental in completing the Han dynastic history her brother left unfinished upon his death. According to her Preface to the Instructions, she wrote the text out of concern that the unmarried women of her family (her daughters and nieces) were unprepared for their future vocation as wives. She hoped to remedy the situation with helpful advice that, as we shall see, fully embraces the wifely way that we have been describing.

She begins by alluding to an ancient practice upon the birth of a girl which was meant to indicate the type of life she was meant to lead.

> On the third day after the birth of a girl, the ancients observed three customs: first to place the baby below the bed; second to give her a potsherd with which to play; and third, to announce her birth to her ancestors by an offering. (Nü-chieh 1:2b–3a, Swann 1932, 83)

The first action indicated that as female she should be lowly and submissive, humbling herself before others, the second that she should be hardworking and diligent in the domestic sphere, and the third that she should enter fully into the wife's responsibilities to the ancestors of her husband's family.

Having thus explained these three fundamental aspects of a woman's vocation as wife, Pan Chao next focuses on the nature of the marriage bond and the wife's duty to her husband. She fully accepts the cosmological correspondences of the husband-wife relationship with that of Heaven and earth, and the implications for differentiation in sex roles. That is, the husband must be strong, firm, and dominant like Heaven, and the wife must be weak, pliant, and subservient like earth. The husband's duty is to superintend or manage the wife, the wife's duty is to serve her husband. Things will go awry if either one fails in his or her duty to the other. Thus men who fail to exert authority over their wives are just as much at fault as wives who are not willing to serve their husbands (Nü-chieh 1:4b–5a, Swann 1932, 84).

The couples owe each other mutual respect and the way to maintain respect is to observe the restrictions placed upon their intimacy by the system of sexual segregation. She warns couples of the dangers of too much familiarity, that it so often leads to excessive lust or anger.

> If husband and wife have the habit of staying together, never leaving one another, and following each other around within the limited space of their own rooms, then they will lust after and take liberties with one another. From such action improper language will arise between the two. This kind of discussion may lead to licentiousness. And out of licentiousness will be born a heart of disrespect to the husband. (Nü-chieh 1:6a–b, Swann 1932, 85)

Pan Chao goes on to describe how this loss of respect often then leads to contempt for one's husband and incessant nagging on the part of the wife, which then evokes anger on the part of the husband who then beats the wife. "The correct relationship between husband and wife is based upon harmony.... Should actual blows be dealt, how could the matrimonial relationship be preserved?" (Nü-chieh 1:6b, Swann 1932, 86).

Though there is to be this typically Confucian reserve and formality in the marriage relationship, there should also be, on the part of the wife, an element of affectionate devotion. Pan Chao quotes an ancient saying: "To obtain the love of one man is the crown of a woman's life; to lose the love of one man is to miss the aim in woman's life" (Nü-chieh 1:8b, Swann 1932, 87). Though this is so, Pan Chao cautions women not to try to win their husbands' hearts through flattery and cheap methods, but through single-minded devotion and correct behavior. Such behavior is broken down into four categories, or aspects of a woman's character. They are womanly virtue, womanly speech, womanly deportment, and womanly work.

Womanly virtue involves being pure and chaste, quiet and reserved, and acting with a sense of honor and integrity in all things. Womanly speech entails talking only when appropriate, not maligning or abusing others in one's talk, and not wearying others with too much talk. Womanly deportment, interestingly enough, focuses entirely on personal cleanliness, that is, washing one's hair and one's body regularly, as well as keeping one's clothes and ornaments fresh and clean. Lastly, as for womanly work,

> With whole-hearted devotion to sew and weave; to love not gossip and silly laughter; in cleanliness and order, to prepare the wine and food for serving guests, may be called the characteristics of womanly work. (Nü-chieh 1:8b–9a, Swann 1932, 86)

Having dealt with a wife's responsibility to her husband, Pan Chao uses the last few sections of the text to deal with the wife's responsibilities to her in-laws. In dealing with all of them, she recommends a heavy dose of modesty and acquiescence, as well as a skillfulness in pleasing them all. Specifically, in terms of one's mother-in-law, one is advised to act as a shadow or an echo to her, that is, she should go along with her in all matters and assert no will of her own. Even if what the mother-in-law commands is wrong, the daughter-in-law should still obey it. The jealousy and haughtiness of sisters-in-law (wives of one's husband's brothers) may be even more of a challenge to the new bride, so she is cautioned to humble herself before them at all times.

The rewards Pan Chao holds out to women who fully follow her advice in this text are typically Confucian: "Parents-in-law boast of her good deeds; her husband is satisfied with her. Praise of her radiates, making her illustrious in district and in neighborhood; and her brightness reaches to her own father and mother" (Nü-chieh 1:11b, Swann 1932, 88). These rewards are consonant with those usually offered to Confucian males: a good name and the happiness of one's parents.

On one level, we can read this text as a guidebook for surviving as a bride in the highly hierarchical, group-oriented Chinese family system. Being a new bride in such a system was not easy, and as Margery Wolf's research has shown, in more recent times the rate of suicide was quite high for young brides. Indeed, at one point in her text, Pan Chao decries the lack of adequate overall education for women, given the difficulties of their roles in the Chinese family system. On a deeper level, the text represents the type of spirituality required of women in the Confucian world.

The religious path presented by Pan Chao, though not as overt as in later texts by women, revolves around the full acceptance of women's inferiority and submission to the relationships involved in marriage: notably, with the husband, his parents, and other in-laws. A woman accepts her inferior status, according to Confucian logic, not because men have told her to but because the authority of the cosmic order demands it. She has a stake in the maintenance of that order just as much as a man. She also has a stake in the maintenance of the family order and thus submits to the discipline of family relationships. Her spiritual path has the same orientation as that of men, that is, that one fulfills oneself by immersing oneself in human life, not going off on one's own. As sacred community, the family is to be a woman's total area of dedication. She takes her place in the larger whole, not upsetting but rather enhancing its order. She does so by not putting herself forward but by working in subtle and humble ways. Though a woman is called upon to be "weak," she is not to be spineless and helpless. Rather what she is called upon to do requires a great amount of inner strength and courage. In fact, one might even say that Confucian women are called upon to go beyond the selflessness, humility, obedience, and dedication expected of men. As outsiders in men's families, they have to doubly prove themselves to gain acceptance. They have to work for the good of the family as a whole even though it is not their natural family; thus in many ways, their dedication is more selfless than a man's dedication to his family.

Pan Chao's Instructions for Women, though only a short piece of 7 sections, nevertheless exerted a tremendous influence on the lives of Chinese women. It became the prototype of all later instructional texts for women, and Pan Chao became the model female instructress, so much so that later women often wrote their texts in her voice rather than their own. Two of the most striking examples of this are a Ms. Ch'eng (ca. 700 C.E.) who wrote the Classic of Filial Piety for Women (Nü hsiao-ching) and Sung Jo-chao (ca. 800 C.E.) who wrote the Analects for Women (Nü lun-yü). These two women capitalized both on the reputation of Pan Chao by adopting her voice in their texts and also on the popularity of the Confucian texts the Classic of Filial Piety and the Analects. The conscious modelling of women's instructional texts on mainstream Confucian classics represents a growing moral seriousness on the part of women and a sense of the need for texts as valuable for their guidance as those already canonized by the tradition for men....

With the fall of the Han dynasty in 220 C.E., Confucianism was eclipsed by Buddhism and Taoism in the area of religion. It was not to play a significant role in that area until its reemergence in the form of Neo-Confucianism in the Sung dynasty (960–1279 C.E.). When it did reemerge in this form, a great shift had occurred which was to have a profound effect on the lives of women.

The early Neo-Confucians zealously worked to revitalize Confucianism to reclaim the territory it had earlier lost to the Buddhists. Their challenge was to reestablish the family and the state as the locus of religious duty. They attacked the Buddhists for selfishly trying to escape from the world rather than direct their energies to building up the human order. Nevertheless, they were quite impressed with the depths of Buddhist spirituality. How could they blend the best of the two? The Neo-Confucianism that resulted was a more overtly religious tradition than earlier Confucianism and was concerned more with metaphysical matters, human interiority, and religious practices such as meditation. There was a new sense of the profound depths of the human self, but with it a greater awareness of the dangers and obstructions which hinder the full development of the self. They saw these dangers in terms of human desires and passions. As a result, in Neo-Confucianism there is a greater preoccupation with self-discipline and with controlling one's desires.

This great wariness about human desires and passions was directed to the area of human relationships, the cornerstone of Confucian religiosity. Ch'eng I (1033–1107), one of the leading Sung Neo-Confucians, reflects this wariness in the following statement which appears in the most famous anthology of Neo-Confucian writings, Reflections on Things at Hand (Chin-ssu lu):

> In family relationships, parents and children usually overcome correct principles with affection and supplant righteousness with kindness. Only strong and resolute people can avoid sacrificing correct principles for the sake of personal affection. (Chin-ssu lu 6:1b, Chan 1967, 173)

Here we see a new element. In classical Confucianism, one fulfilled oneself by immersing oneself in the network of human relationships. Now there is more ambivalence about these relationships, a sense that they may be a source of obstruction rather than a contribution to one's pursuit of sagehood.

Women could not but be influenced by this change, especially because one of the most intimate ties of a Confucian male was with his wife. Women came to be seen as activators of desires both sensual and affective. There was a felt need to ensure that they controlled their desires and not upset men's progress toward sagehood. Thus the moral code for women, while in many ways a continuation of the earlier, classical one, focused to an almost obsessive degree on chastity. And within this, the chastity of widows was singled out for special emphasis.

To be sure, chastity had been an important virtue for women in the classical period, as we have seen in the Biographies of Exemplary Women, and widows were exhorted to remain faithful to their husbands by not remarrying. But nothing in the classical period can match the degree of preoccupation with chastity that Neo-Confucianism exhibited. The most chilling statement in this regard was made by Ch'eng I concerning the remarriage of widows. He is asked whether a widow can remarry in the extenuating circumstance that she is poor, all alone, and about to starve to death. Ch'eng I responds: "This theory has come about only because people of later generations are afraid of starving to death. But to starve to death is a very small matter. To lose one's integrity, however, is a very serious matter" (Chin-ssu lu 6:3a, Chan 1967, 177).

The models of women presented in an influential primer for young men, the Elementary Learning (Hsiao-hsüeh), compiled by the most famous Sung dynasty Neo-Confucian Chu Hsi (1130–1200), staunchly promote this moral code. In one case, we have a woman who progressively mutilates her body with each new exertion of pressure by her parents to remarry. First she cuts off her hair, then her ears, and finally her nose, all the while defiantly asserting her determination to remain faithful to her dead husband. Another example is of two unmarried sisters who are abducted by bandits. They both resist rape, the first by hurling herself off a high cliff and the second by dashing herself on the rocks (there is plenty of blood and gore in these tales) (Hsiao-hsüeh 6:11a–12a). Since the bond of marriage is not just with the husband but with his parents as well, we are also presented with model widows who further prove their faithfulness by giving unstinting care to their mother-in-laws, even in the worst of conditions. One woman's husband dies in war while she is still young, leaving her childless. Rather than succumb to her parent's pressure to remarry, she cares for her mother-in-law even though it entails a life of poverty for her. What little she has at the time of her mother-in-law's death she sells to give the mother-in-law a proper funeral (6:10a-b). Another woman is praised for trying to ward off ten strong bandits when they attack her mother-in-law. She is able to succeed in saving the mother even though she herself is almost beaten to death (6:11b-12a).

What is noticeably absent among these models are mature, astute women of the kind who dispense good advice, who are skillful in the arts of persuasion, and who involve themselves in the political realm. There are no wise, discerning mothers. There are only nun-like martyrs in their young adulthood. This more dramatic and ascetical tone, I must add, also pervades the models set up for men to emulate.

Neo-Confucianism was not adopted as the state orthodoxy until about a hundred years after the demise of the Sung dynasty, that is until the late Yüan and early Ming dynasties (last half of the fourteenth century). As when Confucianism became the state orthodoxy in the Han dynasty, efforts were made to bring women more into the mainstream. But in contrast to the Han emperors, the early Ming emperors were more heavyhanded in promoting Neo-Confucianism.

One aspect of the new orthodoxy was that it brought the chastity cult for women more into the public arena. For example, the first Ming emperor T'ai-tsu announced that chaste widows who lost their husbands before they had reached the age of 30 and who remained chaste until the age of 50 would have a memorial arch built in their honor, and their household would be exempt from corvee labor. The biographical sections of the dynastic histories and local gazetteers are filled with documented cases of women who are celebrated for having preserved their chastity. Ming and Ch'ing China witnessed a great increase in the number of women who mutilated themselves or committed suicide rather than lose their chastity before marriage or enter into a second marriage after the death of a husband. One scholar's estimate, based on dynastic history records, is that the number of deaths by suicide jumped from 383 cases in the Yüan dynasty to 8,688 in the Ming dynasty and then fell to 2,841 in the Ch'ing dynasty. The cases of mutilation jumped even more dramatically from 359 cases in the Yüan dynasty to 27,141 cases in the Ming dynasty and 9,482 in the Ch'ing dynasty (Tung 1970, 112).

The other aspect of the new orthodox worth noting is once again the popularity of texts written by women for women. The most notable one is the Instructions for the Inner Quarters (Nei-hsün) by the second empress of the Ming dynasty, Empress Hsü. Imitating the work her husband, the Yung-lo Emperor, was doing in the area of promoting Neo-Confucian texts for men, she dedicated herself to the instruction of women in the imperial family. Though much of the content of her text echoes that found in the texts we have already discussed, several features are worthy of comment.

The first is her adoption of Neo-Confucian terminology in the area of self-cultivation to discuss the duties and responsibilities of a woman. Great attention is put on one's inner life, a keeping watch over one's thoughts and desires at all times. Though this is not dealt with in nearly the detail or sophistication of texts addressed to men, still, it does go beyond the earlier texts for women where attention to personal character mostly concerned itself with propriety and comportment (be chaste and pure, don't shake your skirts when you stand, be humble and modest).

The second feature of note is that she takes seriously the Neo-Confucian notion that all human beings are called to sagehood. So she encourages women to pursue the path of female sageliness, describing it as a far more precious jewel than either pearls or jade (Nei-hsün 3:22b). As part of this female sageliness, she envisions women as playing a vital role in both family and state morality, thereby restoring to women their role of moral adviser which they had in classical Confucianism but which had been taken away by Sung Neo-Confucians.

Sometime in early or mid-Ming, this text was published together with the three earlier texts (Instructions for Women, Classic of Filial Piety for Women, and Analects for Women) as the Four Books for Women (Nü ssu-shu). Later, in the early seventeenth century, a scholar official Wang Hsiang substituted the instructional text his mother had written for women, A Handy Record of Rules for Women (Nü-fan chieh-lu), for the Classic of Filial Piety for Women, and published that set as the Four Books for Women.

His action came at a time when many Chinese men involved themselves in education for women. One of the most popular texts for women was a new rendering of the Biographies of Exemplary Women from the Han dynasty brought up to date for contemporary women by a man named Lü K'un (Handlin 1975).

Although we have these examples of women who embraced Neo-Confucianism, either by writing in the spirit of its teachings or by sacrificing themselves to be faithful to its teachings, we still have to consider the fact that most women in China were Buddhists. With the rise of Neo-Confucianism, Buddhism suffered a decline, except with women who became its mainstay. Attention needs to be given to the question of what Chinese women found in Buddhism that sustained them in a way Confucianism (or Neo-Confucianism) did not. Because of the secular nature of Confucianism, there was no problem with women participating in both. Though many male Neo-Confucians had no tolerance for Buddhism themselves, they placed no restrictions on their wives or mothers who practiced it.

The legacy of Confucianism in the modern period is a complicated one. By the late nineteenth and early twentieth century, China was in a state of decline, overwhelmed by problems of poverty, overpopulation, corruption, and loss of morale in the government, and imperialism by Western powers. Radicals and reformers turned on Confucianism as one of the prime sources of their problems. Since the position of women was also seen as at an all-time low, as evidenced in the widespread practices of footbinding, female infanticide, and the buying and selling of women, women also turned against the tradition. Probably no other socioreligious tradition has been attacked in such a large-scale, systematic way. Mao Tse-tung was astute enough to see the potential in women as a revolutionary group and achieved much of his success from the support of women. The People's Republic of China has made sweeping reforms to improve the status of women in society, and has included large numbers of them in the work force and in political office. However, as several recent books have shown, much remains to be done to give women full equality. The recent one-child policy has brought to the surface the traditional bias in favor of male heirs.

But the larger question for us is the future of Confucianism. Does it indeed have a future? Can it exist in a scientific and technological world that does not reflect its cosmic orientation? Can it exist apart from the traditional Chinese political and family system? Despite all the repudiation of Confucianism in modern China, do many of its teachings persists, albeit in Communist form?

If there is no future for Confucianism, then there is no use asking what future role women might play in it. Indeed, there are few Chinese women today who want to identify themselves with Confucianism, linked as it is with the oppression of women. But will there come a time when the atmosphere is not so highly charged and when Chinese women will want to evaluate the positive legacy of their tradition as well? From the outsider's point of view, there is such a positive legacy. Though Confucianism contributed to the victimization of women, it also gave them a sense of self-discipline, esteem for education, and respect for public service that has enabled them to enter into today's political and social realm in the number and with the effectiveness that they have.

The Confucian tradition, with its appreciation for the gift of life, with its profound humanistic spirit, its sense of religious practice as building the human community, and its sense of the relational quality of things, has much to contribute to our global religious heritage. The challenge of giving women a more equitable place within that tradition remains. It seems obvious that unless that challenge is met, the appeal of many aspects of Confucianism will be greatly diminished.

References

Andors, Phyllis. 1983. *The Unfinished Liberation of Chinese Women, 1949–1980*. Bloomington: Indiana University Press.

Chan Wing-tsit, trans. 1967. *Reflections on Things at Hand: the Neo-Confucian Anthology*. New York: Columbia University Press.

Ch'en-Tung-yüan. 1937. *Chung-uo fu-nü sheng-huo shih*. Shanghai: Commercial Press.

Chu Hsi, ed. 1173. *Chin-ssu lu*. Ssu-pu pei-yao edition.

———. 1187. *Hsiao-hsüeh*. Ssu-pu pei-yao edition.

Elvin, Mark. 1984. "Female Virtue and the State in China," *Past and Present* 104 (Aug. '84). 111–152.

Guisso, Richard. 1981. "Thunder over the Lake: the Five Classics and the Perception of Women in Early China." In *Women in China*, ed. Guisso and Johannesen. New York: Philo Press.

Handlin, Joanna. 1975. "Lü K'un's New Audience: the Influence of Women's Literacy on Sixteenth-Century Thought." In *Women in Chinese Society*, ed. Wolf and Witke. Stanford: Stanford University Press.

Empress Hsü. d.u. *Nei-hsün*. In *Nü ssu-shu*, ed. Wang Hsiang. Naikaku bunko 1844 edition.

Johnson, Kay Ann. 1983. *Women, the Family and Peasant Revolution in China*. Chicago: University of Chicago Press.

Kelleher, Theresa. 1986. "How to Be the Perfect Woman: Chinese Instructional Texts for Women." Unpublished paper.

———. d.u. *K'ung-tzu chia yü*. Ssu-pu pei-yao edition.

Legge, James, trans. 1966 reprint of 1923 ed. *The Four Books: Confucian Analects, the Great Learning, the Doctrine of the Mean, and the Works of Mencius*. New York: Paragon.

———. 1967 reprint of 1885 ed. *Li chi, Book of Rites*. Edited by C.C. Chai and W. Chai. 2 vols. New York: University Books.

Liu Hsiang. d.u. *Lieh-nü chuan*. Ssu-pu pei-yao edition.

Mann, Susan. 1984. "Suicide and Chastity: Visible Themes in the History of Chinese Women." Unpublished paper.

———. 1984. "Widows in the Kinship and Community Systems of the Qing Period." Unpublished paper.

O'Hara, Albert. 1945. *The Position of Women in Early China*. Washington, D.C.: Catholic University Press.

Pan Chao. d.u. *Nü-chieh*. In *Nü ssu-shu*, ed. Wang Hsiang. Naikaku bunko 1844 edition.

Steele, John. 1966 reprint of 1917 ed. *The I-Ii, or Book of Etiquette and Ceremonial*. Taipei: Ch'ung Wen Publishing Co.

Sung, Marina. 1981. "The Chinese *Lieh-nü* Tradition." In *Women in China,* ed. Guisso and Johannesen. New York: Philo Press.

Sung, Jo-chao. d.u. *Nü lun-yü*. In *Nü ssu-shu*, ed. Wang Hsiang. Naikaku bunko 1844 edition.

Swann, Nancy Lee. 1932. *Pan Chao: Foremost Woman Scholar of China*. New York: Century Co.

Tung, Chia-tsung. 1970. "Li-tai chieh-fu lieh-nü te t'ung-chen." In *Chung-kuo fu-nü shih lun-chi*, ed. Pao Chia-lin. Taipei: Mu-t'ung Publishing Co.

Waltner, Ann. 1981. "Widows and Remarriage in Ming and Early Qing China." In *Women in China*, ed. Guisso and Johannesen. New York: Philo Press.

Wilhelm, Richard, trans. 1967. *I Ching, or Book of Changes*. Rendered into English by Cary F. Baynes. Princeton: Princeton University Press.

Wolf, Margery. 1975. "Women and Suicide in China." In *Women in Chinese Society*, ed. Wolf and Witke. Stanford: Stanford University Press.

Questions for Discussion

1. What similarities and differences among women's experience in the different Asian religious traditions described in this chapter do you find most striking?

2. Kelleher's essay suggests that despite the support of some women for Confucianism, that most women in China were Buddhists. What do you think women found in Buddhism that sustained them in a way that Confucianism did not?

3. Similarly, in twentieth-century Japan, women have found certain of the new religions more appropriate for their needs and interests than either Buddhism or Shinto. What factors may account for this shift in women's religious affiliations?

4. At the end of her essay, Kelleher asks whether there is a future for Confucianism and, if so, what women's role in this tradition might be, given its history of treating women as subordinate and inferior. What do you think?

5. In this chapter, we find, for the first time, religions that can be described as "women's religions."

   • Do you find any significant differences that distinguish them from "men's religions"?

   • What features of culture enable women's religions to flourish?

   • What are the factors that makes the indigenous religion of Okinawa described by Sered different from other religions dominated by women?

6. How would you explain the function of menstruation in determining gendered religious roles in Asian traditions?

References and Materials for Further Study

Books and Articles

Balbir, Nalini. 1999. "Jainism," in Serinity Young, ed., *Encyclopedia of Women and World Religion*. New York: Macmillan Reference.

———. 1994. "Women in Jainism," in Arvind Sharma, ed., *Religion and Women*, Albany: State University of New York Press.

Barholomeusz, Tessa. 1999. "Southeast Asian Buddhism," in Serinity Young, ed., *Encyclopedia of Women and World Religion*. New York: Macmillan Reference.

Bose, Mandakranta, ed. 2000. *Faces of the Feminine in Ancient, Medieval and Modern India*. New York: Oxford University Press.

Cass, Victoria. 1999. "East Asian Religions: An Overview," in Serinity Young, ed., *Encyclopedia of Women and World Religion*. New York: Macmillan Reference.

Chen, Ellen. 1974. "Tao as the Great Mother and the Influence of Motherly Love in the Shaping of Chinese Philosophy." *History of Religions* 14, 1: 51-64.

Cleary, Thomas, Trans. 1989. *Immortal Sisters: Secrets of Taoist Women*. Boston: Shambhala.

Hardacre, Helen. 1992, "The New Religions, Family, and Society in Japan," in Martin E. Marty and R. Scott Appleby, eds., *Fundamentalisms and Society: Reclaiming the Sciences, the Family, and Education*. Chicago: University of Chicago.

Jaini, Padmanabh. 1992. *Gender and Salvation: Jaina Debates on the Spiritual Liberation of Women*. Berkeley: University of California Press.

Jochim, Chris. 1999. "Confucianism: An Overview," in Serinity Young, ed., *Encyclopedia of Women and World Religion*. New York: Macmillan Reference.

Kelleher, Theresa. 1987. "Confucianism," in Arvind Sharma, ed., *Women in World Religions*. Albany: State University of New York Press.

Kendall, Laurel. 1999. "East Asian Religions: Religious Rites and Practices," in Serinity Young, ed., *Encyclopedia of Women and World Religion* New York: Macmillan Reference.

Kirkland, Russell. 1999. "Taoism: An Overview," in Serinity Young, ed., *Encyclopedia of Women and World Religion*. New York: Macmillan Reference.

Levering, Miriam. 1994. "Women, the State, and Religion Today in The People's Republic of China," in Arvind Sharma, ed., *Today's Woman in World Religions*. Albany: State University of New York Press.

Maneck, Susan. 1994. "Women in the Baha'i Faith," in Arvind Sharma, ed., *Religion and Women* Albany. New York: State University of New York Press.

Miller, Alan L. 1993. "Myth and Gender in Japanese Shamanism: The Itako of Tohoku," *History of Religions* 32, 4: 343-367.

Nefsky, Marilyn. 1995. "Liberator or Pacifier: Religion and Women in Japan," in Ursala King, ed., *Religion and Gender*. Oxford, UK: Blackwell.

Reed, Barbara. 1994. "Women and Chinese Religion in Contemporary Taiwan," in Arvind Sharma, *Today's Woman in World Religions*. Albany: State University of New York Press.

Riesebrodt, Martin, and Kelly Chong 1999. "Fundamentalisms and Patriarchal Gender Politics." *Journal of Women's History* 10, 4: 55-77. On women in evangelical groups in South Korea.

Sered, Susan. 1999. *Women of the Sacred Groves: Divine Priestesses of Okinawa*. New York: Oxford University Press.

———. 1994. *Priestess, Mother, Sacred Sister: Religions Dominated by Women*. New York: Oxford University Press. Among the traditions she discusses are *nat* cults in Burma and Korean shamanism.

Smyers, Karen. 1983. "Women and Shinto: The Relationship Between Purity and Pollution," *Japanese Religions*, 12: 7-18.

Young, Serinity. 1999. "Images of the Tao," in Serinity Young, ed., *Encyclopedia of Women and World Religion*. New York: Macmillan Reference.

Yusa, Michiko. 1994. "Women in Shinto: Images Remembered," in Arvind Sharma, ed., *Religion and Women*. Albany: State University of New York Press.

Internet and Media References

Women's Early Eastern Spirituality Web site;
  http://music.acu.edu/www/iawm/pages/reference /masters.html. Contains a
  wealth of writings by and about early women in Japanese, Korean, Tibetan and
  Chinese religions, including Buddhism, Taoism, and Shinto.

Choice for a Chinese Woman: Enlightenment in a Buddhist Convent, Films for the Humanities, Inc., 1993.

Women and Judaism

Overview

Judaism is among the oldest of the world's religions. Its origins are in the ancient Israelite religion; it began to be "Judaism" only after 586 B.C.E. The Jewish religion spread from the ancient near-eastern region in the Middle East, first through the Mediterranean region of the Greco-Roman Empire beginning in about 515 B.C.E., and then into Europe and Russia and the countries of the former Soviet Union, North and South America, and even into parts of Africa and Asia. In spite of its dissemination around the world, Judaism has remained a minority religion almost everywhere it has been (with the exception of contemporary Israel). By 700 C.E., known as the end of the "rabbinic period," the Jewish tradition had achieved virtually all of the major features that it has today.

Jewish people have been oppressed and marginalized in most places they have lived throughout their entire history. After a period when oppressive state policies toward Jews were liberalized in the modern period following the French Revolution, anti-Semitism was renewed in the nineteenth century. This discrimination and denial of rights to Jews reached its peak with the rise of National Socialism and Hitler's Nazi Party in the mid-twentieth century, with the horror of the Holocaust and the extermination of millions of Jews throughout Europe and the Soviet countries. Many who were able to escape fled to the United States, Canada, parts of South and Latin America, and South Africa, where they now have thriving communities.

As with Hinduism, Buddhism, and other Asian religions, there are many variations and differences among the practitioners of the Jewish tradition. However, some generalizations may be made that are fairly accurate across these differences. Compared to some of the other religions we will encounter, Judaism is not only a religious identity, but also a cultural and ethnic one. Because Judaism does not advocate missionizing or conversion, the vast majority of those who practice Judaism were born to Jewish parents (the tradition specifies that the mother's heritage determines that of the children, so children born to non-Jewish fathers are still Jewish, and the children of their daughters are as well, and so on).

Sacred Texts

Compared to many other religious traditions, Jews are a "people of the book." That is, Judaism is a very textually oriented tradition, and thus literacy and study of the sacred scriptures and commentaries are highly valued (such study was, not surprisingly, a vocation or career historically restricted to males). Indeed, one of the central requirements of Judaism is to spend time studying ancient sacred texts. Traditionally, men who spent their lives studying at a *Yeshiva*, or academic institute, were greatly respected.

The most sacred religious text throughout Judaism is the *Torah*, which consists of the first five books of the Hebrew Bible (what is called the "Old Testament" in Christianity), revealed by God to Moses on Mt. Sinai. The most famous part of this revelation is the Ten Commandments. According to the Jewish faith, at Sinai, the Jewish people entered into a covenant with God. In exchange for their faithful adherence to the Ten Commandments, God would provide them with happiness, freedom, health, long life, offspring, and entrance to the promised land of Israel.

In addition to revealing the Torah, Jews believe that there was also an oral tradition transmitted, which is contained in a huge collection of Jewish legal and theological teachings called the *Talmud*. The first part of the Talmud, the *Mishnah*, was composed by a particular group of rabbis, most likely during the first century C.E. The Mishnah, which proposes an ideal vision of the relation between men and women as well as between God and humans, "ultimately became the guidebook and practical pattern for ensuring forms of Jewish life" (Baskin 1985, 4). The second part of the Talmud, the *Gemorah*, is a wide-ranging set of commentaries on the Mishnah that was composed for centuries thereafter. The main legal treatises of Jewish law are called *Halakah*.

Religious Rituals

Ritual and ethical acts are central to Jewish life. The main ritual and ethical obligations are established by the *mitzvoh*, the divine commandments (which only men are required to satisfy). If these commandments are kept, believing Jews understand, God will eventually send a messiah to bring peace and harmony to the whole world. The precepts to be kept by women— lighting the candles to mark the beginning of the Sabbath, burning a bit of dough used in making *Challah* bread, and *niddah*, the ritual cleansing of women after their menstrual period—are not regarded as mitzvoh but as rabbinic precepts established as punishments for Eve's responsibility for the Fall of Adam from the Garden of Eden (Baskin 1985; 7).

The main centers of Jewish religious life are in the synagogue or temple and in the home. The day of sabbath (*Shabbath*) is Saturday, rather than the Sunday sabbath that is dominant throughout most of the Christian world. Religious services in the synagogue (*shul*) were traditionally gender segregated (and still are in the Orthodox tradition), with women restricted to one side of the temple or upstairs. Only men present were counted toward the quorum (*minyan*) of ten people required for religious rituals to be official. Women are not allowed to read the Torah in the synagogue and are not required to pray three times a day, as men are. These prohibitions and "exemptions" have been interpreted by some to indicate that women are less central to maintenance of religious life.

Yet the centrality of the home, and especially of the kitchen, to Jewish religious life has been emphasized by feminist scholars in recent years. In this sphere, at least, there is no question that women have been integral to the maintenance and transmission of the Jewish religion, despite their exclusion or marginalization within the synagogue and from the rituals conducted there.

Holy days in the Jewish calendar include *Rosh Hashanah, Yom Kippur,* and *Purim.* Special ceremonies, both in shul and at home, are performed on these occasions. Orthodox (and some other) Jews keep *kosher,* meaning that they can only eat special foods, specially prepared on special dishes. In most homes, then, the burden of keeping kosher falls on the women, in their traditional roles as homemakers. Extensive cleaning, shopping, and food preparation are required on these holidays. The main coming of age ritual is called *bar mitzvah* for boys and *bas mitzvah* for girls. The *bas mitzvah* is of fairly recent origins, however, and has been promoted by Jewish feminists as a way of redressing some of the imbalance in the status of males and females within Judaism.

Types of Judaism

Within the United States today, there are four main movements of Judaism, generally ranging from the most conservative to the most radical: Orthodox, Reformed, Conservative, and Reconstructionist. These divisions to a significant extent reflect differences in attitudes toward women. Orthodox Judaism is the most prominent and conservative of these four traditions.

Within the Orthodox tradition are a number of different sects, each with its own variations of ritual and rules for moral and social life. One of the more prominent of the Orthodox schools in the United States is the Lubavitch, described in the selection by Shoshana Gelerenter-Liebowitz on "Growing Up Lubavitch." Her essay illustrates the extensive gender segregation that is practiced in almost all aspects of religious observance, with the exception of the community's relationship to the *rebbe* (rabbi).

The Reform movement developed in Europe in the nineteenth century and represented a liberalization of many of the Orthodox practices and traditions. For example, it introduced the bas mitzvah coming of age ceremony for girls and provided opportunities for girls to have spiritual education at non-Orthodox rabbinic schools. The excerpt by Nancy Hausman in the selection from *Daughters of the King* describes the experience of being a member of the Reformed synagogue.

Conservative Judaism began as an offshoot of the Reform movement among Eastern European immigrants to the United States. It represents a more moderate position between Reform and Orthodox Judaism. It was slow in granting women equal rights in synagogue services and still refuses ordination to gays and lesbians.

The Reconstructionist tradition began as an offshoot of the Conservative movement and is based on the distinctive writings of Mordecai Kaplan. It was very progressive in granting women equal rights with men, and in welcoming gays and lesbians as rabbis (see Heschel 1999, 543). The excerpt from *Daughters of the King* by Emily Faust Korzenik describes the experience of being a member of the Reconstructionist tradition.

Relationship of Female-Gendered and Feminine Images and Symbols to "Real" Women

In contrast to several of the other religions covered in this textbook, women in Judaism have been treated with relatively high respect and granted a number of opportunities. However, like all the other world religious traditions, Judaism also has its sexist and patriarchal aspects. These are manifest in gendered imagery and stories that are central to the tradition. Perhaps the most visible symbol of religious identity, circumcision of male Jews, functions also as a symbol of male spiritual superiority. Since women are unable to bear this mark, their religious identity can only be secondary to that of men.

The images and symbols of women in Judaism are varied and diverse. Although images of women as wives and mothers restricted to roles in the private sphere are common, there are also images of women as warriors, prostitutes, leaders, prophets, and wise decision makers.

Eve is the most prominent female figure in Judaism. An apocryphal ("later added") or officially dismissed part of the Jewish religion, however, is the story of Lilith, sometimes referred to as Adam's first wife or the "bad Eve," who did not submissively acquiesce to Adam's domination. Lilith has been promoted by Jewish feminists as a model for resisting patriarchy and male domination.

Women's Relationship to Judaism

Women-Specific or Distinctive Aspects of Judaism

Despite their exclusion from development of the major textual traditions of their faith, Jewish women developed their own prayers and ritual practices. Today, there are all-female prayer groups in the less conservative denominations of Judaism. Orthodox Jewish communities started all-girl schools both in Europe and the United States to protect them from secular influences. Orthodox women also formed social service and Zionist (based on political views favoring Israel as *the* homeland for the Jewish people) organizations for women. In Israel, where women are excluded from most forms of active participation in public religious life, a group founded in 1989 called Women at the Wall arrange their own group worship at the Western Wall, a sacred part of the ancient temple of Jerusalem.

Gender-Based Segregation and Inequalities

Observant male Jews recite a daily prayer which includes the line "Blessed art thou, Lord our God, King of the Universe, who has not made me a woman" (Baskin 1985, 4-6). This prayer suggests that Judaism values males more highly than females and, indeed, other evidence of gender inequality is not difficult to find, although the extent of such inequalities in Judaism today varies widely, depending on the state and denomination in question. In traditional Judaism, and in the more conservative forms (usually Orthodox, which is the prevailing form of Judaism in Europe and Israel today), there is significant gender segregation. This segregation extends even to the extent of separating male and female seating in the synagogues, excluding women from *minyan* (the number of participants required to have a quorum to conduct religious services), as well as excluding women from certain religious rituals, the study of Torah, and development of scriptural interpretation and commentary, interpretation of Halakah, opportunities to become rabbis, and so on.

As the selection by Niditch describes, Jewish Biblical law prescribes a number of restrictions and prohibitions in women's lives, including segregation in the temples and during menstruation, in domestic matters—for example, men are allowed to divorce their wives, but not vice versa; men can have more than one wife, but women are restricted to one husband; sons but not daughters can inherit from their father, and so on. However, within the private sphere, men owe women conjugal rights, a striking reversal of most cultural traditions which make women's sexual needs subservient to those of men.

The strong preference for male offspring, and the disappointment expressed in texts over the birth of a female baby, reinforces the evidence that ancient Israelite society was strongly patriarchal. In ancient Israel, women were in effect regarded as the property of males: At the time of their marriage, their fathers "paid" a dowry to the husband. Virginity was valued so highly that if a husband could prove that his new wife was not a virgin, he could "return" her to her father's home. If evidence showed that he had lied, and she was in fact a virgin, the husband would be required to take her back. Adultery was viewed as a crime against the husband, not the wife, so that only extra-marital sex by the wife was punished. If evidence revealed that the wife had entered the liason willingly, both she and the man were stoned to death. If she was unmarried at the time that she was forced into having sex, the perpetrator could be forced to marry her or to pay compensation to the father for "damaging" her value by removing her virginity. These biblical practices reveal the extent to which women in ancient Judaism had no rights to their own personhood or autonomy to have a voice in how their lives were determined.

The Hellenistic period essentially reinforced the extreme patriarchy of the Israelite period of Judaism. Some of these patriarchal aspects of the tradition have diminished over time, although not until many centuries had passed. For example, laws governing family matters have been altered so that now women are given the same basic rights upon marriage as men. Polygamy died out in the tenth century.

Women's Access to Religious Training and Leadership Roles

The difficulties that Jewish girls and women have had in their attempts to obtain an education, especially in the sacred religious texts and commentaries, were perhaps most popularized by Barbara Streisand in the Hollywood movie "Yentl." Since the beginning of the twentieth century, more opportunities have become available for women in Jewish institutions, especially the more liberal ones (reform and conservative). In 1972, Sally Priesand became the first woman rabbi to be ordained, graduating from the Reformed Seminary of Hebrew Union College. Women were later allowed to attend the Jewish Theological Seminary and become Conservative rabbis. The selection by Shoshana Gelerenter-Liebowitz "Growing Up Lubavitch" describes some of the obstacles that Jewish girls and women still encounter in their efforts to obtain an education and training in the Jewish faith.

As with opportunities for religious education and training, Jewish women are increasingly able to participate as leaders in their communities.

In her book *Women Who Would Be Rabbis: A History of Women's Ordination, 1889–1985*, Pamela Nadell describes the struggles that Jewish women have had in obtaining permission to ordain as rabbis, which came only some years after they were finally admitted to theological studies to gain the requisite training. Since the first woman rabbi was ordained in 1972, increasing numbers of women have begun careers as rabbis and cantors (directors of liturgical music and prayer in the synagogue) in the Reformed and Reconstructionist synagogues.

Women are now allowed to become rabbis in all but the Orthodox tradition (for example, the Conservative Jewish Theological Seminary in the United States decided to ordain women in 1983 and the Reform movement in Israel in 1992). Even in Israel, some synagogues allow women to be assistant rabbis, with responsibilities for teaching, preaching, and pastoral care. Since the 1990s, most synagogues in the United States have offered women the same opportunities to be involved in prayer rituals. (In Israel, by contrast, where Orthodox Judaism is the official state religion, most synagogues exclude women from leadership and active participation in worship and still require segregated seating in synagogues.)

Before this avenue of ordination, however, and still today for Orthodox women, leadership roles within Judaism are basically restricted to either being the wife of a rabbi (a *rebbetzin* in the Lubavitch tradition), or by participating in one of the many Jewish women's organizations that originated mostly in the nineteenth century, as described in the selection by Pamela Nadell entitled "Ladies of the Sisterhood: Women in the American Reform Synagogue."

The selection from *Daughters of the King* by Emily Faust Korzenik—"On Being A Rabbi"—describes how she sees her capacities to be nurturing and connected to others as a rabbi have been shaped by her experiences of being a wife and mother. She also describes the discrimination she has faced as a woman when the norm for spiritual leaders continues to be male. The essay by Nancy Hausman, "On Becoming a Cantor," indicates the strides that Jewish women have made: There are now more women than men entering cantorial school and discrimination against women cantors has diminished since she began her career.

Well-Known and/or Influential Women in the Tradition

Perhaps the most prominent female in the scriptural tradition of Judaism is the figure of Eve, the "first woman," portrayed in the Hebrew Bible's Genesis chapter. There are a number of other prominent women figures in the Hebrew Bible, however, including Deborah, the wives of King David (Michal, Abigail, and Bathsheba); Sarah and Hagar (Abraham's wife and the mother of his son Ishmael, respectively); the warriors Deborah and Jael; Abigail; Ruth; Naomi; and Miriam, the sister of Moses. As Baskin notes, during the Rabbinic period, the authors of the Mishnah made certain to disparage and denigrate these biblical figures, portraying them as adulteresses and in need of chastisement.

In contemporary times, perhaps the most famous Jewish woman remains Golda Meir, the first prime minister of Israel. Well-known Jewish women scholars include Blu Greenberg, Susannah Heschel, Rachel Baskin, Phyllis Trible, Rachel Bia le, and Judith Plaskow.

Changes in the Status of Women in Judaism

Historically

The selection by Susan Niditch, "Portrayals of Women in the Hebrew Bible," provides an excellent overview of the historical development and main tenets of Judaism. Niditch's essay also discusses some of the difficulties in ascertaining the actual status and roles women played in the historical period of a religious tradition that are applicable to many of the other religions discussed in this textbook as well.

Historically, women held power in Judaism predominantly through their roles as wives and mothers in the private sphere. Contact with the Greco-Roman world magnified the distinction between public and private spheres in early Judaism. Yet, as Niditch discusses, women have also had a larger role to play in Jewish life than once imagined, as archeological evidence is revealing that women also held important roles as prophets, judges, and charismatic leaders during the first and second periods. During the second period, for example, women started a female monastic community. In medieval times, some women rose to prominence as scriptural interpreters for other women, suggesting that they were not completely excluded from the study and interpretation of sacred texts.

Future Prospects

Since the 1970s, Jewish feminists have been active in attempting to improve the status of women within the tradition. From this impetus, parallel women's communities that belong to the general movement of alternative congregations have arisen. These feminists have also made significant contributions in reinterpreting the scriptures and developing gender-neutral or female-centered prayers, liturgies, and rituals. It is likely that these developments will continue in the future and that there will be increasing pressure on the Orthodox synagogues to open up their congregations to female rabbis (despite the stated lack of interest in equality by some Orthodox women). In addition, it is likely that Jewish women will continue pressing for equality in other aspects of Jewish life beyond the synagogue, such as in relation to their rights under domestic law governing marriage, divorce, and child custody, and their ability to study and participate in interpreting and defining the tradition in the future.

Portrayals of Women in the Hebrew Bible

Susan Niditch

To study women and the Hebrew Bible is to delve into a variety of fields including not only Bible scholarship but also women's studies, Judaica, literary criticism, anthropology, and sociology. Primary material in the Hebrew Scriptures is rich and varied, the relevant bibliography extensive, and the methodologies employed by students of women and the Bible interdisciplinary, daring, and often at the very crest of scholarship. This essay explores portrayals of women in the Hebrew Bible, discusses the challenges and problems such a study poses, and provides a guide to major trends in recent scholarship.

Methodological Challenges

Challenges in the study of women and the Hebrew Bible are in many ways parallel to challenges faced in Scripture study as a whole. The ways in which biblical authors portray families or women or kings do not necessarily correspond to how families and women actually lived or kings governed in specific, historically datable and definable social realities. In the Bible's own scheme, Israelite history divides into three major periods: (1) the time before the monarchy (before c. 1000 B.C.E.), (2) the period of monarchy (c. 1000–586 B.C.E.), and (3) the post-monarchic period (586 B.C.E. on). Within the Bible's narrative framework the first era includes the patriarchs and matriarchs, the

From Judith Baskin, ed. 1991. *Jewish Women in Historical Perspective.* Detroit, MI: Wayne State University Press, pp. 25–42. Reprinted with permission from Wayne State University Press.

exodus from Egypt, and Moses, Aaron, and Miriam, the conquest and settlement, Joshua and Rahab, and all the judges including Deborah, Samson, and the prophet-judge Samuel. The second era includes the first king, Saul, and his successor, David; David's wives, Michal, Abigail, and Bathsheba; certain "wise women"; the other Northern and Southern kings; and the rise of prophecy. A major theme of this period is the building and maintainance of the Temple and the Holy City, Jerusalem; the epoch ends with the destruction of Solomon's Temple and the exile of the elite of Jerusalem. The third era includes the prophets Zechariah and Haggai and the leaders Ezra and Nehemiah and is the so-called Second Temple period following the Babylonian exile. During this time the Temple is rebuilt and a new theological grounding for Yahwism is established; Israelite religion begins to be Judaism. . . .

Given that the Hebrew Bible is the product of a complex process of growth, what can we hope to learn about women in the Hebrew Scriptures? Can we place individual portraits on a historical time line or are all the portrayals archetypal and timeless? Is it possible to speak of individual authors and their life settings, or should we treat the tradition as a whole?

First, we need not forego all notions of history or sociological setting. Acknowledging that all pieces of Scripture were given final form by someone allows us to speak of composers or authors who belong to particular periods and settings. Certain values and attitudes—often contrasting ones—emerge in how women are presented; in these are found a history of worldviews and ethos, if not simple reliable fact. We do not know if a character named Rahab once saved Israelite spies (Joshua 2), but we know that an author employs the traditional and cross-cultural motif of the helpful harlot at the crossroads in a way that comments on the appeal of Yahwism to non-Israelites and on the marginality of Israelites at a certain point in their history. This author implicitly comments on the potential power for directed action and on the cleverness of a woman, in particular, one who is outside the social order and who in a sense symbolizes the situation of Israel as narrated. Yahweh is with her and she with him. We might then go on to discuss at which periods in real history such a portrait with its implicit messages might be of particular interest to Israelite authors and audiences.

We must also keep in mind that the Hebrew Scriptures, even in its final composed form, is no monolith. It reflects various periods of time, as well as differences among Israelites, even of one period. As Morton Smith has shown, every attitude in favor of a particular position hints at the existence of counterattitudes. "Yahweh-alone-ers" no doubt coexisted in Israel with those who worshipped Yahweh along with other personal gods, some of these perhaps female divine figures. Hints of the attitudes of these Israelites remain in the Hebrew Scriptures in polemics against worshippers of the ancient Near Eastern goddess, Asherah, for example. So, too, while the Hebrew Bible in general is male-centered, interesting nuances and threads emerge when one goes beyond that generalization. Equally misleading can be claims, difficult to substantiate, suggesting women may be responsible for one of the sources believed to underlie the Pentateuch just because many of the stories are about women, children, and the home and that 2 Isaiah may be a woman because some of the Isaianic prophecies employ female imagery to describe God (e.g., Isaiah 42:14, 49:15; and later material in 66:9 and 13).

The situation becomes even more complicated when one thinks of the various life settings and orientations from which authors may have come, and the various options in life-style possible for real Israelite women, especially during the period of the monarchy and beyond. I have found, for example, at least three definable styles and worldviews in Genesis, one more baroque and courtly, one more popular, and one more homiletical and self-consciously theological. Might not authors with such differing orientations present women differently? If one looks behind the literature to real lives, it becomes clear that the eighth-century B.C.E. woman surrounded by the "ivory couches" and other luxuries of the Northern Israelite aristocracy condemned by Amos (6:4–7), would have led a life quite different from the wife of a small landowner or a poor destitute widow. Issues of class within one period are as important as issues of date across several periods. Here, archaeological information becomes critically important even though major archaeological digs have often involved the sites of cities and temples rather than ordinary villages where people ate, and cooked, and worked.

Finally, one must acknowledge that the canon of the Hebrew Bible, like the implicit canon of English literature or Renaissance music, is an explicitly edited work from which many women's roles and important aspects of women's lives have been excluded. As we turn to portrayals of women in the Hebrew Scriptures and explore attitudes toward women implied in its narratives and legal corpora and especially as we speculate on the lives of real Israelite women and on the historical settings of biblical composers, we must always think about what may have been excluded.

Law and Social Setting

The spiritual basis of Israel's history and law is the covenantal relationship enjoined on all believers in Yahweh, who are bound to each other through him in a vow of love and obedience. While such an exalted vision of human equality in the presence of their Creator might seem to be a positive and liberating force in Israelite religion, the statutes preserved in Scripture present the image of a strongly patrilineal culture in which women are in some instances highly marginalized and fenced out and in others neatly fenced in, enclosed, and safely bound. Again, we must always remember that biblical law is material edited, preserved, codified and presented in literature and not necessarily a reflection of actual lives. In discussing this literature, the image of woman as vessel or a house is appropriate. She is to be filled with her husband's seed which (it is hoped) will develop into children, especially male children. As she contains and shelters the future child, so her realm is the home, the private realm of children and procreation. Women are legally governed by their fathers before marriage and by their husbands after marriage. In the former condition they are virgins; those discovered to be sexually active are to be stoned by their father's houses (Deuteronomy 22:21). As wives, they are to be faithful, child-producing spouses, a position they may share with other wives in polygynous marriage. Those who cannot bear successfully or who displease their husbands may be divorced (Deuteronomy 24:1–4, but see the protections offered in Deuteronomy 22:13–19); those who commit adultery are to suffer the same fate as nonvirgins (Deuteronomy 22:22; Leviticus 20:10), though we have no way of knowing whether these laws were consistently carried out. Those accused by their husbands of adultery, in the absence of certain proof, undergo a trial ritual rich in the symbolism of "purity and danger" (Numbers 5:11–31). Adultery involves relations with a married woman. A married man's relations with an unmarried woman are not adulterous, for intimate aspects of women's lives really have to do with relations between men. Thus, a man is executed for lying with another's wife because he has committed a crime of theft against a man. If a man seduces or rapes a virgin, he must pay bride-price to the father and marry her (Deuteronomy 22:28). Rules of incest—information about who is or who is not an appropriate marriage partner—are likewise addressed in the masculine singular to men. Leviticus 18 is a fascinating passage revealing priestly views concerning what constitutes too close a marriage tie, as this thread of Israelite culture steers a course between incest and exogamy.

Women normally do not inherit property, although exceptions are made in families without sons (see Numbers 27:1–11), and the author of the Book of Ruth assumes a wife could inherit her husband's property. All of this paints a portrait of women with very little de jure political or economic autonomy. The married woman who does not bear children is in an especially marginalized position, for she is no longer a virgin in her father's home yet does not fully function in her husband's. It is the children who form her bond with her husband's clan. No specific law applies to her; but the barren wife is a favorite biblical motif, marking the birth of heroes, as in many cultures. The condition of infertility is presented as a special cultural worry for the woman, and the young childless widow is a particular problem case, for she is caught between two stages in her life. This problem is addressed in Deuteronomy 25:5 by a law requiring the dead man's brother to take her as his wife to raise up children in the name of the deceased, thereby regularizing the woman's position in the patriarchal clan.

Perhaps the most noticeable laws of fencing off and boundary making vis-à-vis women are laws pertaining to purity. The menstruating woman is forbidden to her husband sexually for seven days. Her uncleanness (an invisible but real *substance*) contaminates what she sits upon, and a man can contract uncleanness by touching her or a seat or bed where she has been (Leviticus 15:21). This uncleanness from touching lasts until the transitional evening time returns the man's state to cleanness (15:19). The man who has intercourse with her is rendered unclean for seven days (15:24). So, too, the postpartum woman is unclean for seven days after the birth of a son, then must remain an additional thirty-three days in the blood of her purification. She may touch nothing "holy nor enter the sanctuary" in this period. Twice these lengths of time—fourteen and sixty-six days—are prescribed for the birth of daughters, in a sort of anticipation of the female babies' future dangerous states (Leviticus 12). This material is found in a portion of Scripture preserved by priests; it is not entirely clear exactly how rules such as these affected ordinary women's daily lives or their participation in community life. Are these purity laws premonarchic and pre-Temple in date or later? One can conclude that for at least one important group in Israelite culture, all discharges were regarded as rendering unclean. The ordinary woman of child-bearing age has regular discharges and is therefore regularly subject to uncleanness, an uncleanness associated with the psychologically and physically powerful rhythms of fertility, pregnancy, and childbirth. As such, woman becomes a monthly source of danger and power, containing an uncleanness that can spill over and contaminate, making successful mediation between God and humans in ritual impossible. Thus, in the priestly worldview, the woman is bound out of most aspects of cultic life. Do such laws reflect male priests' desires to hold power? Were there other competing options in religious expression open to women, threads not preserved in our sources? There are, after all, cultures in which women's procreative powers render them influential in the realm of the religious.

A few more features of legal material should be mentioned. Men are obligated to perform conjugal duties for their wives in Exodus 21:10, pointing to a power of the woman in the private realm, emphasized in the matriarchal narratives of Genesis discussed below.

While prostitution is outlawed, as in the book law of many cultures, some of the narrative material assumes the existence of independent, working prostitutes, women who are crossroads people, beyond ordinary cultural norms assumed for women and not under the thumb of husband or father. These marginal women are of interest to biblical writers, as shown by the stories of Rahab (Joshua 2) and the disguised Tamar (Genesis 38).

Within the Bible, legal material does not always tally with narrative. Jacob marries two sisters although this is forbidden in Leviticus 18:18; the law of the levirate is contrary to Leviticus 18:16. These differences may reflect different periods and changes in the law or indicate that the priestly laws of Leviticus 18 were not "law" to all.

As we move on to portrayals of women in narrative and other genres, certain sometimes overlapping typologies emerge. Biblical women include matriarchs and tricksters, wise women and warriors, and finally a group whom Phyllis Trible calls the victims.

Women in Narrative

Biblical authors portray Rebecca, wife of Isaac, and the sisters Rachel and Leah, wives of Jacob, as young women in their fathers' homes who marry their paternal cousins, that is, who participate in the time-honored custom of cross-cousin marriage (see Genesis 24 and Genesis 28–30).

Except for the unloved Leah, all the wives of the patriarchs—Sarah, Rebecca, and Rachel—are able to bear children only with difficulty; they are archetypal barren women, as are Hannah, the mother of Samuel, and Samson's unnamed mother. Paradoxically, however, they have power in the private realm over matters of sex and children; in this connection they often play the role of tricksters, of those who use irregular, deceiving means to gain an end. Those who are marginal in their family and culture use wit to derive some benefit from, or power over, those in control. It is in child-related areas, in particular, that the women display their strength and a certain closeness to the divine. Communications about children to be born are some of the few instances in which God is seen to speak to women. The annunciation to Samson's mother in Judges 13 is of special relevance, for the divine emissary makes it quite clear that he wishes to speak to the woman—not with her husband, who is, in fact, portrayed as a doubting, fearful dolt in contrast to his more sensible, down-to-earth wife. Sarah has the nerve to laugh when she hears a child is to be born (Genesis 18:12). Hannah herself prays for a child at the sanctuary and interacts with the priest Eli (1 Samuel 1:9–18). Sarah and Rebecca, moreover, further with God's blessing the careers of their favorite sons, the younger offspring, Sarah in having Hagar and Ishmael expelled and Rebecca in tricking Isaac into giving Jacob his blessing (see also Bathsheba's role in 1 Kings 1:15–21, 28–31). The women, like Manoah's wife, are perceived in these cases as having the inside track to God's will. Similarly, Rachel successfully steals her father's household gods and hides them under her, chasing her father away with the warning that she is in a menstrual state (Genesis 31:34–35). This scene, with its implicit emphasis on the woman's power grounded in her fertility places the power of the hearth over the power of the public realm. Laban, like the patriarchs, is reduced to impotency.

So the blind Isaac is deceived by his wife and son in his old age, so Abraham must acquiesce to Sarah's wishes vis-à-vis Ishmael, so Manoah sees but does not comprehend. A relevant scene is the "selling" of Jacob's marital duties. Rachel, desperate for children, buys fertility-producing mandrake plants from her sister Leah in exchange for Jacob's conjugal services. When he returns from the field Leah gives him his orders. He will sleep with her that night; meekly, without question, he goes and performs his duty (Genesis 30:14–18), yielding Leah an unexpected son. These stories fit traditional narrative patterns: youngest sons always inherit and heroes are born under special circumstances. Nevertheless, the fact that the biblical writers create special roles for the women in the working out of these patterns, that they draw the mothers and wives a certain way, does say something important about their perceptions of the feminine, an important perception apparently shared by the participants in the literary tradition. The portraits of women holding power in the private realm, a power associated with fertility and children, tallies with the portrait emerging in the legal material and is not unique to Israelite culture.

In addition to the portrayals of "mothers," the matriarchs, we find equally penetrating portraits of women warriors and wise women, both of whom share traits with the tricky mothers discussed above and indeed with most of the successful men of the Hebrew Scriptures, who succeed by means of savvy and concealment, wit and deception.

The warriors, Deborah and Jael, make their appearances in the Book of Judges in the context of Israel's battles with Canaanite enemies. While Deborah is a judge, a general, and a tactician who clearly dominates and outshines Barak, her man-at-arms (Judges 4:8–9), Jael is a guerrilla assassin who welcomes the fleeing Canaanite general Sisera into her tent with promises of safety and succor and then runs him through the head with a tent peg (Judges 4–5). In language and imagery richly dripping in eroticism and death, Jael partakes of a wider Ancient Near Eastern and more universal archetype of the seductress-exterminator. Jael is an unlikely heroine, a self-appointed female soldier, who reverses the normal fate of a woman in battle (cf. Judges 5:30). She is not seduced, taken, or despoiled but herself seduces, marginalizes, and despoils a man. An Israelite author and Israelite audiences of various periods clearly identify with her when confronting enemies better armed and more powerful than themselves (so, too, the Maccabean-period Judith, based on Judges 4–5). As JoAnn Hackett has shown, the larger, more active, public, and aggressive roles given Deborah and Jael may well indicate works composed during periods of "social dysfunction" and decentralization, when women emerge from the shadows as more directed, overtly aggressive or powerful figures. Certainly, such characterizations of women are found in the literature about such periods.

Jael, like Judith, seduces and kills via deception, and thus shares in the category of biblical men and women who use their wit to achieve their goals, escape danger, or improve their status. Among such figures are Abigail, Esther, Ruth, and Naomi. Abigail's beautiful appearance, clever rhetoric, and demeanor of self-effacement save her household from the future king David who appears on her husband's estate very much like a bandit or pirate as he flees from Saul (1 Samuel 25). Esther, also assuming the pose of the humble, vulnerable, and beautiful supplicant, saves herself and her people from her foolish but powerful husband, Ahasuerus, the Persian monarch who has fallen under the influence of the evil Haman. Ruth, with Naomi's help, wins a husband to efface her widow status. All of these women share two traits: their husbands are foolish or absent (in the cases of Abigail and Esther, the women clearly outstrip their husbands in intelligence); and they present an appearance of subservient "female behavior," dressing for success, dealing obsequiously with spouses or future spouses, flattering, and using language well and convincingly. The wisdom tradition in Proverbs suggests a similar combination of savvy and subservience as the means of obtaining political success in dealing with the powerful, for spheres of politics and gender are often mirror images. Proverbs 31:10–31 presents a slightly different portrait, that of the respected, capable wife, the jewel in her husband's crown, having various economic as well as familial responsibilities.

Quite different are the so-called "wise women" who appear in two fascinating passages in 2 Samuel. Does the term *wise woman* simply refer to a woman who is wise, or were there professional wise women in ancient Israel? If so, what were their roles? In 2 Samuel 14 a wise woman from Tekoa is summoned to become a living *mashal*, or parable. Joab, general to King David, instructs her as a director would direct an actress to portray the role of bereaved mother and spin a tale to David that will convince him to allow his son Absalom to return to court. She plays the part beautifully, convincing the king. She is, in short, a professional mediator, an improvisationist skilled in the dramatic weaving and enactment of mediating parables. In a similar role, the wise woman of 2 Samuel 20:16 intervenes between her town and the general Joab, who has come on a search-and-destroy mission to capture the rebel Shimei ben Bichri. She uses appropriate proverbs, rhetoric, and skills of mediation to convince her townsmen to give up the offender to the agent of the king and in this way prevents great destruction. These wise women are not unlike Abigail and Esther in their mediating roles but appear also to be titled professionals. Their activities, moreover, have much in common with those of prophets like Nathan, who weaves a parable to mediate between God and David, indirectly accusing the king of murder. Numerous other prophets, named and unnamed, become living dramatizations or symbols of God's message (see 1 Kings 11:29–40, 20:35–43; Jeremiah 13: 1–11). These women and men employ a creative, artistic, and formalized technique to accuse an offender of wrongdoing or to reveal a true situation in order to resolve tensions, ease conflict, and render justice, sometimes shaming a person or persons into acting justly.

One might wonder if women also played the prophetic mediating role or any prophetic role, for prophecy is a form of wisdom. In other Near Eastern cultures women were prophets, dream interpreters, diviners, and singers (and perhaps ecstatic composers) of sacred texts. The Hebrew Bible does include some portrayals of such female figures involved in leadership roles in the publically religious sphere (see Isaiah 8:3; 2 Kings 22:14–20; and Nehemiah 6:14). Hulda, the prophetess (2 Kings 22:14–20), provides the seventh-century B.C.E. King Josiah with a divine warning of doom unless he becomes a pro-Yahwist reformer, casting out idols. Her oracle is framed in rubrics typical of biblical prophecy, although all other examples are delivered by male prophets. The accusations, suggestions for reform, and acceptance of the king's confession and repentance are presented in language completely at home in the canon of prophetic speech. Her prophetic gift is not treated as unusual for a woman. Petition to her is made in the most matter-of-fact way, leading one to wonder whether she was one of a score of female prophets not included in the Hebrew Scriptures or at least a characterization based on such real-life figures. Miriam, sister of Moses, is called "the prophetess" in Exodus 15:20. Passages such as Numbers 12 reveal another thread in the tradition. In its criticism of Moses' sister, the tale of Miriam's "gossiping" about Moses' wife is an attempt to squelch Miriam's pretentions—or more precisely the claims of priestly groups and leaders, perhaps female leaders, claiming Miriam as ancestress heroine. One also thinks of the female spirit medium who raises the ghost of the prophet Samuel for Saul in an eerie and powerful adumbration of the latter's final defeat (1 Samuel 28:7). In an apparent trance state she brings forth the crusty old man to predict Saul's death and then emerges from her state and professional role to offer the depressed king food. Much like Achilles to Priam after the death of Hector in Homer's *Iliad*, she attempts to bring Saul and his thoughts out of the realm of death to the realm of the mundane and ordinary, the realm of eating. Thus the spirit medium is also the nurturer, Woman.

In discussing women able to cross the boundary from earthly to divine, this-worldly to otherworldly, we raise several important issues touched upon above: (1) the question of ordinary women's cultic and religious activities: How did women reach God? (2) special cultic roles for women in various forms of Yahwism; (3) the question of women goddesses in the Ancient Near East and in some forms of Yahwism; (4) images of Yahweh as female.

We do not have the space to discuss each of these matters in detail but direct the reader to fine secondary readings. Phyllis Bird's essay and a forthcoming book discuss the first two of these issues, including biblical and extra-biblical evidence for forms of Israelite popular religion not sanctioned by the framers of the Hebrew Scriptures. For an overview of ancient Near Eastern goddesses, places to start are E. O. James, *The Cult of the Mother Goddess*, an older but still useful work; articles by Judith Ochshorn and C. J. Bleeker in C. Olson's edited *Book of the Goddess Past and Present*; and Carole Fontaine's study of goddess tricksters.

In one spot in the Hebrew Scriptures a goddess-like figure meets Yahwism in the female personification of Wisdom, whose alter ego, or Jungian negative counterpart, is the "strange" woman personifying Antiwisdom. The biblical figure of Wisdom of Proverbs 8 has a certain grand stature, accompanying God at the Creation and exhorting men to follow her ways.

Claudia Camp has explored the female Wisdom figure in detail. Another important area involves the place of the Near Eastern goddess Asherah in the religious life of some Israelites who worshipped her, much to the horror of, and in spite of the condemnation of purist Yahwists (see 1 Kings 15:13, 18:19; 2 Kings 21:7, 23:4, 7). As noted by P. D. Miller, inscriptions from Kuntillet Ajrud described by William Dever as "a 9th–8th century B.C.E. Israelite-Judaean caravanserai and attached shrine" refer more than once to "Yahweh of Samaria and his '*ašerah*." Scholars debate about '*ašerah's* status, though many believe her to have been regarded as a consort of Yahweh. Also relevant are the prophet Jeremiah's condemnations of worship practices involving "the Queen of Heaven" (see Jeremiah 7:17–18, 44:15–25). The possibility that in some forms of Israelite religion women played greater roles in cult or that some Israelites may have worshipped female deities, of course, does not necessarily imply that the workaday lives of women in these traditions differed markedly from the lives of women whose Yahwism is sanctioned by the biblical framers nor that the former enjoyed better or fuller lives, socioeconomically or politically. As for images of Yahweh as mother or nurturer, as a starting point, I recommend Phyllis Trible's *God and the Rhetoric of Sexuality*.

Having raised questions concerning the connections between the patterns of literature and the patterns of real lives, we turn to a group of women whom, after Phyllis Trible, we call the victims. Phyllis Trible explores a number of these characters with her usual great literary sensitivity and thoughtfulness in the book *Texts of Terror*. By *victims* we refer to women who suffer physical and/or mental abuse at the hands of some of the male characters of Scripture. Most troubling is the narrators' neutrality and seeming lack of sympathy for the victims. As Eve Sedgwick has shown for a different corpus of literature, the stories featuring women are not necessarily about women but about relations between men. Thus, the rape of David's daughter Tamar, about which David does nothing, becomes the cause of the blood feud between Absalom, Tamar's brother, and Amnon, the half brother, who has his way with her (2 Samuel 13–18). The rape of Jacob's daughter Dinah similarly becomes the cause for Jacob's sons' vengeance against the men of Shechem (Genesis 34). The nameless concubine in Judges 19 is another rape victim thrown to her fate by her husband to save his own skin from rapists, "evil fellows" among the Benjaminites. The evil deed spills over into a full-scale civil war. Michal, David's first wife, daughter of Saul, is caught between her father and husband, given to David, taken away, retaken by David, and then cast off by him. Jephthah promises as a sacrifice to God the first thing he sees upon return from battle if God helps him to succeed. He succeeds, but the first thing he sees is his daughter. She meekly agrees to become a sacrifice and goes off to the the hills to mourn her virginity with friends her age (Judges 11:29–40). Hagar, Abraham's concubine, is sent away with her son, alone and deserted (Genesis 21:8–21). She is caught in the Ishmael-Isaac contest for succession, though they are both children at the time. The complex texts that present these women are open to interpretation. Do the authors of these tales mean us to sympathize with the women? A modern reader of this material cannot but do so, but is the sympathy reader-generated or author-generated? The men of the narratives are variants of the folk motif of the incompetent, stupid father-husband mentioned above. Like Beauty's foolish father, or the father of the "Girl without Hands" (*Grimms' Fairy Tales*, nos. 88 and 31, respectively), Jephthah thoughtlessly and with concern only for his own success makes a vow dooming his daughter. So the Levite in a more visceral way sacrifices his concubine to a barbaric mob. When Jacob hears of the rape of his daughter, he is more concerned to make peace with the rapist's father than to defend his child. Abraham—and indeed his advisor, God—cast off the mother Hagar. David and Amnon use young women and then discard them, later suffering—or in the case of Amnon, dying—because of the family strife they create. Even the pro-Davidic writer of David's court narratives portrays David as a weak and impotent father and husband, a man whose personal life never reaches the successes of his public achievements. It is as if the artistic demands on this creative and traditional-style author outweigh his pro-Davidic propagandistic motivations. Even the men who defend women, Dinah's brothers and Absalom, might be accused of being self-serving—with honor in the case of Jacob's sons, concerned with ridding himself of a senior prince in the case of Absalom (though this is not certain). These narratives may reflect an interesting anthropological, psychological, and mythological pattern whereby the brother-sister relationship is the love relationship rather than the relationship between father and child (e.g., the birth narratives of Cronos and Zeus and his siblings in *Theogony* 145–210, 453–506, and the folktale "Hansel and Gretel," *Grimms' Fairy Tales* no. 15).

The women submit silently (Dinah, concubine, Hagar) or verbally (Jephthah's daughter) or protest in vain (Tamar). Are the authors of these narratives providing models of how women should be or how they must be? Are the characterizations typological reflections of a cultural reality? How does each author judge this reality if it exists? Do the authors sympathize with the women, or are the narrative voices too silent, too neutral, to read? Jephthah's daughter displays a certain nobility and is described as the founder of a ritual for young women; Tamar and Hagar certainly evoke pathos. These women are surely presented as the heroines of their stories; the men around them are bumbling, cruel, foolish, or all three.

Conclusion

To study women in the Hebrew Bible is to reexamine and reassess a lengthy history of biblical hermeneutics; it is to pose new questions about legal and nonlegal texts and to make what will strike some readers as radical suggestions concerning the religion and culture of Israel. I have explored the characterizations of women, and the tone, texture, and point of view of the compositions in which they appear as a student of literature, asking what sorts of authors and audiences would have found these portrayals meaningful and why. As a student of history, I have faced the challenge that even the so-called historical books of the Bible and the legal texts are not simple reflections of historical fact or verifiable data. Most important, I have tried to convey a sense of the varieties of Israelite religion and culture both in any one period of time and over time as relevant to a study of women. An examination of the provenance and biases of particular authors is critical, as is the realization that information about women's modes of religious expression, about alternate forms of Yahwism, and about particular women leaders and positions of leadership held by women, may have been excluded from the canon. We have explored some of the hints left behind in the edited texts. Perhaps most interesting in our study is the realization that the laws of the Hebrew Bible come from various periods and groups responding to, and reflecting, various perceptions of Israelite mores and worldviews. The priestly view of women, emerging in laws of purity, for example, may not have been the most characteristic view of women in all periods or segments of Israelite culture. Just as Jacob Neusner and other feminist scholars have suggested that early rabbinic law originally may have reflected the cosmology of the rabbis and not Jews in general, so, too, priestly law may reveal the worldview of a small group of Israelites and not the worldview of all or even most participants in Israelite culture.

Ladies of the Sisterhood:
Women in the American Reform
Synagogue, 1900–1930

Pamela S. Nadell
Rita J. Simon

Hostesses of coffee and tea, organizers of meals for the bereaved, planners of "Jewish Home Beautiful" pageants, outfitters of synagogue kitchens, fund-raisers for schools and scholarships, diners at mother-daughter banquets, and discussers of great Jewish books—these were the customary roles of sisterhood women in mid-twentieth-century American Reform, Conservative, and Orthodox synagogues. In the eyes of their members, then, such activities and the parameters they established for Jewish women's behavior within their temples seemed to have been set from time immemorial. When the rabbi appealed to sisterhood women to staff the Sunday school, when they planned Sisterhood Sabbath, or when they studied the rabbinic text "Ethics of the Fathers,"[1] sisterhood women were following what they presumed to be well-established patterns of what women had always done in and for their synagogues.

Yet, an examination of the emergence of Reform synagogue sisterhoods in the early twentieth century and of the founding, in 1913, and programs of the national organization of Reform synagogue sisterhoods, the National Federation of Temple Sisterhoods (NFTS), reveals how recently women had assumed these roles. It also suggests that the early history of women's religious organizations can serve as an example of how, as the historian Paula Hyman notes, women "created a female culture and constructed a community different from the organized community of Jewish men."[2] In this case women shared the space and institutional structure of the synagogue and the values and aspirations of Reform Judaism with their husbands and brothers. But through organized communities of women, they created a culture that enabled them to change the expectations of their proper behavior within its portals and expand Jewish women's public religious roles.[3]

By the end of the second decade of the twentieth century Jewish women's associational life had blossomed into an array of national organizations. In the United States women had organized for their self-education and

From Maurie Sacks, ed. 1995. *Active Voices: Women in Jewish Culture.* Urbana: University of Illinois Press, pp. 63-75. Reprinted with permission of University of Illinois Press.

for social welfare in the National Council of Jewish Women (1893), for Zionism in Hadassah (1912), and for the synagogue in Reform Judaism's National Federation of Temple Sisterhoods (1913) and Conservative Judaism's National Women's League of the United Synagogue of America (1918). Jewish women, in essence, created a "volunteer army" dedicated to serving their community.[4] Yet this efflorescence of women's national organizational activity masks a long history of Jewish women's local activism.

In small Jewish communities across the United States as early as the 1830s, German Jewish immigrant women had begun to band together in Hebrew ladies benevolent societies. Possibly modeled on German Jewish female associations, called Frauen Vereine, from which some took their names, they enabled Jewish women to render aid to one another and social welfare to those less fortunate. Collectively and publicly fulfilling the Jewish commandment of *tzedakah*, the ladies of the benevolent societies aided the sick, sewed for the poor, helped the unemployed, and buried their dead. While many of the associations were communally based, some, espousing that women give personal service to the cause of Judaism and not just to needy Jews, became synagogue auxiliaries. Through bazaars, strawberry festivals, and even oyster suppers, these women raised money to build local synagogues. And once built, their synagogues depended upon them to raise funds to sustain them. Together the women of the ladies' auxiliaries bought chairs and organs, papered Sunday school classrooms, and arranged flowers to decorate the sanctuary.[5] Thus like American women in their churches, they too began to exercise influence in their communities by extending accepted middle-class female roles—sustaining their families, nurturing their children, and beautifying their homes—to their community in the public spaces of their synagogues.[6]

But by the 1900s, as the historian William Toll writes, "the benevolent societies were undergoing an eclipse as ... the concept of general nurturant benevolence was being replaced by more specialized institutions."[7] As synagogues proliferated, rabbis in some places and their wives in others organized sisterhoods as the successors to the Hebrew ladies benevolent societies.

The founding of the sisterhood of Washington Hebrew Congregation, today with twenty-eight hundred family and individual memberships, the leading Reform congregation in the nation's capital, was typical. In 1905, a year after her husband, Abram, became the synagogue's first ordained rabbi, Carrie Obendorfer Simon founded the Ladies Auxiliary Society of Washington Hebrew Congregation. Its goals were "for congregational work, pure and simple, and to endeavor to establish a more congenial and social congregational spirit." Sisterhood lore recalls that fifty women attended the founding meeting, pledged themselves to ten cents dues, promised to raise money to pay off the mortgage, and then promptly recessed to polish the doorknobs. In its first years the sisterhood sponsored bazaars and concerts to reduce the temple's Sinking Fund, presented a gavel to the board and a memorial tablet to the congregation, and gave the children Chanukah candles. These roles, then, fit well within the already accepted patterns of synagogue sustenance, beautification, and nurturance pioneered by the Hebrew ladies benevolent societies.[8]

However, Carrie Simon had higher hopes for women in the temple. She envisioned a national union of women organized specifically for religious work. The historian Jacob Marcus has suggested that the National Federation of Temple Sisterhoods emerged to "counter and rival the National Council of Jewish Women."[9] Founded in 1893 as the first Jewish equivalent of the women's club, the National Council of Jewish Women had originally been interested in both the religious lives of its members and social welfare work. But as Ellen Sue Levi Elwell has demonstrated, by the end of the first decade of the twentieth century, the council had largely shifted its priorities from religious to philanthropic concerns.[10] Possibly troubled by the decline of National Council of Jewish Women's interest in the synagogue and religious affairs, Simon persuaded Reform leaders, like Rabbi David Philipson, of the merit of a national union of sisterhoods within the Reform movement.[11] Working with Rabbi George Zepin, the director of Synagogue and School Extension for the Union of American Hebrew Congregations, Reform's national association of synagogues, Carrie Simon helped bring 156 delegates from fifty-two sisterhoods to Cincinnati in 1913. There she became the founding president of the National Federation of Temple Sisterhoods, then seen as the feminine counterpart of the union and an organization that would "forge a mighty weapon in the service of Judaism."[12]

While women in their local sisterhoods continued to raise funds, take charge of the decor, and concern themselves with the education of their children in their synagogues, the national organization, with its biennial conferences, annual executive board meetings, nationwide correspondence with individual sisterhoods, and printed accounts of many of these, offered to the women of Reform Judaism possibilities for expanding their roles within the synagogue. In his opening address at the founding convention, Rabbi David Philipson, speaking on "Woman and the Congregation," recognized this aspect of the fledgling organization's agenda. First, he enumerated the many steps Reform Judaism had taken to ameliorate women's status within Judaism. Next, he highlighted Reform's introduction of the family pew, which did away with the seclusion of women in their own gallery, the replacement of bar mitzvah with confirmation for boys *and* girls, and the counting of women in the minyan, the quorum of ten adults required for communal worship. He then proposed that "the last word in woman's relation to the congregation will not be spoken until she is received into full membership if she so desires, on the same footing as man."[13] That may have been the most revolutionary reform David Philipson envisioned sisterhood women would achieve. However, over the course of a bit more than the next decade, the women of NFTS would discover that together they could expand old avenues and open up new ones for their participation in synagogue life that Rabbi Philipson had not even imagined.

Not surprisingly, through NFTS, sisterhood women continued their, by then, well-established roles of sustaining and beautifying their synagogues. In addition, almost every sisterhood remained highly involved with the religious education of its children. Sisterhood women raised money to buy furniture and equipment and decorate schoolrooms. They arranged entertainments and refreshments to celebrate holidays. Some organized parents meetings to help bring what was taught in the school into the home. In small communities, where there was often neither a rabbi nor trained teachers, sisterhood women not only sponsored the schools but also taught in them. In so doing, they drew not from the Jewish tradition of the past but rather from the American milieu, which over the course of the second half of the nineteenth century had seen women move in ever greater numbers into teaching. In larger communities they ran free religious schools for the children of the poor and organized teacher training programs to help staff them. In both, sisterhood women created the first synagogue libraries,[14] thereby playing pioneering roles in shaping the emerging American synagogue as an educational center for Jewish youth.

The national organization also enabled women to extend their philanthropic activities. Collectively as NFTS, sisterhood women raised funds for much larger projects than they could undertake as women organized in individual communities. Just as sisterhood women cared for the education of the youth of their congregations, they now expanded their concern to the "boys of the College." In 1921 NFTS pledged to build a dormitory at Hebrew Union College, Reform Judaism's rabbinical seminary in Cincinnati, and appointed Carrie Simon to take charge of the nationwide fund-raising.[15] The National Federation of Temple Sisterhoods gave the women of Reform Judaism a sense of sororality that allowed them to extend their public participation in Reform Judaism beyond their established roles as nurturers and philanthropists. Concerned with religion, with the rites and rituals of Judaism, its ceremonies and services, sisterhood women sought influence over their own religious lives. Through its National Committee on Religion, NFTS was in contact with women throughout the United States interested in religious life in the home and the synagogue. Its reports reveal the range of sisterhoods' religious activities and how sisterhood women, surely working in concert with their rabbis and their rabbis' wives, raised their voices to help shape Reform Judaism. Determined to revive Jewish ceremonials Reform had previously abandoned, NFTS women reclaimed traditions they viewed as too hastily dismissed. Recalling the custom of *shalach mones*, the ritual of giving gifts on Purim, they collected food, clothing, and money for local charities. Concerned with Passover, they hosted communal seders and also celebrated the returning of the seder to the home.[16] In so doing, sisterhood women broadened their participation in Jewish religious life.

The most striking changes, however, occurred in the extension of women's roles in the public religious spaces of Reform Judaism. Because sisterhood women wanted to foster worship, they conceived of the "novel innovation" of providing babysitting at services to allow the mothers of young children the leisure to pray. Not only did the sisterhoods do all they could to enable and encourage attendance at public worship—sometimes even canvassing house-to-house to convince people to come to services—but through the collective of NFTS they came to articulate definite ideas about those services. They called for the reintroduction of congregational singing. They championed the "free pew" movement so that wealth no longer determined where one sat in the congregation. They helped revive the synagogue holiday of Simchat Torah. Citing their own desire for "a book of prayer suitable for every day of the year," they tried to prod the Reform rabbinical association, the Central Conference of American Rabbis, into publishing one. Upset by the fact that, when rabbis vacationed, services were irregular at best, a number of sisterhoods took charge of conducting and leading summer services. In fact, in a striking example of a new idea filtering its way down from the top, the chair of the National Committee on Religion reported that no letter had ever received more response than the one she sent about sisterhoods organizing summer services.[17]

Quickly NFTS came to demand public recognition of women's contributions in an annual Sisterhood Sabbath. Originally, this was conceived as the day when a woman would deliver a "message" to the congregation, that is, speak from the pulpit. In some synagogues, by the early 1920s, it had become the one day outside the summer when women conducted the entire service. In others, women read parts of the service and the rabbi preached a sermon appropriate for the day.[18] By increasing Reform Jewish women's avenues for participation and even religious leadership within their synagogues, the National Federation of Temple Sisterhoods helped change the expectations of the proper female roles within Reform Judaism.

Perhaps recalling David Philipson's remarks at the founding convention, sisterhood women thus continued to champion the emancipation of women within their temples. NFTS reports noted, with satisfaction, that several congregations had admitted married women to full membership and that more temples were admitting women to their boards.[19]

The women of Reform Judaism were by no means unaware of the extent of the transformation made through sisterhood. On NFTS's silver jubilee in 1938 Carrie Simon reflected, "The Ladies Aid Society Grows Up." She noted how the early Hebrew ladies benevolent societies had pioneered new roles for women with their "insistence that women have a place in the practical life of the congregation." But she also stated, "Where formerly the women of the Aid society did not get beyond the threshold of the Temple, recent years … have found them within its very sanctum."[20] Understanding the changes in women's roles that had occurred within Reform Judaism, she wrote elsewhere: "In the past we have considered the Jewish woman as a follower. Within recent years she has become a participant. Does the next step lie in her becoming a leader, religiously speaking?"[21] Thus from her position as the founding president of the National Federation of Temple Sisterhoods, Carrie Simon called for women's ordination, the final barrier to the achieving of full emancipation by women within Reform Judaism.

Quickly, the new avenues for women's activities in Reform synagogues, orchestrated through NFTS, became a comfortable status quo. By the middle of the 1920s Reform sisterhoods' creative "feminist" period was over. The roles first described as indicative of mid-twentieth-century sisterhoods were set. What had once been pioneering new activities for women in the synagogue, such as women leading summer services and speaking on occasion from the pulpit, had apparently, within a bit more than a decade become accepted venues of women's behavior.

Several factors may account for the acceptance of the shifting boundaries of woman's sphere in the synagogue that occurred within the first decade of the founding of NFTS in 1913. Surely, the first lies within Reform Judaism's pioneering stance on women's equality. As Michael Meyer's penetrating study of Reform Judaism has shown, Reform, influenced by Immanuel Kant's ideas of rationally viable faith, came to assert: "The idea that pure religious faith is essentially moral rapidly became the theoretical basis and the practical operative principle of the Reform movement."[22] Because women's inequality within Judaism tested its morality, especially according to nineteenth- and twentieth-century liberal notions of equality of opportunity for all, the amelioration of women's status became a critical test of its theoretical base. Almost from its inception, as David Philipson reminded his audience at NFTS's founding convention, some of the first leaders of Reform Judaism considered it their "sacred duty to declare with all emphasis the complete religious equality of woman with man."[23] As Reform Judaism gained ground in America, Reformers continued to work to improve the position of women within Judaism, despite, as Karla Goldman has carefully documented, real ambivalence about what would happen to gender roles if the full implications of women's emancipation within the synagogue were realized.[24] Hence Philipson's was but another voice in a long tradition of revered Reform leaders calling for women's equality within the synagogue. When NFTS leaders echoed his call, or even daringly, as Carrie Simon did, envisioned a greater emancipation, they stood squarely within Reform's tradition of theoretical equality for women.

Second, NFTS activity must be seen within the larger context of American women's organizational life. Synthesizing twenty years of scholarship in American women's history, William Chafe, in his revision of his path-breaking 1972 study *American Woman*, considers how by the end of the nineteenth century, middle- and upper-class white women had expanded and empowered what had once been a sharply limited "separate sphere" into "more an instrument for political influence than a barrier to freedom." Drawing upon the works of the historians Paula Baker, Suzanne Lebsock, Nancy Cott, and others, he demonstrates how, by the end of the nineteenth century, women's voluntary societies were ubiquitous, that through them women had helped develop the social and educational infrastructures of American life, and that many of these organizations had continued and new ones had emerged to push particular agendas in the 1920s and 1930s.[25] The achievements of NFTS must be viewed as part of this stream. In this case middle- and upper-class Jewish women united in service to the synagogue. In so doing, they forged a community and a culture that enabled them to shift the boundaries of their proper roles there.

Unquestionably, their actions were widely influenced by their intersections with American life and culture. In the 1910s and 1920s that meant the debate about suffrage, the meaning of women's votes, and the emergence of new opportunities for middle- and upper-class women in all spheres—education, the professions, and the labor force. Rabbis and their wives participated in these debates, mutually influencing one another with their ideas about women's roles. Even before 1921 when Martha Neumark, a young student at Hebrew Union College, raised for Reform its first real test case of a woman seeking rabbinic ordination, Carrie Simon's husband, Abram, asserted to his congregation that women had political and social equality and that that should extend to the pulpit.[26] Which came first, his wife's vision of women's emancipation or his, is not clear. But they shared a common stance on the implications of women's emancipation in the wake of the success of the suffrage battle in 1920, one that they carried together to the synagogue. So, too, other rabbis and their wives together paved the way for women's expanded roles within the synagogue.[27]

These debates naturally impacted upon their congregants. NFTS never did endorse suffrage.[28] But as Beth Wenger has revealed, when Stella Bauer of Atlanta's leading Reform synagogue, The Temple, called in 1920 for its board to grant women representation, she did not appeal to Reform's history of ameliorating women's status within Judaism as David Philipson had done. Instead, she justified her call by alluding to "this age of woman's suffrage."[29] Thus at their particular intersection of ethnicity, class, and gender in American life, the women of NFTS extended the sphere of women's roles in the synagogue and allowed their leaders to envision new ones that one day their daughters and granddaughters would champion.

Echoing that earlier period of intense activism, in 1961 Reform sisterhood women, sparked anew by a sense of the changing possibilities for women's lives and prodded by its executive director, Jane Evans, once again took up the call made by its founding president for the ordination of women as rabbis.[30] In so doing, they helped reopen the debate on the women's issue in Reform Judaism at the same time that President John F. Kennedy's Commission on the Status of Women reopened the debate on women's rights that had seemed to close with the passage of the 1920 suffrage amendment. Just when American women began exploring new possibilities for their lives, while high schooler Sally Priesand was planning on becoming a rabbi,[31] the women of the National Federation of Temple Sisterhoods reminded the leaders of Reform Judaism that the time had come for Reform to implement the "complete religious equality of woman with man" that it had championed a century and a half before.

Notes

Pamela S. Nadell wishes to thank the American Jewish Archives for its Marguerite R. Jacobs Memorial Fellowship for 1988–89, which supported part of this research, and the National Federation of Temple Sisterhoods for its assistance. Earlier versions of this essay were presented as "Sisterhood Ladies and Rabbis: Women in the American Reform Synagogue" at the conference "An Age of Faiths: Religion and Society in the Modern World," University of Maryland (Apr. 1990); and as "The Beginnings of the Religious Emancipation of American Jewish Women," at the Berkshire Conference of Women's Historians, Douglass College (June 1990).

1. Minutes of the sisterhood of the Sons of Jacob Congregation, Waterloo, Iowa (1950–66). This Conservative sisterhood in the only synagogue in the area demonstrates activities typical of sisterhoods at mid-century.
2. Paula E. Hyman, "Gender and the Immigrant Jewish Experience in the United States," in Judith R. Baskin, ed. *Jewish Women in Historical Perspective* (Detroit: Wayne State University Press, 1991), p. 223.
3. For an opposing view of sisterhoods, see Jenna Weissman Joselit, "The Special Sphere of the Middle-Class American Jewish Woman: The Synagogue Sisterhood, 1890–1940," in Jack Wertheimer, ed., *The American Synagogue: A Sanctuary Transformed* (Cambridge: Cambridge University Press, 1987), pp. 206–30. There she concludes, "As forces for change within the American Jewish community, the sisterhoods were negligible factors. In every case, the sisterhood left untouched the basic social structure of the synagogue and, by extension, that of the larger Jewish community" (p. 223).
4. Works on these organizations include Ellen Sue Levi Elwell, "The Founding and Early Programs of the National Council of Jewish Women: Study and Practice as Jewish Women's Religious Expression" (Ph.D. diss., Indiana University, 1982); Faith Rogow, *Gone to Another Meeting: The National Council of Jewish Women, 1893–1993* (Tuscaloosa: University of Alabama Press, 1993). On international women's organizations, see Marion A. Kaplan, *The Jewish Feminist Movement in Germany: The Campaigns of the Juedischer Frauenbund, 1904–1938* (Westport, Conn.: Greenwood Press, 1979); Michael Berkowitz, "Transcending 'Tzimmes and Sweetness': Recovering the History of Zionist Women in Central and Western Europe, 1897–1933," in this volume.
5. "Hebrew Ladies Benevolent Societies, 1857–1912," in Jacob R. Marcus, ed., *The American Jewish Woman: A Documentary History* (New York: Ktav, 1981), pp.

204–19. See also Hasia Diner, *A Time for Gathering: The Second Migration, 1820–1880* (Baltimore: Johns Hopkins University Press, 1992), pp. 86–113.

6. See Dianne Ashton, "Grace Aguilar and the Matriarchal Theme in Jewish Women's Spirituality," in this volume. These roles reveal Jewish women's acceptance of the nineteenth-century "cult of true womanhood," first described by Barbara Welter, "The Cult of True Womanhood, 1820–1860," *American Quarterly* 18 (Summer 1966): 151–74. Believing that women were inherently passive, domestic, pious, and pure, prescriptive literature, politicians, and religious leaders instructed women to use the leisure they had attained as they moved into the middle class to be better wives and mothers. American middle-class women seeking public spaces in which to extend the sway of their moral influence had found that through their churches they could apply the standards of "true womanhood" outside their homes. In fact, as early as the 1780s American women began organizing voluntary, charitable associations within their churches (Sara M. Evans, *Born for Liberty: A History of Women in America* [New York: Free Press, 1989], p. 74). The Hebrew ladies benevolent associations could be considered the Jewish counterpart of this American female phenomenon.

7. William Toll, "A Quiet Revolution: Jewish Women's Clubs and the Widening Female Sphere, 1870–1920," *American Jewish Archives* 61, no. 1 (Spring/Summer 1989): 12.

8. Archives of Washington Hebrew Congregation, Washington, D.C., Box SIS 1, Sisterhood Programs, Minutes of the Washington Hebrew Congregation, 5 May, 3 Nov., 24 Apr. 1907, 5 Apr. 1911; "Fiftieth Birthday Sisterhood Highlights," Feb. 1955.

9. Marcus, *American Jewish Woman*, p. 664.

10. Elwell, "Founding and Early Programs," pp. 136–79. On women's clubs, see Karen J. Blair, *The Clubwoman as Feminist: True Womanhood Redefined, 1868–1914* (New York: Holmes & Meier, 1980). David Philipson notes retrospectively that he was aware of a shift in the objectives of the NCJW (*My Life as an American Jew: An Autobiography* [Cincinnati, 1941], pp. 234–37, cited in Marcus, *American Jewish Woman*, p. 666). While rivalry may have been a motive at the national level, at the local level, as Beth Wenger has shown for Atlanta, the two organizations, with very similar memberships, were seen as complementary. Sisterhood was concerned with the synagogue and NCJW with philanthropy (Beth S. Wenger, "Jewish Women of the Club: The Changing Public Role of Atlanta's Jewish Women, 1870–1930," *American Jewish History* 76 [Mar. 1987]: 321).

11. Philipson, *My Life,* pp. 234–37, cited in Marcus, *American Jewish Woman*, pp. 665–68.

12. American Jewish Archives (hereafter cited as AJA), Cincinnati, Ohio, Nearprint Files, National Federation of Temple Sisterhoods, "We Are the Women of Reform Judaism: Celebrating the 75th Anniversary," 21 Jan. 1988.

13. David Philipson, "Woman and the Congregation," *Proceedings of the National Federation of Temple Sisterhoods* (hereafter cited as *NFTS*) 1 (1913): 15–18.

14. "Report of the Committee on Religious Schools, 1918," *NFTS* 1 (1919): 47–48; "Report of the National Committee on Religious Schools, 1923," *NFTS* 2 (1925): 25–28; "Report of the National Committee on Religious Schools, 1922," *NFTS* 1 (1923): 66–68: Rita J. Simon and Gloria Danzinger, *Women's Movements in America: Their Successes, Disappointments, and Aspirations* (New York: Praeger, 1991), pp. 36–95.

15. "Report of the Special Committee on Hebrew Union College Dormitory, 1922" *NFTS* 1 (1922): 24.

16. "Report of the National Committee on Religion, 1920," *NFTS* 1 (1921): 57–59; "Report of the National Committee on Religion, 1922," *NFTS* 1 (1923): 63–65.

17. "Report of the National Committee on Religion, 1923," *NFTS* 2 (1924): 20–23; Carrie Simon, "The President's Annual Message," *NFTS* 1 (1917): 26; "Report of the National Committee on Religion, 1919," *NFTS* 1 (1920): 20–22, Hattie M. Wiesenfeld, "Report of the President, 1922," *NFTS* 1 (1922): 16–18; "Report of the National Committee on Religion, 1920," pp. 57–59; "Report of the National Committee on Religion, 1921," *NFTS* 1 (1922): 22–24.

18. Wiesenfeld, "Report of the President, 1922," pp. 16–18; "Report of the National Committee on Religion, 1921," pp. 22–24; "Report of the National Committee on Religion, 1923," pp. 20–23.

19. "Report of the National Committee on Religion, 1923," pp. pp. 20–23.

20. AJA, Nearprint Files; Mrs. Abram Simon, "Four Presidents on the N.F.T.S. Silver Jubilee," *Topics and Trends* 4, no. 1 (Jan.–Feb. 1938): 3.

21. AJA, MS #267, 1/3, Abram Simon Collection, Sermons and Addresses O–Y, Untitled, "What Can the Women Do for Judaism?" p. 6. It is exceedingly unlikely that this typed, unsigned, undated sermon was given by Rabbi Abram Simon. In several places (p. 5), it speaks of "us women," "our husbands," and "we women." In addition, a handwritten addition at the end seems to correspond with a sample of Carrie Simon's handwriting located in the archives of the Washington Hebrew Congregation, Washington, D.C. Consequently, we are attributing its authorship to Carrie Simon and would suggest that this may have been a text she used when she spoke from the pulpit on behalf of NFTS. See *Washington Star*, 21 Nov. 1913, p. 1, which reported that she spoke from the pulpit of Temple Israel in Boston on "the call of the Sisterhood"; and her biographical sketch in *Who's Who in American Jewry* (New York: Jewish Biographical Bureau, 1926), which claims that she "spoke in many pulpits throughout the country in the interest and advancement of Jewish womanhood."

22. Michael Meyer, *Response to Modernity: A History of the Reform Movement in Judaism* (New York: Oxford University Press, 1988), pp. 64–65.

23. David Einhorn, "Report of a Committee on the Position of Women," cited in Philipson, "Women and the Congregation," p. 16.

24. Karla Goldman, "The Ambivalence of Reform Judaism: Kaufmann Kohler and the Ideal Jewish Woman," *American Jewish History* 79 (Summer 1990): 492.

25. William H. Chafe, *The Paradox of Change: American Women in the Twentieth Century* (New York: Oxford University Press, 1991), pp. 5, 9–10, 35–36.

26. *The Evening Star* (Washington, D.C.), 9 Oct. 1920, 4.

27. When, in 1922, Reform rabbis debated the question of women's ordination, they voted to allow their wives to join in the debate ("Resolution on Ordination of Women," *Central Conference of American Rabbis Year Book* 32 [1922]: 51).

28. Women of Reform Judaism, *Index of Resolutions: Adopted by the National Federation of Temple Sisterhoods, 1913–1985* (New York: Women of Reform Judaism, 1988).

29. Cited in Wenger, "Jewish Women of the Club," p. 327.

30. AJA, National Federation of Temple Sisterhoods, Box 73, 5/3, "Resolutions at the 23rd Biennial, 1961," p.6.

31. In 1972 Sally Priesand became the first woman in America to be ordained a rabbi.

Personal Vignettes

Susan Grossman
Rivka Haut

Growing Up Lubavitch:
Shoshana Gelerenter-Liebowitz

When I was very young I loved to go to *shul* with my father. One of the many privileges I enjoyed as the oldest child was having my father to myself on our long walks to and from 770 (the headquarters and main synagogue of the Lubavitch Movement). My parents came from Poland and became Lubavitch when they arrived in the United States. I am therefore a first generation American and Lubavitcher.

On our walks to and from *shul* my father spoke to me quite freely of his parents who had died in the Holocaust. In Hrubishov, Poland, his mother was the *foreleiner* in *shul*. She was the woman who was able to read the prayers. She would say the prayers, word for word, and the other women would recite right after her. This meant my grandmother was a literate woman, which was atypical, as most women could not read or understand Hebrew. My father would talk about his mother with great pride.

When I was little, I was allowed to enter the men's section with my father. Some other fathers brought in girls older than myself. When a little girl looked a little too old to be in the men's section, around ten years old, the men would become very agitated. Sometimes someone would say something to admonish he, and the big little girl would understand that she was too old to be with the men. Nobody had to explain why girls can not sit with their fathers in *shul* past age ten or why boys and girls don't pray together. Boys and girls don't do anything together. Nobody questions this. The separation of the sexes is accepted throughout the society. Boys and girls are never together. During my childhood, if a girl played with boys outside of *shul* she was called a *Hamor eizel*, a donkey. It was very frowned upon.

I don't remember ever feeling upset that I couldn't pray with the men anymore. The men's section was not a pleasant place in which to pray. It didn't feel peaceful because it was always crowded and hot and there was no room to sit.

From Susan Grossman and Rivka Haut, eds. 1992. *Daughters of the King: Women and the Synagogue: A Survey of History, Halakhah, and Contemporary Realities*. Philadelphia: Jewish Publication Society. Reprinted with permission from the Jewish Publication Society.

Lubavitch women don't ever feel secondary or deprived. Their lives are as busy as the men's. There is always so much activity. An equal responsibility for performing *mitzvot* rests with with the males and females. All children are soldiers in *HaShem's* army. The boys encourage nonobservant men to wear *tefillin;* the girls ask women to light candles: equal roles.

When girls start lighting candles on Friday nights, at three years old, their womanhood really begins. They light and their brothers don't. Candlelighting is stressed very much. Although little boys at age three get their first haircut, receive their first set of *tzitzit* (ritual fringes), and begin to always wear a *yarmulke* (skullcap), the *mitzvot* of *tallit* and *tefillin* only begin at a later developmental stage for boys. Girls do not feel at all like second-class citizens; little girls do not envy boys because there are *mitzvot* for both to observe.

Mothers don't usually go to *shul* on Friday night because they are home with their children. (*Editor's note: Observant Jews do not carry or wheel baby carriages outside on the Sabbath.*) My mother had her children closely spaced so she couldn't go to *shul,* but she davened at home every Shabbes. As I started to learn *tefillos* (prayers) in school, I began to daven at home every Shabbes morning and on Friday nights. My mother would say to my sisters and me, "Let's daven *Kabbalas Shabbes*" (the Friday evening prayers) and we would do so together. As we got older, each of my sisters would take a *siddur* and daven separately, though at the same time.

During the week, I had to say the beginning prayers before I came to breakfast. The rest of the morning prayers were recited in school. On days when there was no school, I was expected to complete the prayers at home after breakfast. My mother would remind me to daven, the same way she would remind me to get dressed in the morning. This was a normal part of the day's routine. At one point, I went through a little phase of davening *Minhah* and *Ma'ariv* (afternoon and evening prayers) of my own volition, and my parents were very pleased. They viewed it as a sort of charming thing. I remember when any of us exceeded their spiritual expectations of us, my parents smiled and my father was very proud of his daughters.

In my family, and, I think, in all Lubavitch families, women's prayers are taken very seriously. The power of a woman's prayers was often stressed as being the most valuable to God when granting blessings of help and health.

Every Shabbes my mother said all of *Tehillim* (Psalms), and she added specific verses to her daily prayers. My mother used to do this as a European custom, but now everyone does this. When someone is sick, there is a lot of focus on praying and saying *Tehillim*. I remember in my girls' school they would often announce on the loudspeaker that so and so, the daughter or son of so and so, is sick, and the children should have *kavannah* (intention) to pray for a *refuah sheleimah* (complete recovery). Girls were repeatedly told that their prayers are very important and that good things happen because of the *zekhut* (merit) of women.

Teenage girls go to *shul* on Friday night. Partly they go to *shul* to daven and partly for the social ambiance. They don't say "I am going to *shul*." They say "I am going to 770." All their friends go to *shul*. They don't talk in *shul*, but once they leave *shul*, they chitchat. There is no mingling between the sexes. The men stand on their side, and the woman on their side, socializing after *shul*. The women start walking, and their husbands usually catch up to them.

On *Yom Tov* (holiday), when baby carriages may be wheeled to *shul*, there is a noticeable increase in the number of women and children present. An entire area outside the *shul* is filled with women, with prayer books or *Tehillim* in their hands, rocking their baby carriages and praying at the same time.

Most married women also go to *shul*. However, some women don't go to 770 because they find that the social aspect of getting dressed, putting on their *sheitels* (the wigs that married women wear), and seeing and talking to friends might be a distraction to their *kavannah* (intention in prayer). Lubavitchers, compared to other kinds of Jews, however, do not dress up to a point that might be considered vain. Social standards are quite subtle though, for vanity can often be a woman's Achilles' heel when it comes to her observance of *mitzvot*.

Part of the focal point of going to 770 is really to see "The Rebbe." That is special in Lubavitch life. The people want to get a glimpse of "The Rebbe." Women daven quietly because, if there is any noise, they can't hear the Torah reading or the *ba'al tefillah* (prayer leader). It is a gigantic place, 770. The downstairs (men's) section is very large. The women's section is built over it. There is a dark-tinted glass partition. The women can see through, but the men can't see in. The window opening is chest high, so women have to bend their heads in order to see down. There are only a limited number of seats in the front row, the only row from which one can see. Usually the young girls come early and get those front seats. When older women see this monopolization, they sometimes fight over seats, because everyone wants the privilege of seeing "The Rebbe."

In *shul*, the women never sing aloud. They only whisper "amen" and the sections that the entire congregation chants aloud. If hundreds of women started to say "Amen," in unison, nobody would hear what was going on. Also, in terms of *tzniut* (modesty) this would be inappropriate. However, in school, when the girls daven, they do daven out loud. They are led by a *hazzanit* (prayer leader). There is no Torah reading. Also, women never sing *zemiros* (Sabbath songs) out loud at home. However, Lubavitch has a girls' choir that sings only for women. They put on plays, always with a Lubavitch theme, such as celebrating the previous Rebbe's release from prison.

Women are supposed to go to *shul* to hear the *shofar* blown on Rosh Hashanah and to hear the *Megillah* read on Purim. They go to the little *shuls* for that. There are many small synagogues in Crown Heights, which serve many kinds of Jews. Now Lubavitchers are the only Jews in the area, and they do their best to maintain these *shteiblakh* (small *shuls*).

Women's responsibility to participate in all the *mitzvot* that are possible is taken very seriously by the women themselves and by the men. If a woman cannot get to *shul*, someone will come to her home to blow the *shofar* or read the *Megillah* for her. If anyone is in the hospital, arrangements will be made for her. Sometimes her husband will do it, or, if he cannot, someone else will.

Women never say *Kaddish*. If there is no male relative, then someone else is given that responsibility. Women do participate in many fund-raising activities for the synagogue and many charities.

"The Rebbe" is a role model for both men and women. There are special *farbrengen* (gatherings to hear "The Rebbe" teach) for women several times a year. "The Rebbe's" wife was a mysterious figure in Crown Heights. It is rather unusual that the rebbetzin of the community was so anonymous. Nobody knew anything about her. She did not have a special place in the *shul* where everyone davens (770) but stayed in a private room in the building.

"The Rebbe" is a transcendental figure, very elevated and spiritually capable of guiding his followers in their personal decisions. Men and women share a respectful reverence toward him. Women and men share a desire to be in "The Rebbe's" presence, often pushing themselves to their physical limits to stay up at *farbrengens* until the early hours of the morning. He activates everybody. Women and men basically have the same role in their relationship to him....

Since 1972, when Sally Priesand became the first woman rabbi to be officially ordained, increasing numbers of women have entered the rabbinate and the cantorate. Despite the official endorsement by their movements, women who seek to enter these professions still experience difficulties. As Rabbi Emily Korzenick and Cantor Nancy Hausman show, congregants are often slow to accept women in roles traditionally reserved for men.

Hausman discusses the process by which women achieve professional equality: by dispelling male fears that the feminization of their profession would lower its status and by persisting in their efforts at communal acceptance. Hausman illustrates that discrimination often dissipates as congregants grow accustomed to women as leaders in the synagogue.

Korzenick details how women bring to the rabbinate special nurturing skills often acquired in their roles as mothers and wives. She is one of a growing number of rabbis who seek to re-establish the home as a focus of religious life. While in the Orthodox community religion was always centered both in the home and the syna-

gogue, during the past century, non-Orthodox synagogues have supplanted the home as the loci for Jewish observance. The inclusion of women in the rabbinate has facilitated the process of integrating home and synagogue.

On Being a Rabbi:
Emily Faust Korzenik

I am one of the oldest women to become a rabbi in the United States, a fact that has significant implications for the way I have perceived my role in this profession. I took my own four children through *Bar* and *Bat Mitzvah* ceremonies, and then had my own *Bat Mitzvah*, before I began to guide other families through that meaningful rite of passage. Most often, I guide mothers who, whether they work or not, usually bear the major responsibility for supervising their child's *Bar* or *Bat Mitzvah* preparation and for arranging the festive celebration.

Being older than most new rabbis also means that I had confronted the death of a loved one, a parent, before I began trying to assist others in the most painful hours of their lives. It also means that I graduated college and began my life as a wife and mother at a time when most middle-class women saw their primary function as serving their families.

Nurturing is good preparation for the rabbinate. For example, I enjoy inviting members of my congregation to my home for Shabbat dinner. I cook the meal as well as prepare a talk on a Jewish theme. This spring I invited my college bound youngsters for a Shabbat dinner and asked them to bring their college catalogues so that together we could look over the Jewish Studies courses available to them. Every Sukkot my very helpful and encouraging husband and some grown children build a *sukkah* in our yard, to which I invite some of the young couples I have married. They are beginning to come with their little ones. Passover is madness for me. I prepare and cook for my own big *seder* at home, and on the second evening I conduct my congregation's community *seder*. It is exhausting but I love it.

Coming to a rabbinical career as an older person and as a woman also means that I am not lonesome. Rabbinical colleagues, notably men, speak about the difficulty of making close friends, of being set apart, of having a religious and public role that complicates intimacy. Long before I became a rabbi, I had formed my cadre of close friends. Now I marry their children and can bring some special comfort, I believe, at sad times. I am first of all their friend, and, as a result, I intuitively approach my congregants as a friend who has a particular role. My way of being a rabbi has been shaped as much by my life as a wife and mother, a high school history teacher, and a social and political activist, as by rabbinical study and preparation itself.

People often ask me if I experience discrimination as a rabbi because I am a woman. From its inception, the Reconstructionist Movement accepted women as peers. Mordecai Kaplan performed the first *Bat Mitzvah* ceremony for his daughter in 1922. There was never any question about the role of women in the Reconstructionist congregation in White Plains, N.Y. to which my husband and I have belonged for thirty years. I read from the Torah, chanted the *haftarah* portion, was president of the synagogue, and even chairperson of the ritual committee. I was just one of many studious, participating women. That was the milieu within which I began to form my desire to become a rabbi. It was a milieu that made discrimination against women elsewhere in the Jewish religious world seem incomprehensible and, therefore, something to be overcome.

There have been disquieting moments, of course. A young woman doctor asked me to officiate at her wedding, and then she discovered her Israeli fiancé and his family would not be comfortable with a woman rabbi. She asked if I would co-officiate with a man. I replied that if I was not rabbi enough to perform the ceremony, I preferred not to participate. She wanted to satisfy her fiancé but she meant to be kind. Didn't I understand that the "social customs" were different in Israel? I did not remind her that "social customs" had kept women from becoming doctors until not long before her own entry into that profession.

The most egregious example of discourtesy toward women in the synagogue that I experienced took place in Poland. In September of 1985, I participated in a Shabbat morning service in Cracow with a *Bar Mitzvah* boy and his family who are members of my congregation in Stamford, Connecticut. A gentleman, whose daughter I had married the year before, returned from a United Jewish Appeal-Federation mission to Poland and Israel with a request from a leader of the remnant of elderly Jews in Cracow. When the American visitors had asked what they could do to help, Maria Jakabowicz said, "Bring us some life. Bring us some youth. Bring us a *Bar Mitzvah*." One of my *Bar Mitzvah* students, his family, and I immediately responded to the request. I also invited a wonderful, traditional Jewish man, a survivor of Auschwitz, to come with us to daven *Shaharit*, as I was sensitive from the first to the probable preferences of the elderly Jews in Cracow; however, I did plan to participate in the service.

In Cracow, I stood upon the *bimah*, *tallit* in hand, to be with the *Bar Mitzvah* boy when he chanted his beautiful *haftarah* portion from Isaiah. I offered a brief commentary, despite the actions of an American rabbi, who pulled my *tallit* from me and attempted to prevent me from speaking.

The experience in the synagogue was not painful because the congregation's sympathy was with us. We had succeeded in bringing some joy to these old people who had suffered so much. We had fulfilled their request. We had handled ourselves with dignity and restraint. It was a triumphant day, the rabbi who had challenged me notwithstanding.

However, it was sad, so very sad, to know that leaders of the Orthodox community at home in the States had, in fact, asked the Jews of Cracow to rescind their invitation to us because, as non-Orthodox Jews, our use of the fifteenth-century Remu Synagogue would have been a desecration in their eyes. The Jews of Cracow responded by arranging to have the *Bar Mitzvah* held in the Templum, a nineteenth-century non-Orthodox synagogue. The day following the Sabbath ceremony, Ed Blonder, the survivor who had led the morning *Shaharit* service and chanted the Torah portion, took us through Auschwitz. The torturers and murderers of over three million Polish Jews had not differentiated between the Orthodox and the non-Orthodox. I remembered stinging words from a Sholem Aleichem story, "You know how we Jews are, if the world does not pinch us, we pinch each other."

I cannot, however, end on so sorrowful a note. It is wonderful to be a woman and a Jew in America at the close of the twentieth century. Without question, the new opportunities for women in the religious world had their impetus in America's open, democratic, secular society. I am blessed to be a rabbi when most Jews are proud to be themselves. And I am so eager to serve.

On Becoming a Cantor:
Nancy S. Hausman

My parents raised me to believe that I could do anything I wanted to do. Partway through my junior year in college I realized that the prelaw program I was taking was not for me. It was then that I considered going to cantorial school. My parents were very active Reform Jews. They were one of the founding families of our temple in Upper Nyack, New York, and I had sung in the temple choir from its inception, eventually becoming the soprano soloist. Cantorial school seemed just the right career for me, a person who loves Judaism and who also loves to sing.

I entered Hebrew Union College–Jewish Institute of Religion's School of Sacred Music in the fall of 1974. I was part of a class of three women and five men—there was a grand total of forty-five students in the School of Sacred Music.

When I think back on my time at the School of Sacred Music, I remember it fondly. Since my class was so small, we were like a family. Everyone knew what was going on in everyone else's life. We tried to support each other during times of stress and cheered each other on during the good times. Our professors, mostly cantors, were still not sure how to teach women the traditional *"nusah"*[1] so every class was an experimental one for both them and us. However, they were all very positive; no exclusionary practices took place.

I do, however, remember negative comments from some of the male students about the female students. Some of the men were afraid that the women would take all of the jobs, leaving them with no employment. Others complained that salaries would suffer because occupations considered "women's" jobs are traditionally underpaid in our society. These kinds of comments made me angry, but as far as I can ascertain, these fears were unjustified.

There are now more women than men entering cantorial school. The number of men applying to cantorial school has always been small; therefore, the current increase in class size is due to the number of women applying. The changing class profile does not seem to be discouraging congregations from applying for cantors. The need for good Jewish music seems to be transcending any latent bias toward women.

One of the teaching techniques used in cantorial school is on-the-job training, or student pulpits. When I was applying for such a position, some congregations specified that they did not want to consider women. Fortunately, it was and still is a policy of the School of Sacred Music that any temple requesting a student cantor has to audition whoever applies for the job, regardless of sex. As it happened, my student pulpit was with a congregation that originally did not want to hear women. However, after the interview process, they were interested in two students, both women.

I worked there for three very happy years. I heard that there were some members who objected so strongly to my being hired that they left the temple. I also learned that those members owed back dues when they left. This appears to be another case of people using women as scapegoats for other, totally unrelated problems.

I taught second and third graders when I was in my student pulpit. I remember once, when we were all together for an assembly, one little second grader said to me, "Cantor, where is the cantor who was here last year?" I responded, "He's working at another temple." A first grader, who had been silently listening to this conversation, blurted out, "A boy cantor? In all my life, I never heard of one!" I had become the role model for these children. They thought that all cantors were women, just as I had once thought that all cantors were men.

These encounters heightened my awareness of the prejudices against women, which exist in varying degrees. I had a fine relationship with the rabbi of my student pulpit; however, he and I had to establish some rules from the outset. When I began at the temple, the rabbi let me know how glad he was that I was there. He said that I could assist him in so many ways. Often, there were appointments he needed to make by phone, but he had no time to do this. He suggested that I could make these calls as well as write some notes for him. I immediately responded, "I won't have the time, and I don't know how to type." He never made a similar suggestion again, and I think we understood each other and had respect for each other as a result of that encounter.

In my last year at the seminary, I was under a great deal of pressure. I worried about where, and even if, I would be working the following year.

Women were still in the minority as students in the school. We were still a relatively untested phenomenon.

There was one job-hunting experience that left a lasting impression on me. A large Southern congregation came to New York to interview cantors. About twenty cantors (both graduating cantors and those out in the field) auditioned. I was one of three cantors, the only woman, that the temple chose to invite to their town for extended interviews. It was a very intensive experience, and I was pretty "green," but I thought it went well. When I came back to New York, some of my professors who were close to people in that temple told me to pack my bags; however, I didn't get the job. I wondered why, but the job I took instead kept me too busy to ponder this for long.

I became Associate Cantor at Hebrew Union College in Jerusalem. While I was in Israel, a convention of the World Union for Progressive Judaism took place. Jews from all over the world attended. I was fairly visible as one of the College's cantors. A member of the Southern congregation where I had been interviewed introduced herself to me. She said she had been on the cantorial search committee the year before but had been out of town when I was interviewed. She had heard very nice reports about me and was disappointed that I had not been hired, but there had been controversy over hiring a woman cantor, so they had hired a man. I was angry about that for a long time. That temple, by the way, now has a woman cantor.

I came back to the States in the spring of 1980 and took a full-time position. I worked at that temple for two years. During my second year, after the High Holy Days, two long-time members (women) told me that at first they were not used to seeing me on the *bimah*, but that now my presence seemed very natural to them. It was interesting that they never said they did not like me; they said they were not used to me.

The next congregation for which I worked was in Florida. I stayed there for four years and left to come back up North. However, it is rewarding to realize that I was able to be a positive role model for so many young girls there. By being exposed to a female cantor, they were made aware of yet another possible occupational choice. After I was at that congregation for a few years, a congregant made an interesting observation. He said, "Your voice seems to have gotten lower." We both laughed and agreed that rather than my voice having changed registers, he had just gotten used to hearing a woman's voice on the *bimah*.

I now have two jobs, one as a cantor in a temple in New Jersey and the other as the placement administrator of a national cantorial association. Through the second job, I speak with many congregations that are considering hiring cantors. They have all kinds of questions and a wide variety of needs. Not one has said that it does not want to hire a woman. In fact, some specifically request a woman cantor. These congregations feel a woman would add an extra dimension to their temple family. I try to convey to them that sex should not be a factor in employment. Their questions should be,

"Does this cantor have the right qualifications for our temple? Can he or she add personally to our congregation?" An interview can only reveal so much about an applicant. When trying to make a positive impression, none of us needs the extra burden of sexual prejudice weighing us down.

Note

1. The traditional musical modes to which certain parts of the liturgy are sung.

Questions for Discussion

1. How has the status of Jewish women changed from the days of the Israelite religion?
2. Would you say the similarities or the differences are more significant in Jewish women's experiences?
3. Is it possible to eliminate male bias from Judaism?
   - Why or why not?
4. Do the gender-distinctive aspects of Jewish religious practice, which largely specify the domestic sphere as the space for women's religious ritual practice, signify complementary roles for men and women, or hierarchical, male-dominant ones?
5. How are the lives of Jewish women spiritual leaders (rabbis and cantors) different from those of Jewish men?
6. How do the lives of Jewish women spiritual leaders compare with those of women in other religious traditions we have examined so far?

References and Materials for Further Study

Books and Articles

Adler, Rachel. 1998. *Engendering Judaism: An Inclusive Theology and Ethics.* Philadelphia: Jewish Publication Society.

Baskin, Judith, ed. 1991. *Jewish Women in Historical Perspective.* Detroit, MI: Wayne State University Press.

———. 1985. "The Separation of Women in Rabbinic Judaism," in Yvonne Yazbeck Haddad and Ellison Banks Findly, eds., *Women, Religion, and Social Change.* Albany: State University of New York Press.

Biale, Rachel. 1984. *Women and Jewish Law: An Exploration of Women's Issues in Halakhic Sources.* New York: Schocken Books.

Brooten, Bernadettte. 1982. *Women Leaders in the Ancient Synagogue: Inscriptional Evidence and Background Issues.* Chico, CA: Scholars Press.

Cantor, Aviva. 1995. *Jewish Women/Jewish Men: The Legacy of Patriarchy in Jewish Life.* San Francisco: HarperSanFrancisco.

Carmody, Denise. 1994. "Today's Jewish Women," in Arvind Sharma, ed., *Today's Woman in World Religions.* Albany: State University of New York Press.

Goldman, Karla. 1999. "Judaism: Contemporary Jewish Life," in Serinity Young, ed., *Encyclopedia of Women and World Religion.* New York: Macmillan Reference.

Greenberg, Blu. 1981. *On Women and Judaism: A View from Tradition.* Philadelphia: Jewish Publication Society of America.

Grossman, Susan, and Rivka Haut, eds. 1992. *Daughters of the King: Women and the Synagogue: A Survey of History, Halakhah, and Contemporary Realities.* Philadelphia: Jewish Publication Society.

Hackett, Jo Ann. 1985. "In the Days of Jael: Reclaiming the History of Women in Ancient Israel," in Clarissa W. Atkinson et al., eds., *Immaculate and Powerful: The Female in Sacred Image and Social Reality*. Boston: Beacon Press.

Hauptman, Judith. 1998. *Rereading the Rabbis: A Woman's Voice*. Boulder, CO: Westview Press.

Heschel, Susannah. 1999a. "Judaism: An Overview," in Serinity Young, ed., *Encyclopedia of Women and World Religion*. New York : Macmillan Reference.

———. 1999b. "Judaism: Modern Era," in Serinity Young, ed., *Encyclopedia of Women and World Religion*. New York: Macmillan Reference.

———, ed. 1983. *On Being a Jewish Feminist: A Reader*. New York: Schocken Books.

Hyman, Paula, and Deborah Dash Moore, eds. 1997. *Jewish Women in America: An Historical Encyclopedia*, Vol. 2. New York: Routledge.

Kraemer, Ross. 1992. *Her Share of the Blessings: Women's Religions Among Pagans, Jews, and Christians in the Greco-Roman World*. New York: Oxford University Press.

Levinson, Prina Nave. 1990. "Women and Sexuality: Traditions and Progress," in Jeanne Becher, ed., *Women, Religion, and Sexuality*. Philadelphia: Trinity Press.

Nadell, Pamela. 1998. *Women Who Would Be Rabbis: A History of Women's Ordination, 1889-1985*. Boston: Beacon Press.

———. 1995a. "'Top Down' or 'Bottom up': Two Movements for Women's Rabbinic Ordination," in Jeffrey Gurock and Marc Raphael, eds., *An Inventory of Promises: Essays on American Jewish History in Honor of Moses Rischin*. New York: Carlson Publishing, Inc.

———. 1995b. "Ladies of the Sisterhood: Women in the American Reform Synagogue, 1900-1930," in Maurie Sacks, ed., *Active Voices: Women in Jewish Culture*. Urbana: University of Illinois Press.

———. 1995c. "The Women Who Would Be Rabbis," in T.M. Rudavsky, ed., *Gender and Judaism: The Transformation of Tradition*. New York: New York University Press,

Niditch, Susan. 1991. "Portrayals of Women in the Hebrew Bible," in Judith Baskin, ed., *Jewish Women in Historical Perspective*, Detroit, MI: Wayne State University Press.

Plaskow, Judith. 1990. *Standing Again At Sinai: Judaism from a Feminist Perspective*. San Francisco: HarperSanFrancisco.

Sawyer, Deborah. 1996. "Sisters in Christ or Daughters of Eve?" in *Women and Religion in the First Christian Centuries*. New York: Routledge. Also Chap. 2, "Women within Judaism and Christianity," and Chap. 5 "The Religion of Jewish Women."

Simon, Rita, and Pamela Nadell. 1995. "In the Same Voice or Is It Different?: Gender and the Clergy." *Sociology of Religion*. 56, 1: 63-70.

Trible, Phyllis. 1984. *Texts of Terror: Literary-Feminist Readings of Biblical Narratives*. Philadelphia: Fortress Press.

Umansky, Ellen. 1991. "Spiritual Expressions: Jewish Women's Religious Lives in the Twentieth-Century United States," in Judith Baskin, ed., *Jewish Women in Historical Perspective*. Detroit, MI: Wayne State University Press.

———. 1985. "Feminism and the Reevaluation of Women's Roles within American Jewish Life," in Yvonne Yasbeck Haddad and Ellison Banks-Findly, eds., *Women, Religion, and Social Change*. Albany: State University of New York Press.

Wegner, Judith Romney. 1988. *Chattel or Person?: The Status of Women in the Mishnah*. New York: Oxford University Press.

Internet Resources

Annotated Bibliography and Guide to Archival Resources on the History of Jewish Women in America, compiled by Phyllis Holman Weisbard, Women's Studies Librarian, University of Wisconsin System:
http://aleph.lib.ohio-state.edu/www/jewomen.html#bib.

Bibliography of Jewish Women's Resources: compiled by Tsiporah Wexler-Pashkoff:
http://aleph.lib.ohio-state.edu/www/jewomen.html.

Bridges: A Journal for Jewish Feminists and Our Friends:
http://www.pond.net/~ckinberg/ bridges/.

The Fanya Gottesfeld Heller Center for the Study of Women in Judaism:
http://www.biu.ac.il/JS/jwmn/.

Hadassah International Research Institute on Jewish Women at Brandeis University:
http://www.brandeis.edu/hirjw/about.html.

Jewish Feminist Web site:
http://world.std.com/~alevin/jewishfeminist.html.

Lilith: The Independent Jewish Women's Magazine:
http://www.lilithmag.com/.

Maven, The Jewish Portal:
http://www.maven.co.il/subjects.asp?S=201.

Soc. Culture.Jewish Newsgroups Reading Lists:
http://www.scjfaq.org/rl/gen-women.html.

Torah Continuum: Women's Study:
http://www.rainmall.com/tcws/.

Women and the Holocaust:
http://www.interlog.com/~mighty/.

Women in Judaism: A Multidisciplinary Journal:
http://www.utoronto.ca/wjudaism/.

Women in Rabbinic Literature—An Online Course from JTSA:
http://courses.jtsa.edu/registration.

Media Resources

Blessed Deception. Video, 60 min. Films for the Humanities, 1996. Focuses on the story in which Rebekah procures Isaac's blessing for Jacob through deceit. Explores sibling rivalry, the idea of women as the carriers of faith, the nature of blessing, and the uses of deception.

Miriam's Daughters Now. Video, 30 min. Center for Visual History, New York, 1986. Discusses the changing roles of Jewish women and their demand for equal rights.

Not a Job for a Nice Jewish Girl: Becoming a Woman Rabbi. Video, 60 min. Films for the Humanities, 1994.

Women Serving Religion. Video, 29 min. Films for the Humanities, 1991. Roles of women in traditional and contemporary Christianity, Judaism, and Islam.

The Return of Sarah's Daughters. Video, 56 min. Patchworks, 1997. Three Jewish women discuss their relationship to Judaism.

Chapter 6

Women and Christianity

⌣∙ ∶⌣

Overview

Christianity is a "historical religion" in that it was founded upon specific historical events: the birth, life, and death of Jesus of Nazareth. It arose in the ancient Near East, in Judea and Galilee, in the context of Judaism and the Greco-Roman pagan religions. The New Testament of the Bible (considered to be Revelation or the word of God by many but not all Christians) offers a partial description of the earliest years of the Christian narrative. The earliest written evidence of Christianity is contained in the letters of St. Paul (52–62 C.E.), one of Jesus' key disciples. The Pauline letters not only provide us with some clues about the earliest Christian communities; they also set forth prescriptions for the appropriate gender roles of men and women in those communities. Key events include Jesus's divine birth by the Virgin Mary in a manger in Bethlehem, his modest upbringing and education as a carpenter, his teachings from the Sermon on the Mount, his opposition to the use of the sacred temple—the house of God—as a place for conducting "worldly" activities such as business transactions, his profession of the coming of God's judgment and ensuing Kingdom, and the presence of the divine spirit.

The New Testament also recounts Jesus's miraculous activities, like turning loaves into fishes to feed the multitudes, walking on water, and rising from the dead three days after he had died on the cross and been interred in the tomb. Jesus' teachings can be considered millenarian in the sense that he preached the imminent end of the world, the "eschaton," at which point God's plan for the world would be fulfilled and the ungodly powers would be conquered. Thus, the first Christian communities formed after Jesus's death were based upon the belief that the end was near, and the hierarchical and patriarchal structures of the rest of society were unnecessary.

Judaism is Christianity's "parent" religion. Jesus and his family and disciples were Jewish. In its initial years, it was a Jewish "renewal" movement or "Jesus movement" rather than a self-consciously separate religion. Jesus' teachings themselves relied on Jewish scripture in his message of repentance and salvation. Christianity did not arise as a new religion until the end of the first century C.E., when Judaism and Christianity began to define themselves in opposition to one another (Sawyer 1996, 42). However, there were some distinct differences in how the "Jesus movement" was organized and operated, especially its nonhierarchical and egalitarian organization.

The various books of the New Testament were not sealed together into a single canon until the end of the second century C.E. Some of the contemporaneous writings of Christians, such as those of the Montanists, discussed later, were excluded as illegitimate. Disagreements over biblical interpretation and practice in the early Church led to the development of a number of different sects of Christianity. One of the earlier major splits was between the "Western" church and the Eastern Orthodox. As a result of the Reformation in Europe in the sixteenth century, dissenters, unhappy with the Pope and what they perceived to be deviations from the original Gospel, split off from Roman Catholicism and became the Protestant church. In turn, different sects of Protestantism have developed over time, leading to a wide variety of different denominations of Protestant Christianity today. In addition, the Mormon Church, started by Joseph Smith in the nineteenth century United States, has become a "third type" of Christianity, as it rejects being identified as either Catholic or Protestant.

Although the Roman Catholic Church remains one centralized and hierarchical entity, with the ultimate authority being vested in the Pope, who resides at the Vatican in Rome, there are nonetheless a range of different interpretations of Catholicism. Because Catholicism often mixed together with the indigenous religions of the areas where it was introduced through missionizing and colonialism, there are radically different forms of "Catholic" worship (although some of these are not recognized as legitimate by Rome). In addition to a number of theological and liturgical differences, one prominent opposition between the Protestant and Catholic Churches is their attitude toward monasticism. Whereas Catholicism developed orders of both monks and nuns fairly early on, celibate and renunciant lifestyles were opposed by Protestant reformers, and monasticism was never established in Protestant sects.

All three types of Christianity have been disseminated widely throughout the world as a result of colonialism, missionizing, and proselytizing. As a result, the vast majority of peoples living in North and South America, Europe, Australia, and New Zealand are Christian. In Canada, Roman Catholicism arrived with French traders and missionaries, but in 1763, when England took over the territory, the Church of England became the official religion. In the United States, Catholicism came with the Spanish explorers to the Southwest (also to Mexico and Latin and South America), whereas Protestantism arrived first in the northeast with the English colonists. Deborah Sawyer emphasizes that "Christianity's understanding of the nature and role of men and women has been the single most influential ingredient in the construction of gender roles and behaviour in western society and its domination" (Sawyer 1996, 41). In addition, substantial numbers of people living in Asian and African countries have also converted to Christianity over the past few centuries. There are over 900 million Roman Catholics in the world today, the majority of whom are poor and live in the former European colonies.

Relationship of Female-Gendered and Feminine Images and Symbols to "Real" Women

The Christian religion includes prominent gender images that are in tension or outright conflict with the roles of actual women in society. Perhaps the earliest example of this is in the Old Testament account of Genesis, a creation story which Christianity shares with Judaism. Eve, the "first woman," in this cosmological account of the creation of the world, is made "from" Adam in one of two accounts of how God created humans (Genesis 2) rather than as, in "real life," being born from a woman. The Genesis account of creation makes Eve, symbolizing "woman," subordinate to Adam, the original and archetypal "man," because of succumbing to the temptation of eating fruit from the tree of knowledge and then dragging Adam into complicity in her sin against God's orders.

The New Testament account of Jesus' birth by the "Virgin Mother" perpetuates the view that all other women's natural birth-giving is inferior. Mary's immaculate conception (not accepted by all Christian sects) presents an unattainable model for all other women to emulate and thus symbolizes their lack of divinity. In addition, the gendered symbolism which makes God male and links males with reason and spirit and women with emotion and embodiment and/or sexuality suggests that women are inferior.

In Catholicism, with its pantheon of male and female saints, some "cults," such as those to the Virgin Mary (see The Mary Page Web Site) and St. Jude (see Orsi 1996), have been predominantly worshiped by women. In Protestantism, which banned representations of the saints, women have been left with no female representations of the divine to balance against the male trinity of God, Jesus Christ, and the Holy Spirit. Feminist theologians have created new "models of God" which are female or have feminine attributes, however (see, e.g., McFague 1987).

Women's Relationship to Christianity

Women-Specific or Distinctive Aspects of Christianity

As in several other world religions, women form the majority and major support for Christian Churches in both Catholicism and Protestantism. For example, in contemporary churches in North America, the majority of congregants in mainstream churches are women. The central role of women was evident in the very beginnings of Christianity.

In the second century, an institution called the "order of widows" enabled women of any age who had been married to join together with other similarly situated women to be supported by the community and opt out of marriage and family life. I Timothy specifies, however, that the order of widows was only available to women over age 60, suggesting that women of childbearing age should be married and raising children. This limited the options of younger women to stay unmarried, in direct contradiction to Paul's earlier teaching that it was preferable for women (as well as men) to remain single if possible (see Sawyer 1996, 110).

Nonetheless, communities of celibate Christian women have existed from the earliest days of Christianity through the present. The Catholic Church made monasticism available to women as well as men. These female monastic communities were mostly devoted to prayer until the twelfth century, when evidence suggests that they became more active in "apostolic" activities of charity and social service, corresponding to the period when many Christians were attempting to imitate Christ and his disciples through such works (see Mooney 1999, 175). A papal bull issued in 1298 mandated the enclosure of all nuns, forcing them to severely curtail or terminate their charitable activities in the community and withdraw into cloisters. Those who refused enclosure were subject to charges such as heresy and rarely survived.

Nonetheless, several orders of Catholic nuns were established, including the Company of St. Ursala ("Ursalines," the counterpart of the Jesuits) in the middle of the sixteenth century, and the Daughters of Charity, formed by Vincent de Paul (1580–1600) and Louise de Marillac (1591–1660). For a time, the Ursalines were able to avoid the legislative mandate of enclosure imposed on all nuns at the Council of Trent (1545–1563) (and enforced by civil authorities) by wearing secular dress and living individually in their homes. The Daughters of Charity did likewise by circumventing the definition of "nuns" for its members by calling themselves "secular sisters" (see Mooney 1999, 175).

Religious orders were widely repressed during the revolutions of the eighteenth century at the same time that women were becoming more emancipated. They experienced a revival during the nineteenth century, however, and spread to European colonies, though indigenous communities of religious women grew slowly in Latin America, Africa, and Asia (see Mooney 1999, 176). While growing in Africa, women's religious orders in Europe and North America have experienced a sharp decline in recent years. Some women have left monastic life out of disaffection for the continuing patriarchal and sexist character of the Church, and as older nuns have died, younger women have not been attracted to either the religious beliefs or the monastic life. These developments have put some orders in danger of extinction.

Joining a religious order as a nun has given Catholic women an alternative to the conventional roles of wife and mother and enabled them to pursue a spiritual vocation. After religious orders began educating girls and young women, they became an avenue by which women could improve their opportunities in life. Paradoxically, while the Reformation eliminated this option for most Protestant women (there are a very few Protestant female religious orders in the Anglican-Episcopal Church in Great Britain and the United States), it made the text of the Bible accessible to them and in fact obligated them to be able to read it. It also (eventually) removed the prohibitions on their assuming roles of religious leadership in their congregations (although this would take centuries in some denominations, in which women have only had the opportunity to become ordained priests and ministers in the past several years). However, the Protestant emphasis on biblical authority and conservative, restricted literal interpretations of the Bible have the effect of restricting women's activities, making them subject to the authority of their husbands and silencing them in church.

As in Judaism, many Christian women's religious practices and rituals have taken place informally in the domestic sphere rather than within institutionalized settings. Within the Eastern Orthodox and Roman Catholic traditions, these have included activities such as reciting rosaries, prayers, reciting novenas, making and offering votive candles, making traditional foods for religious holidays, making devotion to particular saints, worshiping at home altars, and reciting feminist liturgies. In some indigenous Mexican regions, Catholic women hold prayer vigils for the deceased and chant the rosary all night (see Bailey 1999, 152). Women also dominate traditions of folk healing in several Christian cultures, including Greek Orthodox. Healers use some combination of traditional prayers and religious objects such as icons, amulets, and charms to heal or protect against illness.

In Protestant traditions, women in nineteenth-century Europe and America were considered to be the moral center of the home, responsible for instilling Christian virtues in their husbands and children. Women in some Protestant denominations, however, rejected the Christian gender ideology which restricted them to domestic and subservient roles. Quaker women, for example, developed a theology based on biblical interpretations supporting women's spiritual equality with men (Keller 1999, 170). Women in evangelical and pentecostal Protestant denominations (distinguished by practices such as speaking in tongues and faith healing), as well as in "fundamentalist" churches (so-called because of their belief in the inerrancy of the Bible as God's revelation), tend to be more traditional in their gender roles than women in more liberal Protestant denominations.

Gender-Based Segregation and Inequalities

The selection by Deborah Sawyer, from her book *Women and Religion in the First Christian Centuries*, provides an excellent overview and introduction to the place of women in the early Christian Church. Her piece indicates that gender hierarchy and the denigration of women have been present since the very beginnings of the Christian religion, despite the presence of some egalitarian aspects. Sawyer reveals how the early church "Fathers," including St. Paul, Tertullianm, Ambrose, St. Chrysostom and St. Augustine, interpreted scripture in ways which established male dominance and superiority over females.

Despite this sexist and patriarchal context, there is contextual evidence that Jesus himself viewed women as spiritual equals to men. This evidence, however, is largely dependent upon contrasting what is said in the Gospels (the Books of Matthew, Mark, Luke and John) about the life and teachings of Jesus with negative reconstructions of the lives of Jewish women during that time (see D'Angelo 1999, 156). Although he never married, Jesus associated with a number of different women over the course of his life, including women regarded by some as "unrespectable," such as Mary Magdelene. It was women who were present at his death (his mother Mary, Mary Magdelene, Mary, mother of the Apostle James, and Salome), witnessed his burial, and discovered that he had arisen from the tomb.

By the end of the first two centuries of Christianity, however, the main paradigm for women's status and roles had shifted from full inclusion to marginalization and subordination to the authority of husbands and fathers. The "Household Codes" contained in the New Testament books of Colossians, Ephesians, I Timothy, Titus, and I Peter command women's, children's, and slaves' submission to their husbands, fathers, or masters. This is thought to have been done, at least in part, to accommodate Christianity to prevailing Roman "family values" (see D'Angelo 1999). But it is also given a divine mandate in Ephesians, which specifies that a woman's subordination to her husband is analogous to the church's submission to Christ (Ephesians 5:23-24), and that husbands are obligated to sanctify their wives, just as Christ sacrificed himself to make the church holy (Ephesians 5: 25-27), thereby suggesting the women are fundamentally impure (see Pastis 1999, 158).

The contradictory messages of Corinthians, endorsing both marriage and celibacy, were associated with women as the "problem" of sexuality. Paul's statements in Romans (1: 26-27) that the "unnatural" intercourse of women with women was the outcome of the idolatrous worship of images suggests that Paul condemned lesbianism. Although women were expected to be chaste, and Paul had recommended single, celibate lifestyles for those who were able, Timothy makes women's salvation dependent upon submission to their husbands and upon childbearing and rearing (Tim. 2:9-15). Paul taught that women were to wear head coverings (since a man is the image and glory of God, whereas woman is the glory of man, and woman was created from man and for man) and be silent in church (since woman's voice is shameful in public worship) (I Corinthians 11:2-16; 14:34-35). The same restrictions were not imposed on men.

The milllenarian Montanist movement of the second century was led by the prophecies of one man, Montana, and two women, Prisca and Maximilla, who had a significant following, including the Church father Tertullian. Opposition to the Montanists (both because of their millenarianism and having women leaders) was actually the motivation for the formation of the New Testament Canon, based on fears that otherwise the Montanists' prophecies would have to be accepted as Christian doctrines (see Sawyer 1996, 108-09).

During the persecution of Christians by the Romans in the fourth century (303–311 C.E.), women were prominent among the martyrs, Christians who were willing to go to their death rather than renounce their faith. After Christianity was established as the religion of the Roman Empire in 391, women influenced the religious policies adopted by the emperors (see Cardman 1999, 149). But church patriarchs such as Tertullian, Chrysostom, and Augustine viewed women primarily as passive reproductive vessels or fetal containers for active male seed and attributed original sin to be the fault of woman (Eve's eating of the forbidden fruit in the Garden of Eden). Their views became dominant and resulted in severely curtailing women's leadership roles.

Without question, the severest repression of women occurred between the fourteenth and seventeenth centuries, when as many as 300,000 women in Europe and the Americas were prosecuted and condemned to death for being witches. Christianity was also especially oppressive for indigenous and African Americans in the Americas colonized by Europeans. The colonialists demonized indigenous religious traditions and in many cases actively repressed them; imposed European practices of Christianity as the exclusive religious faith; and also required adherence to religiously legitimated patriarchal, hierarchical, and sexist norms (Aquino 1999, 166-67).

Within the larger Catholic Church, most women have been limited to distinctly secondary roles, generally those of wives and mothers. The Church has counseled women that their primary responsibility is to the home and family and has discouraged them from outside occupations. The American Catholic bishops have concurred with this view. In the twentieth century, with the development of Catholic Liberation Theology and Protestant "base communities' in Latin America (radical forms of Christianity which incorporate socialist principles and dictate a "preference for the poor"), Christianity has also become a vehicle for liberating people—especially women—from oppression rather than imposing it upon them. However, these liberationist movements are being threatened by pentecostal and right-wing Protestant groups, which have heavily missionized in these areas in recent years (Aquino 1999, 167).

In contrast to traditional Roman Catholicism, Protestant Christianity reflects a broad spectrum of different views of women. Although Protestantism shares the Catholic heritage of sexist and patriarchal views about women, many mainstream denominations have incorporated contemporary social norms that promote equality for women. In particular, the principle that the heart of the gospel is the free gift of grace, given by God through the life and death of Christ, is egalitarian in its view that salvation is available to all regardless of merit or dessert, not merely to one sex or gender.

Other Protestant churches continue to reflect more traditional sexist and patriarchal attitudes that promote rigid notions of gendered social roles and restrict women's primary roles to those of wife and mother. This is especially true of many fundamentalist and evangelical churches. In these churches, such views are often accompanied by an insistence on the subservient role of women and the dominant role of men. Traditional family values promoted by many conservative Protestant groups such as the Promise Keepers include the beliefs that the father is the natural leader and head of the household, the woman's place is in the home, and that the wife and children are obligated to obey the male head of household and are subject to physical punishment as a legitimate response for their disobedience.

In Canada, as in the United States and elsewhere, Christianity has functioned to empower some women and oppress others. Because Christianity is the socially and politically dominant religion in both Canada and the United States, it has also been used to perpetuate the imperialist privileges of women of European extraction at the expense of indigenous and non-Caucasian women. African-American women have faced discrimination not only as women within a patriarchal and sexist religion, but also as minorities within Protestant denominations, including the Church of England and the Methodist and Baptist churches, which have excluded them. Many African Americans have responded by beginning their own denominations. But even here, for example, in the African Methodist Episcopal Church women were discriminated against and excluded from preaching authority. Perhaps it is needless to say that lesbians have faced varying degrees of discrimination, with a few exceptions in a few, mostly liberal, Protestant denominations in the past few decades.

Women's Access to Religious Education
and Opportunities for Leadership Roles

Opportunities for women's leadership within Christianity have varied widely, depending upon the time period and type of Christian community involved. Over time, confidence in the imminence of Christ's return diminished. Along with this waning of hope came increased pressure to reduce the status of women to the secondary place it occupied outside of Christian circles, both because of the pressures to conform to the norms of outside communities in order to avoid persecution and the prospect of having to settle into a long-term existence in the world before the end-time would take place.1 In addition, with increasing institutionalization and legitimation of Christianity as a state religion came a diminishment of the status and roles for women. Even though the tradition of single celibate women active within the Church continued, acceptance of their central leadership roles did not. Indeed, by the turn of the fifth century, women had been excluded from most formal ministries other than acting as deaconesses. Some Christian women have always been exceptions to the prescribed rules, however.

The Gospels and Acts indicate the central involvement of women in the earliest days of the Christian church. Paul's letters indicate that at least one of the Apostles, Junia, was a woman (Rom. 16:7). Paul also refers to Phoebe as a deacon and Prisca as a co-worker and head of a church. Several missionaries and prophets in the first era of Christianity were also women, including the "three Marys" and Salome (see Gospels of Mark, John, Matthew, and Luke). The evidence that women were "on the road to Galilee" preaching with Jesus in what was a loosely structured, egalitarian, wandering, and mendicant group of missionaries suggests that women were centrally involved in the early Christian movement (see D'Angelo 1999, 156).

Since the early Christians met secretly in the houses of members, and since the domestic sphere was regarded as women's domain, this might have enhanced women's authority in the early church. In Galatians, Paul states that in God there are no distinctions, "neither Jew nor Greek, slave nor free, female nor male," suggesting an egalitarian basis for Christian society. The Book of Timothy, however, precludes women from teaching. In the fourth century C.E., there were some celibate women who either lived in ascetic communities or on their own. Some of the collections of sayings of the "Desert Fathers," ascetics who lived in the deserts of Egypt, Palestine, and Syria, include the teachings of desert mothers as well. In the early Middle Ages, some women in the West entered monasteries to pursue a religious vocation (although some women were required to enter the monastery, either because their parents had promised them to the church or because they were deemed unmarriagable [see Cardman 1999, 150]).

During the early modern period, women in radical Protestant groups claimed leadership authority from the egalitarian nature of the spirit.

Anabaptist women, for example, were martyrs, visionaries, and prophets (Cardman 1999, 151). Women in Moravianism, early Methodism and revivalism were able to gain authority because of the emphasis on affective religious experience in those sects. Despite the discrimination against them by both white and black Protestant churches, some African-American women in the eighteenth and nineteenth centuries succeeded in developing their own ministries as educators, revivalists, church social welfare advocates, and missionaries. In addition to black and white women missionaries, some Chinese American, Native American and Latina women were also involved in this work.

In early nineteenth-century Europe, it was women's religious communities that were responsible for opening up opportunities for universal education for girls. Being excluded from leadership roles in institutional church settings, Protestant women established a wide range of missionary, charitable, and other social service organizations, and some became actively involved in missionary work themselves, roles that had been closed to them prior to the nineteenth century. During the early years of evangelical and pentecostal Protestant churches, women held prominent roles as preachers, healers, and teachers. Aimee Semple McPherson (1890–1944) established the International Church of the Foursquare Gospel, for example.

Whereas before the nineteenth century women were excluded almost completely from leadership roles, most markedly in the Catholic Church, this has changed significantly in recent decades. The Catholic Church still bars women from ordination as priests and deacons and thus precludes them from performing many sacramental functions. Despite efforts by Catholic women in recent decades for fuller participation in the Church, the hierarchy has thus far refused to change its policy on women's ordination, thereby continuing to prohibit women from participation in the leadership and policy-setting functions of ecclesiastical life. Many women have felt so strongly about this bar to holding leadership roles in the church that they have left in protest.

New voluntary lay roles, such as lay professional ministers, have opened up for Catholic women, however. In Canada, sisters have been appointed to vacant parishes. In China, perhaps because of a shortage in clergy, women preach, lead prayers, and offer pastoral prayer, even though they still are prohibited from offering the sacraments.

The first woman was ordained in North America in 1853 in the Congregational church. Beginning in the late nineteenth century, but not fully until the mid-1950s through the 1970s, many Protestant churches opened their churches to women ministers and priests and made efforts to eliminate gender bias in ecclesiastical life, including liturgy, hymns, administration, and leadership. Opportunities for women to receive theological education have expanded phenomenally over the past couple of decades. While during the 1970s only a small proportion of seminary students in U.S. theological schools were women, by 1987 more than half the students were women in the more liberal Protestant theological schools.

However, these high percentages of women do not reflect a general trend within Christian institutions to embrace women as full leaders on a par with men. Some Protestant churches have been far slower to affirm women's equality, especially at the institutional level of opening full ordination to women. At European theological institutions, there are very few female faculty. In both Europe and North America, women in Christian institutions are still paid less than men and have overall lower ranks and administrative status.

Progress in women's institutional status within Christianity has been made overall. Nonetheless, women in some of these resistant congregations, both white and African American, dominate public worship, especially through "testifying," a kind of informal preaching (see Bailey 1999, 153-54).

Well-Known and/or Influential Women in the Tradition

Christians share the female biblical figures like Eve, Hagar, and Rebecca, and so forth, with Judaism. Prominent among the women associated with Jesus are his mother, the Virgin Mary, Mary Magdalene, and Mary, the wife of Clopas. Jesus' mother Mary was regarded as the redeemer of women after the sins of Eve, the first woman, who was thrown out of the Garden of Eden for eating the fruit of the tree of knowledge.

In the medieval era, Hildegaard de Bingen (1098–1179) was a renowned theologian, musician, and spiritual leader. She was the abbess of a convent and an accomplished writer and musical composer. Women mystics and visionaries found receptive audiences in the medieval West but were viewed suspiciously by the Church hierarchy. These included Gertrude the Great (died 1301), Mechthild of Magdeburg, Julian of Norwich, Catherine of Siena, and Bridget of Sweden. While these women mystics were allowed to speak and write unharmed, others, like Joan of Arc (c. 1312–1434), were burned at the stake for heresy and witchcraft.

In later centuries of Catholicism, a number of prominent women emerged, including Teresa of Avila (1515–1582), a mystic and reformer of the Carmelite order, and Catherine of Sienna (1347–1380), who was also a mystic as well as a caretaker for the poor and a diplomat for the Church (see Redmont 1999, 849). Sor Juana de la Cruz (c. 1648–1695) was a Mexican nun, philosopher, and poet who read widely in Spanish, Portuguese, and Latin in an era when education was generally not available to women.

During the early modern period (1500–1800), some European queens, including Mary Stuart (Queen of Scots, r. 1561–1567) and Mary Tudor ("Bloody Mary," r. 1553–1558), defended the Roman Catholic Church against the Protestants, whereas others, such as Elizabeth I (1558–1603), forwarded the cause of Protestantism. Mary of the Incarnation (1599–1672), a member of the French Ursuline order of Catholics, started the first school for girls in Quebec (1639) and compiled dictionaries of several Native American languages.

Some radical Protestant women, such as Anne Hutchinson (1591–1643) and Margaret Fell (1614–1702) became very prominent leaders who claimed their authority by virtue of the egalitarian nature of the spirit. In the eighteenth and nineteenth centuries, Mother Ann Lee established the Shakers, and Mary Baker Eddy the Christian Scientists, both Protestant denominations founded upon the view of the feminine as the higher element in the perfection of humanity. In 1853, Antoinettte Brown became the first woman to be ordained as a minister in the United States (by the Congregationalist Church).

In the contemporary era, prominent Christian women include Dorothy Day (1897–1980), who co-founded the Catholic Worker movement in the early twentieth century, Simone Weil, a French mystic writer who died at a young age in the midst of the World Wars; and Mother Theresa of Calcutta (1910–1997), a Nobel Peace Prize winner whose mission was to serve the "poorest of the poor."

Changes in the Status of Women

Historically

Protestant feminists, followed by Catholic and Jewish feminists, began challenging the sexism and patriarchy of their churches in the late nineteenth and early twentieth centuries in America. Prominent among them were Sojourner Truth, an African-American woman and former slave who challenged the racial prejudice as well as the sexism of white Christians, and Elizabeth Cady Stanton, whose revisionist "Woman's Bible" drew both praise and condemnation for eliminating sexist scriptural passages.

In the so-called "second wave" of the women's movement in the 1970s, increasing numbers of feminists worked to transform the church to be a more accessible and accepting institution for women.

In the late 1960s, the radical feminist philosopher and theologian Mary Daly, a former Catholic, published *The Church and the Second Sex* which brought to light and scathingly criticized the male domination, sexism, and patriarchy of the Christian church. In 1971, Daly was the first woman invited to preach at Harvard Memorial Church. She ended her sermon entitled "The Woman's Movement: An Exodus Community," by walking out of the church in protest of Christianity's institutionalized sexism and invited other women to do the same (see Eller 1993, 4). Daly summarized her position on the sexism of Christianity by saying that, in effect, "If God is male, male is God," that is, superior. Daly has now left the church, and proposed that women establish their own, "gyno-centric" religious traditions. Her lawsuit against Boston College for wrongful termination (for refusing to allow male students in one of her classes) received national news coverage.

Subsequent to Daly's groundbreaking work, a number of other feminist theologians have gained prominence for their work to reform and/or radicalize the Church to make it more egalitarian. These include the Catholic theologians Elisabeth Schüssler Fiorenza and Rosemary Ruether, and Protestants Sharon Welch, Katie Cannon, Rita Nagashima Brock, Susan Thistlewaite, Beverly Harrison, and Carter Heyward. They also include critics like the poet Audre Lorde, whose "Open Letter to Mary Daly" points out the ways that Daly completely ignores the experience of women of color in her radical feminist perspective on religion.

Within Western Christian churches, both Catholic and Protestant women have expressed discontent with several aspects of their religious institutions. These include lack of attention to women's experiences, including domestic violence, sexual abuse, and poverty; restrictions on reproductive freedoms; gender ideology; and the lack of ordination for women in Catholic and Anglican churches.

More "public" religious roles for women have become available in recent decades, in part because of the influence of the feminist movement. "Woman Church," for example, is an organization founded by a group of Catholic women disaffected by the secondary status of women in Catholicism and the firm opposition of Church authorities to change the institution so as to improve women's status. Many Catholic feminist women have been developing alternatives to the prohibition on women giving the Eucharist (a role restricted to priests, who are required by church rules to be male) by creating alternative Eucharists (see Bailey 1999, 154). Areas where some Christian churches have responded to feminist critiques and proposals for reform include gender-inclusive language, clergy-lay relations, and new liturgies. Even in China, there are limited, but seemingly growing, opportunities for Christian women to attend seminaries, travel abroad, and lead prayer groups.

Future Prospects

If churches are open to the demands of many Christian women for greater participation and inclusion in the religious life, it is possible that they will become more egalitarian. If they are not, however, more and more women may abandon their churches for other avenues of spiritual exploration and expression, such as Woman Church, more liberal Christian denominations where women do have a greater status and opportunity to participate, or Wicca or goddess spirituality, which are alternatives to a Christian-based religiosity altogether.

Broader changes within Christian denominations will require the continued enrollment of women in theological schools, ordination as religious specialists (ministers, lay pastoral counselors, and other religious professionals), infusion of feminist ideas into theological school curriculum and Church doctrines and liturgies, and so forth.

The selection included here by Carter Heyward, an Episcopal minister, feminist theologian and "out" lesbian, provides an overview of some of the main strands of feminist Christian thought. Heyward provides a synopsis of Mary Daly's groundbreaking feminist insights about the patriarchy and sexism of traditional Christianity and critiques Daly's lack of attention to the differences among Christian women. Heyward then contrasts the award-winning African-American feminist author Alice Walker's writing, which reveals the different kinds of oppression that African-American women have faced in the Church. Finally, Heyward provides some of her own views about what is necessary to bring about justice for women and other oppressed peoples in the Church.

The final selection, by Mujerista theologian Ada Maria Isasi-Diaz, provides an introduction and exemplar of feminist theology being done by Latinas. She explains why she uses the term "Mujerista" rather than simply "feminist theologian." In describing some of the similarities and differences between feminist theology being written by "First World" and "Third World" feminists today, Isasi-Diaz clarifies how the intersectionality of nationality and ethnicity with gender and religion complicates the analysis of liberation for Latinas.

NOTES

1. Sawyer suggests that because of the link between women and millenarianism, as long as the end time was perceived as near, the equality of women was not perceived as a problem, since it was only for an interim period (see Sawyer 1996, 107-09).

Sisters in Christ or Daughters of Eve?

Deborah Sawyer

When we set Christianity beside Greco-Roman religion and Judaism, it does seem distinct in its explicit attempts to define the nature of women in relation to men. What we discover as implicit in the other traditions is clearly articulated by Christian writers from the first century onwards. Earlier in our discussion of the role of women within the early Christian communities, we noted a diversity of practice that reflected alternative notions of organization and structure.[1] It is this diversity that prompts Christianity's explicit definition of gender, particularly in relation to the nature and role of women. Because there is diversity in terms of women's self-understanding and experience, when Christianity does consciously realize the need to conform to, rather than to challenge, society, it is compelled to argue for a particular understanding of gender. This early development formed the basis for subsequent Christian beliefs about the essential nature of women and men, and the prescriptions regarding the roles each has to fulfil within church and society. The charismatic communities of the first half-century provide the antithesis to the Christian concept of womanhood that emerged by the end of the century.

Within the context of the charismatic communities that were characteristic of the Jesus movement and the early Pauline foundations, gender roles were constructionist rather than essentialist. Men and women could work side by side, preaching and spreading their beliefs about Jesus of Nazareth. Women could opt out of the domestic sphere and enter the public world; they could exist apart from their fathers, husbands or children. The order of "widows" was a means of realizing this option.[2] By taking on the dress of a widow, a woman gained the ability to move freely within the public sphere, protected from sexual harassment or assault. The guise of widowhood was a means of bypassing the norms of patriarchy, and allowing for an alternative form of existence for women.

This phenomenon within early Christianity begs comparison with the Jewish Therapeutrides of Egypt described by Philo,[3] and, perhaps, the order of Vestal Virgins.[4] All three groups prescribe roles for women that are in stark contrast to the usual expectations of the patriarchal societies to which they belong. In the case of the Vestal Virgins their role is one deliberately constructed by the power-group of their society. Their relative freedoms, which at times place them on a par with men, are granted to them by men. They are a controlled incongruity, as opposed to a challenge to society's norm. The

From Deborah Sawyer, 1996. *Women and Religion in the First Christian Centuries*. New York: Routledge. Reprinted with permission of Routledge.

Therapeutrides, along with their male counterpart community of Therapeutae, were a group that withdrew from society. As women who turned their backs on marriage in preference for wisdom "as a life partner,"[5] the Therapeutrides did not seek a role in wider society, rather an option to be apart from it, living in their own society.

In comparison to the Vestal Virgins and the Therapeutrides, the "widows" of early Christianity, the women co-workers that St Paul mentions in his letters, strike a chord of dissonance within their society. They are not a category that society has formalized, nor are they prepared to withdraw and constitute a community apart. They were women who wished to exercise the same freedoms that men enjoyed in the public sphere, so that they could preach the gospel in which they fervently believed as effectively as the men, if not more so. The impetus for their non-conformity seems to lie within their own psyche. They were convinced that their inward self had been transformed by the death and resurrection of Jesus of Nazareth. Such a belief is well attested in the Pauline letters which constitute the earliest extant evidence we possess of Christianity, and it had profound implications for the understanding of gender roles within the early Christian communities. We noted earlier the baptismal formula in Galatians, for example, which reflected the belief that all social, racial and gender boundaries are dissolved in the community of Christ.[6] At baptism the new believer puts to death the "old" self, and rises out of the water a new creation:[7]

> Do not lie to one another, seeing that you have stripped off the old self with its practices and have clothed yourselves with the new self, which is being renewed in knowledge according to the image of its creator. In that renewal there is no longer Greek and Jew, circumcised and uncircumcised, barbarian, Scythian, slave and free; but Christ is all and in all.
> (Col. 3.9–11)

This concept of a transformation of the self in early Christianity allowed women to cross boundaries and challenge their identity in radical terms. Being a woman could be redefined in this new context in such a way as to make possible for her a self-understanding and experience that had previously been exclusive to men.

A tension necessarily arose between experience within this new believing community and life outside it where the "old" norms and expectations for women prevailed. The order of widows is testimony to the compromise that had to exist between the old and the new. If women were to live the new life, spread the gospel and support the embryonic communities in the public sphere, they still had to observe the restrictions society placed on their freedom. They therefore had to present themselves publicly as non-sexual beings, that is, as widows who enjoyed society's protection from men's sexual advances. They did not constitute a group of women who could function in public without their sexuality being their most significant feature. Rather, they were a group who had to "suspend" their sexuality in order to function freely outside their normative domestic sphere.

The inclusion of women in the earliest phases of Christianity is a feature that is not universal, and to present it as a "golden age" for women's participation does not represent fully the divergent nature of Christian practice. In contexts where non-conformity to the wider society could have resulted in scapegoating and persecution, the compulsion to reflect rather than to challenge society's structures can easily be understood. The first major persecution of Christians began in 65 C.E., instigated by the Emperor Nero who made them responsible for the fire of Rome, but even before this particular incident, sporadic outbreaks of disorder had met with the Empire's heavy fist.[8] In such contexts other structures were appearing, parallel to the charismatic communities we have been considering, and they mirrored the norms of society in terms of organization as well as gender roles.[9]

There was another factor in this too. The beliefs that underpinned women's inclusion in the charismatic communities were bound up with convictions about the imminent return of Christ and the eschatological overturning of earthly authority and power structures.[10] Once those convictions weakened, and Christian beliefs focused on the role of the church in this world rather than the next, the practice of conformity within society had to outweigh any tendency to challenge from without. Women's roles then had to be articulated clearly in the light of divergent practices which did reflect a challenge to, and therefore a criticism of, the endemic patriarchal society.

In order to prescribe modes of behaviour for men and women that reflected rather than challenged the norms of Greco-Roman society, Christianity had to provide the theology that would support its teaching. To be convincing, this theology had to demonstrate that these roles had been part of divine revelation since the time the world was created, or to put it another way, that in God's mind there could be no alternative.

Christianity shared with Judaism the account of Adam and Eve as the primal couple, made by the hand of God to enjoy the fruits of divine creation. The story recounts how the couple quickly demonstrated their independence from God by eating fruit from a tree that had been expressly forbidden to them. Although there is evidence to show that early Christian commentators interpreted the culpability of this act to lie with Adam,[11] Eve soon became the central figure in this primeval act of disobedience:

> I permit no woman to teach or to have authority over a man; she is to keep silent. For Adam was formed first, then Eve; and Adam was not deceived, but the woman was deceived and became a transgressor. Yet she will be saved through childbearing, provided they continue in faith and love and holiness, with modesty.
>
> (1 Tim. 2.12–15)

Christian theology invested Eve with a unique position, not only regarding the Fall, but also in the theology of redemption. She became the representative and type of all women, so that even the Blessed Virgin Mary was interpreted as the New Eve as Christ was the New Adam. The figure of Eve lies at the heart of Christianity's understanding and estimation of women. In contemporary Christian theological debate she deserves the closest attention of anyone who wishes either to revise that estimation of women or to uphold it.

It is possible to characterize three types of argument in Christian theology regarding Eve. These, although distinctive, are interrelated and to some extent interdependent through the biblical proof-texts they share and the conclusions they reach.[12] The first argument supports the notion that in gender terms a hierarchy exists in which women are the second sex. It is founded on the order of creation described in Gen. 2 where the text can suggest that Eve is created after Adam and for Adam's needs: "Then the Lord God said, 'It is not good that man should be alone; I will make him a helper fit for him'" (Gen. 2.18). In Christian theology this verse became the proof-text for maintaining a sexual hierarchy in the Christian family and in ecclesiastical office. The Genesis account of the order of creation was used in our earliest accounts of Christianity, the Pauline epistles, to define the position of women. Two of these texts, 1 Cor. 11.7ff. and 1 Tim. 2.13, most clearly bring to mind the Genesis text. In 1 Corinthians 11 Paul attempts to persuade the women in the congregation not to reveal their hair while leading prayers or prophesying,[13] "For a man ought not to cover his head, since he is the image and glory of God; but woman is the glory of man. (For man was not made from woman, but woman from man. Neither was man created for woman, but woman for man.)" (1 Cor. 11.7–9). This passage relates to a particular problem regarding a particular Christian community at a particular time in history, but since it is part of the Christian canon of scripture it has been recognized by churches as normative throughout the centuries. One conclusion deduced from this passage, that women did not bear the image of God in an identical way or proportion to that of men, was, perhaps, the most influential in Christianity's deliberate determining of the male gender as normative. John Chrysostom, writing in the fourth century, for example, interprets this passage to imply that women lost their divine image as a result of the "Fall." He notes that the Greek word *exousia*, usually translated "veil" in 1 Cor. 11.10, actually means "authority" which is something that women lack since God made them subservient to men as punishment for Eve's disobedience:

> For the "image" is not meant in regard to essence, but in regard to authority, as we shall make clear by bringing forth arguments in an orderly manner. To grasp the point that the form of man is not that of God, listen to what Paul says: "For the man ought not to be veiled, for he is the image and glory of God. But woman is the glory of man. Therefore she ought to have a veil (Greek: "authority") on her head."

Indeed if Paul here says this was the "image," making clear the un-changeableness of the form that is patterned on God, then man is called the "image of God" because God has stamped him in this way. Not so, according to our opponents, who argue that not only the man must have the "image," but the woman as well. Our answer is that the man and the woman do have one form, one distinctive character, one like-ness. Then why is the man said to be in the "image of God" and the woman not? Because what Paul says about the "image" does not per-tain to form. The "image" has rather to do with authority, and this only the man has; the woman has it no longer. For he is subjected to no one, while she is subjected to him; as God said, "Your inclination shall be for your husband and he shall rule over you" (Gen. 3.16). Therefore the man is in the "image of God" since he had no one above him, just as God has no superior but rules over everything. The woman, however, is "the glory of man," since she is subjected to him.[14]

This type of argument ensures that sexual hierarchy becomes an essential part of Christian theology. Not only is Eve the second sex because she was created after Adam, but through her disobedience she is distinct from men in that she no longer shares God's image.

The other Pauline passage, 1 Timothy 2, makes the same two points about women by declaring first that "Adam was formed first, then Eve," and then reinforcing the concept of the "second sex" by mentioning her disobe-dience. By setting out these arguments in a passage which is about ecclesias-tical organization, the idea of women assuming any significant role within the power hierarchy is not viable.

New Testament scholars are divided on the question of the Pauline au-thorship of 1 Timothy.[15] Fiorenza seeks to understand them as late first-cen-tury attempts by Christian communities to conform to the norms of their Greco-Roman context, and notes the influence of Aristotle's ideas, of sexual hierarchy and domestic and political hierarchy.[16] One of the most important features of her work is the insistence that such texts must be read "against the grain": such strongly worded admonitions are themselves evidence that there were situations where women were teaching men and asserting au-thority outside their proper domestic sphere.

When these admonitions were taken alongside the sexual hierarchy re-flected in the New Testament's household codes (e.g., "Wives, be subject to your husbands, as to the Lord" Eph. 5.22),[17] the Church Fathers had firm scriptural foundations for developing a Christian attitude to womankind that was in sympathy with tendencies in Greco-Roman culture to preserve and disseminate Aristotelian values. Augustine, for example, puzzles over the very creation of woman: what was the point of God creating such a crea-ture? Does the description of woman as man's "helper" (Gen. 2.18) imply that she would help the man with manual labour?[18] In fact he dismisses this since, before the Fall, such hard labour did not exist, and, furthermore, if God had wanted a manual labourer, then another man would have been more suitable. He continues:

> One can also posit that the reason for her creation as a helper had to do with the companionship she could provide for the man, if perhaps he got bored with his solitude. Yet for company and conversation, how much more agreeable it is for two male friends to dwell together than for a man and woman![19]

His eventual answer to the problem of why women were created at all is based on his view of the order of creation in which women are by nature subordinate to men:

> If it is necessary for one of two people living together to rule and the other to obey so that an opposition of wills does not disturb their peaceful cohabitation, then nothing is missing from the order we see in Genesis directed to this restraint, for one person was created before, the other afterwards, and most significantly, the latter was created from the former, the woman from the man. And nobody wants to suggest, does he, that God, if he so willed, could only make a woman from a man's side, yet that he couldn't create a man as well? I cannot think of any reason for woman's being made as man's helper, if we dismiss the reason of procreation.

Procreation, then, for Augustine, was the only valid reason behind God's decision to create woman, and the ultimate peak in this process comes when a unique woman, without tarnish of sin, brings forth the Christ child into the world.

This concept of a "natural order" among the sexes reflects basic Aristotelian concepts:

> There are by nature various classes of rulers and ruled. For the free rules the slave, the male the female, the man the child in a different way. And all possess the various parts of the soul but possess them in different ways; for the slave has not got the deliberative part at all, and the female has it but without full authority, while the child has it but in an undeveloped form.
>
> (*Politics* I.1260a)[20]

John Chrysostom applies this natural order of the sexes some centuries later:

> Our life is customarily organized into two spheres: public affairs and private matters, both of which are determined by God. To woman is as-

signed the presidency of the household; to man, all the business of state, the marketplace, the administration of justice, government, the military, and all other such enterprises.... Indeed, this is a work of God's love and wisdom, that he who is skilled at the greater things is downright inept and useless in the performance of the less important ones, so that the woman's service is necessary. For if the man were adapted to undertake both sorts of activities, the female sex could easily be despised. Conversely, if the more important, more beneficial concerns were turned over to the woman, she would go quite mad.[21]

The combination of the Aristotelian notion of the natural order of things with the Genesis account of the creation of male and female furnished Christianity with the theoretical underpinning of its practice of sexual hierarchy.

The second type of argument characteristic of Christian theology about Eve concerns her particular responsibility for introducing sin into the world. This belief that the "Fall" of the human race came about through Eve's act of eating the fruit of the tree in the "midst of the Garden" (Gen. 3.6) can be found in Christian writing from as early as the New Testament period.[22] The first evidence we find of Eve being deemed uniquely culpable is in Paul's letter to the Corinthians: "But I am afraid that as the serpent deceived Eve by his cunning, your thoughts will be led astray from a sincere and pure devotion to Christ" (2 Cor. 11.3). This observation of Eve's vulnerability later becomes a pronouncement of her guilt: "Adam was not deceived, but the woman was deceived and became a transgressor" (1 Tim. 2.14). The argument for female subordination based on the order of creation is now overtaken by the belief that woman is the originator of sin. This one passage from a short epistle became the foundation text in Christian theology about women and their role and status in the church. In it the figure of Eve is of central importance: she is the first sinner and she is also the embodiment of all womankind. It would seem that her sin was so great that she and the rest of womankind even fall outside the redemptive power of Christ. Salvation for them comes through child-bearing and modest dress and behaviour rather than through the Christian soteriological scheme of the death and resurrection of the Son of God. The theology of this verse was certainly one factor in Augustine's belief, quoted above, that the only reason for woman's existence was procreation.

We find the same attitude regarding the necessity for modesty amongst Eve and her daughters expressed by the late second-century Christian writer Tertullian. He begins his discourse *On the Dress of Women* as follows:

> If such strong faith remained on earth, as strong as the reward of faith is expected in heaven, not one of you, dearest sisters, from the time she acknowledged the living God and learned about herself, that is, about the condition of women, would have desired a more charming dress,

not to speak of a more exquisite one. She would rather go about in cheap clothes and strive for an appearance characterised by neglect. She would carry herself around like Eve, mourning and penitent, that she might more fully expiate by each garment of penitence that which she acquired from Eve—I mean the degradation of the first sin and the hatefulness of human perdition. "In pains and anxieties you bring forth children, woman, and your inclination is for your husband, and he rules over you" (Gen. 3.16)— and you know not that you also are an Eve?

(I,1,1)

As in the case of the passage from 1 Timothy, Tertullian steeps his arguments in material from Genesis 3; and, again like the writer of 1 Timothy, sees Eve as "everywoman":

God's judgment on this sex lives on in our age; the guilt necessarily lives on as well. You are the Devil's gateway; you are the unsealer of that tree; you are the first foresaker of the divine law; you are the one who persuaded him whom the Devil was not brave enough to approach; you so lightly crushed the image of God, the man Adam; because of your punishment, that is death, even the Son of God had to die. And you think to adorn yourself beyond your "tunics of skins" (Gen. 3.21)?

(I,1,2)

Here the female gender has a particular responsibility not only for the first sin, but also for the death of Christ. The more one particular interpretation of Genesis 3 became embedded in Christian theology, the more marginalized from the heart of that religion women became. They came to be identified with the "other," in opposition to the normative male gender which had now been perfected in the incarnation of the divine into human male form.[23]

In the century following Tertullian, both Ambrose and Augustine echo and reinforce the theological basis of sexual hierarchy through the belief in Eve's primary responsibility for the Fall, constantly referring back to the words of 1 Timothy. First Ambrose: "The woman, therefore, is the originator of the man's wrongdoing, not the man's of the woman's. Hence Paul says, 'Adam was not deceived, but the woman was deceived and committed sin'" (1 Tim. 2.14).[24] And then Augustine:

The apostle Paul's words were not meaningless when he said, "For Adam was formed first, then Eve. And Adam was not led astray, but the woman was, and was made guilty of transgression" (1 Tim. 2.13–14), i.e., that through her the man became guilty of transgression. For the apostle calls him a transgressor as well when he says, "In the likeness of the transgression of Adam, who is a figure of him who is to come" (Rom. 5.14), but he does not say that Adam was "led astray." For even when asked, Adam does not reply, "The woman whom you gave me led me astray and I ate," but rather he says, "She gave me from the tree and I ate." She, to be sure, did speak the words, "The serpent led me astray."

(Gen. 3.13)[25]

In this comment, comparing Adam with Eve, we see how Augustine singles the woman out as having particular responsibility for the Fall. Although Adam is not without sin, he was not "led astray."

A third line of argument addressed by early Christianity to the figure of Eve concerned her typological link with Mary, the mother of Jesus. This link can be traced to as early as the middle of the second century in the work of Justin Martyr. Towards the end of that century Irenaeus, Bishop of Lyons, discussed the similarities and contrasts between these two women. Having noted first how Eve shares the same status as Mary in having a husband and yet remaining a virgin, he continues:

Eve, having become disobedient, was made the cause of death both for herself and for all the human race. Thus also Mary had a husband selected for her and nonetheless was a virgin, yet by her obedience she was made the cause of salvation both for herself and for all the human race. For this reason the law calls a woman engaged to a man his wife, while conceding that she is still a virgin. This indicates a link that goes from Mary back to Eve.

… Moreover, the knot of Eve's disobedience was loosened through the obedience of Mary. For what the virgin Eve bound through unbelief, this the Virgin Mary loosed through faith.[26]

Mary's faith is expressed in her affirmatin of God's intention to make her, a virgin, conceive the Christ child: "Behold, I am the handmaid of the Lord; let it be to me according to your word" (Lk. 1.38).

Although evidence identifying Mary as the New Eve is not explicit in the New Testament, the Church Fathers found texts to support their typology, for example, the contrasting imagery of the Whore of Babylon (Rev. 17) and the Queen of Heaven (Rev. 12) in the *Book of Revelation*.

In considering the negative interpretations of Eve that lie at the heart of Christianity, we must note that there is also a certain ambivalence concerning her sin. Although, in Christian terms, it led to the "Fall," and is the greatest sin ever committed, without it there would have been no act of redemption. Eve and Mary are both central characters in ensuring the inevitability of Christ's redemptive work, and Christianity recognizes a bond between these two women in their cooperation in bringing about the birth of Christ. Eve is then the type of the one that is to come: Mary. This is evident in Jerome's Vulgate version of Gen. 3.15b where God castigates the serpent. The Hebrew is rendered in English as follows: "he [Hebrew *hu*] shall bruise your head, and you shall bruise your heel." But Jerome has the feminine: "She it is who shall bruise your head" (*ipsa conteret caput tuum*). In the repercussions of Eve's act of disobedience is found the promise of redemption through the act of another woman.[27]

Christianity produced two types to represent all of womankind: Eve and Mary. In reality Mary was the one and only example of her type, and all women were daughters of Eve. As Augustine defined his concept of Original Sin, identifying concupiscence as the primary cause and Eve as its source and instigator, so Mary became more and more elevated in her unique status. As the drastic consequences of Eve's sinful disobedience became apparent, her sinful nature was laid bare to stand in stark contrast to the perfect, untainted nature of Mary.

With the concept of congenital sin came speculation on the possible sinlessness of Christ, and by degree, the sinlessness of his mother. If Christ was to be without taint of congenital sin then his mother had to be without sin. The moment that sin is passed on from one generation to another, according to Augustine, is the moment during the act of sex when conception takes place. It can be recognized by the lust that accompanies all such acts. It is woman who awakens this lust in man, just as Eve has sparked off Adam's lust for the fruit of the tree in the midst of the Garden. Christ's conception bypassed this process and was therefore devoid of concupiscence. Mary's own immaculate conception meant that she also bypassed the inheritance of sin and therefore could not pass any stain on to the son in her womb.

To conclude, within Christian theology as expressed in its first centuries, two theories of gender are apparent. The first, noted in the charismatic organization of the Jesus movement and the first urban communities, manifests Plato's vision of the *grove of academe*, where equality of opportunity allows for the development and inclusion of both genders.[28] The second, resting on the Aristotelian notion of natural order, not only makes sexual hierarchy visible both in the domestic and public spheres, but also adds theological underpinning through reflection on the implications of Eve's sin in order to ensure a uniformity of belief and practice in the universal church. We noted at the beginning of this section on Christianity that this tradition was distinctive in comparison to Greco-Roman cults and Judaism in its explicit articulation of the nature and roles of male and female. In this context it is more useful to set Christianity beside classical Aristotelian and Platonic philosophy which did concern itself with the meaning of matter formed as male and female.[29] Such a study falls outside the limits of this project, allowing us only to note that from its earliest days Christianity identified itself as a religion that presumed to regulate for every aspect of life and thought for the individual, the community and, eventually, the Empire.

Notes

1. "A Mother in Israel: Aspects of the Mother Role in Jewish Myth," in R.M. Gross, ed., *Beyond Androcentrism: New Essays on Women and Religion*, Missoula, MT: Scholars Press, 1977, pp. 237–255.
2. Ibid., pp. 109–110.
3. Ibid., pp. 78–79.
4. Ibid., pp. 68–70.
5. Philo, *On the Contemplative Life*, from section 68–69.
6. Gal. 3.28; Adler, note 1, pp. 101–103.
7. Rom. 6.3–4.
8. See, e.g., the expulsion of the Jews from Rome by Claudius in 49 C.E. According to Suetonius' record this was the result of disorder among them over beliefs about "Chrestus"; see *Life of Claudius* 25.4.
9. Adler, note 1, pp. 113–114.
10. A vivid description of these beliefs is given by Paul, 1 Cor. 15.23–28; also *Revelation*.
11. Rom. 5 and 1 Cor. 15.
12. I rehearsed these arguments for the first time in an earlier article, Morris and Sawyer (eds), *A Walk in the Garden*, pp. 271–289.
13. The question regarding women's hair-style in Corinth is discussed in Adler, note 1, pp. 103–105.
14. *Discourse 2 on Genesis*, translation from Elizabeth A. Clark, *Women in the Early Church*, pp. 35–36. All translations from the Church Fathers in this section are taken from Clark.
15. This observation applies to certain other Pauline texts where there are passages that are central to the debate concerning the status of women, namely, Colossians, Ephesians and the other pastoral epistles: 2 Timothy and Titus.
16. Fiorenza, *In Memory of Her*, pp. 251–284; Adler, note 1, pp. 111–115.
17. Adler, note 1, pp. 110–113.
18. On Augustine's ideas concerning sexual hierarchy see Genevieve Lloyd, "Augustine and Aquinas," in Ann Loades (ed.), *Feminist Theology: A Reader*, pp. 90–98.
19. *Literal Commentary on Genesis*, IX,5.
20. Translation from H. Rackham, *Aristotle, Politics*, Loeb Classical Library, Cambridge, Mass., Harvard University Press, 1926; see the discussion of household codes in Adler, note 1, pp. 110–113.
21. *The Kind of Women Who Ought to be Taken as Wives* 4.
22. The same tendency is evidenced in the Jewish apocryphal work *Sirach; see* Adler, note 1, pp.134–135.
23. For a critique of Christianity's understanding of woman as the "other," with its focus on Eve, see Mary Daly, *Beyond God the Father; Toward a Philosophy of Women's Liberation*, Boston, Beacon Press, 1974, pp. 13–68.
24. Ambrose, *On Paradise*, XII, 56.
25. Augustine, *Literal Commentary on Genesis*, XI, 42.
26. *Against Heresies*, III,22,4.
27. This same theology is heard in the following poem:

> Ne had the apple taken been
> The apple taken been,
> Ne hadde never our Lady
> A been heaven's queen.
> Blessed be the time

> That apple taken was!
> Therefore we may singen
> "Deo Gratias!"

From the work of a fifteenth-century anonymous poet; Helen Gardner (ed.), *Oxford Book of English Verse 1250–1950*, Oxford, Oxford University Press, 1972, pp. 13–14.

28. See Ibid., pp. 5–7.
29. In relation to current feminist dialogue with classical philosophy and gender theory see J. Butler, *Bodies that Matter: On the Discursive Limits of Sex*, London, Routledge, 1993, pp. 27–55.

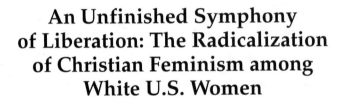

An Unfinished Symphony of Liberation: The Radicalization of Christian Feminism among White U.S. Women

A Review Essay

Carter Heyward

This essay is dedicated to Katie G. Cannon, Ada Maria Isasi-Diaz, and other racial/ethnic feminists who've helped me grasp the urgency of acknowledging that I'm white and Anglo and …

Prelude

In this review essay, I propose to discuss several recent theological contributions to the tasks of Christian feminism as it is being practiced among white women in the United States. The legitimate scope of this discussion is both

From *Journal of Feminist Studies in Religion* I/I, 1985, pp. 99-118. Reprinted with permission of *Journal of Feminist Studies in Religion* and Carter Heyward.

broad and narrow: vast insofar as the vision which inspires the labor of many white Christian feminists is global, strenuous in its demand that we seek connections between and among ourselves and those whose races, religions, cultures, and relationships may be quite different from our own. But my focus is narrow in that most of the texts I have chosen to examine, as well as the interpretive framework I bring to this work, are shaped by the narrow particularities of experience that is white, Christian, and academic. As such, this piece emerges from the Euroamerican "enlightened" consciousness which for so long has been presumptuous enough to provide "universal" definitions of both "theology" and "God," and thereby to lend moral justification to the structures of domination by which most people on earth continue to be kept in their subordinate places.

I do not apologize for what I am about to do, but rather I want to state clearly the limits of what I am attempting. For among the most compelling insights emerging currently among feminist theologians of all colors and different religions is that our theological creativity is enhanced, not diminished, by understanding the particularities, thus limits, of our own lives as lived in relation to—not as identical with—others. Not only our creativity, but also our moral agency, is strengthened as we struggle to know and name the relativities and contingencies of our actions and credos.

While I emphasize the white and Christian praxis of this essay to underscore the significance of particularity to the theological enterprise, I do so not without realizing the double-edged effect of this particular racial and religious emphasis in a society beset by white racism and anti-Semitism. At a time like ours, when our nation is being swept swiftly along in fascist currents, the attachment of special significance to either the white race or the Christian faith is potentially very dangerous. If done, or understood, from a segregationist or isolationist posture, it can only be reprehensible.

But fascism is steeped not in the dominant racial or religious group's acknowledgment of the limits of its particular historical experiences, cultures, or credos, but rather in the refusal of dominant peoples to accept the limits of their particular visions, values, and faith-claims. For white Christian women to shut their eyes to the meaning of either their racial or their religious (as well as economic and national) roots is to fuel the fires of bigotry and violence. We need to comprehend the meaning of our lives precisely in relation to the social privilege we hold. Only insofar as we do so can we who belong to the superordinate racial/ethnic groups enter into theological collegiality and feminist solidarity with Black, Hispanic, Asian, and Native women. Similarly, to own the limits of our Christian faith-claims can contribute to our capacity to work with, rather than against, Jewish, Moslem, Hindu, Buddhist, wicca, post-Christian, and other feminists. Then too, our failure to assess honestly the particularities of our lives continues to divide white Christian feminists among ourselves—especially as lesbians and straight women; women of different economic classes and strata; and, perhaps to a lesser degree, women of Catholic heritage and those who share a Protestant construction of the world and God.

It is with these separate places in mind, both among white Christian feminists and between us and others, that I approach this review.

The Earlier, Simpler Sounds and a Movement
Toward a More Comple ¿ Voice

Sixteen years ago, Mary Daly dared to suggest that the Church is sexist and that Christian women have an uphill struggle.[1] The Christian feminism of the late twentieth century United States was born of the angry and expectant proposal that women could fight for their rights within and beyond the church. Thus, the liberation of women was the crucible in which Christian feminist impulses were revitalized among many otherwise traditional religious women—most of us white—during the late 1960s and early 1970s. Daly's 1968 book and the collection of essays edited by Sarah Bentley Doely[2] were among the first efforts by churchwomen of our generation to signal the value of women's lives in counterpoint to the disvaluation of women in Christian tradition.

While few, if any, of us white women intended to exclude the lives of women of color from our concerns, we simply had not begun to comprehend the extent to which women of different racial/ethnic groups have disparate historical and contemporary experiences of sexism. In proclaiming the centrality of *our* lives to the Christian theological enterprise, we did not realize how loudly we were heralding the centrality and importance of *white* lives in particular. And so we sang with gusto, more or less oblivious to the fact that we were not singing for all women.

A few voices and, in time, an expanding chorus of white Christian women had begun singing the stories of our lives as the arena in which the legitimacy of all Christian theology was to be tested. Our time was simple: we shall be free. We sang of pain and passion, sexuality and friendship, support networks and institutional change. Once isolated from each other, we were becoming sisters and, some of us, lovers. In our ecclesial and educational settings, we were becoming irrepressible agents of reformation. We were proud. We knew it was no sin to be proud. We were right. Our tune was direct and clear and good. We will not forget it.

The import of this early movement among many white Christian women during the last decade and a half should not be underestimated. It is to this day the spark of much of the best theological work being done in this country, because its basic methodological assumption—that theology begins with daily lived experiences—posed a hearty and occasionally effective challenge to the established theological tenets of Euroamerican male Christian academics. We broke away from the assumptions of ecclesial and academic fathers that constructive Christian theology is, by definition, systematic in shape, linear in movement, and dispassionate in ambience.

Close to two decades later, white Christian feminists have come struggling into a theological "place" marked by dissonant and complex movements among us. At issue is still the liberation of *women*—but which women? What about those whose lives and, therefore, theologies are not "like" ours? Women of other races and religions? Women in different economic situations? Those with different kinds of work and choices, or no choice at all?

One of our earliest indictments of patriarchal religion was that male theologians have tended to universalize their experience and faith-claims, thereby trivializing women's insistence that the church is sexist. As Daly suggested, "The difficulty with this approach is that the [universal] words used may be 'true' but when used to avoid confronting the specific problems of sexism they are radically untruthful."[3] But what if our words, the truths we speak, we who are white Christians, serve to "avoid confronting the specific problems" raised by Jewish women, Black women, other women—problems like anti-Semitism, racism, economic exploitation? How do we, or can we, both hold to the truth of our experience and participate in the birth of new truths which can be ours only in relation to the experiences of women whose lives are, in many ways, remarkably different from our own?

Criteria for Assessing Christian Feminism: Consciousness and Solidarity

Thus, in reading Christian feminist literature, I look for signs of the author's awareness, or consciousness, of the problem of injustice and of its dissonance and complexity in the world of women's lives. I look also for movement into solidarity with those whose daily work and relationships may be foreign to the author's first-hand experience.

I have chosen to review five books written by women in the United States. Four of them reflect, each in its own way, interest in the liberation of women from the perspective of white Christian women. The fifth text, which I think must be included in any serious discussion of recent theological resources for white Christian feminists, is a renowned novel by a Black woman whose formal religious affiliation, if any, I do not know. I trust that Alice Walker will not be bewildered by the inclusion of *The Color Purple* in an essay primarily about the Christian feminism being practiced by white women. Perhaps more than any other, her book has inspired the labor of white Christian feminists throughout this and other lands.[4]

As primary texts for review, I have selected, along with *The Color Purple,* Elisabeth Schüssler Fiorenza's luminous work, because it is an exemplary critical effort by a Christian feminist to reconstruct—historically, socially, politically, theologically—the biblical foundation upon which Christian women have been understood and have experienced themselves. Schüssler Fiorenza is "must" reading for any serious student of Christian history or theology interested in whether women have had a constructive past in the church, a past upon which we may construct a creative, redemptive future.

In her most recent book, as in each of its predecessors. Virginia Ramey Mollenkott speaks boldly and compassionately to a broad spectrum of Christian women—that is, to most Christian women, those not wrestling in the web of academic theological concepts and/or not prepared (or willing) to reassess the singular, fundamental, and normative status of scripture as the primary resource of Christian feminism. Mollenkott is an evangelical Christian with a long-standing feminist commitment. An articulate representative of the evangelical tradition, Mollenkott has been too often dismissed by those Christian and other religious feminists who tend to think of themselves as more "radical" than women who actually believe that Jesus was divine and that Paul was inspired. The fact is, if we are related—we who are Christians and, more broadly, we who are religious women—we cannot afford to shut our minds to those whom we perceive to be in a different place—which is, of course, inferior to our own. How utterly masculinist to do so, how imitative of the way the church fathers have dealt with everyone "beneath" them.

Rosemary Radford Ruether's powerful *Sexism and God-Talk* should silence the lingering wail among some male Christian theologians that "feminists have no systematic theology." Rosemary Ruether has produced one, a book valuable and provocative in its scope and precise in its doctrinal attentiveness. It is also potentially dangerous—to the extent that it may be read through the lens of a masculinist mentality which seeks to impose logic and order upon human and divine life, thereby stuffing human experience into the container of "systematics." Ruether is aware of this and seeks to avoid laying herself or us open to such manipulation. But her work, because its far-reaching merits demand serious attention, begs to be studied critically among feminists. For it is our responsibility to see that *Sexism and God-Talk* is not wielded as a weapon against other feminists by those men and women who cannot think theologically unless they begin with God and move in a straight line toward eschatology.

I have included Marjorie Hewitt Suchocki's *God, Christ, Church* as a work being publicized as an implicitly feminist theology. Unlike Walker, Schüssler Fiorenza, Mollenkott, and Ruether, Suchocki has not chosen either women or feminism as her subject. Consider the question posed by John Cobb in his foreword to this book: "What will happen when feminist theologians turn their attention away from the discussion of woman and man and feminine and masculine and join in writing about God and human beings, the church and the wider world?" (p. vii). However banal the suggestion that writing about women and men is, in fact, not "writing about God and human beings," Suchocki's work invites attention to a difficult and increasingly essential question: In what sense can theology be feminist if women's experience is accorded no epistemological privilege?

Alice Walker's book raises a complementary issue: In what sense can feminist fiction, theory, poetry, or drama be theological if its author states no particular or explicit interest in theology as an academic discipline or as a field of inquiry within the bounds of institutional religion? We can move immediately into a response to this question, for it is hard to imagine a more compelling example of feminist consciousness, so critical to feminist theology, than Alice Walker's sensitivity to the dynamics of women's lives in *The Color Purple*.

Feminist Consciousness and the Movement into Solidarity

"When I found out I thought God was white, and a man, I lost interest."[5]

Finding out what we think. That's what consciousness is—not simply thinking but knowing what we think and why, and where it comes from, and what difference it makes. Honest theological thought is generated by consciousness.

In *The Color Purple*, Alice Walker weaves a liberation story through the life and relationships of Celie, as told in her letters to God. Celie is a poor woman bought by Mr. ___ as his girl-wife. She is abused by Mr. ___ and his son, separated from her own infant children and her sister Nettie, stuck—as if it were her lot—in gross relational and economic poverty. Her prayers meet us at the top of almost every page: "Dear God," her letters begin, their every word echoing an interminable lament. Celie's pathos is cemented in an abysmal self-image, itself the construct of her hostile environment, unmitigated by any awareness of what she thinks about her situation. Racial bigotry, alienated labor, the abuse of women and children, the lack of any apparent ways to break free, have bred, in Celie and just about every other character in this book, a passive resignation to coping as best they can with what God has given them. You don't think about it, you just live with it. That is, until Shug Avery comes along.

Shug "got a long pointed nose and a big fleshy mouth. Lips look like black plum. Eyes big, glossy. Feverish. And mean" (p. 42). The woman every man loves and fears, and every woman hates and envies, Shug is Mr. ___'s special lady-friend, and she's ill.

> Even the preacher got his mouth on Shug Avery, now she down. He take her condition for his text. He don't call no name, but he don't have to. Everybody know who he mean. He talk about a strumpet in short skirts,

smoking cigarettes, drinking gin. Singing for money and taking other women's mens. Talk about slut, hussy, heifer and streetcleaner. (p. 40)

Mr. ___ takes her in, has Celie nurse her, and thus initiates the liberation not only of Celie from his violence but also of himself and many others, including Shug, from the brutalizing effects of a loveless world. Celie and Shug "hear each other into speech."[6] Each takes the other seriously as a friend, woman, lover, healer, liberator. Taking women seriously: the first fruits of rising consciousness.

As their relationship deepens, so too does Celie's capacity to know what she thinks about herself, Mr. ___, and everything else. Her letters to God are displaced by letters to and from her long-absent sister Nettie. The abstract gives way to the concrete. And the "old ... tall ... gray-bearded ... white man ... who don't seem to listen to your prayers" (pp. 165–66) begins to give way to a God which "ain't a he or a she, but a it" (p. 167).

Don't look like anything, she say. It ain't a picture show. It ain't something you can look at apart from anything else, including yourself. I believe God is everything, say Shug. Everything that is or ever was or ever will be. And when you feel that, and be happy to feel that, you've found it.... She say, My first step from the old white man was trees. Then air. Then birds. Then other people. But one day when I was sitting quiet and feeling like a motherless child, which I was, it come to me: that feeling of being part of everything, not separate at all. I knew that if I cut a tree, my arm would bleed. And I laughed and I cried and I run all round the house. In fact, when it happen, you can't miss it. It sort of like you know what, she say, grinning and rubbing high up on my thigh.

Shug! I say.

Oh, she say. God love all them feelings. That's some of the best stuff God did.... Listen, God love everything you love— and a mess of stuff you don't. But more than anything else, God love admiration.

You saying God vain? I ast.

Naw, she say. Not vain, just wanting to share a good thing. I think it pisses God off if you walk by the color purple in a field somewhere and don't notice it.

What it do when it pissed off? I ast.

Oh, it make something else. People think pleasing God is all God care about. But any fool living in the world can see it always trying to please us back.

Yeah? I say.

Yeah, she say. It always making little surprises and springing them on us when us least expect.

You mean it want to be loved, just like the bible say.

Yes, Celie, she say. Everything want to be loved. (pp. 167–68)

Alice Walker's consciousness of what goes into the making of a Black woman's liberation carried me, with Celie, Shug, and Mr. ___, not into a visionary realm of idealization but rather into an experience of immersion in the redemptive currents of actual human life in which stirs the hope of the world. It is not that a large sum-total of Celie–Shug relationships can "save the world," but rather that the power born between Celie and Shug, and named by them, is God. And the reader is left with the buoyant expectation that this God—which "gets pissed off if you walk by the color purple in a field and don't notice it"—is the resource of justice for all.

Liberation theologians contend that theology is "the second act," the first being the act of human commitment to liberation from injustice. The problem with this assumption is that, like the traditional Euroamerican theology it is meant to critique, it perpetuates a split between action and theory. Should we maintain that whereas we may find theological implications—the consciousness rising out of real human struggle—in Walker's novel, we must turn to academic theologians for theology per se? Should we assume simply that an Alice Walker provides the story about which a Rosemary Ruether provides the theological meaning?

Or should we try to imagine that, as different as their literary genres may be, both of these women present works laden with theological meaning to the extent that each is imbued with investment in actual human life? If this is true, as I would contend, then it is the author's knowledge of what she thinks about human well-being, and why, and where it has come from, and what difference it makes—that is, the value and meaning of her own perceptions—that gives a work its theological formation, rather than the work's conformity to certain conceptual academic or ecclesial patterns.

And so it is that the intellectual integrity of Ruether's *Sexism and God-Talk* lies not primarily in the logic of its systematic shape. The reader can begin this book with nearly any chapter and find coherence (which is not true of many systematic theologies). Rather, the theological power of this book is rooted in Ruether's transparent desire for the affirmation of female personhood and her knowledge of the damage done to women by the historical streams of Christian misogyny which still flow strong and terribly. The strength of Ruether's consciousness of women's oppression—specifically under the authority of Christian teachings—has carried her over the years into an expansive terrain, in which she sees sisterhood both as a global utopic vision and as the immediate arena of redemptive work, wherever we may be.

> It is not our calling to be concerned about the eternal meaning of our lives, and religion should not make this the focus of its message. Our responsibility is to use our temporal life span to create a just and good community for our generation and for our children. It is in the hands of Holy Wisdom to forge out of our finite struggle truth and being for everlasting life. (p. 258)

Ruether's constructive suggestions, whether about christology, evil, economics, or ecology, are made in sharp contrast to the bulwark of Christian doctrine and practice. She is attempting to demonstrate that Christian feminism can move at once critically and constructively in relation to the dominant tradition. We who are white Christian feminist theologians can do so insofar as we are aware that women's liberation is, necessarily, a fundamental movement in relation to all movements for liberation. Ruether insists that oppressed peoples and other creatures all suffer under Christianity's global impact, and that all have much to gain from a Christian feminist commitment shaped not only by the prophetic principle shared by Jews and Christians, but also by "countercultural" egalitarian movements in Christianity, pagan resources, and modern "post-Christian" resources of liberal, romantic, and Marxist oppositions to certain forms of Christian imperialism (inequality, rationalism, capitalism, respectively).

Throughout her many contributions to Christian feminist theology, Ruether's commitment has been to the radicalizing of Christian faith and practice—to a church re-formed in relation to justice in its many real-life dimensions. In *Sexism and God-Talk*, she explicates this broad-based allegiance as held fast in her faithfulness to God/ess. And she reveals her particular role among us as consciousness-raiser. She writes to and for Christians who are ready to think critically and creatively. We are alerted to be on the lookout. For behind, beneath, or above any Christian doctrine, image, or story lurks something which may do us harm or good....

Elisabeth Schüssler Fiorenza's *In Memory of Her* goes a long way toward showing why Christian women ought not to stake their faith-claims in the dogma of the church. In this historical study of religious and social movements in the early church, Schüssler Fiorenza examines, as if under a microscope, the conflicting strands of scriptural teachings on the male–female relation.

She is aware that "the Christian gospel cannot be proclaimed if the women disciples and what they have done are not remembered" (p. xiv). Her historical research has suggested to her that women were both creative participants in the early movements around the person and memory of Jesus and those who, by the end of the first century, were becoming subjugated under the domination of men in the manner of the Greco-Roman household (which, in the Pastoral Epistles, becomes the "household of God"). Thus, Schüssler Fiorenza's intention in writing is to remember women—not only as the oppressed but also as agents of liberation.

In Memory of Her portrays women and other underclass peoples, such as slaves, as full and lively members of the Jesus movement within Judaism and of its spirit-filled missionary movements. As the young church spread, women's standing was in bold contrast to their inferior status in the wider social order. "The Christian missionary movement thus provided an alternative vision and praxis to that of the dominant society and religion" (p. 251). But, as Schüssler Fiorenza maintains, there was tension.

... the praxis of coequal discipleship between slaves and masters, women and men, Jews and Greeks, Romans and barbarians, rich and poor, young and old brought the Christian community in tension with its social-political environment. This tension engendered by the alternative Christian vision of Gal. 3:28, and not by "enthusiastic excesses," became the occasion for introducing the Greco-Roman patriarchal order into the house church. (p. 279)

A feminist consciousness provides the mill into which Schüssler Fiorenza pours the grist of her historical critical research and her liberation hermeneutic. She concludes that if women know history as ours, and view ourselves as we really have lived—rather than through the androcentric lens of most historical perspectives—we will know our power to "gather as the ekklesia of women, the people of God" (p. 344).

When I speak of the ekklesia of women, I have in mind women of the past and of the present, women who have acted and still act in the power of the life-giving Sophia-Spirit. Such an understanding of catholic sisterhood that spans all ages, nations, and continents does not need to deny our hurt and anger or to cover up the injustice and violence done to women in the name of God and Christ. It ... also does not need to claim salvific powers for women and to narrow its understanding of sisterhood to those women who are the elect and the holy. (p. 350)

In Schüssler Fiorenza's work, we are met by an author's realization of her own situation as one female Christian reaching beyond herself into something larger, broader, more complex: a "catholic sisterhood," itself a resource for global solidarity.

Feminist biblical spirituality must be incarnated in a historical movement of women struggling for liberation. It must be lived in prophetic commitment, compassionate solidarity, consistent resistance, affirmative celebration, and in grassroots organizations of the ekklesia of women. (p. 349)

Stumbling on towards Stronger Solidarity

Racism

Dating back at least as far as the publication of her *Liberation Theology: Human Hope Confronts Christian History and American Power*,[7] Rosemary Ruether's theological movement, like Schüssler Fiorenza's, has been toward solidarity with women and men who suffer injustices, often, at least in part, due to the hostility or apathy of the church. Ruether has never taught an individualistic theology or one intended to speak only to other white, affluent Christian women. *Sexism and God-Talk* is no exception. What distinguishes this new book from her earlier works is its global scope as a book about Christian women in solidarity with each other, with other women, and with men. Ruether paints with large strokes across an ever-expanding canvas of human need. She intends to omit no one, and she goes about as far as any theologian in her efforts toward inclusivity.

She is superb, as ever, in her knowledge of and respect for Jewish religion and history in relation to Christian tradition. And in this latest work, she has come well into an appreciation of wicca and Goddess religions in relation to our own. Her constructive work is suggestive. Ruether's critical work—especially in relation to Christian doctrine and practice—is indispensable to Christian feminism. This major book signals a call to solidarity not only among Christians, but also between and among all people who value human and other created life.

And yet there seems to be a stumbling-block in this book. Ruether can be faulted here for having paid little attention specifically to race as a theological issue. This struck me as a curious slight, given her previously expressed awareness of racism, and I found myself wondering whether Ruether was attempting consciously not to trespass on the prerogatives of women of color to speak for themselves. This would not justify in any case her lack of focus on racism as a problem as central as sexism and classism to a feminist liberation hermeneutic.

Pursuing my own question about how such a justice advocate as Ruether could forego critical attention to racism as a theological issue, I began to realize that, with the exception of Schüssler Fiorenza in her historical explication of the condition of slaves and other marginated people, none of the white authors in this review has accorded racism a central focus in her analysis of what has made us what we are or of what we must now do. At the same time, each indicates her awareness of white supremacy as a devastating force in our common life.

In fact, Ruether and Schüssler Fiorenza go further than many white Christian feminists in articulating their understanding that racism is a feminist concern. For this, we can be glad. But it is difficult for white people to grasp the immediacy of white supremacy as a constant and immediate dilemma which can never be far from the surface of any study which professes to take racism seriously. It is easy for us to overlook white supremacy as we attempt to unravel the fabric of male gender superiority, economic injustice, homophobia, or as we try to comprehend various nuances of "dualism" or "biblical authority."

In relation to this oversight, such resources as *This Bridge Called My Back: Writings of Radical Women of Color*, edited by Cherrie Moraga and Gloria

Anzaldua,[8] become essential to our work. White women need to hear what feminists of color are saying about our books, our words, our omissions.

> The fact is, white wimmin are oppressed; they have been "colonized" by white boys.... Lately, having worked free of the nominal and/or personal control of white boys, white wimmin are desperately reactionary. As a result, they identify with and encourage short-sighted goals and beliefs.... As a reactionary oppressed group, they exhibit a strange kind of political bonding or elitism, where white wimmin are the only safe or valid people to be with; all others are threatening.... that, in part, is why they create "alternatives" for themselves and put up psychological signs saying WHITE WOMEN ONLY.[9]

We white women need to probe our own work, and respond to that of others, with such questions as, In what sense is our work "reactionary"—still hooked into the very theological presuppositions we reject and, in particular, to subtle, unexamined assumptions about human and divine life which may serve to exclude or demean people of color? In what ways do our theological visions "put up psychological signs saying WHITE WOMEN ONLY"? The failure to elaborate racism as a lead-theme in any book about women's liberation is surely such a sign.

Christocentrism

Because Jesus Christ has been proclaimed by Christians as the divine man, churchmen have encouraged each other, understandably, to believe that they have a special relation to God. More special, that is, than anyone else. This is hardly the ground on which to cultivate solidarity with women, Jews, or the vast majority of the human family. For this reason, the most accurate barometer of a white Christian theologian's openness to solidarity is her/his christology.

Schüssler Fiorenza presents Jesus as a Jewish man, in whose ministry "God is experienced as all-inclusive love ... a God of graciousness and goodness who accepts everyone and brings about justice and well-being for everyone without exception" (p. 130). Moreover, Jesus proclaims, "The *basileia* of God is in the midst of you" (Luke 17:21)—given to the impoverished; available in the healing activities of Jesus; and inclusive not only of the poor and the morally destitute ("sinners"), but moreover of social outcasts who, by patriarchal definition, were frequently assumed to be "sinners" (e.g., prostitutes) or who, because they were poor, had to do disreputable work in order to survive (e.g., tax collectors).

For Schüssler Fiorenza, Jesus is inspired by a "solidarity from below," a vision of community inclusive of the poor and the marginal in society.

The "church of the poor" and the "church of women" must be recovered at the same time, if "solidarity from below" is to become a reality for the whole community of Jesus again. As a feminist vision, the *basileia* vision of Jesus calls *all women without exception to wholeness and selfhood, as well as to solidarity with those women who are the impoverished, the maimed, and outcasts of our society and church.* (p. 153; emphasis added)

Jesus' vision and the movement which grew around him—a movement among women and poor men—constitute a call to consciousness and solidarity.

Similarly, Ruether portrays Jesus as a liberating figure.

Implicit in the early Jesus movement is a challenge to religious authority embodied in past revelation and institutionalized in the hands of a privileged group of interpreters. Jesus declares that God has not just spoken in the past but is speaking *now*.... Those of low or marginal status (Jesus and his disciples) speak not simply as interpreters of past traditions but as the direct word of God.... And Jesus does not think of himself as the "last word of God," but points beyond himself to "One who will come."

Thus Jesus restores the sense of God's prophetic and redemptive activity taking place in the present-future, through people's present experiences and the new possibilities disclosed through those experiences. *To encapsulate Jesus himself as God's "last word" and "once-for-all" disclosure of God, located in a remote past and institutionalized in a cast of Christian teachers, is to repudiate the spirit of Jesus and to recapitulate the position against which he himself protests.* (pp. 121–22; emphasis added)

We should not miss the radical implications of the christological vision shared by Ruether and Schüssler Fiorenza in their discussions of Jesus and the Jesus movement. For here is no "male God," nor an individual able to be reified and glorified as the unique and only Son of God. For these women, the focus then and now is *on us*, as participants who are empowered by the same Spirit which moved Jesus and his earlier disciples. This is, in my opinion, the christological basis of our Christian feminist movement into solidarity—with all women and men of all races, religions, economic situations, and nations.[10] ...

... Both Ruether and Schüssler Fiorenza convey acute understanding of the historical relation between the Jewish and Christian religions and of the doctrinal claims on which Christian anti-Semitism has thrived. It is surely no coincidence that, for both of these Christian women, Jesus is a human being who was moved by God, who loved God, and in whose life and work God's liberating acts are perceived to have been abundant. This is a far cry from the triumphalist Christus Rex, before whom every knee shall bow.

Coming full circle back to *The Color Purple,* we have what I read as a testimony to incarnational reality. There need not be any reference to Jesus of Nazareth for a book to spill over with incarnational innuendos, as evidenced by the power human beings share to effect a more just world. The characters in the book seem to reflect their author's passion for a God who casts down the mighty from their thrones and lifts up the poor and brokenhearted. For Alice Walker dedicates her book "to the Spirit.

> Without whose assistance
> Neither this book
> Nor I
> Would have been
> Written."

And on the last page, Walker states simply, "I thank everybody in this book for coming. A. W., author and medium."

Walker presents the movement of women and of God as one movement, thus expanding our christological sensibilities beyond all traditional Christian affirmations—except, if Schüssler Fiorenza is right, those incipient among women and other marginalized people who were first drawn to the Jesus story. The praxis of Christian feminist theology is most fertile whenever and wherever we are able to hear the symphony of multicultural, multicolored sounds and recognize the voices as at once human, female, and divine.

Notes

1. Mary Daly, *The Church and the Second Sex* (New York: Harper & Row, 1968).
2. Sarah Bentley Doely, ed., *Women's Liberation and the Church* (New York: Association Press, 1970).
3. Mary Daly, *Beyond God the Father* (Boston: Beacon Press, 1973), p. 6.
4. There is at least one other recent publication which should be paid serious attention in any attempt to examine significant contributions to Christian feminism. Beverly Wildung Harrison's *Our Right to Choose: Toward a New Ethic of Abortion* (Boston: Beacon Press, 1983) has been cited as "a milestone in feminist ethics ... a gift to secular [and theological] feminists" (Kathryn Pyne Addelson, in *Women's Review of Books* I, no. 8 [May 1984]: 11–12). Having worked closely with Harrison in the creation of this valuable resource, I feel I am not the reviewer to explore its insights, oversights, or relation to other texts. Still, it must be mentioned here, because Harrison is unsurpassed among Christian ethicists/theologians in the consistency and brilliance of her liberation hermeneutics which demand that every feminist and every Christian posture be grounded in a passion for human well-being.
5. Alice Walker, *The Color Purple,* p. 166.

6. Nelle Morton, "The Rising Woman Consciousness in a Male Language Structure," *Andover Newton Quarterly* 12, no. 4, pp. 177–90.
7. New York: Paulist Press, 1972.
8. Watertown, MA: Persephone Press, 1981.
9. Davis Davenport, "The Pathology of Racism: A Conversation with Third World Women, in *This Bridge Called My Back*, pp. 88–89.
10. Cf. my book *The Redemption of God: A Theology of Mutual Relation* (Washington: University Press of America, 1982) and also Susan Thistlewaite's *Metaphors for the Contemporary Church* (New York: Pilgrim Press, 1983), in which she examines the ecclesiological implications of feminist christology.

References

Elisabeth Schüssler Fiorenza, *In Memory of Her: A Feminist Theological Reconstruction of Christian Origins*, New York: Crossroad, 1983.

Virginia Ramey Mollenkott, *The Divine Feminine: The Biblical Imagery of God as Female*, New York: Crossroad, 1983.

Rosemary Radford Ruether, *Sexism and God-Talk: Toward a Feminist Theology*, Boston: Beacon, 1983.

Marjorie Hewitt Suchocki, *God, Christ, Church: A Practical Guide to Process Theology*, New York: Crossroad, 1982.

Alice Walker, *The Color Purple*, New York and London: Harcourt, Brace, Jovanovich, 1982.

Mujerista Theology:
A Challenge to Traditional Theology

Ada María Isasi-Diaz

One of the reviewers of my book *En la Lucha* pointed out that I have spent the last ten years of my life working at elaborating a *mujerista* theology. When I read this, I realized the reviewer was right: the elaboration of *mujerista* theology has been and will continue to be one of my life-projects. Since I know myself to be first and foremost an activist, an activist-theologian, the reason why *mujerista* theology is so important to me is because to do *mujerista* theology is a significant and important way for me to participate in the struggle for liberation, to make a contribution to the struggle of Latinas in the USA.

What is *mujerista* theology? In the first part of this chapter, after a general description of *mujerista* theology, I will explain some of the key characteristics and elements of *mujerista* theology. In the second part I will deal with the challenges that *mujerista* theology presents to traditional theology. So, what is *mujerista* theology?

General Description

To name oneself is one of the most powerful acts a person can do. A name is not just a word by which one is identified. A name also provides the conceptual framework, the point of reference, the mental constructs that are used in thinking, understanding, and relating to a person, an idea, a movement. It is with this in mind that a group of us Latinas[1] who live in the United States and who are keenly aware of how sexism,[2] ethnic prejudice, and economic oppression subjugate Latinas, started to use the term *mujerista* to refer to ourselves and to use *mujerista* theology to refer to the explanations of our faith and its role in our struggle for liberation.[3]

The need for having a name of our own, for inventing the term *mujerista* and investing it with a particular meaning became more and more obvious over the years as Hispanic women attempted to participate in the feminist Anglo-European movement in the United States. Latinas have become suspicious of this movement because of its inability to deal with differences, to share power equally among all those committed to it, to make it possible for Latinas to contribute to the core meanings and understandings of the move-

From *Mujerista Theology: A Theology for the Twenty-first Century*, 1996. Maryknoll, NY: Orbis Books. Reprinted with permission of Orbis Books.

ment, to pay attention to the intersection of racism/ethnic prejudice, classism, and sexism, and because of the seeming rejection of liberation as its goal, having replaced it with limited benefits for some women within present structures, benefits that necessitate some groups of women and men to be oppressed in order for some others to flourish. These serious flaws in the Euro-American feminist movement have led grassroots Latinas to understand "feminism" as having to do with the rights of Euro-American middle-class women, rights many times attained at the expense of Hispanic and other minority women. As the early 1992 national survey conducted by the Ms Foundation in New York City and the Center for Policy Alternatives in Washington, D.C., called the "Women's Voices Project" showed:

> the term feminism proved unattractive ... women of color saying it applied only to white women. The survey shows that, while 32 percent of all women reported they would be likely to join a woman's group devoted to job and educational opportunities, or supporting equal pay, and equal rights for women, substantially fewer reported they would join a "feminist" group devoted to these tasks. Thus we must demonstrate to women that "feminism" *means* devotion to the concerns of women report, or we must find another term for women's activism.[4]

Mujerista is the word we have chosen to name devotion to Latinas' liberation.

A *mujerista* is someone who makes a preferential option for Latina women, for our struggle for liberation.[5] Because the term *mujerista* was developed by a group of us who are theologians and pastoral agents, the initial understandings of the term came from a religious perspective. At present the term is beginning to be used in the other fields such as literature and history. It is also beginning to be used by community organizers working with grassroots Hispanic women. Its meaning, therefore, is being amplified without losing as its core the struggle for the liberation of Latina women.

Mujeristas struggle to liberate ourselves not as individuals but as members of a Hispanic community. We work to build bridges among Latinas/os while denouncing sectarianism and divisive tactics. *Mujeristas* understand that our task is to gather our people's hopes and expectations about justice and peace. Because Christianity, in particular the Latin American inculturation of Roman Catholicism, is an intrinsic part of Hispanic culture, *mujeristas* believe that in Latinas, though not exclusively so, God chooses once again to lay claim to the divine image and likeness made visible from the very beginning in women. *Mujeristas* are called to bring to birth new women and new men — Hispanics willing to work for the good of our people (the "common good") knowing that such work requires the denunciation of all destructive sense of self-abnegation.[6]

Turning to theology specifically, *mujerista* theology, which includes both ethics and systematic theology, is a liberative praxis: reflective action that has as its goal liberation. As a liberative praxis *mujerista* theology is a process of enablement for Latina women which insists on the development of a strong sense of moral agency and clarifies the importance and value of who we are, what we think, and what we do. Second, as a liberative praxis, *mujerista* theology seeks to impact mainline theologies, those theologies which support what is normative in church and, to a large degree, in society — what is normative having been set by non-Hispanics and to the exclusion of Latinas and Latinos, particularly Latinas.

Mujerista theology engages in this two-pronged liberative praxis, first by working to enable Latinas to understand the many oppressive structures that almost completely determine our daily lives. It enables Hispanic women to understand that the goal of our struggle should be not to participate in and to benefit from these structures but to change them radically. In theological and religious language this means that *mujerista* theology helps Latinas discover and affirm the presence of God in the midst of our communities and the revelation of God in our daily lives. Hispanic women must come to understand the reality of structural sin and find ways of combating it because it effectively hides God's ongoing revelation from us and from society at large.

Second, *mujerista* theology insists on and aids Latinas in defining our preferred future: What will a radically different society look like? What will be its values and norms? In theological and religious language this means that *mujerista* theology enables Hispanic women to understand the centrality of eschatology in the life of every Christian. Latinas' preferred future breaks into our present oppression in many different ways. Hispanic women must recognize those eschatological glimpses, rejoice in them, and struggle to make those glimpses become our whole horizon.

Third, *mujerista* theology enables Latinas to understand how much we have already bought into the prevailing systems in society — including the religious systems — and have thus internalized our own oppression. *Mujerista* theology helps Hispanic women to see that radical structural change cannot happen unless radical change takes place in each and every one of us. In theological and religious language this means that *mujerista* theology assists Latinas in the process of conversion, helping us see the reality of sin in our lives. Further, it enables us to understand that to resign ourselves to what others tell us is our lot and to accept suffering and self-effacement is not a virtue.

Notes

1. There is no agreement among Latinas whether to refer to ourselves as "Hispanic women" or as "Latina women." My choosing to use "Latina" is done indiscriminately.
2. In mujerista theology heterosexism is understood to be a distinct element of sexism.

3. It is important to notice that we do *not* use the term *mujerismo* since it can be understood to indicate that Latinas' natural entity is based on being woman when in fact our natural entity as women is based on being human. See Raquel Rodríguez, "La marcha de las mujeres ...," *Pasos*, no. 344 (March–April 1991): 11, n. 6.

4. Linda Williams, "Ending the Silences: The Voices of Women of Color," *Equal Means* 1, no. 4 (Winter 1993): 13.

5. Though the rest of this chapter refers more directly to *mujerista* Latinas, we intend here to make explicit that Latino men as well as men and women from other racial/ethnic groups can also opt to be *mujeristas*.

6. Rosa Marta Zárate Macías, "Canto de mujer," in *Concierto a mi pueblo*, tape produced by Rosa Marta Zárate Macías, P.O. Box 7366, San Bernardino, CA 92411. Much of this description is based on this song composed and interpreted by Rosa Marta in response to several Latinas' insistence in the need for a song that would help to express who they are and what would inspire them in the struggle. For the full text of her song in English and Spanish see Ada María Isasi-Díaz, "*Mujeristas:* A Name of Our Own," *Christian Century* (May 24–31, 1989): 560–62.

Questions for Discussion

1. In what ways do the status and experience of Christian women differ from those of Jewish women? Is it even possible to generalize enough to answer this question?

2. How do the status and opportunities available to Christian women after the first century change from the period of Jesus' life and the following first century?

3. How did the status of Christian women change as a result of the institutionalization and official recognition of Christianity as the dominant religion?

4. What parallels, if any, do you see in the opportunities made available to celibate and/or monastic women in some forms of Christianity and Buddhism?

5. Does monasticism for Catholic women provide resources for women's liberation from sexist or patriarchal oppression?

   • If so, why are women's monastic institutions having such a difficult time surviving today?

   • How does the role of female monasticism in Catholicism compare with the female role in Buddhism?

References and Materials for Further Study

Articles and Books

Aquino, Maria Pilar. 1999. "Christianity: In Latin America and the Caribbean," in Serinity Young, ed., *Encyclopedia of Women and World Religion*. New York: Macmillan Reference.

Bailey, Deborah Ann. 1999. "Christianity: Religious Rites and Practices," in Serinity Young, ed., *Encyclopedia of Women and World Religion*. New York: Macmillan Reference.

Bednarowski, Mary Farrell. 1999. *The Religious Imagination of American Women*. Bloomington: Indiana University Press.

Brock, Rita Nakashima. 1992. *Journeys by Heart: A Christology of Erotic Power*. New York: Crossroad Publishing Co.

Cannon, Katie Geneva. 1989. *Black Womanist Ethics*. Atlanta, GA: Scholars Press.

Cardman, Francine. 1989. "Christianity: Historical Overview from 300 to 1800," in Serinity Young, ed., *Encyclopedia of Women and World Religion*. New York: Macmillan Reference.

Chaves, Mark. 1997 *Ordaining Women: Culture and Conflict in Religious Organizations* Cambridge, MA: Harvard University Press.

Chong, Kelly. 1999. "Fundamentalisms and Patriarchal Gender Politics." *Journal of Women's History*. 10, 4: 55-77. Explores evangelical groups of South Korea for their ideology and politics of gender relations.

Daly, Mary. 1978. *Gyn/Ecology: The Metaethics of Radical Feminism*. Berkeley, CA: Shambala Press.

———. 1975. "The Qualitative Leap Beyond Patriarchal Religion." *Quest* 1,4: 20-40.

———. 1973. *Beyond God the Father: Toward a Philosophy of Women's Liberation* Boston: Beacon Press.

———. 1968. *The Church and the Second Sex*. New York: Harper & Row.

D'Angelo, Mary Rose. 1999. "Christianity: New Testament Canon," in Serinity Young, ed., *Encyclopedia of Women and World Religion*. New York: Macmillan Reference.

Eck, Diana, and Devaki Jain, eds. 1987. *Speaking of Faith: Global Perspectives on Women, Religion, and Social Change*. Philadelphia: New Society Publishers.

Eller, Cynthia. 1993. *In the Lap of the Goddess: The Feminist Spirituality Movement in America*. New York: Crossroads Publishing Company.

Heyward, Carter. 1999. *Touching Our Strength: The Erotic as Power and the Love of God*. San Francisco: Harper & Row.

———. 1985. "An Unfinished Symphony of Liberation: The Radicalization of Christian Feminism Among White U.S. Women." *Journal of Feminist Studies in Religion* 1, 1: 99-118.

———. 1984. *Our Passion for Justice: Images of Power, Sexuality, and Liberation*. New York: The Pilgrim Press.

Isasi-Diaz, Ada Maria. 1996. "Mujerista Theology: A Challenge to Tradtional Theology," in *Mujerista Theology: A Theology for the Twenty-first Century*. Maryknoll, NY: Orbis Books.

———. 1993. *En la Lucha (In the Struggle): A Hispanic Women's Liberation Theology*. Minneapolis, MN: Fortress Press.

Keller, Rosemary. 1999. "Christianity—United States," in Serinity Young, ed., *Encyclopedia of Women in World Religion*. New York: Macmillan Reference.

Kraemer, Ross Shepard, and Mary Rose D'Angelo, eds. 1999. *Women and Christian Origins*. New York: Oxford University Press.

Kraemer, Ross Shepard. 1992. *Her Share of the Blessings: Women's Religions Among Pagans, Jews, and Christians in the Greco-Roman World*. New York: Oxford University Press.

Lorde, Audre. 1981. "An Open Letter to Mary Daly," in Cherrie Moraga and Gloria Anzaldua, eds., *This Bridge Called My Back: Writings by Radical Women of Color*. New York: Kitchen Table Press.

McFague, Sallie. 1987. *Models of God: Theology for an Ecological, Nuclear Age*. Philadelphia: Fortress Press.

Miles, Margaret. 1989. *Carnal Knowing: Female Nakedness and Religious Meaning in the Christian West*. Boston: Beacon Press.

Mooney, Catherine. 1999. "Aposolic Religious Orders and Communities," in Serinity Young, ed., *Encyclopedia of Women and World Religion*. New York: Macmillan Reference.

Orsi, Robert. 1996. *Thank You, St. Jude : Women's Devotion to the Patron Saint of Hopeless Causes*. New Haven, CT: Yale University Press.

Pastis, Jacqueline. 1999. "Christianity: Paul and the Pauline Tradition," in Serinity Young, ed., *Encyclopedia of Women and World Religion*. New York: Macmillan Reference.

Ranke-Heinemann. 1990. *Eunuchs For the Kingdom of Heaven: Women, Sexuality, and the Catholic Church*. New York: Doubleday.

Redmont, Jane. 1999. "Roman Catholicism," in Serinity Young, ed., *Encyclopedia of Women and World Religion*. New York: Macmillan Reference.

Ruether, Rosemary R., ed. 1996. *Women Healing Earth: Third World Women on Ecology, Feminism, and Religion*. Maryknoll, NY: Orbis Books.

———, ed. 1985. *Womanguides: Readings Toward a Feminist Theology*. Boston; Beacon Press.

———. 1983. *Sexism and God-Talk: Toward a Feminist Theology*. Boston: Beacon Press.

———. 1983. "Christianity and Women in the Modern World," in Arvind Sharma, ed., *Today's Woman in World Religions*. Albany: State University of New York Press.

Ruether, Rosemary R., and Rosemary Skinner Keller, eds., 1995. *In Our Own Voices: Four Centuries of American Women's Religious Writing*. New York: HarperCollins.

Russell, Letty, Kwok Pui-Lan, Ada Maria Isasi-Diaz, and Katie Cannon, 1988. *Inheriting Our Mothers' Gardens: Feminist Theology in Third World Perspective*. Philadelphia: Westminster Press, 1988.

Sawyer, Deborah. 1996. "Sisters in Christ or Daughters of Eve?" in *Women and Religion in the First Christian Centuries*. New York: Routledge.

Scaraffia, Lucetta, and Gabriella Zarri, eds. 1999. *Women and Faith: Catholic Religious Life in Italy from Late Antiquity to the Present*. Cambridge, MA: Harvard University Press.

Schüssler Fiorenza, Elisabeth. 1995. *Bread Not Stone*, 2d ed. Boston: Beacon Press.

———. 1989. "In Search of Women's Heritage," in Judith Plaskow and Carol P. Christ, eds., *Weaving the Visions: New Patterns in Feminist Spirituality*. San Francisco: Harper & Row.

Smith, Karen Sue. 1990. "Catholic Women: Two Decades of Change," in Mary Segers, ed., *Church Polity and American Politics: Issues in Contemporary Catholicism*. New York: Garland Publishing, Inc.

Watt, Paul. 1999. "New Buddhist Movements," in Serinity Young, ed., *Encyclopedia of Women and World Religion*. New York: Macmillan Reference.

Weaver, Mary Jo. 1995. *New Catholic Women: A Contemporary Challenge to Traditional Religious Authority*, 2d ed. San Francisco: Harper & Row.

———. 1993. *Springs of Water in a Dry Land: Spiritual Survival for Catholic Women Today*. Boston: Beacon Press.

Welch, Sharon. 1989. *A Feminist Ethic of Risk*. Minneapolis, MN: Fortress Press.

Westerkamp, Marilyn. 1999. *Women and Religion in Early America, 1600–1858: The Puritan and Evangelical Traditions*. New York: Routledge.

Internet Resources

Catholic Network for Women's Equality Web Site:
http://www.sarnia.com/groups/cnwe.
A support and advocacy group for women and men in the Roman Catholic tradition based in Canada.

Catholic Perspective on Women in Society and in the Church Web Site:
http://www.cco.caltech.edu/~newman/women.html.
Links to many articles on women from the perspective of the Catholic Church. Maintained by the Newman Center, a Catholic student center at CalTech.

Christian Resource Index: Women Web Site:
http://ChristianBest.com/index.html.
Collection of links to Web resources supportive of evangelical Christian women.

Christianlesbians.com Web Site:
http://www.geocities.com/WestHollywood/Heights/2685.
Articles, support, chat rooms, and links to related sites for Christian lesbians.

Diotima: Materials for Study of Women and Gender in the Ancient World Web Site:
http://www.stoa.org/diotima/ about.shtml.
An interdisciplinary resource for studying patterns of gender around the ancient Mediterranean world.

Feminist-Theology Web Site:
http://www.jiscmail.ac.uk/lists/feminist-theology.html.
An unmoderated forum for the academic discussion of Jewish and Christian feminist theology. Topics discussed include a feminist critique of traditional ways of doing theology.

Hulda: Feminist Theology Web Site:
http://www.dike.de/hulda/english.html.
Guide to Internet sites relating to Christian and Jewish feminist theology.

The Mary Page Web Site:
http://www.udayton.edu/mary/.
Maintained by the Marian Library/International Marian Research Institute at the University of Dayton in Ohio. An international center of research and study on the role of Mary in Christian life. Page encompasses an extensive range of resources on all aspects of Marion worship, including images, documents, and Web resources.

Sistersnchrist Web Site:
http://www.egroups.com/group/SistersnChrist.
For "born-again" Christian ladies who aim for a deeper walk with the Lord, basically "women who homeschool, allow God to plan our families, dress modestly, and aim to submit to God, and our husbands."

Sister Site Web Site: http://www.geocities.com/Wellesley/1114.
Focuses on "the history and contemporary concerns of Catholic women religious (sisters and nuns)." The list is open to scholars, practitioners, and others interested in these issues.

WATER Web Site: http://www.his.com/~mhunt.
Women's Alliance for Theology, Ethics, and Ritual, a feminist educational center and network of justice-seeking people that began in 1983 as a response to the need for serious theological, ethical, and liturgical development for and by women.

Media Resources

Battle for the Minds. Video, 52 min. New Day Film Library, 1997. Documents the rise of Protestant fundamentalism and its impact on women, especially those in leadership roles.

Faith Even to the Fire. Video, 58 min. Filmakers Library, 1993. U.S. nuns living out a mission of social justice.

God Is Not Through with Me Yet. Video, 27 min. PAACT Productions, 1995. Examines the past and present lives of ordinary, Afro-American Baptist women in Marion County, Florida, including their role in the establishment, management, and support of Baptist churches.

Hildegard von Bingen's Ordo Virtutum. Video, 70 min., color. Films for the Humanities, 1997. The oldest extant Western musical drama written by the medieval mystic and female composer.

Mother Teresa's First Love. Video, 26 mins. Filmakers Library, 1999. Documentary with the last authorized footage of Mother Teresa working with the dying in Calcutta.

The Need to Know: Women and Religion. Video, 47 min., color. Films for the Humanities, 1996. Covers women in early Christianity, the goddess tradition that Christianity supplanted, and Islam's oppression of women.

The Other Side of the Fence: Conversations with a Female Fundamentalist. Video, 28 min. Filmakers Library, 1994.

Religions of the Book: Women Serving Religion. Video, 29 min., color. Films for the Humanities, 1991. Roles of women in traditional and contemporary Christianity, Judaism, and Islam.

The Witches of Salem: the Horror and the Hope. Video, 34 min. Learning Corporation of America, 1986. Dramatization, based on authentic records, of the 1692 witchcraft trials in Salem, Massachusetts.

Yo, la Peor de Todas (I, the Worst of All). Video, 108 min. First Run/Icarus Films, 1990. Historical drama relating the story of Juana Inéz de la Cruz, one of the greatest poets of the Spanish Siglo de Oro and her intimate relationship with the vicereine of her convent at the time of the Inquisition.

Chapter **7**

Women and Islam

Overview

Islam means submission to the will of God, which Muslims believe is specified in the Qur'an, the holy book of the Muslim people. Muslims, the followers of Islam, believe that the Qur'an is the collection of the word of God as transmitted to and recorded by Prophet Muhammad via the Angel Gabriel in the eighth century C.E. Muhammad was born in Arabia in the seventh century and declared himself to be a prophet of God in eighth-century C.E. Mecca, when he recorded the Qur'an. After teaching in Mecca for several years, he received a message from God to move to Medina, and many of his followers accompanied him there in what is known as "the Haj." After his death, Muhammad became known as "the seal of the Prophets," that is, the final prophet of God in a lineage beginning with Adam, and including Moses, Noah, Abraham, Imram, and Jesus, whose message was to correct the errors in God's message that earlier communities had accepted.

As revelation, the Qur'an holds the same status for Muslims that the Hebrew Bible does for Jews and the New Testament does for Christians. Indeed, because Muslims consider their religion to be the culmination of the Judeo-Christian tradition that began with Abraham, much of the material in the Qur'an contains narratives of persons and events from the Bible. Muslims thus consider Jews and Christians to be "people of the book," who were also given God's revelation. However, they believe that this revelation was cor-

249

rupted over time and inaccurately transmitted down through the centuries, so that the Jewish and Christian religions do not accurately embody God's true word. The religion of Islam shares the same roots and the same God as Judaism and Christianity and thus may be considered to be a relative, albeit in some respects a distant one, to these Western monotheistic traditions.

The Qur'an is comprised of 23 books or Surahs, each bearing a different title. The Qur'an's overarching message can be characterized as revealing God's will for humanity to create a just society and institute a variety of social reforms, including in the status of women (see Sonn 1999a, 488). In addition to the Qur'an, other important texts in Islam include the Hadith, a record of everything that the Prophet said and did, and Tafsir, the accompanying scriptural commentary. The notion of Sunna, God's law or tradition as revealed by his prophets and messengers, is based on the Hadith. The Sharia'a, a religiously based secular law derived from a patriarchal reading of the Qur'an and Sunna, is regarded as being of divine origin, and thus irrefutable. Sharia'a governs in several predominantly Islamic countries today. There are now five major schools of law and many different legal codes (Sonn 1999a, 491).

Islam was first established in the Arab countries of the Middle East. It spread early on (c. 639) into Northern Africa when Arab Muslim armies invaded Egypt, and it has now become a major religion in much of Africa, including the southern sub-Saharan regions. The largest number of Muslims in the world now live in Asia, especially India, Afghanistan, Pakistan, Bangladesh, Malaysia and Indonesia. Islam has also been practiced in Eastern and Western Europe, Russia, and the former Soviet Republics since the fifteenth century, and to a lesser extent in North and South America. Islam now encompasses about a billion adherents and is the fastest growing religion worldwide. As with other world religions we have examined, there is tremendous diversity in how Islam is practiced in different countries and regions, based on such factors as the prevailing political and economic institutions, the nationalization of Islam into dominant political institutions, and so forth.

The major split between forms of Islam is between the "Shi-ite" or Shia and "Sunni" sects and relates to succession, since Muhammad did not designate a successor before his death. Sunnis (the majority of Muslims) follow Abu Bakr, one of the earliest converts and the father of Muhammad's youngest wife Aisha, who assumed the highest office of Caliph not long after Muhammad's death. Shi-ite Muslims reject Abu Bakr and believe that Muhammad appointed Ali, his cousin and the husband of his daughter Fatima, as successor. In addition to these more institutionalized forms of Islam is the mystical tradition of Sufism (which tends to be more prominent in Asia). Sufism is generally more personalistic and less legalistic than the other sects of Islam and focuses more on cults of saints and pilgrimages than it does on institutionalized forms of worship.

Despite the regional and ethic differences in Islamic faith and practice, all Muslims are expected to observe the "Five Pillars of Islam." These require professing one's faith in God's oneness and Muhammad as God's prophet, praying five times a day, fasting during the holy month of Ramadan, giving alms, and making a pilgrimage to Mecca at least once in one's lifetime.

Relationship of Female-Gendered and Feminine Images and Symbols to "Real" Women

In contrast to most of the religions we have explored so far, Islam opposes the use of gendered imagery for the divine, based on Muslims' interpretation of God's commandment, recorded by Moses, to forsake idolatry and graven images. Thus, most Islamic art is nonrepresentational. Nonetheless, within a broader interpretation of gender imagery and symbolism, the feminist Islamic scholar Leila Ahmed observes that the study of Islamic discourse regarding women is always partly symbolic (Ahmed 1992, 2). In other words, Islamic discourse about women includes a wider variety of issues and concerns than simply the status of women. It also functions as a "code" for discussing other issues, such as liberation from colonial domination, Islamic nationalism, and so on. Especially in Asia, women have been at the center of the debate about whether to secularize government and society, as in India, or to Islamicize, as in Pakistan and Bangladesh. This has created some confusion about women's appropriate roles in society, as traditional Islamic teaching comes into conflict with modernization and globalization. Thus, interpretations of Qur'anic verses regarding women function not only to regulate women's lives, but also to order Islamic society as a whole through categories based on gender.

Women's Relationship to Islam

Women-Specific or Distinctive Aspects of Islam

The essay by Bouthania Shaaban included in this chapter points out that the first person to believe in the truth of the Prophet Muhammed's teachings was a woman, as was the first person to be martyred for the cause of Islam. Women were also present at the first Acaba conferences where the Islamic state of Yathrib is thought to have been founded. The Prophet himself had 11 wives, some of them simultaneously. The Qur'an recounts that God ordered Muhammad to offer his wives the option of divorcing him, which he did, and that all of them declined the offer. Thus, women were central to the very establishment and growth of the Islamic religion.

As the selection of verses from the Qur'an shows, gender is a central concern of Islam. Many passages relate to women's bodies, their sexuality and reproductive capacities, their sexual morality, how they should behave, how men should behave in relation to them. Marriage, divorce, adultery, and child custody and support are the subjects of several regulations. The text is explicitly written from a male perspective, addressing how men should behave in relation to women.

Relative to the Quran's historical context, however, its teachings regarding women are quite progressive. The Qur'an grants women certain rights which they did not have previously in Arab culture. It created prohibitions on female infanticide and on men inheriting wives from their fathers, raised the age at which females were allowed to marry, and gave women certain property, inheritance, and marital rights they were previously denied. These include provisions for child support and alimony and the right of women to keep their marriage dower and their own earnings as their own property, which provided them with a form of financial independence. The Qur'an also prohibits a husband from divorcing while his wife is pregnant and builds a waiting period of three months into the divorce process to ensure that she is not.

Nonetheless, as the selection of Qur'anic verses included here shows, women are still regarded as lesser than men in certain areas, including divorce, the value of their legal testimony as witnesses, and with respect to their inheritance, property, and marital rights. In addition to what is included in the Qur'an about women, the Hadith and Sharia'a further limit women's rights and status.

As several other religious traditions discussed in this volume teach, menstruation is a kind of pollution. These polluting effects are used as the justification for segregating women, treating them as inferior, and excluding them from the mosque, especially during the period of their menstruation or pregnancy. Menstruating women are also prohibited from praying or touching a Qur'an until their period is over and they have taken the ritual, cleansing bath (see Sonn 1999a, 491). It can also be inferred that women's sexual difference from men altogether is viewed as impure, given the widespread practice of female circumcision in Islamic countries.

In addition, in some Muslim societies, women are kept in *purdah* (hidden, both within the home and/or behind veils), segregated, excluded from paid employment, and from most interaction with the outside world, at least if not accompanied by an adult male. In traditional Islamic practices, the mosques are strictly segregated, with women seated behind the men or in a separate area from the main hall. More conservative schools declare women legally incompetent to contract a marriage (or effect other major decisions in their lives) without the permission of a legal male guardian. They also allow women to be coerced into marriage without their consent by their father or grandfather.

Women, unlike men, are not expected to observe all of the five pillars of Islam regularly. In particular, women are not expected to pray five times a day or to fast, in part because of women's alleged ritual impurity during menstruation. It is also less likely that women will make the pilgrimage to Mecca, or make the annual alms donation (because men generally control the family's finances). Nonetheless, some Muslim women strictly observe all five pillars (see Beck 1999, 494).

Muslim women often perform some religious practices together as a group, which fosters solidarity and opportunities for women to expand their horizons beyond the four walls of their homes. These practices include reciting passages from the Qur'an and Hadith, reciting prayers, making pilgrimages to the local saints' tombs and places where miracles are believed to have occurred, commemorating the births and deaths of saints, holding vow ceremonies in their homes, and mourning the deaths of family and community members before the funeral services, as well as at the cemeteries at ritually significant designated intervals thereafter. In some regions, Muslim women also participate in spirit cults together, either as observers or mediums. Women are the majority of participants in spirit cults, consistent with the belief that women are more closely connected with the spirits than men are. Some other rituals, such as fortune telling, dream interpretation, and divining, which Western cultures might consider to be magic, are regarded by Muslim women as part of their religious practices and observances.

Life-cycle events such as births, puberty, marriage, divorce, and death usually include Islamic related rituals. Although female circumcision is not mentioned in the Qur'an, it is in the Hadith and is accepted by all but one of the schools of Islamic law (see Sonn 1999a, 492). Where female circumcision is practiced, it is believed to be mandated by Islam. In addition, women have responsibility for cleaning, preparing food, and welcoming guests for religious rituals that are performed in the home. Certain religious observances, such as the Feast of Sacrifice (commemorating Abraham's willingness to give up his son at God's command) are important to Muslim women (see Beck 1999, 495).

Gender-Based Segregation and Inequalities

Even given Islam's relatively progressive attitudes toward women (relative to those that prevailed in pre-Muslim Arab countries), because Islam is androcentric and male-biased, Islamic scholars and writers (who have been almost exclusively all men) have most likely ignored the contributions of women who were significant to the development and sustenance of the tradition. The Qur'an states that men are a degree above women (Surah 2: 228), and that "men are in charge of women, because Allah hath made the one of them to excel the other, and because they spend of their property (for the support of women)" (Surah 4:34, quoted in Pickthall 1977, 83). Men have the right to marry up to four wives if they can provide for them all, but women have the right to only one husband. Husbands are granted an almost absolute right to obtain a divorce (see Pickthall 1977), whereas women must petition the courts in order to obtain a divorce (see Badawi 1994, 102, 106). Muslim men can marry a Jewish or Christian woman, whereas Muslim women are not allowed to marry outside of their faith. In addition, the Qur'an accords women's legal testimony only half the value given to men's.

As Beverly Thomas McCloud notes (1991), it is difficult to generalize about the status of women in American Islam. This is in part because most of the Muslims in this country—with the exception of the Nation of Islam and the American Muslim Mission (AMM, the Black Muslims)—immigrated from other cultures in recent generations, and in part because American women convert to Islam for a wide variety of reasons.

The regional and institutional diversity of Islam in America make American Muslims the most diverse of any Muslim community in the world. This diversity means that Muslim practices and beliefs differ significantly regarding women's status and roles, including the extent to which women are allowed to work outside the home, take active roles in the Muslim centers and community life, and interact with members of the non-Muslim community. In addition, social practices of Islam have been influenced by American culture as well and are thus apt to differ from either Islam as practiced in its cultures of origin or from those set forth in the Qur'an. McCloud's essay describes some "ideal types" of African-American women who have converted to Islam and discusses some of the positive as well as the negative consequences of their decisions.

One of the most controversial issues in Islam today concerns the practice of *hijab*, or veiling of women, a practice which predated Islam but was adopted by some Muslim communities. The extent of veiling practices differs widely in different Muslim communities, from a simple headscarf to the full *burqua* or complete covering, which sometimes even covers the eyes (with netting so the woman can see). Political leaders in some predominantly Muslim countries, such as Turkey, have banned *hijab*. Others, in more conservative Islamic countries such as Iran, have mandated it. Shaaban's essay describes Zin al-Din's reasoned opposition to the practice of *hijab* as not authentically called for by the Qur'an. In recent years, however, some highly educated Muslim women have spoken out *in favor* of *hijab*, as a way for women to gain a certain kind of autonomy, independence, and respect as virtuous women that they would not receive if they were not so attired (see Sonn 1999a, 493). In Iran, women voluntarily donned *hijab* and adopted segregation as a form of political protest against perceived imperialism and Western domination in Islamic countries after the overthrow of the Shah in the 1979 revolution (see Tohidi 1991; Darrow 1995; Haddad 1985).

Women's Access to Religious Training and Education and Opportunities for Leadership Roles

In general, women's access to religious education and training is not good anywhere in the Islamic world. However, significant variations exist, depending upon factors such as class, area of residence (urban versus rural), and sectarian differences. Starting with the reform movement that began in the late nineteenth century, there has been more emphasis placed on education for women, but the primary purpose is seen as preparing women to become better mothers and citizens, not for their own empowerment or to expand their opportunities to become leaders or professionals.

As the Shaaban reading informs us, there have been prominent Muslim women military and political leaders, poets and literary critics, medical researchers, and so forth, but their accomplishments have largely been marginalized by male scholars. Today, there are relatively few opportunities for spiritual leadership for women in institutionalized forms of Islamic religious observance. With only a few exceptions, all roles in religious and legal institutions are held by men. A few women in Egypt teach the Qur'an and Hadith, but only to other women. In Indonesia, the Aisyihah movement (named after Muhammad's wife A'isha) enables women to teach other women about Islam, and a few women act as imams (prayer leaders) (Smith 1994). In Turkey, some women have gained unofficial recognition as mullahs (low-ranking religious officials), and in Iran, a few women are recognized as *mojtaheds* (high-ranking religious officials), but in both cases, they are not allowed to have followers (see Bauer 1999, 499). Some women in Jordan have become sheikhs of women's mosques. In Algeria, women are allowed to proselytize on behalf of Islamicists. Outside of institutionalized Islam, however, Muslim women have more opportunities for religious leadership, especially within segregated female groups which worship together.

Well-Known and/or Influential Women in the Tradition

There are several important women in the history of Islam, including Muhammed's wives, especially the first, Khadija Bint Khuwaylid, and his youngest wife (among several) A'isha. Muhammad's daughter Fatima also had a significant role in the early development and teachings of Islam. The Qur'an mentions a number of virtuous women as exemplars of the faith. It, along with the Hadith, includes several narratives relating to women, including the wives of Muhammad and Abraham, Mary, the mother of Jesus, and the mother of Moses. The two latter receive revelations directly from God. Muhammad's wives have a special status in the Qur'an.

Rabi`a al-'Adawiyya al-Qaysiyya (known as Rabi`a of Basra), the subject of Margaret Smith's essay included in this chapter, is revered as one of the earliest and greatest Sufi mystic ascetics in Islam. Although little is known of her life, it is understood that she was born into poverty: the fourth girl (hence her name Rabi`a meaning "fourth") about 717 C.E. in Basra, Iraq. It is thought she was captured after being orphaned and sold into slavery, becoming a flautist. She was apparently freed after her owner observed an enveloping radiance (*sakina*) around her while she was rapt in prayer. She is then believed to have retreated into the desert and begun a life of worship. Rabi`a led a life of poverty, rejecting numerous offers of marriage. She is probably best known for her emphasis on unselfish love for Allah.

Rabi'a's life demonstrates how religious vocations provided women in early Islam with alternatives to domestic lifestyles as wives and mothers. Rabi'a is understood to have made a significant contribution to the development of Sufi doctrine. The excerpts from her biography included here provide a taste of what spiritual life was like for spiritually devoted women in early Islam. (More information about Rabi'a and other well-known Muslim women is included in the Maryam's Net Web site cited in the "For Further Reference" section at the end of this chapter.)

In North Africa, the thirteenth-century woman Lalla 'Aisha Manoubia is regarded as a patron saint of the city of Tunis in Tunisia. Her miraculous works are recorded in hagiographical literature and transmitted in the oral tradition. A nineteenth-century Algerian woman Lalla Zaynab succeeded her father as regional leader of a Sufi order due to a number of factors, including social privilege, educational training, and being regarded by her followers as a saint, mystic, and miracle-worker. Her tomb remains a pilgrimage site to this day (see Clancy-Smith 1999, 502).

The selection by Bouthaina Shaaban discusses women in more recent centuries who were interpretors of the Qur'an. Shaaban notes the roles that women have played in the history of Islamic interpretation, focusing on the thought of one of these, Nazira Zin al-Din, and how her thought has been marginalized by contemporary Islamic scholars.

Changes in the Status of Women

Although the establishment of Islam brought a marked improvement in the status of women, and some women have had increasing opportunities to control their own lives, women in many parts of the Islamic world have continued to occupy a distinctly secondary and segregated status. Since the early twentieth century, Islamic women have established organizations to improve their position in society. These include both secular organizations, such as the Union of Egyptian Women founded in 1923, as well as religious groups, like the Egyptian Muslim Women's Association, founded in 1936 by

Zayna al-Ghazali. Muslim reformers who favor gender equality and equal rights for women have met with mixed success in Islamic regions, being influenced by the levels of education in the populace, the form of government, and whether women's rights are viewed as associated with Western countries, which many Muslims, especially in Arab countries, view with suspicion. Regarding the latter, Islamic nationalistic regimes and independence ("Islamist") movements, such as those of Iran, Iraq, Syria, Lebanon, and the Taliban in Afghanistan, generally advocate restricting women's rights in conformity with a very conservative reading of the Qur'an (see Sonn 1999b, 497).

Under the Taliban, for example, the status of women has declined dramatically. The Taliban are a group of fundamentalist Muslims, originally formed by students opposing corruption and the Soviet invasion of Afghanistan and Pakistan. When they seized power in Afghanistan in 1996, they imposed a fundamentalist Islamic government rule and severely restricted the rights of women. Freedom of religion is restricted severely, and Taliban members vigorously enforce their interpretation of Islamic law.

It is indisputable that the so-called Islamic laws instituted by the Taliban violate women's basic human rights and have instituted a virtual gender apartheid. Women are required to wear full-length shrouds, called *burqa,* that completely cover their bodies, including their faces, wrists, and ankles, whenever they are out in public and risk being beaten when they are not. The denial of women's right to basic freedom of movement includes being discouraged from appearing in public, prohibited from taking buses or taxis unaccompanied by a father or husband, and prevented from obtaining a passport or leaving the country without the authorization of a male relative. Members of the Ministry for the Promotion of Virtues and Suppression of Vice, which was raised to the status of a ministry in May 1999, regularly check passersby to ensure that women are dressed in strict traditional Taliban-approved garb and are not in the company of men who are unrelated to them. Women are also prohibited from voting or holding public office. They are often permitted to go only to hospitals where there are no males present.

Women who resist these highly gender discriminatory laws are beaten. Under principles of male guardianship, husbands are permitted to beat their wives for refusing to do their will. Women accused of offenses like adultery are stoned to death (Waxman 1999, C1). Family honor is central to the structuring of marriage and family life. Women and girls who are suspected of losing their virginity before their wedding night have been killed by male relatives, including brothers and fathers, as "destroyers of family honor." It has been argued that the Taliban's restrictions on women's rights are not strictly Islamic but, rather, use Islam as a way of legitimating or justifying the oppression of women. Even so, some of the Taliban's practices, like male guardianship and inequalities in marital rights, certainly are.

There are a number of contemporary Islamic feminist scholars who are reinterpreting the Qur'an to emphasize its basic message of gender egalitarianism and thereby cast into suspicion the validity of the kinds of oppressive and restrictive interpretations offered by groups like the Taliban. These include Riffat Hassan, Azizah al-Hibri, Zaynab al-Ghazali, and Amina Wadud. From a different angle, women in some Islamic regions in Africa are taking on significant roles as having special powers, which is described in the Hackett essay in the chapter on women and African religion.

The Meaning of the Glorious Koran: An Explanatory Translation

Mohammed Marmaduke Pickthall, trans.

SÛRAH II: The Cow

221. Wed not idolatresses till they believe; for lo! a believing bondwoman is better than an idolatress though she please you; and give not your daughters in marriage to idolaters till they believe, for lo! a believing slave is better than an idolater though he please you. These invite unto the Fire, and Allah inviteth unto the Garden, and unto forgiveness by His grace, and expoundeth thus His revelations to mankind that haply they may remember.

222. They question thee (O Muhammad) concerning menstruation. Say: It is an illness, so let women alone at such times and go not in unto them till they are cleansed. And when they have purified themselves, then go in unto them as Allah hath enjoined upon you. Truly Allah loveth those who turn unto Him, and loveth those who have a care for cleanness.

223. Your women are a tilth for you (to cultivate) so go to your tilth as ye will, and send (good deeds) before you for your souls, and fear Allah, and know that ye will (one day) meet Him. Give glad tidings to believers, (O Muhammad)....

From *The Meaning of the Glorious Koran*, trans. by Mohammed Marmaduke Pickthall, 1963. Reprinted with permission of Routledge, Inc.

226. Those who forswear their wives must wait four months; then, if they change their mind, lo! Allah is Forgiving, Merciful.

227. And if they decide upon divorce (let them remember that) Allah is Hearer, Knower.

228. Women who are divorced shall wait, keeping themselves apart, three (monthly) courses. And it is not lawful for them that they should conceal that which Allah hath created in their wombs if they are believers in Allah and the Last Day. And their husbands would do better to take them back in that case if they desire a reconciliation. And they (women) have rights similar to those (of men) over them in kindness, and men are a degree above them. Allah is Mighty, Wise.

229. Divorce must be pronounced twice and then (a woman) must be retained in honour or released in kindness. And it is not lawful for you that ye take from women aught of that which ye have given them; except (in the case) when both fear that they may not be able to keep within the limits (imposed by) Allah. And if ye fear that they may not be able to keep the limits of Allah, in that case it is no sin for either of them if the woman ransom herself. These are the limits (imposed by) Allah. Transgress them not. For whoso transgresseth Allah's limits: such are wrongdoers.

230. And if he hath divorced her (the third time), then she is not lawful unto him thereafter until she hath wedded another husband. Then if he (the other husband) divorce her it is no sin for both of them that they come together again if they consider that they are able to observe the limits of Allah. These are the limits of Allah. He manifesteth them for people who have knowledge.

231. When ye have divorced women, and they have reached their term, then retain them in kindness or release them in kindness. Retain them not to their hurt so that ye transgress (the limits). He who doeth that hath wronged his soul. Make not the revelations of Allah a laughing-stock (by your behaviour), but remember Allah's grace upon you and that which He hath revealed unto you of the Scripture and of wisdom, whereby He doth exhort you. Observe your duty to Allah and know that Allah is Aware of all things.

232. And when ye have divorced women and they reach their term, place not difficulties in the way of their marrying their husbands if it is agreed between them in kindness. This is an admonition for him among you who believeth in Allah and the Last Day. That is more virtuous for you, and cleaner. Allah knoweth: ye know not.

233. Mothers shall suckle their children for two whole years; (that is) for those who wish to complete the suckling. The duty of feeding and clothing nursing mothers in a seemly manner is upon the father of the child. No one should be charged beyond his capacity. A mother should not be made to suffer because of her child, nor should he to whom the child is born (be made to suffer) because of his child. And on the (father's) heir is incumbent the like of that (which was incumbent on the father). If they desire to wean the child by

mutual consent and (after) consultation, it is no sin for them; and if ye wish to give your children out to nurse, it is no sin for you, provided that ye pay what is due from you in kindness. Observe your duty to Allah, and know that Allah is Seer of what ye do.

234. Such of you as die and leave behind them wives, they (the wives) shall wait, keeping themselves apart, four months and ten days. And when they reach the term (prescribed for them) then there is no sin for you in aught that they may do with themselves in decency. Allah is Informed of what ye do.

235. There is no sin for you in that which ye proclaim or hide in your minds concerning your troth with women. Allah knoweth that ye will re-member them. But plight not your troth with women except by uttering a recognised form of words. And do not consummate the marriage until (the term) prescribed is run. Know that Allah knoweth what is in your minds, so beware of Him; and know that Allah is Forgiving, Clement.

236. It is no sin for you if ye divorce women while yet ye have not touched them, nor appointed unto them a portion. Provide for them, the rich according to his means, and the straitened according to his means, a fair pro-vision. (This is) a bounden duty for those who do good.

237. If ye divorce them before ye have touched them and ye have ap-pointed unto them a portion, then (pay the) half of that which ye appointed, unless they (the women) agree to forgo it, or he agreeth to forgo it in whose hand is the marriage tie.1 To forgo is nearer to piety. And forget not kindness among yourselves. Allah is Seer of what ye do....

240. (In the case of) those of you who are about to die and leave behind them wives, they should bequeath unto their wives a provision for the year without turning them out, but if they go out (of their own accord) there is no sin for you in that which they do of themselves within their rights. Allah is Mighty, Wise.

241. For divorced women a provision in kindness: a duty for those who ward off (evil)....

SÛRAH IV:
Women: Revealed at Al-Madînah

In the name of Allah the Beneficent, the Merciful.

1. O mankind! Be careful of your duty to your Lord Who created you from a single soul and from it created its mate and from them twain hath spread abroad a multitude of men and women. Be careful of your duty to-ward Allah in Whom ye claim (your rights) of one another, and toward the wombs (that bare you). Lo! Allah hath been a Watcher over you.

2. Give unto orphans their wealth. Exchange not the good for the bad (in your management thereof) nor absorb their wealth into your own wealth. Lo! that would be a great sin.

3. And if ye fear that ye will not deal fairly by the orphans, marry of the women, who seem good to you, two or three or four; and if ye fear that ye cannot do justice (to so many) then one (only) or (the captives) that your right hands possess. Thus it is more likely that ye will not do injustice.

4. And give unto the women, (whom ye marry) free gift of their marriage portions; but if they of their own accord remit unto you a part thereof, then ye are welcome to absorb it (in your wealth).

5. Give not unto the foolish (what is in) your (keeping of their) wealth, which Allah hath given you to maintain; but feed and clothe them from it, and speak kindly unto them.

6. Prove orphans till they reach the marriageable age; then, if ye find them of sound judgement, deliver over unto them their fortune; and devour it not by squandering and in haste lest they should grow up. Whoso (of the guardians) is rich, let him abstain generously (from taking of the property of orphans); and whoso is poor let him take thereof in reason (for his guardianship). And when ye deliver up their fortune unto orphans, have (the transaction) witnessed in their presence. Allah sufficeth as a Reckoner.

7. Unto the men (of a family) belongeth a share of that which parents and near kindred leave, and unto the women a share of that which parents and near kindred leave, whether it be little or much—a legal share.

8. And when kinsfolk and orphans and the needy are present at the division (of the heritage), bestow on them therefrom and speak kindly unto them.

9. And let those fear (in their behaviour toward orphans) who if they left behind them weak offspring would be afraid for them. So let them mind their duty to Allah, and speak justly.

10. Lo! Those who devour the wealth of orphans wrongfully, they do but swallow fire into their bellies, and they will be exposed to burning flame.

11. Allah chargeth you concerning (the provision for) your children: to the male the equivalent of the portion of two females, and if there be women more than two, then theirs is two-thirds of the inheritance, and if there be one (only) then the half. And to his2 parents a sixth of the inheritance, if he have a son; and if he have no son and his parents are his heirs, then to his mother appertaineth the third; and if he have brethren, then to his mother appertaineth the sixth, after any legacy he may have bequeathed, or debt (hath been paid). Your parents or your children: Ye know not which of them is nearer unto you in usefulness. It is an injunction from Allah. Lo! Allah is Knower, Wise.

12. And unto you belongeth a half of that which your wives leave, if they have no child; but if they have a child then unto you the fourth of that which they leave, after any legacy they may have bequeathed, or debt (they may have contracted, hath been paid). And unto them belongeth the fourth of that which ye leave if ye have no child, but if ye have a child then the eighth of that which ye leave, after any legacy ye may have bequeathed, or

debt (ye may have contracted, hath been paid). And if a man or a woman have a distant heir (having left neither parent nor child), and he (or she) have a brother or a sister (only on the mother's side) then to each of them twain (the brother and the sister) the sixth, and if they be more than two, then they shall be sharers in the third, after any legacy that may have been bequeathed or debt (contracted) not injuring (the heirs by willing away more than a third of the heritage) hath been paid. A commandment from Allah. Allah is Knower, Indulgent....

15. As for those of your women who are guilty of lewdness, call to witness four of you against them. And if they testify (to the truth of the allegation) then confine them to the houses until death take them or (until) Allah appoint for them a way (through new legislation).3...

18. The forgiveness is not for those who do ill deeds until, when death attendeth upon one of them, he saith: Lo! I repent now; nor yet for those who die while they are disbelievers. For such We have prepared a painful doom.

19. O ye who believe! It is not lawful for you forcibly to inherit the women (of your deceased kinsmen), nor (that) ye should put constraint upon them that ye may take away a part of that which ye have given them, unless they be guilty of flagrant lewdness. But consort with them in kindness, for if ye hate them it may happen that ye hate a thing wherein Allah hath placed much good.

20. And if ye wish to exchange one wife for another and ye have given unto one of them a sum of money (however great), take nothing from it. Would ye take it by the way of calumny and open wrong?

21. How can ye take it (back) after one of you hath gone in unto the other, and they have taken a strong pledge from you?

22. And marry not those women whom your fathers married, except what hath already happened (of that nature) in the past. Lo! it was ever lewdness and abomination, and an evil way.

23. Forbidden unto you are your mothers, and your daughters, and your sisters, and your father's sisters, and your mother's sisters, and your brother's daughters and your sister's daughters, and your foster-mothers, and your foster-sisters, and your mothers-in-law, and your step-daughters who are under your protection (born) of your women unto whom ye have gone in—but if ye have not gone in unto them, then it is no sin for you (to marry their daughters)—and the wives of your sons who (spring) from your own loins. And (it is forbidden unto you) that ye should have two sisters together, except what hath already happened (of that nature) in the past. Lo! Allah is ever Forgiving, Merciful.

24. And all married women (are forbidden unto you save those (captives) whom your right hands possess. It is a decree of Allah for you. Lawful unto you are all beyond those mentioned, so that ye seek them with your wealth in honest wedlock, not debauchery. And those of whom ye seek con-

tent (by marrying them), give unto them their portions as a duty. And there is no sin for you in what ye do by mutual agreement after the duty (hath been done). Lo! Allah is ever Knower, Wise.

25. And whoso is not able to afford to marry free, believing women, let them marry from the believing maids whom your right hands possess. Allah knoweth best (concerning) your faith. Ye (proceed) one from another;4 so wed them by permission of their folk, and give unto them their portions in kindness, they being honest, not debauched nor of loose conduct. And if when they are honourably married they commit lewdness they shall incur the half of the punishment (prescribed) for free women (in that case). This is for him among you who feareth to commit sin. But to have patience would be better for you. Allah is Forgiving, Merciful....

32. And covet not the thing in which Allah hath made some of you excel others. Unto men a fortune from that which they have earned, and unto women a fortune from that which they have earned. (Envy not one another) but ask Allah of His bounty. Lo! Allah is ever Knower of all things....

34. Men are in charge of women, because Allah hath made the one of them to excel the other, and because they spend of their property (for the support of women). So good women are the obedient, guarding in secret that which Allah hath guarded. As for those from whom ye fear rebellion, admonish them and banish them to beds apart, and scourge them. Then if they obey you, seek not a way against them. Lo! Allah is ever High Exalted, Great.

35. And if ye fear a breach between them twain (the man and wife), appoint an arbiter from his folk and an arbiter from her folk. If they desire amendment Allah will make them of one mind. Lo! Allah is ever Knower, Aware....

43. O ye who believe! Draw not near unto prayer when ye are drunken, till ye know that which ye utter, nor when ye are polluted, save when journeying upon the road, till ye have bathed. And if ye be ill, or on a journey, or one of you cometh from the closet, or ye have touched women, and ye find not water, then go to high clean soil and rub your faces and your hands (therewith). Lo! Allah is Benign, Forgiving....

124. And whoso doeth good works, whether of male or female, and he (or she) is a believer, such will enter paradise and they will not be wronged the dint in a date-stone....

127. They consult thee concerning women. Say: Allah giveth you decree concerning them, and the Scripture which hath been recited unto you (giveth decree), concerning female orphans unto whom ye give not that which is ordained for them though ye desire to marry them, and (concerning) the weak among children, and that ye should deal justly with orphans. Whatever good ye do, lo! Allah is ever Aware of it.

128. If a woman feareth ill-treatment from her husband, or desertion, it is no sin for them twain if they make terms of peace between themselves.

Peace is better. But greed hath been made present in the minds (of men). If ye do good and keep from evil, lo! Allah is ever Informed of what ye do.

129. Ye will not be able to deal equally between (your) wives, however much ye wish (to do so). But turn not altogether away (from one), leaving her as in suspense. If ye do good and keep from evil, lo! Allah is ever Forgiving, Merciful.

130. But if they separate, Allah will compensate each out of His abundance. Allah is ever All-Embracing, All-Knowing....

177. They ask thee for a pronouncement. Say: Allah hath pronounced for you concerning distant kindred. If a man die childless and he have a sister, hers is half the heritage, and he would have inherited from her had she died childless. And if there be two sisters, then theirs are two-thirds of the heritage, and if they be brethren, men and women, unto the male is the equivalent of the share of two females. Allah expoundeth unto you, so that ye err not. Allah is Knower of all things.

SÛRAH V:
The Table Spread

5. This day are (all) good things made lawful for you. The food of those who have received the Scripture is lawful for you, and your food is lawful for them. And so are the virtuous women of the believers and the virtuous women of those who received the Scripture before you (lawful for you) when ye give them their marriage portions and live with them in honour, not in fornication, nor taking them as secret concubines. Whoso denieth the faith, his work is vain and he will be among the losers in the Hereafter.

6. O ye who believe! When ye rise up for prayer, wash your faces, and your hands up to the elbows, and lightly rub your heads and (wash) your feet up to the ankles. And if ye are unclean, purify yourselves. And if ye are sick or on a journey, or one of you cometh from the closet, or ye have had contact with women, and ye find not water, then go to clean, high ground and rub your faces and your hands with some of it. Allah would not place a burden on you, but He would purify you and would perfect His grace upon you, that ye may give thanks.

SÛRAH XXIV

An-Nûr, "Light," takes its name from vv. 35–40, descriptive of the Light of God as it should shine in the homes of believers, the greater part of the Sûrah being legislation for the purifying of home life. All its verses were revealed at

Al-Madînah. Tradition says that vv. 11–20 relate to the slanderers of Ayeshah in connection with an incident which occurred in the fifth year of the Hijrah when the Prophet was returning from the campaign against the Banî'l-Mustaliq, Ayeshah, having been left behind on a march, and found and brought back by a young soldier who let her mount his camel and himself led the camel. A weaker tradition places the revelation of vv. 1–10 as late as the ninth year of the Hijrah.

The period of revelation is the fifth and sixth years of the Hijrah.

LIGHT:
Revealed at Al-Madînah

In the name of Allah, the Beneficent, the Merciful.

2. The adulterer and the adulteress, scourge ye each one of them (with) a hundred stripes. And let not pity for the twain withhold you from obedience to Allah, if ye believe in Allah and the Last Day. And let a party of believers witness their punishment.

3. The adulterer shall not marry save an adulteress or an idolatress, and the adulteress none shall marry save an adulterer or an idolater. All that is forbidden unto believers.

4. And those who accuse honourable women but bring not four witnesses, scourge them (with) eighty stripes and never (afterward) accept their testimony—They indeed are evil-doers.

5. Save those who afterward repent and make amends. (For such) lo! Allah is Forgiving, Merciful.

6. As for those who accuse their wives but have no witnesses except themselves; let the testimony of one of them be four testimonies, (swearing) by Allah that he is of those who speak the truth;

7. And yet a fifth, invoking the curse of Allah on him if he is of those who lie.

8. And it shall avert the punishment from her if she bear witness before Allah four times that the thing he saith is indeed false,

9. And a fifth (time) that the wrath of Allah be upon her if he speaketh truth....

23. Lo! as for those who traduce virtuous, believing women (who are) careless, cursed are they in the world and the Hereafter. Theirs will be an awful doom....

26. Vile women are for vile men, and vile men for vile women. Good women are for good men, and good men for good women; such are innocent of that which people say: For them is pardon and a bountiful provision.

27. O ye who believe! Enter not houses other than your own without first announcing your presence and invoking peace upon the folk thereof. That is better for you, that ye may be heedful....

30. Tell the believing men to lower their gaze and be modest. That is purer for them. Lo! Allah is Aware of what they do.

31. And tell the believing women to lower their gaze and be modest, and to display of their adornment only that which is apparent, and to draw their veils over their bosoms, and not to reveal their adornment save to their own husbands or fathers or husbands' fathers, or their sons or their husbands' sons, or their brothers or their brothers' sons or sisters' sons, or their women, or their slaves, or male attendants who lack vigour, or children who know naught of women's nakedness. And let them not stamp their feet so as to reveal what they hide of their adornment. And turn unto Allah together, O believers, in order that ye may succeed.

32. And marry such of you as are solitary and the pious of your slaves and maid-servants. If they be poor, Allah will enrich them of His bounty. Allah is of ample means, Aware.

33. And let those who cannot find a match keep chaste till Allah give them independence by His grace. And such of your slaves as seek a writing (of emancipation), write it for them if ye are aware of aught of good in them, and bestow upon them of the wealth of Allah which He hath bestowed upon you. Force not your slave-girls to whoredom that ye may seek enjoyment of the life of the world, if they would preserve their chastity. And if one force them, then (unto them), after their compulsion, Lo! Allah will be Forgiving, Merciful.

Sûrah XXXIII:
The Clans: Revealed at Al-Madînah

4. Allah hath not assigned unto any man two hearts within his body, nor hath he made your wives whom ye declare (to be your mothers) your mothers,5 nor hath he made those whom ye claim (to be your sons) your sons. This is but a saying of your mouths. But Allah sayeth the truth and He soweth the way.

5. Proclaim their real parentage. That will be more equitable in the sight of Allah. And if ye know not their fathers, then (they are) your brethren in the faith, and your clients. And there is no sin for you in the mistakes that ye make unintentionally, but what your hearts purpose (that will be a sin for you). Allah is Forgiving, Merciful.

6. The Prophet is closer to the believers than their selves, and his wives are (as) their mothers. And the owners of kinship are closer one to another in the ordinance of Allah than (other) believers and the fugitives (who fled from Mecca), except that ye should do kindness to your friends.6 This is written in the Book (of nature)....

28. O Prophet! Say unto thy wives: If ye desire the world's life and its adornment, come! I will content you and will release you with a fair release.

29. But if ye desire Allah and His messenger and the abode of the Hereafter, then lo! Allah hath prepared for the good among you an immense reward.

30. O ye wives of the Prophet! Whosoever of you committeth manifest lewdness, the punishment for her will be doubled, and that is easy for Allah.

31. And whosoever of you is submissive unto Allah and His messenger and doeth right, We shall give her reward twice over, and We have prepared for her a rich provision.

32. O ye wives of the Prophet! Ye are not like any other women. If ye keep your duty (to Allah), then be not soft of speech, lest he in whose heart is a disease aspire (to you), but utter customary speech.

33. And stay in your houses. Bedizen not yourselves with the bedizenment of the Time of Ignorance. Be regular in prayer, and pay the poor-due, and obey Allah and His messenger. Allah's wish is but to remove uncleanness far from you, O Folk of the Household, and cleanse you with a thorough cleansing.

34. And bear in mind that which is recited in your houses of the revelations of Allah and wisdom. Lo! Allah is Subtile, Aware.

35. Lo! men who surrender unto Allah, and women who surrender, and men who believe and women who believe, and men who obey and women who obey, and men who speak the truth and women who speak the truth, and men who persevere (in righteousness) and women who persevere, and men who are humble and women who are humble, and men who give alms and women who give alms, and men who fast and women who fast, and men who guard their modesty and women who guard (their modesty), and men who remember Allah much and women who remember— Allah hath prepared for them forgiveness and a vast reward.

36. And it becometh not a believing man or a believing woman, when Allah and His messenger have decided an affair (for them), that they should (after that) claim any say in their affair; and whoso is rebellious to Allah and His messenger, he verily goeth astray in error manifest.

37. And when thou saidst unto him on whom Allah hath conferred favour and thou hast conferred favour: Keep thy wife to thyself, and fear Allah. And thou didst hide in thy mind that which Allah was to bring to light, and thou didst fear mankind whereas Allah had a better right that thou shouldst fear Him. So when Zeyd had performed the necessary formality (of divorce) from her, We gave her unto thee in marriage, so that (henceforth) there may be no sin for believers in respect of wives of their adopted sons, when the latter have performed the necessary formality (of release) from them. The commandment of Allah must be fulfilled....

49. O ye who believe! If ye wed believing women and divorce them before ye have touched them, then there is no period that ye should reckon. But content them and release them handsomely.

50. O Prophet! Lo! We have made lawful unto thee thy wives unto whom thou hast paid their dowries, and those whom thy right hand posses-

seth of those whom Allah hath given thee as spoils of war, and the daughters of thine uncle on the father's side and the daughters of thine aunts on the father's side, and the daughters of thine uncles on the mother's side and the daughters of thine aunts on the mother's side who emigrated with thee, and a believing woman if she give herself unto the Prophet and the Prophet desire to ask her in marriage—a privilege for thee only, not for the (rest of) believers—We are aware of that which We enjoined upon them concerning their wives and those whom their right hands possess—that thou mayst be free from blame, for Allah is Forgiving, Merciful.

51. Thou canst defer whom thou wilt of them and receive unto thee whom thou wilt, and whomsoever thou desirest of those whom thou hast set aside (temporarily), it is no sin for thee (to receive her again); that is better; that they may be comforted and not grieve, and may all be pleased with what thou givest them. Allah knoweth what is in your hearts (O men) and Allah is Forgiving, Clement.

52. It is not allowed thee to take (other) women henceforth, nor that thou shouldst change them for other wives even though their beauty pleased thee, save those whom thy right hand possesseth. And Allah is Watcher over all things.

53. O ye who believe! Enter not the dwellings of the Prophet for a meal without waiting for the proper time, unless permission be granted you. But if ye are invited, enter, and, when your meal is ended, then disperse. Linger not for conversation, Lo! that would cause annoyance to the Prophet, and he would be shy of (asking) you (to go); but Allah is not shy of the truth. And when ye ask of them (the wives of the Prophet) anything, ask it of them from behind a curtain. That is purer for your hearts and for their hearts. And it is not for you to cause annoyance to the messenger of Allah, nor that ye should ever marry his wives after him. Lo! that in Allah's sight would be an enormity.

54. Whether ye divulge a thing or keep it hidden, lo! Allah is ever Knower of all things.

55. It is no sin for them (thy wives) (to converse freely) with their fathers, or their sons, or their brothers, or their brothers' sons, or the sons of their sisters or of their own women, or their slaves. O women! Keep your duty to Allah. Lo! Allah is Witness over all things....

58. And those who malign believing men and believing women undeservedly, they bear the guilt of slander and manifest sin.

59. O Prophet! Tell thy wives and thy daughters and the women of the believers to draw their cloaks close round them (when they go abroad). That will be better, that so they may be recognised and not annoyed. Allah is ever Forgiving, Merciful....

73. So Allah punisheth hypocritical men and hypocritical women, and idolatrous men and idolatrous women. But Allah pardoneth believing men and believing women, and Allah is Forgiving, Merciful.

SÛRAH LX:
She Who Is to Be Examined

10. O ye who believe! When believing women come unto you as fugitives, examine them. Allah is best aware of their faith. Then, if ye know them for true believers, send them not back unto the disbelievers. They are not lawful for the disbelievers, nor are the disbelievers lawful for them. And give the disbelievers that which they have spent (upon them). And it is no sin for you to marry such women when ye have given them their dues. And hold not to the ties of disbelieving women; and ask for (the return of) that which ye have spent; and let the disbelievers ask for that which they have spent. That is the judgement of Allah. He judgeth between you. Allah is Knower, Wise.

11. And if any of your wives have gone from you unto the disbelievers and afterward ye have your turn (of triumph), then give unto those whose wives have gone the like of that which they have spent, and keep your duty to Allah in whom ye are believers.

12. O Prophet! If believing women come unto thee, taking oath of allegiance unto thee that they will ascribe nothing as partner unto Allah, and will neither steal nor commit adultery nor kill their children, nor produce any lie that they have devised between their hands and feet, nor disobey thee in what is right, then accept their allegiance and ask Allah to forgive them. Lo! Allah is Forgiving, Merciful....

Sûrah LXV:
Divorce: Revealed at Al-Madînah

In the name of Allah, the Beneficent, the Merciful.

1. O Prophet! When ye (men) put away women, put them away for their (legal) period and reckon the period, and keep your duty to Allah, your Lord. Expel them not from their houses nor let them go forth unless they commit open immorality. Such are the limits (imposed by) Allah; and whoso transgresseth Allah's limits, he verily wrongeth his soul. Thou knowest not: it may be that Allah will afterward bring some new thing to pass.

2. Then, when they have reached their term, take them back in kindness or part from them in kindness, and call to witness two just men among you, and keep your testimony upright for Allah. Whoso believeth in Allah and the Last Day is exhorted to act thus. And whosoever keepeth his duty to Allah, Allah will appoint a way out for him,

3. And will provide for him from (a quarter) whence he hath no expectation. And whosoever putteth his trust in Allah, He will suffice him. Lo! Allah bringeth His command to pass. Allah hath set a measure for all things.

4. And for such of your women as despair of menstruation, if ye doubt, their period (of waiting) shall be three months, along with those who have it

not. And for those with child, their period shall be till they bring forth their burden. And whosoever keepeth his duty to Allah, He maketh his course easy for him.

5. That is the commandment of Allah which He revealeth unto you. And whoso keepeth his duty to Allah, He will remit from him his evil deeds and magnify reward for him.

6. Lodge them where ye dwell, according to your wealth, and harass them not so as to straiten life for them. And if they are with child, then spend for them till they bring forth their burden. Then, if they give suck for you, give them their due payment and consult together in kindness; but if ye make difficulties for one another, then let some other woman give suck for him (the father of the child).

Notes

1. *i.e.* the bridegroom.
2. The deceased.
3. See XXIV, 2–10.
4. This expression, which recurs in the Koran, is a reminder to men that women are of the same human status as themselves.
5. The Prophet had ordained brotherhood between individuals of the Ansâr (Muslims of Al-Madînah) and the Muhâjirîn (fugitives from Mecca) a brotherhood which was closer than kinship by blood. This verse abolished such brotherhood, in so far as inheritance was concerned.
6. The reference is to a custom of the pagan Arabs by which a man could put away his wife by merely saying: "Thy back is as my mother's back for me."

Rabi'a the Mystic and Her Fellow-Saints in Islam

Margaret Smith

Part One / Chapter I /
Rabi'a al-'Adawiyya: Her Birth and Early Years

In the history of Islam, the woman saint made her appearance at a very early period, and in the evolution of the cult of saints by Muslims, the dignity of saintship was conferred on women as much as on men. As far as rank among the "friends of God" was concerned, there was complete equality between the sexes.

It was the development of mysticism (Sufism) within Islam, which gave women their great opportunity to attain the rank of sainthood. The goal of the Sufi's quest was union with the Divine, and the Sufi seeker after God, having renounced this world and its attractions, being purged of Self and its desires, inflamed with a passion of love to God, journeyed ever onward, looking towards his final purpose, through the life of illumination, with its ecstasies and raptures, and the higher life of contemplation, until at last he achieved the heavenly gnosis and attained to the Vision of God, in which the lover might become one with the Beloved, and abide in Him for ever.

Such a conception of the relations between the saint and his Lord left no room for the distinction of sex. In the spiritual life there could be "neither male nor female." All whom God had called to be saints could attain, by following the Path, to union with Himself, and all who attained, would have their royal rank, as spiritual beings, in the world to come.

Attar, to prove that saintship may be found in a woman as naturally as in a man, says:

> The holy prophets have laid it down that "God does not look upon your outward forms." It is not the outward form that matters, but the inner purpose of the heart, as the Prophet said, "The people are assembled (on the Day of Judgment) according to the purposes of their hearts." ... So also 'Abbas of Tus said that when on the Day of Resurrection the summons goes forth, "O men," the first person to set foot in

From Elizabeth Warnock Fernea and Basima Qattan Bezirgan, eds. 1977. *Middle Eastern Muslim Women Speak*. Austin: University of Texas, pp. 37–45. Reprinted with permission of University of Texas Press.

that class of men (i.e. those who are to enter Paradise) will be Mary, upon whom be peace.... The true explanation of this fact (that women count for as much as men among the saints) is that wherever these people, the Sufis, are, they have no separate existence in the Unity of God. In the Unity, what remains of the existence of "I" or "thou"? So how can "man" or "woman" continue to be? So too, Abu 'Ali Farmadhi said, "Prophecy is the essence, the very being, of power and sublimity. Superiority and inferiority do not exist in it. Undoubtedly saintship is of the same type."

So the title of saint was bestowed upon women equally with men, and since Islam has no order of priesthood and no priestly caste, there was nothing to prevent a woman reaching the highest religious rank in the hierarchy of Muslim saints. Some theologians even name the Lady Fatima, daughter of the Prophet, as the first *Qutb* or spiritual head of the Sufi fellowship. Below the *Qutb* were four *'Awtad'*, from whose ranks his successor was chosen, and below them, in the next rank of the hierarchy, were forty *'Abdal'* or Substitutes, who are described as being the pivot of the world and the foundation and support of the affairs of men. Jami relates how someone was asked, "How many are the 'Abdal'?" and he answered, "Forty souls," and when asked why he did not say "Forty men," his reply was, "There have been women among them." The biographies of the Muslim saints, such as those compiled by Abu Nu'aym, Farid al-Din 'Attar, Ibn al-Jawzi, Jami and Ibn Khallikan and many others, are full of the mention of women Sufis, their saintly lives, their good deeds, and their miracles. The influence which these women saints exercised both during their lives and after their deaths, is perhaps best proved by the fact that Muslim theologians, opposed to the Sufi movement, denounce also these women saints and the worship known to be given to them.

The high position attained by the women Sufis is attested further by the fact that the Sufis themselves give to a woman the first place among the earliest Muhammadan mystics and have chosen her to be the representative of the first development of mysticism in Islam.

This was the saintly Rabi'a, a freedwoman of the Al-'Atik, a tribe of Qays b. 'Adi, from which she was known as al-'Adawiyya or al-Qaysiyya, and also as al-Basriyya, from her birth-place: of whom a modern writer says, "Rabi'a is the saint par excellence of the Sunnite hagiography." Her biographer 'Attar speaks of her as

That one set apart in the seclusion of holiness, that woman veiled with the veil of religious sincerity, that one on fire with love and longing, that one enamoured of the desire to approach her Lord and be consumed in His glory, that woman who lost herself in union with the Divine, that one accepted by men as a second spotless Mary—Rabi'a al-'Adawiyya, may God have mercy upon her. If anyone were to say, "Why have you made mention of her in the class of men?" I should say … "God does not look upon the outward forms…. If it is allowable to accept two thirds of our faith from 'A'isha the Trustworthy, it is also allowable to accept religious benefit from one of her handmaids [i.e. Rabi'a]. When a woman walks in the way of God like a man, she cannot be called a woman."

A later biographer, al-Munawi, says of her:

> Rabi'a al-'Adawiyya al-Qaysiyya of Basra, was at the head of the women disciples and the chief of the women ascetics, of those who observed the sacred law, who were God-fearing and zealous … and she was one of those who were pre-eminent and experienced in grace and goodness.

He gives the names of several well-known women saints and goes on to say, "She was the most famous among them, of great devotion and conspicuous in worship, and of perfect purity and asceticism."

Unfortunately there is no writer very near her own time to give us her biography, and for an account of her early life we can find material only in the *Memoir of the Saints* of 'Attar, already mentioned, who lived more than four hundred years after Rabi'a. Much of what he tells of her must be regarded as purely legendary. Yet though the legends which surround Rabi'a's name may not, and in many cases certainly do not, correspond to historic facts, at least they give some idea of her personality and shew the estimation in which she was held by those who lived after her and had heard of her fame.

She was born probably about A.H. 95 or 99 (= A.D. 717) in Basra, where she spent the greater part of her life.

Born into the poorest of homes, according to 'Attar (though a modern writer says she belonged to one of the noble families of Basra), miraculous events were reputed to have taken place even at the time of her birth. 'Attar tells us that on the night of her birth there was no oil in the house, no lamp nor swaddling clothes in which to wrap the new-born child. Her father already had three daughters, and so she was called Rabi'a (= the fourth). The mother asked her husband to go and ask for oil for the lamp from a neighbour, but he had made a vow that he would never ask anything of a creature (*i.e.* as a true Sufi he would depend only upon God to supply his needs), and so he came back without it. Having fallen asleep in great distress at the lack of provision for the child, he dreamt that the Prophet Muhammad appeared to him in his sleep and said, "Do not be sorrowful, for this daughter who is born is a great saint, whose intercession will be desired by seventy thousand of my community." The Prophet said further:

Tomorrow send a letter to 'Isa Zadhan, Amir of Basra, reminding him that every night he is wont to pray one hundred prayers to me and on Friday night four hundred, but this Friday night he has neglected me, and as a penance (tell him) that he must give you four hundred *dinars*, lawfully acquired.

Rabi'a's father awoke, weeping; he rose up, wrote the letter as directed and sent it to the Amir through the latter's chamberlain. The Amir, when he had read the letter said:

Give two thousand *dinars* to the poor as a thank-offering, because the prophet had me in mind, and four hundred *dinars* to that Shaykh and say to him that I desire that he should come before me that I may see him, but it is not fitting that such a person as he is should come to me, but I will come and rub my beard on his threshold.

But in spite of this event of good augury, 'Attar relates that misfortunes fell upon the family, and when Rabi'a was a little older, her mother and father died and she was left an orphan. A famine occurred in Basra and the sisters were scattered. One day, when Rabi'a was walking abroad, an evil-minded man saw her and seized upon her and sold her as a slave for six *dirhams* and the man who bought her made her work hard. One day a stranger (one who might not look at her unveiled) approached her. Rabi'a fled to avoid him and slipped on the road and dislocated her wrist. She bowed her face in the dust, and said, "O Lord, I am a stranger and without mother or father, an orphan and a slave and I have fallen into bondage and my wrist is injured, (yet) I am not grieved by this, only (I desire) to satisfy Thee. I would fain know if Thou art satisfied (with me) or not." She heard a voice saying, "Be not sorrowful, for on the day of Resurrection thy rank shall be such that those who are nearest to God in Heaven shall envy thee."

After this Rabi'a returned to her master's house and continually fasted in the daytime and carried out her appointed tasks and in the service of God she was standing on her feet till the day. One night her master awoke from sleep and looked down through a window of the house and saw Rabi'a, whose head was bowed in worship, and she was saying, "O my Lord, Thou knowest that the desire of my heart is to obey Thee, and that the light of my eye is in the service of Thy court. If the matter rested with me, I should not cease for one hour from Thy service, but Thou hast made me subject to a creature." While she was still praying, he saw a lamp above her head, suspended without a chain, and the whole house was illuminated by the rays from that light. This enveloping radiance or *sakina* (derived from the Hebrew Shekina = the cloud of glory indicating the presence of God) of the Muslim saint, corresponding to the halo of the Christian saint, is frequently mentioned in the biographies of the Sufis.

Rabi'a's master, when he saw that strange sight, was afraid and rose up and returned to his own place and sat pondering until day came. When the day dawned, he called Rabi'a and spoke kindly to her and set her free. Rabi'a asked for leave to go away; so he gave her leave, and she left that place and journeyed into the desert. Afterwards she left the desert and obtained for herself a cell and for a time was engaged in devotional worship there. According to one account, Rabi'a at first followed the calling of a flute player, which would be consistent with a state of slavery. Then she became converted and built a place of retreat, where she occupied herself with works of piety.

Among other stories related of this period of her life, is one telling how she purposed performing the pilgrimage to Mecca and set her face towards the desert; she had an ass with her to carry her baggage, and in the heart of the desert the ass died. Some people (in the caravan) said to her, "Let us carry thy baggage." She said, "Go on your way, for I am not dependent upon you (for help)," *i.e.* she placed her trust in God and not in His creatures.

So the people went on and Rabi'a remained alone, and bowing her head, she said, "O my God, do kings deal thus with a woman, a stranger and weak? Thou art calling me to Thine own house (the Ka'ba), but in the midst of the way Thou hast suffered mine ass to die and Thou hast left me alone in the desert."

She had hardly completed her prayer, when the ass stirred and got up. Rabi'a put her baggage on it and went on her way. The narrator of this story said that some time afterwards he saw that same little ass being sold in the bazaar.

Another story tells us how she went into the desert for a few days and prayed, "O my Lord, my heart is perplexed, whither shall I go? I am but a clod of earth and that house (the Ka'ba) is only a stone to me. Shew Thyself (to me) in this very place." So she prayed until God Most High, without any medium, spoke directly within her heart, saying, "O Rabi'a ... when Moses desired to see My Face, I cast a few particles of My Glory upon the mountain (Sinai) and it was rent into forty pieces. Be content here with My Name."

It is told how another time she was on her way to Mecca, and when half-way there she saw the Ka'ba coming to meet her and she said, "It is the Lord of the house whom I need, what have I to do with the house? I need to meet with Him Who said, 'Whoso approaches Me by a span's length I will approach him by the length of a cubit.' The Ka'ba which I see has no power over me; what joy does the beauty of the Ka'ba bring to me?"

In connection with this legend, which indicates how highly favoured by God Rabi'a was, in the eyes of her biographers, it is related that Ibrahim b. Adham spent fourteen years making his way to the Ka'ba, because in every place of prayer he performed two *raka's*, and at last when he arrived at the Ka'ba, he did not see it.

He said, "Alas, what has happened? It may be that some injury has overtaken my eyes." An unseen voice said, "No harm has befallen your eyes,

but the Ka'ba has gone to meet a woman, who is approaching this place."
Ibrahim was seized with jealousy, and said, "O indeed, who is this?" He ran
and saw Rabi'a arriving and the Ka'ba was back in its own place. When
Ibrahim saw that, he said, "O Rabi'a, what is this disturbance and trouble
and burden which thou hast brought into the world?" She said, "I have not
brought disturbance into the world, it is you who have disturbed the world,
because you delayed fourteen years in arriving at the Ka'ba. He said "Yes I
have spent fourteen years in crossing the desert (because I was engaged) in
prayer." Rabi'a, said, "You traversed it in ritual prayer (*namaz*) but I with personal supplication (*niyaz*)." Then, having performed the pilgrimage, she returned to Basra and occupied herself with works of devotion.

For these early years only legends are available, but they give us a clear
idea of a woman renouncing the world and its attractions and giving up her
life to the service of God, the first step on the mystic Way to be trodden by the
Sufi saint.

Chapter II /
Rabi'a's Choice of Celibacy: Her Associates

Rabi'a al-'Adawiyya received many offers of marriage, but rejected them all,
feeling that in the celibate life only could she pursue her quest unhindered.
Among those who sought her hand in marriage was 'Abd al-Wahid b. Zayd,
who was renowned for his asceticism and the sanctity of his life, a theologian
and a preacher and an advocate of solitude for those who sought the way to
God; the reputed writer of verses declaring that

> The Ways are various, the Way to the Truth is one,
> Those who travel on the way of Truth must keep themselves apart.

He was the founder of one of the first monastic communities near
Basra, and died in A.D. 793. Rabi'a did not welcome his offer but shunned
him with the greatest loathing, and said to him, "O sensual one, seek another
sensual like thyself. Hast thou seen any sign of desire in me?"

Another who sought her hand was Muhammad b. Sulayman
al-Hashimi, the 'Abbasid Amir of Basra from A.H. 145, who died in A.H. 172.
He offered a dowry of a hundred thousand *dinars* and wrote to Rabi'a that he
had an income of ten thousand *dinars* a month and that he would bestow it
all on her, but she wrote back, "It does not please me that you should be my
slave and that all you possess should be mine, or that you should distract me
from God for a single moment."

Another account of this offer says that the governor wrote to the people
of Basra asking them to find him a wife, and they agreed upon Rabi'a, and
when he wrote to her expressing his wishes, her reply was as follows:

Renunciation of this world means peace, while desire for it brings sorrow. Curb your desires and control yourself and do not let others control you, but let them share your inheritance and the anxiety of the age. As for yourself, give your mind to the day of death; but as for me, God can give me all you offer and even double it. It does not please me to be distracted from Him for a single moment. So farewell.

Another story tells how Hasan of Basra, with whom the legends persistently associate her (though he died more than seventy years before her death), and others are also said to have come to Rabi'a, urging her to take a husband, and to choose from among the Sufis of Basra whom she would. She replied, "Yes, willingly. Who is the most learned of you, that I may marry him?" They said, "Hasan of Basra," so she said to him, "If you can give me the answer to four questions, I will be your wife." He said, "Ask, and if God permit, I will answer you."

She said then, "What will the Judge of the world say when I die? That I have come out of the world a Muslim or an unbeliever?"

Hasan answered, "This is among the hidden things, which are known only to God Most High."

Then she said, "When I am put in the grave and Munkar and Nakir question me, shall I be able to answer them (satisfactorily) or not?" He replied, "This also is hidden."

She said next, "When the people are assembled at the Resurrection and the books are distributed, and some are given their book in the right hand and some in the left, shall I be given mine in my right hand or my left?" He could only say, "This also is among the hidden things."

Finally she asked, "When mankind is summoned (on the Day of Judgment), some to Paradise and some to Hell, in which of the two groups shall I be?" He answered as before, "This, too, is hidden, and none knows what is hidden save God, His is the glory and majesty."

Then she said to him, "Since this is so, and I have these four questions with which to concern myself, how should I need a husband, with whom to be occupied?"

She is said to have emphasized her refusal with the following beautiful lines, but they cannot be attributed to her with any certainty:

My peace, O my brothers, is in solitude,
And my Beloved is with me alway,
For His love I can find no substitute,
And His love is the test for me among mortal beings,
When-e'er His Beauty I may contemplate,
He is my "mihrab," towards Him is my "qibla"
If I die of love, before completing satisfaction,
Alas, for my anxiety in the world, alas for my distress,

O Healer (of souls) the heart feeds upon its desire,
The striving after union with Thee has healed my soul,
O my Joy and my Life abidingly,
Thou wast the source of my life and from Thee also came my ecstacy.
I have separated myself from all created beings,
My hope is for union with Thee, for that is the goal of my desire.

This story is given in more than one account, and though chronologically it is almost impossible that Hasan of Basra should be the suitor in the case, it is possible that it refers to some other offer of marriage.

Another legend also gives an account of an offer said to have been made by Hasan of Basra, in which the same feeling is evident in Rabi'a's answer. Hasan is reputed to have said, "I desire that we should marry and be betrothed." Her reply was:

The contract of marriage is for those who have a phenomenal existence (*i.e.* who are concerned with the affairs of this material world). Here (*i.e.* in my case) existence has ceased, since I have ceased to exist and have passed out of Self. My existence is in Him, and I am altogether His. I am in the shadow of His command. The marriage contract must be asked for from Him, not from me.

So, like her Christian sisters in the life of sanctity, Rabi'a espoused a heavenly Bridegroom and turned her back on earthly marriage even with one of her own intimates and companions on the Way....

The Muted Voices
of Women Interpreters

Bouthaina Shaaban

There are very few women interpreters in the history of Islam because women are seen to be the subject of the Islamic *shari'a* and not its legislators. Yet even the few interpreters who have appeared during the long history of Islam have been kept at the periphery, their views never allowed to influence Islamic legislation. Moreover, even men interpreters who were open-minded about women were marginalized and, in some cases, found their authority questioned. In this chapter I shall discuss the contribution to Islam of Muslim women interpreters, the concurrence between their views and the views of later men interpreters, and the deliberate marginalization of their thought by contemporary Islamists. I will focus on Nazira Zin al-Din as one of the more serious and knowledgeable Muslim women scholars of our time.

The first person to believe the message of the Prophet and to become a Muslim was Muhammad's wife Khadija Bint Khuwaylid, of whom the Prophet said: 'She believed when people did not, and believed me when others did not, and consoled me with her money when I was abandoned by others.'[1] The first martyr for the Islamic cause was a woman (Summiyya). Women attended the first and the second Aqaba Conferences (Bay'at al-Aqaba al-Awla wa'l-Thaniyya) believed to have founded the Islamic state in Yathrib.[2]

The first Muslim woman whose views have been important to Muslims throughout Islamic history was Aisha, wife of the Prophet. Muhammad's contemporaries, among them both the *muhajerun* (emigrants who followed him from Mecca) and the *ansar* (those who helped the Prophet in Medina) considered Aisha a source of religious rules and an expert on issues of Islamic legislation. When she was mentioned to Ata Bin Abi Rabah, he said: 'Aisha was the most knowledgeable Muslim and had the best opinion in public affairs; she related 2210 sayings of the prophet Muhammad among which are 170 which have been approved and Bukhari took sayings from them.'[3] In *Arab Women in Jahiliya and Islam*, Abdol Sir Afifi writes: 'Muslim women scholars are known for their honesty in relating *hadith* and for their objectivity, which have rendered them free of intellectual suspicion, the things that most men were not fortunate enough to have.' In *Mizan al-I'tidal* (The Scales of Moderation), al-Hafez al-Zahabi (died 748 IE, 1347 CE) a

From Mahnaz Afkhami, ed. 1995. *Faith and Freedom: Women's Human Rights in the Muslim World.* London: I.B. Tauris, pp. 61–77. Reprinted with permission of I.B. Tauris.

renowned Muslim authority on *hadith*, points to four thousand suspect Muslim *hadith* tellers and then adds: 'I have not known of any woman who was accused of falsifying *hadith*. To this we add, that from the time of Aisha, the mother of believers, until the time of al-Zahabi the sayings of the prophet Muhammad were not kept or related by anyone as they were kept in the hearts of women and related by them.'[4]

The wives and women relatives of the prophet Muhammad were not an exception in their age. Many women were scholars and teachers.[5] Muhammad Bin Sa'id mentions over 700 women who related *hadith* from the prophet Muhammad or from the *muhajirun* and *ansar*. Men scholars and pillars of Islam quoted these women.[6] Thus Asma Bint Yazid bin al-Sakan al-Ansariyya is known to have related 81 sayings from the prophet Muhammad and her uncle Mahmud Bin Amr al-Ansari and Abu Sufian and others reported and quoted her. She is also known to have been a woman of science and a defender of women's rights. It is reported that she led a delegation of women to the Prophet Muhammad and said to him 'I am the envoy of women to you. God has sent you to both men and women. We believed in you and in your God, but we as women are confined to our homes, satisfying your desires and carrying your children while you men go out to fight, and go to *haj* and lead holy wars for the sake of God. When one of you goes to the battle field we keep your money for you, weave your clothes and bring up your children. Do we deserve to share your wages?'[7] The Prophet Muhammad acknowledged that she represented women, and he answered her and the women who stood behind her.

Muslim women assumed political power as well as literary authority. They became queens, warriors, doctors, poets, and literary critics. Many won reputations for valor in battle and received praise from the Prophet and his followers. Clearly, the role of women was not confined to encouraging men and treating their wounds; they also played an active part in defending their tribe and their cause. Ismat al-Din, known as Shajarat al-Dur, was the first woman in Islam to assume a throne in her own right. Her husband, King Sala al-Din, died during the crusaders' invasion of Egypt. She continued to issue military and operational orders, keeping the news of his death secret for over two months to avoid undermining the morale of the troops. She found a man named Swab al-Suhayla who forged her husband's handwriting so well that no one doubted that the orders were issued by the king himself. She drew up plans, encouraged soldiers and instructed officers to lead the battle against the crusaders, during which King Louis IX of France (Saint Louis) was captured, making Shajarat al-Dur's victory final. Once the battle was over and victory secured, Shajarat al-Dur announced her husband's death, gave him a royal funeral, and openly assumed the throne. Shajarat al-Dur was mentioned in Friday prayers and money was coined in her name.[8] She was known as a 'knowledgeable queen who is deeply informed of matters, big and small. People felt optimistic during her rule and the poor enjoyed her good deeds. Her government was not authoritarian and she would not make a decision until she convened a council of consultants and listened to the opinions of her ministers and advisers.'[9] Women have also ruled in other Muslim countries. In Yemen there was more than one queen after the fifth/tenth century. The best known among them, Queen Orpha (died 484/1090) assumed total political authority which included planning and executing wars. In the thirteenth century many women were top leaders in Islamic countries, among them Sultana Radia in Delhi and Turkan Khatun, Safwat al-Din Malik Khatun, Sati Bik Khan and Tendo in Central Asia. In the same century, queens ruled Indonesia for 24 years without interruption and carried names such as 'Taj al-Alam' (The Crown of the World), and 'Nur al-Alam' (The Light of the World).

Muslim women were poets and literary critics. First among such critics is Sukayna Bint al-Husayn who was the ultimate judge of poetic production in her time. Poets travelled long distances in order to recite their poetry and obtain her judgement, which could affect the future course of a poetic career.[10] Aisha Bint Talha followed in the steps of Sukayna, meeting with poets and men of letters. Amra al-Jamihiya from Beni Jumah met with poets and story tellers at her home, listened to them, and judged their literary production.[11] Women also played an important role in medicine for which Arabs were renowned. They practiced in Baghdad, Qurtaba, and other cities in Iraq and Andalus.[12] However, their names and their contributions in different fields still await proper recording and authoritative documentation. The information, scattered in books, journals, and newspapers, has not been classified properly in archives and therefore is not yet a part of the mainstream historiography of Islam. Indeed, more often than not, the role of women in Muslim history has been marginalized and obscured, sometimes totally reversed, depending on the whims of men scholars.

Nazira Zin Al-Din and Textual Interpreters

'As women have the right to participate in public governing they also have the explicit right to participate in Qur'anic interpretation and explanation. Women are better qualified than men to interpret the Qur'anic Verses speaking of their rights and duties because everyone is better equipped to understand his or her right and duty,'[13] writes Nazira Zin al-Din in *al-Fatat wa'l-shiukh*. Nazira Zin al-Din is the most serious and knowledgeable of the women Muslim scholars and interpreters to date. She is the daughter of Shaykh Sa'id Zin al-Din, a judge and the first president of the court of appeal in Lebanon in the 1920s. She was encouraged by her father to study. She tried to understand why Muslim women at the time were kept at home wrapped in darkness that covered not only their bodies but also their minds. The answer was that Islam was responsible. She studied the Qur'an and *hadith* and arrived at her own conclusions regarding the position of women in Islam. Although she was only 20 years of age when her books were published, her work is a significant source of reference on the relations between men and women in Islam. Very little is known about her personal life except that she is from a Druzi (Shi'i) sect. Her conclusions showed that Islam is not the reason behind the inferior status of women. The main reason is the gender-biased interpretation of the Qur'anic text by men of religion. When her first book was published, men of religion announced their stand against Zin al-Din and started distributing pamphlets against her; they incited demonstrations against the book and threatened the owners of bookshops who carried it. They accused her of atheism and treason. Her answers were sober, based on logic and clear evidence.

Nazira Zin al-Din made a thorough study of the Qur'anic texts and *hadith* concerning women, their rights, and their duties. Her two books, *al-Sufur wa'l-hijab*[14] and *al-Fatat wa'l-shiukh*, are perhaps the best scholarly studies available of Islamic texts and their interpretations dealing with women. Both are controversial, but the first is more so because it touches on the most sensitive issue in contemporary Islam, namely *hijab*.

In the introduction to *al-Sufur wa'l-hijab*, Nazira Zin al-Din writes that although she had always been interested in women's rights, what prompted her to write this book were the incidents in Damascus in the summer of 1927, in which Muslim women were deprived of their freedom and prevented from going out without *hijab*. 'I took my pen trying to give vent to the pain I feel in a brief lecture,' Zin al-Din says, 'but I could not stop writing and my pen had to follow in the trace of my injured self until the lecture became lectures too long to be delivered or attended.' In this book, Zin al-Din starts from the premise that she is a Muslim woman who believes in God, in his Prophet Muhammad, and in the holy Qur'an, and that all her arguments are informed by those beliefs.

According to Zin al-Din, the Islamic *shari'a* is not what this or that Muslim scholar says, but what is in the Qur'an and in the *hadith*. She argues that men have drawn up laws without the slightest participation by women. Yet even major interpreters of Islam such as Baydawi, al-Nusufi, and Tabari did not agree on the meaning of the Qur'anic text in such matters as geography, history, and astronomy, or, for that matter, on rituals and appropriate behavior, one should, therefore, go back to the Qur'an and the *sunna* to attain knowledge on all religious matters. She writes:

> When I started preparing my defence of women, I studied the works of interpreters and legislators but found no consensus among them on any subject; rather, every time I came across an opinion, I found other opinions that were different or even contradictory. As for the *aya(s)* concerning *hijab*, I found over ten interpretations, none of them in harmony or even agreement with the others as if each scholar wanted to support

what he saw and none of the interpretations was based on clear evidence.[15]

Zin al-Din argues that Islam is based on freedom of thought, will, speech, and action, and that no Muslim has authority over another Muslim in matters of religion, mind, and will. She cites many verses from the Qur'an to show that God did not want even his Prophet to watch over the deeds or misdeeds of Muslims: 'He who obeys the Apostle, obeys God; But if any turn away, We have not sent thee To watch Over their evil deeds' (*Sura al-Nisa'*, *Aya* 80). God also said, addressing his Apostle: 'If it had been God's Plan, they would not have taken False gods: but We Made thee not one To watch over their doings, Nor art thou set Over them to dispose of their affairs' (*Sura al-An'am, Aya* 107). And then in another *sura*: 'Therefore do thou give Admonition, for thou art One to admonish. Thou art not one To manage (men's) affairs' (*Sura al-Gashiya, Aya* 21–22). Zin al-Din then argues that if God did not allow the Prophet Muhammad to watch over people's deeds, how do other Muslims assume for themselves such a privilege? Through well-chosen and well-placed quotations from the Qur'an and *hadith*, Zin al-Din establishes that Islam is the religion of freedom and that Muslims are only accountable to their God. The claims of some Islamists to be the custodians of Islamic practices are therefore against the very spirit of Islam. The Prophet was also instructed to 'Invite all to the Way of thy Lord with wisdom And beautiful preaching; And argue with them In ways that are best And most gracious: For thy Lord knoweth best, Who have strayed from His Path' (*Sura al-Nahl, Aya* 125). God also said: 'And dispute ye not With the People of the Book, Except with means better (Than mere disputation), unless It be with those of them Who inflict wrong (and injury): But say, 'We believe In the Revelation which has come down to us and in that Which came down to you' (*Sura al-Ankabut, Aya* 46).

Through these citations and many similar ones, Zin al-Din argues that the question of belief or non-belief and the question of carrying out the instructions of Islam are matters between God and the individual. No one on earth, not even God's apostle, is responsible for those who believe or those who do not, and no measures should be taken against those who refuse to be Muslims. Only logical arguments should be used, and used kindly; true belief should stem from the heart and generate a feeling of satisfaction and inner peace, for 'If it had been thy Lord's Will, They would all have believed, All who are on earth. Wilt thou then compel mankind Against their will, to believe!' (*Sura Yunus, Aya* 99). In an *aya* that bears no possible other interpretation, God says 'Let there be no compulsion in religion: Truth stands out clear from Error' (*Sura al-Baqara, Aya* 256). In citing these and many other similar *ayas* from the Qur'an, Zin al-Din establishes that Muslims are responsible only to their God and that no authority on earth has the right to be God's representative, especially as God's Apostle was not allowed to watch over the deeds of Muslims. She convincingly argues that this is a lesson to all Muslims that no one on earth, not even the Prophet Muhammad, is authorized by God to punish people for their lack of faith, as all Muslims are free in will and thought; it follows, then, that Muslim women are free. The problem lies with the laws legislated in the name of the Islamic *shari'a*; laws that are in total contradiction to the spirit of Islam. She complains that the practices of some religious authorities violate Islam and God's *shari'a*; 'It is a great shame that some Muslim local authorities dare to disobey the words of God and impose constraints on the freedom of Muslim women in towns, while non-Muslim women in towns and Muslim women in the countryside enjoy their full freedom.'[16]

There is no basis in the Qur'anic text for the idea that men are better than women. God prefers the most pious regardless of gender: 'O mankind! We created You from a single (pair) Of a male and female, And made you into Nations and tribes that Ye may know each other (Not that ye may despise Each other). Verily The most honored of you In the sight of God Is (he who is) the most Righteous of you, And God has full knowledge And is well acquainted (With all things)' (*Sura al-Hujurat, Aya* 13). God also stated in the Qur'an: 'O mankind! reverence Your Guardian Lord, Who created you From a single Person, Created, of like nature, His mate, and from them twain Scattered (like seeds) Countless men and women' (*Sura al-Nisa', Aya* 1). Again it is stated in the Qur'an 'It is He Who hath Produced you From a single person' (*Sura al-An'am, Aya* 98).

Zin al-Din attributes the idea that men are superior to women to the state of servitude to which women have been reduced throughout the ages. She draws a parallel with slavery: 'That was the case of each nation reduced into slavery and of each people deprived of their freedom. No slave has ever excelled before gaining his freedom because the injustice imposed on him exhausts the powers of his mind and prevents its effects from emerging.'[17] Women's inferior social status has nothing to do with their mind or religion. Was the inequality that prevailed between the serf and the master the result of the former's shortcomings? There is not a single *aya* that grants men a degree over women in either mind or religion: 'If any one do deeds Of righteousness, Be they Male or Female And have faith, They will enter Heaven, and not the least injustice Will be done to them' (*Sura al-Nisa', Aya* 124).

Zin al-Din's advocacy against the veil does not aim at depriving women of their status as mothers, nor does she wish to lower their status to that of mere imitators of men. Her advocacy is prompted by her belief that 'knowledge rather than ignorance preserves women's dignity and morality.'[18] She cites Muslim scholars, including Shaykh Muhammad Abduh, Shaykh Badr al-Din al-Na'sani, Shaykh Yusuf al-Faqih, Shaykh Jamal al-Din al-Afghani, Muhyi' Din al-Arabi and Shaykh Mustafa al-Ghalayini, who decried the distortion of the *hadith* and insisted that Islam does not accept judgment without evidence and clear proof. Those authorities insisted that we only follow what God Himself has stated in the Qur'anic text and what his Apostle has explained.'[19]

Zin al-Din divides her evidence against *hijab* into two parts: intellectual and religious. She first cites intellectual and historical arguments contending that *hijab* encourages immorality rather than morality and decent behaviour. Masking identity is an obvious incentive for wrongdoing: 'Can't men see that thieves and murderers mask their true identities in order to have the nerve to commit crimes?'[20] She explains that 'fear of social disgrace is one of the strongest imperatives that restrain people from wrong doing. Why do men deny women this important imperative?'[21] She goes on to ask 'How could serfdom be an incentive to morality? Only if darkness could be the source of light and death the cause of life and annihilation the reason for existence!' Zin al-Din stipulates that the morality of the self and the cleanness of the conscience are far better than the morality of the *chador*. No goodness is to be hoped from pretence; all goodness is in the essence of the self.

Zin al-Din also argues that imposing the veil on women is the ultimate proof that men suspect their mothers, daughters, wives and sisters of being potential traitors to them. This means that men suspect 'the women closest and dearest to them. What quality of life do they live if they are in a perpetual state of suspicion about their mothers, daughters, sisters and wives, fearing all the time their betrayal?'[22] How can society trust women with the most consequential job of bringing up children when it does not trust them with their faces and bodies? How can Muslim men meet rural and European women who are not veiled and treat them respectfully but not treat urban Muslim women in the same way? She concludes this part of the book by stating that it is not an Islamic duty on Muslim women to wear *hijab*. If Muslim legislators have decided that it is, their opinions are wrong. If *hijab* is based on women's lack of intellect or piety, can it be said that all men are more perfect in piety and intellect than all women?

Zin al-Din then wonders how some people can consider *hijab* and the total withdrawal of women from public life a sign of their honor and dignity. An honorable woman is someone who does useful things for both herself and for others. If all women are locked behind walls or behind *hijab*, how can we distinguish one from the other? The spirit of a nation and its civilization is a reflection of the spirit of the mother. How can any mother bring up distinguished children if she herself is deprived of her personal freedom? She concludes that in enforcing *hijab*, society becomes a prisoner of its customs and traditions rather than of Islam.

In the second part of the book, Zin al-Din sets out to prove that neither the text of the Qur'an nor the *hadith* require Muslim women to wear *hijab*. The *ayas* in the Qur'an concerning *hijab* are four, two of them addressed to the wives of the Prophet and two to Muslim women in general. She cites each of the two groups of *ayas*, discusses all the explanations stated in interpretive texts, cites the *ayas* against these interpretations, and finally reaches her own conclusions. The first two *ayas* about the wives of the Prophet Muhammad (32 and 53) of *Sura al-Ahzab* read as follows:

> O consorts of the Prophet! Ye are not like any Of the (other) women: If ye do fear (God), Be not too complaisant Of speech, lest one In whose heart is A disease should be moved With desire: but speak ye A speech (that is) just. And stay quietly in Your houses, and make not A dazzling display, like That of the former Times Of Ignorance; and establish Regular Prayer, and give Regular Charity; and obey God and His Apostle. And God only wishes To remove all abomination From you, Members Of the Family, and to make You Pure and spotless. And recite what is Rehearsed to you in your Homes, of the Signs of God And His Wisdom: For God understands The finest mysteries and Is well-acquainted (with them). (*Ayas* 32–4, of *Sura al-Ahzab*).

The second *aya* concerning the wives of the Prophet (53) says:

> Ye who believe! Enter not the Prophet's houses, Until leave is given you, For a meal, (and then) Not (so early as) to wait For its preparation; but when Ye are invited, enter; And when ye have taken Your meal, disperse, Without seeking familiar talk. Such (behaviour) annoys The Prophet; he is ashamed To dismiss you, but God is not ashamed (To tell you) the truth. And when ye Ask (his ladies) For anything ye want, Ask them from before A screen; that makes For greater purity for Your hearts and for theirs. Nor is it right for you That ye should annoy God's Apostle, or that Ye should marry his widows After him at any time. Truly such a thing is In God's sight an enormity.

Zin al-Din reviews the mainstream interpretations of these *ayas* in the best known books of *tafsir* (the interpretation of the Qur'an), namely *al-Tafsir al-mawsum bi-anwar al-tanzil wa asrar al-ta'wil* (The Interpretation Characterized by the Lights of Inspiration and the Secrets of Understanding) by the judge Baydawi, *Tafsir al-Qur'an al-jalil* (The Interpretation of the Glorious Qur'an) by Imam Ala al-Din al-Sufi known as al-Khazin; *Madarik al-tanzil wa haqa'iq al-ta'wil* (Domains of the Text and Truths of Interpretation) by Imam Abdullah al-Nasafi, which is a comment on al-Khazin's interpretation, and *Mujama' al-bayan fi tafsir al-Qur'an* (The Cluster of Evidence in Interpreting the Qur'an) by Imam al-Tabari. They all agree that these *ayas* are addressed to the wives of the Prophet and not to other Muslim women, although they differ on the reasons that caused these *ayas* to be sent by God to his Prophet. Al-Nasafi adds that when these *ayas* were addressed to the wives of the Prophet, other Muslim women asked why were they not addressed by God? After that the *aya* 'Muslim men and Muslim women, etc.' was conveyed to the Prophet. Challenging those Muslim interpreters who claim that these *ayas* call on the wives of the Prophet or all Muslim women to stay at home and inactive, Zin al-Din draws upon many examples of women active in all walks of life during the time of the Prophet and his caliphs. In *The Status of Woman in Islam* by Prince Ali Khal and in *The Rights of Woman in Islam* by Ahmad Agayeeve, it is stated that Fatima al-Zahra, the daughter of the Prophet, gave lessons and lectures to both men and women and that Shaykha Shahda (5th/11th), known as the Pride of Women, gave lectures and lessons in the schools and mosques of Baghdad in literature, history, *fiqh* and religion. Imam Shafi'i learned at the hands of Nafisi, who was the grand-daughter of Ali Bin Abi Talib and wife of Ishaq, son of Jafar al-Sadiq. Qatar al-Nada, wife of the caliph al-Mu'tad and mother of al-Muqtadir, met in the presence of ministers the ambassadors of foreign countries and reviewed people's cases every Friday with judges and advisors in her audience. In brief, Muslim women remained in mixed company with men until the late sixth century IE (eleventh century CE). They received guests, held meetings, and went to wars helping their brothers and husbands defend their castles and bastions.[23]

The other two *ayas* that are usually taken to justify the imposition of *hijab* on Muslim women are *Aya* 30 from *Sura al-nur* and *Aya* 59 from *Sura al-ahzab*. The first *aya* reads:

> Say to the believing men That they should lower Their gaze and guard Their modesty: that will make For greater purity for them: And God is well acquainted with all that they do. And say to the believing women That they should lower Their gaze and guard Their modesty; that they Should not display their Beauty and ornaments except What (must ordinarily) appear Thereof; that they should Draw their veils over Their bosoms and not display Their beauty except To their husbands, their fathers, Their Husband's fathers, their sons, Their husband's sons, Their brothers of their brothers' sons, Or their sisters' sons, or their women, or the slaves Whom their right hands Possess, or male servants Free of physical needs, Or small children who Have no sense of the shame of sex; and that they Should not strike their feet In order to draw attention To their hidden ornaments.

Aya 59 from *Sura al-Ahzab* reads: 'Prophet! Tell Thy wives and daughters, And the believing women, That they should cast Their outer garments over their persons (when outside): That is most convenient, That they should be known (As such) and not molested.'

Zin al-Din reviews the interpretations of these two *ayas* by al-Khazin, al-Nasafi, Ibn Masud, Ibn Abbas and al-Tabari and finds them full of contradictions. Yet, almost all interpreters agreed that women should not veil their faces and their hands and anyone who advocated that women should cover all their bodies including their faces could not base his argument on any religious text. If women were to be totally covered, there would have been no need for the *ayas* addressed to Muslim men: 'Say to the believing men that they should lower their gaze and guard their modesty.' (*Sura al-Nur, Aya* 30). She supports her views by referring to the sayings of the Prophet Muhammad, always taking into account what the Prophet himself said, namely, that everything has to be referred back to the book of God and anything that is inconsistent with it is an ornament. 'I did not say a thing that is not in harmony with God's book.'[24] When ordering the wives of the Prophet to wear *hijab* for special reasons relating to the house of the Prophet, God, as if He feared that Muslim women might imitate the wives of the Prophet, stressed: 'O consorts of the Prophet! ye are not like any of the (other) women' (*Ahzab*, 53). Thus it is very clear that God did not want us to measure ourselves against the wives of the Prophet and wear *hijab* like them and there is no ambiguity whatsoever regarding this *aya*. Therefore, those who imitate the wives of the Prophet and wear *hijab* are disobeying God's will. In *Islam ruh al-madaniyya* (Islam: The Spirit of Civilization) Shaykh Mustafa Ghalayini reminds his readers that veiling pre-dated Islam and that Muslims learned from other peoples with whom they mixed. He adds that 'hijab as it is known today is prohibited by the Islamic *shari'a*. Any one who looks at *hijab* as it is worn by some women would find that it makes them more desirable than if they went out without *hijab*.'[25] A similar argument is produced by Zin al-Din based on interviews she conducted with women before and after wearing *hijab*.

Zin al-Din points out that Islam is not confined to a few urban Muslim women or to some known families in rural societies. Veiling was a custom of rich families as a symbol of status. She quotes Shaykh Abdul Qadir al-Maghribi who also saw in *hijab* an aristocratic habit to distinguish the women of rich and prestigious families from other women. She concludes that *hijab* as it is known today is prohibited by the Islamic *shari'a*.[26]

In the fourth part of the book Zin al-Din discusses the answers, objections, and reactions that she received from such important Muslim authorities as Shaykh Sa'id al-Baghdadi, Shaykh Muhammad Ibrahim al-Qayati al-Azhari from the school of Azhar University in Cairo, Shaykh Muhammad Rahim al-Tarabulsi and Shaykh Mustafa al-Ghalayini. It appears that the heated arguments that followed the publication of her first book only made her stronger in her defence of women's rights. She dedicated her first book to her father, her second book to all women: 'Because you have the spirit of the mother and because I believe that reform in the East is built on the basis of your freedom and your struggle for what is right. May you have an overflow of God's light.'

Nazira Zin al-Din had her supporters. Writer Amin al-Rihani, head of the Syrian government Taj al-Din al-Husni, and Education Minister Muhammad Kurd Ali[27] sent her letters of support. The French Consul in Beirut wrote to her that he ordered parts of her book to be translated so that he could study it. She was the talk of Cairo, Alexandria, Damascus, Aleppo, and Baghdad. The Lebanese emigrants in Argentina, the United States, and Brazil sent her letters and wrote in their local newspapers in her support. The book was reviewed in major journals and newspapers in Damascus, Beirut, Cairo, New York, Buenos Aires, São Paulo, Baghdad, Aleppo and she received letters from men of religion, heads of state and governments, and from editors and publishers all over the world.

At least three Muslim scholars agreed with Zin al-Din's arguments and raised similar concerns about the necessity of sifting Islamic legislation from rumors and falsifications which later became part of Islamic practices. Shaykh Muhammad al-Ghazali in his book *Sunna Between Fiqh and Hadith*[28] argues that women can assume any post they are qualified to assume except that of the caliph and this, he insists, is the rule of true Islam. He declares that those who claim that women's reform is conditioned by wearing the veil are lying to God and his Prophet. None of the four Imams has said that seeing a woman's face is an offence. In total harmony with Zin al-Din's arguments Shaykh Muhammad al-Ghazali expresses the opinion that the contemptuous view of women has been passed on from the first *jahiliya* (the Pre-Islamic period) to the Islamic society. He uses the same argument, citing the same *aya* as cited by Mustafa Ghalayini[29] in order to prove that Muslim women do not have to cover their faces and hands. Al-Ghazali's argument is that Islam has made it compulsory on women not to cover their faces during *haj* and *salat* (prayer) the two important pillars of Islam. How then could Islam ask women to cover their faces at ordinary times?[30] Through his detailed study of the time of the Prophet Muhammad he reaches the conclusion that it was a time when *sufur* was prevalent.[31] He stresses that 'looking down at women is a crime in Islam, and that true Islam rejects the customs of nations which impose constraints on women or belittle their rights and duties.'[32] Hence, according to al-Ghazali, our customs and habits should be scrutinized in order to leave only what is closely connected with the Islamic *shari'a* and our adherence to these rules should be in proportion to their harmony with the Qur'anic text.

Like Zin al-Din, al-Ghazali is a believer and is confident that all traditions that function to keep women ignorant and prevent them from functioning in public are the remnants of *jahiliya* and that following them is contrary to the spirit of Islam. God said in the Glorious Qur'an: 'The Believers, men and women, are protectors, One of another; they enjoin What is just, and forbid What is evil: they observe Regular prayers, practice Regular charity, and obey God and His Apostle. On them will God pour His mercy: for God Is Exalted in power, Wise.' (*Sura Tauba, Aya* 71) Like Zin al-Din, Shaykh Ghazali insists on a basic Muslim right to compare different interpretations and different versions of Islamic sayings and to choose the more reasonable and the more useful to follow. The easier to adopt for Islam is the religion of *yusur'* (flexibility) and not of *usur* (intransigence). As a Muslim scholar, he rejected the undermining of women's will in marriage and was not against her initiating marriage if her situation required it. Efficient and knowledgeable women should be able to assume any post they like except that of the caliph. Women can consult and give their opinion and the weight of their opinion is in proportion to its validity and correctness. He says 'we don't yearn to make women heads of state or government, but we yearn for one thing, a head of state or government should be the most efficient *person* in the nation.'[33] Commenting on all these wrong attitudes to women al-Ghazali says that during the time of the Prophet women were equals at home, in the mosques and on the battlefield. Today true Islam is being destroyed in the name of Islam.

Another Muslim scholar, Abd al-Halim Abu Shiqa, who wrote a scholarly study of women in Islam entitled *Tahrir al-mara'a fi 'asr al-risalah*: (The Emancipation of Women during the Time of the Prophet)[34] agrees with Zin al-Din and al-Ghazali about the discrepancy between the status of women during the time of the Prophet Muhammad and the status of women today. He says:

> Through my study of the time of the Prophet I found texts and sayings of the Prophet which show women acting in all kinds of professions in total difference to what we see, understand and interpret today. This great discrepancy explained to me why so many women got away from (Islam) because it simply deprived them of the rights of life; that is why I felt it my duty to offer the women from the habits and rules of *jahiliyya* which are mistakenly thought to be Islamic.[35]

He agreed with Zin al-Din and al-Ghazali that Islamists have made up sayings which they attributed to the Prophet such as 'women are lacking in both intellect and religion' and in many cases they brought sayings which are not reliable at all and promoted them among Muslims until they became part of the Islamic culture.

Like Zin al-Din and al-Ghazali, Abu Shiqa finds that in many countries very weak and unreliable sayings are invented to support customs and traditions which are then considered to be part of the *shari'a*. Like Zin al-Din, he argues that the text of the Qur'an proves that both men and women are from the same self and quotes the same *aya* that Zin al-Din quotes: 'O mankind! Reverence Your Guardian Lord, Who created you From a single Person, Created, of like nature, His mate, and from them twain Scattered (like seeds) countless men and women; Reverence God, through Whom Ye demand your mutual (rights), and (reverence) the wombs (That bore you): for God Ever watches over you.' (*Sura Nisa', Aya* 1) He Argues that it is the Islamic duty of women to participate in public life and in spreading good: 'The Believers, men and women, are protectors, One of another: they enjoin what is just, and forbid what is evil.' (*Sura Tauba, Aya* 71) It is the same *aya* quoted by Imam Muhammad al-Ghazali to prove the same point.

As for those who prevent women from going out to work, Abu Shiqa answers: 'if women are prevented from going out to work, what is the meaning of the following *aya*: 'Do not desire what God had granted to others; For men a share of what they earn and for women a share of what they earn' (*Sura Nisa'*, *Aya* 32). He also agrees with Zin al-Din and Ghazali that *hijab* was for the wives of the Prophet and that it was against Islam for women to imitate the wives of the Prophet. If women were to be totally covered, why did God ask both men and women to lower their gaze. (*Sura al-Nur*, *Aya*(s); 30–1) In most of his arguments he cites the same verses cited by Zin al-Din and shows a similar understanding of them. There is no difference at all between Zin al-Din, al-Ghazali and Dr Abdol Halim Abu Shiqa.

Shaykh Muhammad Husayn Fadl Allah, in his book *Ta'amulat Islamiyya hawl al-mara'* (Islamic Speculations About Women),[36] also agrees with these three Muslim scholars on most issues concerning women's *hijab*, freedom, work and political responsibilities. He stresses that Islam sees men and women as one in humanity and responsibility.[37] Islam neither absolves women from their responsibilities nor does it undermine their femininity. Quite the contrary: Islam stresses that women should feel and enjoy their beauty but without any display or attempts to provoke desire. This is precisely the understanding of Zin al-Din and al-Ghazali of *Aya* 59 of *Sura al-ahzab* that is taken by some Muslim scholars to mean the imposition of *hijab* on all Muslim women. It is almost certain that a comparative study of the works of these four Muslim scholars would yield fruitful results. It was Muhammad al-Ghazali who wrote an introduction to Abu Shiqa's book, *Tahrir al-mara' fi 'asr al-risalah*. In this introduction, al-Ghazali says: 'I wish this book had appeared centuries ago and exposed women's issues in Islamic society in such a mature way. Because Muslims have deviated from the instructions of their religion in dealing with women, dark rumors and fabricated *hadith* spread among them leaving Muslim women in deep ignorance, quite removed from religion and life.... This book takes Muslims back to the correct *sunna* of their prophet with no minus or plus.'[38]

While the views of the three Muslim men writing over half a century after Zin al-Din are given some space in Arabic papers and journals, Zin al-Din has not been referred to either by them or even by a woman scholar like Fatima Mernissi who addresses the same subject.[39] One wonders what would have happened to Zin al-Din had she published her books in the 1990s instead of the 1920s? Would she find any *shaykh* to answer her arguments or would she be silenced in one way or another? One cannot help drawing comparisons with Taslima Nasrin, whose statements on Islam are not yet properly quoted, nor is it precisely known what she actually said. Yet some Islamists have called on Muslims to kill her. There is no *aya* in the Qur'an that allows any Muslim, not even the Prophet Muhammad himself, to subscribe to killing another person simply because he or she has expressed views that contradict the views of a certain Muslim scholar, school, or group. I can only agree with what Lisa Beyer wrote in her article 'Life Behind the Veil': 'if the wives of Muhammad lived in parts of the contemporary Islamic world, they might be paying a high price for their independence.'[40]

Notes

1. Qadariyya Husayn, *Chahirat al-nisa' fi'l-alam al-Islamiyya* (Famous Women in the Muslim World). Translated from Turkish by Abdol Aziz Amin al-Khanji (Cairo: Matba'at al-Sa'adeh, 1924), p. 33.
2. Muhammad Shahrur, *al-Kitab wa'l-Qur'an* (The Book and the Qur'an) (Damascus: al-Ahali publishers, 1992), p 594.
3. Husayn, *op. cit.*, p. 74.
4. Abdol Sir Afifi, *al-Mara'a al-arabiyya fi jahiliyatiha wa Islamiha* (Arab Woman in her Jahiliya and Islam), (Cairo: Matba'at al-Ma'arif, 1933), p. 138.
5. *Ibid.*, p. 139.
6. *Ibid.*, p. 142.
7. Fatima al-Batoul Mersa, 'Muslim Women in Arab History,' *al-Ahram*, Cairo, 15 April 1989, p. 5.
8. Hussein, *op. cit.*, p. 179.
9. *Ibid.*, pp. 179–80.
10. See Afifi, *op. cit.*, part two, p. 147.
11. *Ibid.*, pp. 147–9.
12. *Ibid.*, pp. 153–4.
13. *al-Fatal wa'l-shiukh*, printed by Nazira Zin al-Din's father Sa'id Bik Zin al-Din (Beirut, 1929), p. 75.
14. Nazira Zin al-Din, *al-Sufur wa'l-hijab* (Beirut: Quzma Publications, 1928), p. 37.
15. *Ibid.*, p. 37.
16. *Ibid.*, p. 21.
17. *Ibid.*, p. 69.
18. *Ibid.*, p. 27.
19. See *ibid.*, pp. 42–8.
20. *Ibid.*, p. 125.
21. *Ibid.*, p. 125.
22. *Ibid.*, p. 135.
23. See *Ibid.*, pp. 191–2.
24. *Ibid.*, p. 226.
25. Shaykh Mustafa al-Ghalayini, *Islam ruh al-madaniyya* (Islam: The Spirit of Civilization) (Beirut: al-Maktabah al-Asriyya, 1960), p. 253.
26. *Ibid.*, pp. 255–56.
27. Zin al-Din, *al-Fatal wa'l-shiukh, op. cit.*, part 3, pp. w–6.
28. Shaykh Muhammad al-Ghazali, *Sunna Between Fiqh and Hadith* (Cairo: Dar al-Shuruq, 1989, 7th edition, 1990).
29. Ghalayini, *op. cit.*, p. 254.
30. al-Ghazali, *op. cit.*, p. 44.
31. *Ibid.*, p. 49.
32. *Ibid.*, p. 52.
33. *Ibid.*, p. 56.
34. Abd al-Halim Abu Shiqa, *Tahrir al-mara' fi 'asr al-risalah* (Kuwait: Dar al-Qalam, 1990).
35. *Ibid.*, p. 5.

36. Shaykh Muhammad Husayn Fadl Allah, *Ta'amulat Islamiyya hawl al mara'* (Beirut: Dar al-Milak, 1992).
37. *Ibid.*, p. 25.
38. Abu Shiqa, *op. cit.*, p. 5.
39. *al-Harim al-siyassi; al Nabi wa'l-nisa'* (Political Harim; The Prophet and Women) Translated by Abd al-Hadi Abbas (Damascus: Dar al-Hasad, 1990).
40. *Time*, Fall 1990, p. 37.

~:~

Questions for Discussion

1. Looking only at the excerpted surahs from the Qur'an included here, what conclusions do you reach about the status of women in Islam?
2. How do the readings in the chapter change your views, if at all?
3. How might understandings of Islam be different if more women had been allowed to participate in the development of the interpretive tradition?
4. How might you explain discrepancies between women's formal status in the Qur'an and the actual conditions of most women's lives in Islamic countries?
5. Should gender differences in interpretation of religious scriptures be affirmed or eliminated?
6. What *might* prompt African-American women to convert to Islam?
7. What factors contribute to Muslim women's willingness to support fundamentalist Islamic movements? Can or should religion be kept separate from political influences?
8. *Is* Islam oppressive to women? Is it possible to make a blanket conclusion one way or another?

References and Materials for Further Study

Articles and Books

Abu-Lughod. 1985. "A Community of Secrets: The Separate World of Bedouin Women." *Signs* 10: 637-57.

Ahmed, Leila. 1992. *Women and Gender in Islam: Historical Roots of a Modern Debate.* New Haven, CT: Yale University Press.

Anmar, Nawal H. "On Being A Muslim Woman: Laws and Practices." *The Religious Consultation on Population, Reproductive Health and Ethics*; http://www.consultation.org/ consultation/ammar.htm.

Awde, Nicholas, trans. 2000. *Women in Islam: An Anthology from the Quran and Hadiths.* New York: St. Martin's.

Badawi, Leila. 1994. "Islam," in Joan Helm and John Bawker, eds., *Women in Religion.* London: Pinter Publishers.

Bauer, Janet. 1999. "Islam: In Iran and Turkey," in Serinity Young, ed., *Encyclopedia of Women and World Religion*. New York: Macmillan Reference.

Beck, Lois. 1999. "Islam: Religious Rites and Practices," in Serinity Young, ed., *Encyclopedia of Women and World Religion*. New York: Macmillan Reference.

Brooks, Geraldine. 1995. *Nine Parts of Desire: The Hidden World of Islamic Women*. New York: Anchor.

Clancy-Smith, Julia. 1999. "Islam: In Africa," in Serinity Young, ed., *Encyclopedia of Women and World Religion*. New York: Macmillan Reference.

Darrow, William. 1985. "Woman's Place and the Place of Women in the Iranian Revolution," in Yvonne Yasbeck Haddad and Ellison Banks-Findley, *Women, Religion, and Social Change*. Albany: State University of New York Press.

Elias, Jamal. 1988. "Female and Feminine in Islamic Mysticism." *Muslim World.* 78: 209-24.

Fernea, Elizabeth Warnock, and Basima Qattan Bezirgan, eds. 1977. *Middle Eastern Muslim Women Speak.* Austin: University of Texas. Collection of excerpts from various Islamic sources, including the Qur'an, biographies of women, and literature and poetry written by women.

Haddad, Yvonne Yazbeck. 1985. "Islam, Women and Revolution in Twentieth-Century Arab Thought," in Yvonne Yasbeck Haddad and Ellison Banks-Findley, eds., *Women, Religion, and Social Change*. Albany: State University of New York Press.

Hassan, Riffat. "Are Human Rights Compatible with Islam? The Issue of the Rights of Women in Muslim Communities." *The Religious Consultation on Population, Reproductive Health and Ethics*. http://www.consultation.org/consultation/hmnrgtha.htm.

———. "'Members, One of Another': Gender Equality and Justice in Islam." *The Religious Consultation on Population, Reproductive Health and Ethics*. http://www.consultation.org/consultation/hassamoa.htm.

———. "Muslim Women's Empowerment and Self-Actualization: Moving From I.C.P.D. into the 21st Century." *Religious Consultation on Population, Reproductive Health and Ethics*: http://www.consultation.org/consultation/ongomus.htm.

———. 1991. "Muslim Women and Post-Patriarchal Islam," in Paula Cooey, William Eakin, and Jay McDanial, eds., *After Patriarchy: Feminist Transformations of the World Religions*. Maryknoll, NY: Orbis Books.

———. 1990. "An Islamic Perspective," in Jeanne Becher, ed., *Women, Religion, and Sexuality*. Philadelphia: Trinity Press.

——— and John L. Esposito, eds. 1998. *Islam, Gender, and Social Change*. New York: Oxford University Press.

Jeffery, Patricia, and Amrita Basu, eds. 1998. *Appropriating Gender: Women's Activism and Politicized Religion in South Asia*. New York: Routledge. Especially essays by Feldman on Islam in Bangladesh and Metcalf.

Kimball, Michelle, and Barbara R. von Schlegell. 1997. *Muslim Women Throughout the World: A Bibliography*. Boulder, CO: Lynne Rienner Publishers.

Luth, Huda. 1991. "Manners and Customs of Fourteenth Century Cairene Women: Female Anarchy versus Male Shar'ia Order in Muslim Prescriptive Treatises," in Nikki Keddie and Beth Baron, eds., *Women in Middle Eastern History*. New Haven, CT: Yale University Press. Provides evidence of a current of unrest among medieval Muslim women.

McCloud, Beverly. 1991. "African-American Muslim Women," in Yvonne Yazbeck Haddad, ed., *The Muslims of America*. New York: Oxford University Press.

Mernissi, Fatima. 1991. *The Veil and the Male Elite: A Feminist Interpretation of Women's Rights in Islam*. Mary Jo Lakeland, ed. and trans. Reading, MA: Addison-Wesley.

Murata, Sachiko. 1992. *The Tao of Islam: A Sourcebook on Gender Relationships in Islamic Thought*. Albany: State University of New York Press.

Ralph, Austin. 1983. "Islam and the Feminine," in D. MacEoin and Ahmed al-Shahi, eds., *Islam in the ModernWorld*. London: Croom Helm.

Shaaban, Bouthaina. 1995. "The Muted Voices of Women Interpreters," in Afkhami, Mahnaz, ed., *Faith and Freedom: Women's Human Rights in the Muslim World*. London: I.B. Tauris.

Smith, Jane. 1994. "Women in Islam," in Arvind Sharma, ed., *Today's Woman in World Religions*. Albany: State University of New York Press.

———. 1985. "Women, Religion, and Social Change in Early Islam," in Yvonne Yazbeck Haddad and Ellison Banks Findly, eds., *Women, Religion, and Social Change*. Albany: State University of New York Press.

Smith, Margaret. 1977. Excerpts from *Rabi'a the Mystic and Her Fellow-Saints in Islam*, in Elizabeth Warnock Fernea and Basima Qattan Bezirgan, eds., *Middle Eastern Muslim Women Speak*. Austin: University of Texas.

Sonn, Tamara. 1999a. "Islam: An Overview," in Serinity Young, ed., *Encyclopedia of Women and World Religion*. New York: Macmillan Reference.

———. 1999b. "Islam: In the Arab Middle East," in Serinity Young, ed., *Encyclopedia of Women and World Religion*. New York: Macmillan Reference.

Tohidi, Nayereh. 1991. "Gender and Islamic Fundamentalism: Feminist Politics in Islam," in Chandra Talpade Mohanty, Ann Russo, and Lourdes Torres, eds., *Third World Women and the Politics of Feminism*. Bloomington: Indiana University Press.

al-Turabi, Hassan, "On the Position of Women in Islam and Islamic Society," *BICNews Global Newsletter Service*, Belfast Islamic Centre, http://www.iol.ie/~afifi/BICNews/Personal/ personal11.htm.

Wadud-Muhsin, Amina. 1999. *Qur'an and Woman: Rereading the Sacred Text From a Woman's Perspective*. New York, Oxford University Press.

Waxman, Sharon. 1999. "A Cause Unveiled: Hollywood Women Have Made the Plight of Afghan Women Their Own—Sight Unseen." *Washington Post* (March 30), pp. C1, C8.

Webb, Gisela, ed. 2000. *Windows of Faith: Muslim Women Scholar-Activists in North America*. Syracuse, NY: Syracuse University Press. Introduction by the editor is entitled "May Muslim Women Speak for Themselves, Please?"

Internet Resources

Maryam's Net: Muslim Women and Their Islam Web Site: http://www.maryams.net. Provided "in the spirit of encouraging Muslim women and supporters of Muslim women to arise and reinterpret shari'a so that the Muslim world might achieve the essential Qur'anic spirit of egalitarianism and equality."

Muslim Sisters Online Web Site:
  http://www.sistersonline.net/.
  Informational site geared toward providing useful information for women everywhere.

Muslim Women's League Web Site:
  http://www.mwlusa.org.
  "MWL is a nonprofit American Muslim organization working to implement the values of Islam and thereby reclaim the status of women as free, equal and vital contributors to society." Web site contains essays and position papers on a number of issues relevant to Islamic Women, including "honor killing," female genital mutilation, equality, violence against women, sexuality, inheritance, hijab, women in politics, spiritual role, and sex and sexuality in Islam.

Sisterhood Is Global Institute Web Site (SIGI):
  http://www.sigi.org/index.htm.
  Produces and circulates international educational tools and research papers aimed at clarifying concepts, deepening understanding, and building consensus on issues of priority to women, especially the human rights of Muslim women.

Sisters Net Web Site:
  http://www.msa-natl.org/SISTERS.
  A women-only list for Muslim women.

Women's Alliance for Peace and Human Rights in Afghanistan Web Site (WAPHA):
  http://womeninafghanistan.ontheweb.nu/.
  A Washington, DC-based, nonpartisan, nonprofit, independent organization dedicated to the promotion of peace and human rights in Afghanistan.

Woodlock, Rachel, "Western Feminists, Muslim Women and the 'Veil' That Separates Them," Maryam's Net:
  http://www.maryams.net/articles_veil03.shtml.

Media References

Beyond Borders: Arab Feminists Talk about their Lives. Video, 50 min., color. Films for the Humanities,1999.

Beyond the Veil. Video, 52 min. Filmakers Library, 1999. Part 3, "The Born Again Muslims," explores variations in veil policies in Sudan, Turkey, and Iran which reflect variations in Islam in these three countries.

Daughters of Allah. Video, 49 min. Filmakers Library, 2000. On religious freedom for Palestinian Muslim women.

Fire Eyes: Female Circumcision. Video, 60 min. Filmakers Library, 1995. Made by an African woman who underwent the practice at age 13.

In the Name of God: Helping Circumcised Women. Video, 29 min. Filmakers Library, 1997. On Ethiopian women hospitalized after infibulation.

Iranian Journey. Video, 60 min. Filmakers Library, 2000. About the first woman bus driver in the Muslim World.

The Need to Know: Women and Religion. Video, 47 min., color. Films for the Humanities, 1996. Covers women in early Christianity, the goddess tradition that Christianity supplanted, and Islam's oppression of women.

Not Without My Veil: Amongst the Women of Oman. Video, 29 min. Filmakers Library, 1995.

Paradise Lies at the Feet of the Mother. Video, 50 min. Ambrose Video Publishing (in association with the BBC), New York, 1993. Explores women, the Muslim family, the pressure to change, and the forces which hold change back as it looks at the role of women in Islam and in Muslim societies in the Middle East, Asia, and Nigeria.

Prose, Politics, and Power: Conversation with Muslim Women Leaders. Video. SIGI, 1996. Conversations with Muslim women from different countries and backgrounds address the complexities of the issues that weave tradition with modernity, faith with freedom, and universalism with diversity in Muslim societies and beyond.

Rites. Video, 52 min. Filmakers Library, 1991. On female circumcision in Africa.

Shackled Women: Abuses of a Patriarchal World. Video, 41 min., color. Films for the Humanities, 1999.

Under One Sky: Arab Women in North America Talk About the Hijab. Video, 44 mins, color. Films for the Humanities, 1999.

Women in Bangladesh: Taslima Nasreeen. Video, 23 min. Filmakers Library, 1996. On the Bangladesh writer who gained international attention when Islamic leaders issued a death threat against her for writing about the oppression of women in Islam.

Women in the Arab World. 3 videos, 25 min. each. Filmakers Library, 1997. Portraits of educated Muslim women in different countries.

Women Serving Religion. Video, 29 min., color. Films for the Humanities, 1991. Roles of women in traditional and contemporary Christianity, Judaism, and Islam.

Women and Islam. Video, 30 min., color. Films for the Humanities, 1993. Women's Studies professor Leila Ahmed argues the case for revising widely held views in Islam about the role of women.

Chapter 8

Women and African Religions

∿ : ∿

Overview

In this chapter, we will examine African women in religion from a variety of different perspectives. The main focus will be on women's religiosity in traditional societies in sub-Saharan Africa, since much of Northern Africa came to be dominated by Islam several centuries ago. However, this introduction and some of the selections which follow also touch upon how Christianity and Islam have influenced African women's religious lives (Islam is the fastest growing religion on the African continent). Rosalind Hackett's essay "Women in African Religions" provides an overview of the depth and breadth of African women's religious perspectives as well as some of the problems encountered in trying to study this subject. Mercy Amba Oduyoye's essay from *Daughters of Anowa: African Women and Patriarchy* discusses African religion from the perspective of a Christian African woman.

In addition, we will note how African women's religious practices and rituals have had an impact outside of Africa, especially in the Caribbean countries and Brazil. Karen McCarthy Brown's essay describes the experiences of an Afro-Caribbean woman from Haiti who becomes a Vodou spirit priestess after she has immigrated to Brooklyn and experiences a series of life-threatening illnesses. This variety will enable us to gain a broader perspective on the varieties of women's experience with African religions than we would obtain by looking at only one of these dimensions. As we will see, gender—and the differentiation of men and women—is central to African religions, as it is to African society more generally.

As Rosiland Hackett tells us, it is extremely difficult to generalize about women and African religion because the diversity of cultures and traditions is so vast. In addition to the wide variety of indigenous African traditions, African women's religious experience also includes the religions transplanted into Africa by (mainly) Christian and Islamic missionaries and colonialists and the "new religions" which combine elements of these different traditions..

In addition to their tremendous diversity and variety, another problem with studying African religions is the ethnocentrism of traditional scholarship on this subject. Most studies in the past have been written from a Western, Judeo-Christian perspective which considers religions to be text-based. Because traditional African religions are based more in oral than written traditions and emphasize ritual rather than scripture, they have been portrayed to be "primitive" and unsophisticated. This problem has been addressed in more contemporary scholarship on African religions. In fact, Hackett argues (not in her essay included here) that the whole idea of "Traditional African Religion" (TAR) as a monolithic, homogeneous phenomenon is an erroneous Western invention that bears little relation to the multiplicity and diversity of religions in traditional Africa. She points to the ironic twist that it is now primarily *African* educational institutions, universities, and secondary schools that are perpetuating this myth of TAR (Hackett 1990). Another misimpression that many Western viewers have of Africa is that religion is separate and distinct from culture (as it generally is in their Western religious traditions) when, in reality, religion is intertwined with and inseparable from other aspects of African society and culture (as is the case in Native American and many other indigenous religious traditions around the world).

Beyond the African continent, indigenous religions of African peoples have had a significant impact for over 500 years in shaping the religiosity of Africans and others outside of the continent. African slaves coming to the Americas brought their religious traditions with them. Although many of them were forced to convert to Christianity, they incorporated elements of their traditional religious practices into their new lives. Significant aspects of those religious traditions are present today in African-American, Afro-Brazilian, Afro-Caribbean, Afro-Cuban, and other African-centered religious practices, be they superficially Christian or otherwise (in fact, many initiates into New World African religions are members of Roman Catholic churches). Some of these elements have been transmitted down through the generations, and others have been self-consciously adopted or appropriated as part of an effort by African women living in diaspora to retrieve their cultural background.

The reading by Karen McCarthy Brown on "Alourdes," for example, explains that the Haitian Vodou spirit Ogou has origins in the Goun of the Yoruba, a god connected to occupations connected with metal, including hunting and warfare. In addition to Vodou, other African-derived or influenced religious traditions in the Western hemisphere include Santeria ("the way of the Saints") in Cuba, Espiritualismo in Puerto Rico, and Candomble and Umbanda in Brazil.[1] Many African-based or derived religions throughout the Caribbean and North America have Christian, usually Catholic, dimensions as well, often the result of slavery and missionizing during the colonial period. It is estimated that there are approximately 50 million members of Afro-Atlantic religions, 25 million of them in Brazil alone (Fandrich 1999, 12).

Despite these many difficulties in gaining an accurate understanding of African religions, it is possible to make a few generalizations. Perhaps the most significant similarity among African religions is the belief in the imperfection of human life, and the possibility of using ritual means to alleviate sickness, conflict, and other forms of suffering. In contrast to the Western monotheistic and Asian world religions, the focus of African religions is on relationships within this world, not on attaining salvation in an afterlife. Thus, ritual practice is often directed, implicitly or explicitly, to healing fractured social relations and renewing community bonds. Sacred knowledge and ritual practice are transmitted through initiation.

African religions also generally share a "spiritual hierarchy," that is, a belief in one supreme creator god, as well as numerous lesser gods, who, along with spirits and ancestors, have some but lesser spiritual power (such as the relation between the Nigerian Yoruba people's supreme god Olodumare and the Orisha, or secondary divinities). These supreme deities are often of ambiguous or dual gender, such as Chukwu, the supreme being for the Nigerian Igbo, or Mawu-Lisa, the dual-gendered supreme being of the Fon people of Benin. The cosmos is commonly characterized in African myth and ritual as an anthropomorphic entity, and the human body as a microcosm of the cosmos.

The secondary divinities are present in every aspect of life and are more often involved in the fate of human affairs than are the creator gods (Grillo 1999, 12). Thus, careful devotion to them through prayer, ritual, and sacrifice is required (see Fandrich 1999, 14). Ritual is yet another element of commonality across African religious traditions. Ritual plays a variety of significant roles in the life of African peoples, especially in reestablishing harmonious relations between individuals, among members of the community, or with ancestors, spirits, the gods, or the natural forces in the universe. Contact with divinities may take place directly through spirit possession, or through intermediaries such as diviners, who are ritual specialists.

Because belief in fate and predestination is ubiquitous throughout the African diaspora religions, the role of diviners in conducting "readings," and contacting the spirits through possession to forecast the future, and to recommend the best ritual and other means to prepare for it, is in high demand. The popularity of Alourdes, the subject of Brown's essay, illustrates the significance of diviners in the lives of practitioners of African-based religions.

As mentioned above, Christianity and Islam have also become significant religious forces on the African continent. These traditions have been woven together with indigenous tribal religions to form syncretic mixes of traditional and "imported" religious beliefs and practices. For example, Islamic practices of veiling and female seclusion have been adopted in very different ways by different African Muslim communities (see Clancy-Smith 1999, 501).

Relationship of Female-Gendered and Feminine Images and Symbols to "Real" Women

It is perhaps not surprising that many religious images of females and the feminine in African societies relate to women's procreative powers. Thus, women are often linked to the creativity of nature and are viewed as essential to the maintenance and continuity of the community, which is the highest value in most African cultures. Associated with nature, women are frequently viewed in African religions as both a source of generation and of destruction. They are often regarded ambivalently—their powers are respected as awesome, yet also as mysterious and uncontrolled, polluting, and a potential threat to be controlled, especially in order to prevent disorder or misfortune. Thus, women are often linked to witchcraft, especially in relation to infertility and adultery, and regulated by menstrual and pregnancy taboos. These associations are used to justify male control. Because women's power is both revered and feared, rituals involving it are often veiled in secrecy and mystery, making it difficult for the researcher to obtain access. As with stereotypes of women in many other cultures, women are considered to be more emotional than men, and thus as more susceptible to spirit possession (Hackett 1994, 65).

There are some interesting surprises about women's place in traditional African religions, however. One of these is the existence of female-gendered gods or goddesses in several of these religions. Among the Yoruba of Nigeria, for example, are Orisanla, or Oduduwa, "creator" deities; Aje, the female deity of wealth and fertility; Odu, the deity who controls all others; and Yemoja ("Mother of Fishes"), who is the progenitor of all water deities (Paper 1997, 193). The Ewe people of the Republic of Benin worship a bisexual supreme deity called Mawu-Lisa (Hackett 1994, 68). As Hackett notes, however, "the existence of a strong female deity is no guarantee of female ritual authority" (Hackett 1994, 76). Thus, while the existence of female gods may signify a respect for women, this is not necessarily the case. Understanding the relationship between female deities and "real" women is also complicated by the androcentric character of most of the scholarship on African religions that has been produced to date.[2]

Many of the secondary divinities in African religions are of androgynous sexuality or dual-gendered, in keeping with a looser relationship of sex to gender in African societies generally. Thus, the divinities may shift from one gender to another within the same setting. This understanding of gender as shifting and amorphous rather than fixed and unchanging helps explain why gender-role shifts and cross-gender impersonations sometimes occur during rituals.

Women's Relationship to African Religions

As Hackett observes, one of the challenging aspects of studying women in African religions is the ambiguity, complexity, and shifting nature of women's place in relation to religion. Aspects of African religious traditions that may appear to the outside (Western) perspective to show women's subordination may in fact function to empower the women who participate in these traditions.

Even when African women's religiosity has been the subject of study, it has generally been from a distanced perspective of an "outside" (usually Western, white, Christian male) researcher rather than from African women's own perspective. The reading by Mercy Amba Oduyoye is included here as an attempt to respond to this problem. Oduyoye writes not only as an African woman, but also an African *religious* woman, which gives her an insider perspective on at least some of the traditional African religious traditions she writes about. As a Christian woman educated in the West, however, Oduyoye also brings something of an "outsider" perspective to her research, which enables us to observe perhaps more of the negative aspects of traditional African religion for African women than we would otherwise.

Despite the difficulties in learning about women's relationship to African religions, it is clear that women are centrally involved in these religious traditions. In many instances, women are the majority of participants, as in the Afro-Atlantic religions of Candomble and Umbanda of Brazil. Participation in these religious traditions are based on initiation into a "society" of a small, family-like worship community. The relationship between the diviner or spirit possessor and her "initiates" is based on the family model, with members of the same "house" usually having a lifelong commitment to one another (see Fandrich 1999, 15).

Women-Specific or Distinctive Aspects of African Religions

Despite the difficulties in making any generalizations about African religions, as Hackett suggests, there are a number of commonalities that allow *some* generalizations to be made about the roles and status of women. Oduyoye tells us that African women are "demonstrably more religious than men." There are connections between women's ritual roles and their (perceived) physical and emotional natures (Hackett 1994, 65). Women do not often play primary ritual roles, but are generally relegated to subordinate ones, especially in the central public rituals. In fact, they are often restricted to domestic space, especially during important ritual occasions (Hackett 1994, 66). As in many other traditional societies, women's rituals are embedded in and related to their daily lives—as wives, child bearers, child rearers, and so on.

Like other religious traditions covered in this textbook, African religions generally devalue women and marginalize their participation in ritual activities, with some exceptions. Since religion in Africa tends to be integrated with the rest of social life, however, women's subordinate status in the religious realm follows logically from their overall social status. Women have mostly been in asymmetrical relations with men in African societies. Prior to colonialism, women in many parts of Africa held economic independence (as the primary agriculturalists and marketers) and a political voice, yet they were not dominant, or even equal (Hackett 1994, 64). Most of African kinship is arranged on patrilineal lines, and women have held subordinate roles to those of men in most spheres, which are largely gender segregated. One of the major exceptions is their roles in spirit possession cults as diviners and mediums, roles which are about the most important and public ritual roles available to women. Unlike the negative connotations that are generally associated with spirit mediums in the West, in the African context spirit mediums are highly regarded as ritual specialists possessing the ability to "channel" or embody the essence of the gods. Thus, like the devadasis discussed in the Hinduism chapter, African women who lack status in conventional society may gain it through their religious roles. Mediumship is regarded as a form of service to the divine and to the community, as Brown notes with respect to Alourdes.

Some African cultures do have distinctive rituals for women, many of which revolve around aspects of reproduction, such as the onset of menstruation, pregnancy, childbearing, and the lack thereof (infertility). For example, contrary to most religious or other cultural traditions, Yoruaba societies practice a female puberty ritual to mark the transformation of girls into women. Although initiation rituals are more common for boys than girls, this ritual is participated in by all postpubescent young women who have not yet participated in such a ritual. Participation makes young women eligible to take on the primary female roles in Yoruba society of wives, mothers, and market women (see Paper 1997).

Another widespread female initiation ritual is female clitoridectomy, sometimes called FGM or Female Genital Mutilation or "genital cutting" in Western countries. Although the female variation of circumcision is far more radical a procedure than that for males and may involve cutting away parts or all of the clitoris and labia minora, both are part of a ritual process of clearly defining differentiating male and female genders.[3] FGM also accomplishes a separation of sexuality from reproduction and transforms women into mothers, the most esteemed gender role for women in Africa.

A different sort of gendered ritual in Africa is the *gelede* masquerade of the Yoruba. These parades, which take place in the female domain of the marketplace, involve elaborate costumes designed to honor the "Great Mothers" or witches, primarily older women who possess extraordinary powers. Of the two main masks used in these rituals, one is of a bearded woman, signifying the inability to contain her power within a single gender. Just as women are associated with birth, they are also associated with death and consequently often have important ritual roles to play at these times in their communities—or to have enacted upon them, such as when their husbands die.

Scholars differ, however, in their assessments about whether such ritual roles afford any real power to women, or only further entrench them within the larger patriarchal system. For instance, women are frequently excluded from leading or participating in rituals while they are in their childbearing years and/or in public spaces. As Hackett discusses, when women do occupy ritual roles, it is generally either because they are exceptional or because they have lost the characteristics that identify them as women (Hackett 1994, 76). The women who do participate in rituals as spirit mediums or diviners are often illiterate and childless.

Gender-Based Segregation and Inequalities

As noted earlier, many aspects of African women's religious lives takes place in gender-segregated activities. For example, perhaps as a means of balancing women's "natural" creative powers in childbearing, some African societies prohibit women from skills as craftsmen, especially wood carvers and iron working. This does not necessarily imply women's subordination, however. As Hackett suggests elsewhere, segregation of women in relation to menstruation "may be a source of empowerment for women, a validation of their spiritual potency" (Hackett 1995, 290). While gender divisions are carefully established in African religions, there is often a fluidity or shifting of gender designations, as in the case of the ambiguous, multiple, or shifting gender identities of many African divinities.

Some West African religions, such as some tribes of the Yoruba and Poro societies of Sierra Leone, have secret male societies. Their annual festivals serve to demonstrate male power and control over females and help perpetuate patriarchy (Oduyoye 1995, 32). However, there are also some African women's secret socio-religious societies, which Hackett describes (Hackett 1994, 87-88), although most of these did not survive passage to the New World (Fandrich 1999, 16). Thus, although African religions in general are highly gender segregated, this segregation does not necessarily mean that men dominate and control all aspects of religious life.

Women's Access to Religious Training and Education and Opportunities for Leadership Roles

Women in African societies do have relatively open access to religious training and education. Many women have been recognized as diviners or spirit possessors, as Brown's story of Alourdes indicates. Both male and female diviners have trained female initiates in their craft.

In some African religions, women have a relatively prominent role. Among the Ondo, the Eastern practitioners of the Yoruba religion, women are considered to have actual power. This is especially true of older women, who, along with female title holders, mediums, and priests, are called "Our Mothers." The mediums, who allow their bodies to be taken over by deities (called "Orisha") so they can manifest to their worshipers, are mostly female. Men who are mediums are called "wives" of the possessing deity and often adopt female clothing and hairstyles. Mediums are highly respected in their communities and are considered to have power from their connection to the deity who "possesses" them.

There is a hierarchy of female as well as male leaders within each Yoruba subculture whose primary role is to appoint the king. The head of these female leaders is called the *Lobun* ("owner of the market") or the *Oba Obinrin* ("woman king"). The former term corresponds to Yoruba women's role as being in charge of the markets. As Hackett tells us, however, there is divided opinion about whether these women are exceptions to the general rule, and whether they actually hold political power (Hackett 1994, 75).

In the mainstream Christian churches, African women mostly have influence in women's associations and prayer bands rather than as ministers or church leaders. More opportunities are available to women in the new religious movements (which Oduyoye discusses), which have usually grown out of and broken away from more mainstream churches. As Hackett discusses in another essay, these new religious movements have provided significant new roles for women that are denied to them by traditional Christian and indigenous African religious institutions (Hackett 1995).

Well-Known and/or Influential Women in the Tradition

Hackett describes several women who have played significant roles in African religions, either as founders of new movements, or as ritual specialists or diviners or spirit mediums. Although a few of these women, such as Kongo Dona Beatrice (Kimpa Vita), probably founded the earliest African new religious movement in the early eighteenth century, most of these women are from the nineteenth and twentieth centuries. Brown's essay "Alourdes" describes a very influential contemporary Haitian female spirit medium living and performing spiritual services in Brooklyn. Another is the "Vodou Queen" Mari Laveaux, who lived and practiced in nineteenth-century New Orleans (see Fandrich 1999, 14).

Because African religions have been primarily based on oral rather than written traditions, at least until recently and because male researchers have focused primarily on African men's religious activities, it is hard to know how many influential women religious leaders, diviners, and spiritual adepts may have been lost to history.

Changes in the Status of Women

Historically

Both within Africa and particularly in the diaspora Afro-Atlantic religions, women have been able to play more prominent religious roles as they have moved from rural locations, where patriarchal social roles and values are heavily entrenched, to urban areas where there are more freedom and flexibility of gender role definitions. Brown's essay portrays this trend with respect to Haitian Vodou practitioners who have immigrated to New York City. This phenomonon can also be seen in the practice of Candomble in Salvador de Bahia as well as Umbanda in Rio de Janeiro (Fandrich 1999, 14).

Hackett describes how, in contrast to traditional African religions, mission Christianity promotes women's rights. Women's involvement in the new religious movements has provided opportunities for their religious activity that has been foreclosed to them in other religious institutions. Some of the women who founded new religious movements legitimated themselves as female leaders by being exceptional in some respects, such as being childless and unmarried, having passed through menopause or otherwise renouncing their femaleness, or being affiliated with a spirit as mediums and diviners. Women are attracted to new religions mostly for pragmatic reasons, such as seeking cures for illnesses, infertility, or poverty rather than for more political reasons such as opportunities for power and authority in a religious context. But having the opportunity for more responsibilities may function to keep women involved with a new religious movement after their initial affiliation (Hackett 1995, 277). Nonetheless, the main function of mission Christianity is to prepare women for traditional domestic and support roles.

Future Prospects

Since Hackett addresses this topic at the end of her essay, I will not say much here, except to note, as she discusses, that women have been playing key roles in the resurgence of interest in certain African religious rituals, both in Africa and elsewhere, some spearheaded by white (and some European) women. Several African religious traditions, some involving women diviners and spirit mediums, have taken root as a result of slavery outside of Africa, especially in Brazil, Haiti, Cuba, and the Caribbean. In addition, African goddess traditions are of particular interest to women outside of Africa, especially African Americans, as Sabrina Sojourner's essay in Chapter 9 discusses. New African religious movements (most associated with Christianity) are also creating new roles for women, some in positions of leadership. Some women have founded their own movements or taken over leadership after male founders have died. These trends are expected to continue in the future, but there appears to be little potential for radical shifts on the horizon.

Notes

1. Candomble, Santeria, and Umbanda are all influenced by the Orisha religion of the Yoruba (see Fandrich 1999, 13).
2. As Jordan Paper observes with respect to West African religions, since there are many prominent female deities in the sculpture, "it is quite surprising to find most descriptions of the religions of these regions downplaying female spirituality. There seems to be a disjunction between the visual evidence and descriptive rhetoric" (Paper 1997, 193).
3. As you may be aware, FGM is one of the most controversial moral issues today, especially among feminists committed to both the empowerment of women from oppression as well as the significance and value of traditional cultural practices. See references on FGM in Internet and Media References.

Women in African Religions

Rosalind I. J. Hackett

> The Great Mother has power in many things.... [She] is the owner of everything in the world. She owns you. We must not say how the whole thing works.
>
> (Drewal and Drewal 1983, 7)

The belief in women's creative and mystical powers is widespread in many parts of Africa. Such powers may be channeled in a variety of ways through ritual authority, spirit mediumship and possession, divination, healing, and mythical knowledge. As attested to above by the elderly Yoruba participant in the Gelede festival in western Nigeria, which pays tribute to and seeks to derive benefit from female mystical power, these powers are frequently perceived as shrouded in secrecy and mystery, and both venerated and feared. It is this very complexity, secrecy, and ambiguity that render our task of studying women's religious lives in Africa a very challenging one.

There is an urgent need to be aware of the religious factor in African women's lives, not just because of the intrinsic interest for scholars of religion, but because of the capacity of religion to construct meaning, shape community, and influence behavior and self-perception. Religious beliefs and values also provide an excellent insight into a society's gender ideology and attitudes to women (Strobel 1984, 88). Such concerns are regrettably absent for the most part from the consideration of women's issues and development in Africa in general. More generally, as Zuesse rightly emphasizes, we may note that the boundaries and interrelations between humans and spirits, village and forest, children and adults, and male and female are matters of the deepest spiritual significance to Africans (Zuesse 1979, 11).

This essay examines what is known of women's religious roles and experience in traditional African societies, attempting to do justice to both the unity and diversity therein. The survey type of approach, while much needed given the dearth of such comprehensive studies (Kilson 1976; Ezeanya 1976; Strobel 1984; Mbon 1987), has significant limitations. It runs the risk of being static and synchronic, ignoring the dynamism, subtleties, and complexities of the forms of women's religious expression and experience. It may lead to oversimplified generalizations about women's religious

From Arvind Sharma, ed. 1994. *Religion and Women*. Albany: SUNY Press. Pp. 61–92 (excerpted). Reprinted with permission of SUNY Press.

status (or lack of it) or unnecessary sentimentality about their fertility and virtue. It may lead to an overemphasis on the exceptional rather than the ordinary, focusing on overt, elite religious authority rather than the more covert, everyday forms of power and experience.

In order to avoid such possible shortcomings, I have sought, wherever possible, to draw on firsthand and indigenous sources. Examples are also drawn from my own fieldwork among the Yoruba, Efik, and Ibibio peoples of Nigeria. While not proceeding as systematically as Marion Kilson does in her article "Women in African Traditional Religions" when she selects religions from societies on seven different levels of social differentiation (Kilson 1976, 134), a range of examples has been selected from the various regions of Africa. The main focus is on the "traditional" religions of sub-Saharan Africa but some mention will be made of the transformations of African religions in the New World, and in the newer religious movements in Africa as well as the changes engendered by Islam and Christianity.

To ensure a well-rounded approach to women's religious lives in Africa, rather than being limited to theological concepts or ritual participation as a way of organizing the diverse and abundant data on the subject, Ninian Smart's six-dimensional model of religion is used (Smart 1983). This divides the phenomenon of religion into its doctrinal, mythical, ritual, ethical, experiential, and institutional aspects. While any such divisions may be artificial, Smart is keen to emphasize the organic nature of religion—the interdependency between beliefs and practices, for example. Alternatively, themes or types of religion (such as hunting or agricultural religions, as used by Zuesse in his book on African religions, *Ritual Cosmos* [1979]) or regions, as suggested above, could have formed the basis of this study. However, for comparative purposes and given the orientation of the present book, the six-dimensional model provides a more illuminating and productive approach.

Most importantly, however, the present essay is informed by a more flexible approach to gender and sex roles, and the way these are reflected in or shaped by religion. Gender should be viewed as a cultural construct and sex is the term for biological differences (Strobel 1984, 88). Ritual is an important forum for the articulation of the discourse, or even the dialectics, of gender (Glaze 1986). Representations of "maleness" and "femaleness," together with the crossing of boundaries and reversal of roles may be an integral part of the performance. We need to recognize the multiplicity of signs of female religious power and authority—iconography, verbal and musical expression, dress, dance, architecture, rather than just public office.

Women's religious roles and activities in Africa may be sexually exclusive, parallel, or complementary. They deserve a more thorough and adequate treatment than they have enjoyed in the past, and to some extent the present. For, as D. Amaury Talbot astutely observed in the introduction to her book, *Woman's Mysteries of a Primitive People*, in 1915, "primitive woman is still unknown save through the medium of masculine influence." This requires, as outlined above, the descriptive analysis of women's religious participation and symbolic differentiation, but also an awareness of the interplay and complementarity of men and women and the expression of their power conflicts through the medium of religion.

First, some discussion of the characteristics of African "traditional" societies and their religious systems is required, for this has methodological implications. Despite the enormous geographical and cultural diversity of the African continent, including diversity in the status of women, an underlying asymmetry (of various kinds) between men and women is a recurring feature. Prior to the imposition of European rule, most African economies were based on agriculture, trade, or iron technology. Some were made up of pastoralists or hunting and gathering peoples. Women were (and still are) responsible for much of the agricultural and domestic labor. The majority of slaves in precolonial Africa were women. Women played an important commercial role, particularly in terms of the retail food trade, which they dominated in West Africa. They were able to achieve some degree of economic autonomy often because they were able to retain control of their property in marriage. Women's position was also affected by varying family structures. Most African peoples are broadly patrilineal, tracing descent through the paternal line, but there was a greater incidence of matrilinearity in Africa than elsewhere. Even in patrilineal groups, descent through women still often constitutes a "submerged" line of descent through which spiritual qualities can be carried. Marriage was, as now, predominantly a social, political, and economic affair. Nuclear families were rare, as polygyny served to generate wealth and children for men.

In many African societies women's and men's spheres have traditionally been distinct. The delimitation of these spheres is fluid and varies according to ethnic, social, geographic, and historical factors. Women frequently act collectively within their own sphere, either through voluntary associations or through institutions that parallel those of men. In many parts of the continent it has been demonstrated that women had considerable economic independence and a political voice, but they were not dominant, nor were they equal. Some observers attribute this to a general bias toward male superiority, others to unequal access to resources, while some would point to the various cultural restrictions that may keep women subordinate, such as long puberty and mourning rites involving seclusion, menstrual and childbirth taboos, and male secret societies, which are culturally legitimated ways of suppressing women.

It is generally agreed that colonialism weakened the position of African women, both politically and economically, with the importation of Western culture, bureaucratic structures, and military technology. It served to heighten gender stratification, adding European sexism to the patriarchal elements in indigenous cultures (Robertson and Berger 1986, 6).

Since women's religious roles and experience are embedded in their socio-historical context, it is impossible to isolate their religious lives from their lives in general. Religion is such an integral part of traditional societies that many African languages (if not all) have no word for "religion." Zuesse, in his book on African religions, *Ritual Cosmos*, describes the main focus of African religions as being "the transcendental significance of everyday life" or the "sanctification of life" (Zuesse, 3,7). He further observes that "All energies are directed to the ritual sustenance of the normal order—"normal" in two senses, as imbedded in norms going back to the beginning of time, and as usual and commonplace reality (Zuesse, 3). Therefore it is important to include (wherever feasible given the comprehensiveness of the present essay) the possible interpretations and explanations (both internal and external) that point to the embeddedness of women's religious roles, such as the therapeutic benefits of spirit possession or the function of ritual in validating bonds between women beyond the domestic sphere. We now turn to ideas concerning female mystical power.

Ideas Regarding Women's Religious Power and Female Divinities

Ambivalency seems to characterize the ideas about women and their mystical powers in Africa. They are respected for their procreative powers and nurturing role, and their links with the earth and the ancestors. However, in some societies, women may be regarded as the purveyors of evil and misfortune, often in the guise of witches, and polluters of the sacred. This is attributed by some to the uncertainty about women's allegiances to their husbands' lineages. Their generative powers are often associated with the uncontrollable forces of nature. On account of their perceived greater affectivity, they are often believed by certain peoples to be more subject to spirit possession. Their powers of intuition are associated with clairvoyance and equip them in some societies to be diviners.

It is clear that there are strong links between the religious status and participation of women and their (perceived) physiology and psychology. Cultural perceptions of women's power vary from society to society, but some degree of mystery and fear is usually present. It is important to sound a note of caution here, since these are predominantly male perceptions of women recorded and reproduced by male anthropologists. According to Zahan, these dominant perceptions among the Bambara of Mali relate woman to the "night" and "darkness" because she is more enigmatic and unfathomable than any other creature. They relate this to her physical constitution, which is seen as mysterious and very different from that of the male.

In her entirety, the woman "is" the earth—that is, the inert matter that encloses "life within it, and supports all that is necessary for man's existence.

She 'is' also water, the element of proliferation and abundance. Each of the woman's sexual organs, as well as its adjacent parts, reveals by the analogies it evokes the different parts of the creation, each as mysterious as the next." (Zahan, 94)

Thus, like the earth, woman is inert and passive. Like water, she is multiform and changeable (Zahan, 95) and does not let herself be mastered. Like the night and the shadows, woman is difficult to fathom, and like a cavity or hollow, she does not allow herself to be grasped. Alongside this is the view, as among many other African peoples, that women do not know how to impose limits on their words and speak too directly (Zahan, 114). Similarly the dominant ideology among the Dogon asserts that women's chattering is a fault attributed to them by their nature, directly relating them to sickness and death, since a surfeit of words engenders illness (Zahan, 113). This both reflects reverence for the power of the spoken word in Africa, and men's fear of women's powers in this regard.

It will be seen that the various ideas concerning female nature and sexuality are translated into the ritual roles that are ascribed to women, such as night sorcerers, shrine caretakers, "wives" of deities, healers, life cycle ritual specialists. These ideas also influence their metaphysical status as witches or ancestors (all of which will be dealt with in later sections). In some cases, women may only perform key ritual functions when they have reached the postmenopausal stage or are childless, and have become "like men." They also account for why women are often restricted to neutral or domestic space, particularly for important ritual occasions, because they are considered both vulnerable and dangerous (Douglas, 7). Clearly, such an ideology serves male interests socially.

Sacred images also express ideas concerning female spirituality. Yoruba religious art frequently depicts, in wooden sculptural form, a kneeling woman with a child on her back or at her breasts or sometimes uplifting her breasts, all symbolizing not just fertility but devotion to the deity. The woman's dignity and devotion are regarded as exemplary for both men and women. Among the Igbo and Ibibio, also of Nigeria, their "cool," female masks and masquerades, which are usually colored white and emerge in the afternoon, dance and move gracefully like women, in contrast to "hot" male aggression. Certain priests of the Yoruba thunder god, Sango—whether male or female—are known as the wives (*iya*) of Sango and are endowed with the power to soothe and placate the god, just as females are believed to have a soothing effect on their husbands (Drewal and Drewal, 166). Their hair is plaited in a bridal coiffure to communicate that their heads (the site of one's personal essence, potential, and destiny) have been prepared for a special relationship with the deity. The Yoruba perceive patience to be inherent in femaleness (Drewal and Drewal, 15). The Great Mother epitomizes patience—in other words, her inner head is composed. She is believed to exact covert revenge and does not display visible anger. These ideas about women are expressed in the channeled and controlled steps of the female Gelede festival dances, which are powerful yet restrained. The mothers—that is to say, all spiritually powerful women whether elders, ancestors, or deities—"who are united with all women by the 'flow of blood,' embody the concept of balance, a female quality that men must understand—indeed emulate—in order to survive" (Drewal and Drewal, 15).

Another important idea that needs to be mentioned here, although it will receive fuller treatment below and in the section on mythology, is that in former times women had much greater mystical and creative power, and were superior to men. They were held to have founded the great secret societies or even been the prime movers of creation. Whether because of their perceived inability to keep secrets or their loquaciousness, or their unwillingness to wage war (Tonkin 1982), men appropriated the mystical secrets and wrested the power from women....

Ritual

In this section on ritual, I shall first treat women as ritual specialists, then as ritual participants, examining the rites associated with womanhood. Examples of women playing primary ritual roles, with their attendant political power in the traditional African context, are relatively few. One of the classic examples is the Lovedu Rain Queen of the Transvaal. The queen was believed to be of divine origin; her mystical powers were linked to the welfare of society. Her powers were not absolute; combining her own divinity with the use of medicine and charms, she worked in conjunction with the ancestor to control rain and ensure the cyclic regularity of the seasons. She was believed to be so bound up with nature that her very emotions affected the rain. Various royal institutions preserved her sanctity, such as celibacy, seclusion, and suicide. Her death was considered to dislocate the rhythm of nature, causing drought and famine, and necessitating rites of purification, to ensure the harmonious succession of the new queen. The prestige of the queen as ruler helped maintain the high status of women in a patrilineal society. Heads or "mothers" of districts (who might also be men) also served as mediators to the queen. The queen's feminine attributes—appeasement, reciprocity, reconciliation—were viewed as positive, diplomatic qualities.

Among the Yoruba, women are admitted into the priesthood of the main cults such as Sango (thunder god), Obatala (god of creation), and Osun (goddess of fertility). Women are more likely to predominate as officials in cults devoted to female or bisexual deities, or where there is a powerful consort, such as in the case of Oya (wife of Sango). Opinions are divided about whether these women who held high religious office, such as head of the king's market, the worship of departed kings, or the cults of Oduduwa or Ososi and the royal women, were exceptions to the rule and whether they wielded any real political authority. Afonja argues that the religious roles offered these women as advisers to the king are in addition to the general respect accorded their office as intermediaries between people and the divinities (Afonja, 151).

The existence of a strong female deity is no guarantee of female ritual authority. The majority of Igbo cult groups are exclusively male preserves, even that of Ala, the earth goddess (Arinze, 73). Possible exceptions could occur at the family cult level, when elderly women could sacrifice directly to their personal *chi* (guardian spirit) in their compounds, but never at the public level. Igbo women may become diviners, *ndi dibia*, but usually as elderly widows.

In order to gain ritual authority, women sometimes need to have exceptional status or they must lose the characteristics of womanhood. For example, the figure of Mother Ndundu, the female overseer of the Kimpasi, is sometimes an albino (*ndundu*), but is generally an old woman past childbearing age, and who had not given birth to children or they had died. In ordinary life, therefore, she is an unfortunate figure, yet within the context of the cult she is given an elevated status. Her infertility provides her with a central ritual role as mother of the cult members (Janzen, 91; Lewis, 95). Among the Azande, certain women diviners gain authority to mediate between the human and spirit world following a symbolic death, where they claim to witness and experience their death and resurrection (Zahan, 83). No training is required in this type of initiation.

Let us turn now to the role of women as spirit mediums and diviners, both of which are widespread phenomena in Africa, but sometimes difficult to distinguish. Frequently the call to mediumship begins with psychological or physical disturbances, which may worsen if the call is ignored (Horton, 34). Sometimes mediumship is expressed in marital terms—the woman becomes a "wife" of a spirit or deity. The main deities in the Bunyoro and Buganda kingdoms in East Africa had women dedicated to them as wives (Berger, 174). These women were to remain unmarried while in the deity's service. Two of the most important were Mukakiranga, wife of Kiranga in Burundi, who played a major part in the great national ceremony and annual spiritual renewal of the Rundi kingdom, and the medium of Mukasa, the god of Lake Victoria, who was popularly held to have the power to cure the king and work miracles (Berger, 175–76). Gã mediums of southeastern Ghana have been studied by both Field (1937) and Kilson (1972, 1975). Traditional Gã religion (or *kpele* consists of a number of cults, addressed to particular divinities, which are served by two categories of specialists: priests and mediums. The priesthood is a kinship-ascribed male status chiefly concerned with representing humans to the gods; mediumship is an achieved female status concerned with communicating the messages of gods and humans to one another. Priests and mediums cooperate to perform certain calendrical rites (priestly authority tends to be greater), but the medium (*woyei* or *wongtse*) may operate independently, as a diviner, to serve clients. Field argues that these women have no authority except when possessed. Kilson states that most of the mediums are illiterate, and often childless, women; yet their ritual possession and success as insightful mediums may serve to redress much of the inferiority they would normally experience in Gã society.

Berger lists a number of varied ways in which East African women achieved higher status as mediums, symbolized through their use of male stools, male ceremonial dress, and spears, for example, and expressed through the authority they were able to exert over women's (and sometimes men's) affair in the community (Berger 1976). For two years (1971–1973) during the war for independence in Zimbabwe, an aged female medium, known as Kunzaruwa, serving the great spirit Nehanda, gave advice to the guerillas on how to win the war. She imposed ritual prohibitions, told them what food to eat and which paths to take—"she hated all European things" (Lan, 3–7). There was a tradition of resistance and liberation associated with Nehanda mediums, which dated back to Shona resistance against colonial oppression in the 1890s and was expressed in many important works of Shona literature from the 1950s onward.

Let us now turn to those women who practice divination. Among the BaLuba specialists who serve as intermediaries between the souls of the dead and the living, there are numerous women who serve in the highest class (Zahan, 83). All Gusii diviners in Nyansongo in Kenya are female. Following an apprenticeship and elaborate initiation ceremony, the diviners of a given area are said to meet secretly from time to time. As Levine states: "The parallel between the female diviners meeting together, training and inducting novices, and the female witches who also meet, recruit and train, is striking one" (Levine, 232–33).

Sandobele (female diviners) among the Senufo of Côte d'Ivoire believed to mediate between land spirits and clients, are generally revered for their ability to "cool" or heal people from the illnesses and troubles resulting from their unintentional offences against the spirits (Glaze 1986, 37). Yoruba women are not excluded from the divination system known as Ifa. In fact, in Yoruba mythology it is told how the goddess Osun was initiated into Ifa. Some would claim that several verses (*odu*) of the Ifa corpus, particularly those associated with female or androgynous deities (Oya, Olokun, Oduduwa), were composed by women. However, few women attain the status of *babalawo* (father of mysteries; sometimes the term, *iyalawo* is used) because of the lengthy and rigorous apprenticeship involved. Many families consider divination to be an undesirable and impractical career for women. Barber (288–90) maintains that women are not debarred from becoming *babalawo*, only that they choose not to—preferring to avoid likely accusations of witchcraft. Among the Temne of Sierra Leone, distinctions between male and female are reflected in the contrasts between private/public and individual/social divination (Shaw, 289). In private divinations, the majority of clients are women and, apart from a few female private diviners, divination is predominantly a male preserve. Public divination, the domain of men, is more positively evaluated, since it is performed in the open and is associated with the upholding of community interests.

Numerous rituals and accompanying taboos concern women alone. Women's religious devotions among the Igbo of Nnobi in southeastern Nigeria begin with private worship known as *ilo chi* (remembering the deity) at their personal shrines before proceeding to group worship, *ilo chi Idemili* (remembering the goddess Idemili) (Amadiume 1987, 103–4). *Ekwe* titled women have their own exclusive day of worship. In a number of parts of Africa, it is commonly believed that pregnant women need special protection from witches and evil spirits. Gã women (Ghana) would bathe in a bath of herbs and morsels of food (believed to deceive the preying witch) (Field 1937, 164). To ensure a safe delivery, libations might be made to the gods, the priest might draw symbolic markings on the body, and rites to ascertain the wishes of the unborn child might also be performed. The Ila of Zambia forbid pregnant women from entering the hut where a woman has just given birth, from entering a calabash garden, and from getting too close to a nest of eggs. Zuesse explains this in terms of a basic antipathy between the not-yet formed (primordial) and the formed (cosmically structured) (1979, 83). Death in childbirth is greatly feared; the Asante of Ghana remove the undelivered child, for they believe it will prevent the dead woman's soul from entering the place of the dead, transforming it into a vengeful ghost (Field, 122).

Barrenness, the fear of women throughout Africa, is generally attributed to witchcraft or the failure to propitiate regularly family gods and spirits. Many women turn to fertility gods or goddesses. Ibibio women might still supplicate Eka Abassi as they did in the past, going with their husbands to lay a sacrifice at her rock shrine:

> O Abassi Ma! Keeper of Souls! What have I done to anger thee! Look upon me, for from the time I left the fatting-room in my mother's house I have never conceived, and am a reproach before all women. Behold! I bring gifts, and beg Thee to have pity on me and give me a child. Grant but this prayer, and all my life I will be thy servant! (Talbot 1968, 19)

In some societies such as the Efik and Ibibio, women were ostracized if they gave birth to twins—the sign of a woman's association with evil spirits. Twin killing was a major target for reform by Christian missionaries. Among other peoples such as the Yoruba, Bambara, Dogon, and Senufo, multiple births are viewed as sacred and special rites may be performed in the event of the death of a twin (Houlberg 1973).

Menstruation is often the source of ritual seclusion and numerous taboos, reflecting the ambivalent attitudes toward women's reproductive powers. Ndembu women have to go and live in special huts and are advised to throw the water used for washing the cloth used at such times in the river, not in the bush, where it might impair hunters' medicines or be used by sorcerers (Turner, 248). Among the !Kung Bushmen of the Kalahari Desert, menstruating women are supposed to keep away from their husbands and not touch their husband's weapons, for fear of destroying their power. The Ila of central Zambia do not allow menstruating women to tend the fire, for fear of polluting the ancestral essence (Zuesse, 82).

Yet the first menstruation is often a sign of rejoicing and marks the beginning of the ritual preparation of the young girl for womanhood and marriage. Throughout the matrilineal central Bantu cultures, these initiation rites for women are basically similar, indicating their importance (Zuesse, 83). Everywhere the novice is separated from her mother, taken from the hut, and in the bush and later in an instructress's hut is reshaped into the archetypal fertile woman. The culmination is often the wedding of the young woman. Ritual serves to delineate this transition, dramatizing and resolving the social conflicts. Ndembu women in Zaire believe that the shades, *mukishi*, will be angry and cause infertility if a girl does not pass through the rites before her marriage (Turner 1968, 200). The focal point of the Ndembu girls' puberty ritual, *Nkang'a*, is the sacred *mudyi* tree, whose milky white latex symbolizes both the mother's milk and the matrilineal and social customs of the Ndembu. The tree also serves to delineate womanhood from manhood, and mother from daughter (Turner, 17).

The importance of these rites in symbolically expressing female identity and defining women's domestic roles is attested to by their persistence in the urban context. In Lusaka, Zambia, for example, these initiation rituals are on the increase, often being jointly performed by several ethnic groups (Bemba, Ngoni, and Crewa). Modified forms have been incorporated into the life cycle rituals of the indigenous or independent churches (Jules-Rosette 1980).

Fertility rites are often celebrated exclusively by women at strategic times of the agricultural year. Ibibio women and girls would go naked, unseen by men, at the time of the New Yam Festival to the shrine of the (male) deity, Isemin, protector of women and bestower of fertility (Talbot 1968, 109–10). They would present sacrifices of corn and fish, symbolizing fertility of earth and the waters. Because of their association with life, women often have major responsibilities at the time of death. Among the Gã of Ghana, an old woman assists the surviving partner to perform the *kwa* or separation ceremony, to convince the dead of the grief of the survivor. The woman is not a priestess (although the appointment is hereditary), just an old woman belonging to a family that the dead know and respect (Field 1937). The difficult and important task of identifying a particular reincarnated ancestor among the Anlo of Ghana, known as *megbekpokpo*, the rite of reincarnation, is a female diviner's prerogative (Gaba, 181). Women are also the principal or key functionaries in a number of other Anlo rituals associated with birth and death. In the past, Ibibio women had responsibility for the burial of their dead warriors in a ritual reminiscent of the Isis and Osiris myth of regeneration. Secret rites were performed, which involved the drawing of sacred boughs over the body of the deceased in an attempt to extract his virility for the community (Talbot 1968, 206–8). Efik women, also from southeastern Nigeria, are responsible for announcing the death of the king or *obong* to the community.

In many parts of Africa, women may be subjected to numerous rites of purification at the death of their husbands. These were often condemned by Christian missionaries, for they involved months of seclusion for the women, where she was not allowed to wash, plait her hair, or wear clothes; she was expected to wail publicly and sometimes undergo physical ordeals by way of purification. Among the Efik and Ibibio these mourning rites (*mbukpisi*) have been much reduced and modified in recent times.

As many have observed, it would seem that women are generally relegated to subordinate ritual roles in the central, communal, and public cults. They rather dominate in the personal rituals of status transformation or life cycle rituals (Kilson 1976, 138–39; Richards 1956). Even when women's involvement appears to be peripheral, in the rituals that men dominate and control, it may be subtle and strategic, pointing not only to men's recognition of female mystical and procreative powers, but also their former higher status. For example, the new ruler, or Ntoe, of the Qua people of southeastern Nigeria is crowned by the Queen Mother, who represents the populace. A senior, royal woman may be called upon to retrieve the *ekpe* (leopard) or mysterious and invisible being from the forest, upon which the Ekpe society is founded (Hackett 1989, 35; Talbot 1968, 193). As part of one of the main festivals of the Ekong or warriors' society among the Ibibio, on the periphery of the proceedings, sat singing a man dressed in women's clothes. He represented "The Mother of Ekong" ensuring blessings for the coming year and reminding people of the female origins of the society (Talbot 1968, 203–4).

The use of ritual space may be significant in understanding perceptions of gender. The Lele of Zambia regard the forest as almost exclusively a male sphere; women are generally prohibited from entering it on all important religious occasions until the proper rites have been performed by men. Women are allocated to the neutrally perceived grasslands. Douglas explains this ritual exclusion in terms of religious conceptions of women's fertility powers—they are both highly vulnerable and highly polluting (Douglas, 7). The Yoruba Gelede festival to appease the "mothers" or witches of the society is appropriately conducted in the marketplace, at once the domain of women and the worldly domain of spirits, where homage can be paid to the special powers of women (Drewal and Drewal, 10; see also Lawuyi and Olupona 1988).

Religious Experience

The area of women's religious experience yields little information. This is attributable to the fact that most accounts of women's religious activities are androcentric, generally viewing women as insignificant or subordinate. In addition, there is a general lack of interest in (or avoidance of) the experiential dimension by researchers. The intangibility and psychological nature of experience, especially when related to the divine or the spiritual, represents a methodological challenge. There is a need for more biographical and autobiographical accounts, such as the one of Julia, an East African diviner, whose extraordinary calling brings about a reversal of an oppressive family structure (Binford, 3–14) and that of Nisa, a !Kung woman, who describes the trance states of women during the drum dance and their intimate connection with *n/um* or the power of healing (Shostak, 297–300). In the absence of such accounts, artistic images offer visual statements—kneeling, nurturing, offering, paying homage, uplifting breasts—of female emotions—namely, serenity, devotion, submission, calmness—in the presence of the divine. The product of male sculptors, these images nonetheless condense and articulate through female symbolism the ideas and norms of divine/human relationships.

The marginalized and privatized world of women may be deceptive and misleading to observers, whether inside or outside the culture. Women may not always be center stage, but their experiences in ritual seclusion may not necessarily be characterized by powerlessness and fear. Instead they may display tolerance of male coercion, such as in masking traditions, and enjoy ideological freedom (Tonkin, 171). Women are not supposed to know the secrets of male cults and associations, but they frequently do.

Since it is the spirit-mediumship cults that have offered women some of the greatest possibilities for active participation, it is here that we are provided with accounts and interpretations of women's religious experience. Berger rightly distinguishes between spirit mediumship (discussed earlier), where the person is conceived of as serving as intermediary between the divine and human realms, and spirit possession, a form of trance in which the behavior indicates spirit control (Berger, 161). The latter has engendered the formation of a number of cults, which Lewis has labeled marginal or "peripheral" since they provide therapeutic assistance to the powerless. He describes the Sar cult among Muslim women in Somalia, where women's ailments are interpreted by them as possession by traditional *sar* spirits. These spirits demand luxuries and finery from their husbands and expensive cathartic dances to effect the recovery of the women. The men generally acquiesce to these demands, which usually occur at times of neglect and abuse in a conjugal relationship. Through the cult Lewis argues that women are able to air their grievances and gain some measure or redress in a world dominated by men. Similar patterns of possession are observable in Ethiopia (where it is known as the Zar cult), Egypt, other parts of northern Africa and Arabia, as well as in the Bori cult in northern Nigeria and Niger (Lewis, 75–79).

Wilson disagrees with Lewis's interpretation of these cults in terms of sexual antagonism; he proposes instead that spirit possession is linked to tensions between women, often caused by marriage (Wilson 1967). Spring is critical of the above social/functional perspectives, because they depict women negatively as "pawns" or "agents of conflict." Based on her research among the Luvale of Zambia, she argues that spirit possession is a way of treating physiological disorders among women and binding them together into a wider symbolic community (Spring 1978). Mernissi shows how Moroccan women seek material power through saint cults, the type of power denied to them through trade unions and political parties. She maintains that this form of religiosity, while offering some therapeutic benefits, only serves to entrench their marginality in an "ever-strengthened" patriarchal system (Mernissi 1977). In his examination of spirit possession among the Kalabari in southeastern Nigeria, Horton (1969, 35ff.) provides important information on women's possession (*oru kuro*), particularly the circumstances of its onset, the ensuing consequences for behavior and life-style, and acceptance or rejection of the possessing spirit (*oru*). He regards such possession as a response to childlessness, terming it more generally as a "loophole for the socially miscast." However he does see this type of spirit possession as a means of recasting social roles, and also as a platform for the introduction of innovation into a highly conservative culture. . . .

Conclusion

It may be argued that the distinction between men and women is the primary social distinction for many societies (e.g., Whyte, 182; Shaw 1985). Sometimes myths and rituals serve to emphasize and explain these contrasting categorizations of reality, sometimes they are more implicit. It has been demonstrated that social models and their representation through religious ideology and related ritual practice are elaborated from the dominant male position (E. Ardener 1975). This view represents men as central and identifies them with the essence of society itself. Such ideological discourse defines women as "other" than men, either by placing them peripherally in nature, or as possessed by spirits that are marginal, foreign, or little (Whyte, 180–81; Lewis 1971). Several authors have argued that despite social differences, men and women still share the general social model and are part of the same social structure (Whyte, 189). The counterpart models and alternative views generated by women, which seemingly repudiate the male subject, are not completely independent or autonomous. They are interactively shaped by the general ideological and structural model. We have seen throughout this chapter how this complementarity, rather than equality, is expressed in a number of ways both symbolically and ritually, transcending everyday hierarchical social relationships. Religion serves both to legitimate male dominance as well as to provide a (sometimes subtle or covert) channel of communication for the muted or subdominant groups such as women to express their interests, to challenge male control and revalidate their identities. African ritual has been aptly described as "dialogic in form, and always a process of competition, negotiation and argumentation" (H. J. Drewal 1988, 25). West African secret societies and their attendant masquerades represent particularly rich contexts for such processes and perceptions (Glaze 1986).

When studying African traditional religious systems and women's roles in these religions, it is important to guard against the too ready imposition of Western values and over objectified interpretations (Holden, 3–4). It is too simplistic to dismiss women's ritual roles as subordinate because they are linked to their sexual status and biological functions (Hoch-Smith and Spring, 2–4) or to say that women achieve authority only by becoming and behaving like men. Complexities and ambiguities abound. We are challenged to be attentive to the female symbols atop male masquerades, the sexual metaphors of architecture, the cross-dressing of ritual participants, the androgynous character of many religious leaders, the transformative capacity of spirit possession. Both perceptions and behavior are marked by fluidity—men, as well as women, may become "wives" and "cooks" of the deity, just as women may be "husbands" and "kings." Exclusion from the religious life, such as initiation rites, may not necessarily entail exclusion from the spiritual life, since it may be held that women naturally carry (spiritual) knowledge within them (Zahan, 54–55).

It is this very ambiguity and fluidity that generates debate, such as over whether ritual segregation gives women a greater or a different power or serves to alienate them, or whether female ritual authority shapes, questions, or even undermines male authority in any way. More research is required in this field. It must treat women as subjects and not just as objects. It must seek to hear the multiplicity of voices involved in order to see more clearly, even reconstruct, women's religious worlds not just in contradistinction to, but also in interaction with, men's religious lives. Likewise, the historical perspective is integral to an appreciation of the dynamic of gender discourse.

It seems appropriate to end this chapter on women and religion in Africa, not so much by looking back, but rather by looking forward, by highlighting areas of persistence and transformation. Evidence abounds for the demise of traditional religious institutions, yet there are some interesting examples of women playing strategic roles in preserving and revitalizing religious traditions both in Africa and the New World.

For example, the annual festival of the river goddess, Osun, in Osogbo, western Nigeria, has become a very popular event, drawing thousands of people from all over Nigeria. They come to seek her blessings since "she is the wisdom of the forest where the doctor cures the child and does not charge the father. She feeds the barren woman with honey and her dry belly swells up like a juicy palm fruit."

Susanne Wenger, an Austrian artist who settled in Yorubaland in the 1960s, and became a priestess in Osogbo, has done much to revitalize the traditional festival of Osun (Wenger and Chesi, 1983). Yoruba goddesses have an appeal beyond national boundaries. In her book *Oya: In Praise of the Goddess*, Judith Gleason traces the various manifestation of Oya in nature—the great river Niger, strong winds and tornadoes, lightning and fire, and the mighty African buffalo, and her associations with funerals and masquerades constructed of secret, billowing cloth, from Africa to the New World, where she has devotees in Brazil, the Caribbean, and New York City (Gleason 1987). Oya is also linked to market women, to transformations, to the dynamic interplay of edges, to concealment, and to female leadership. African goddesses have tremendous appeal for African-American women (Sojourner 1982).

In both Zimbabwe and Nigeria, white women have been active in revitalizing traditional cults. In addition to Susanne Wenger, referred to above, a white spirit medium, Elsie Thompson, in eastern Zimbabwe, claims to have been possessed by and ordained to bring back the spirits of Mzilikazi and Chamunika. A white American women, Norma Rosen, whose initiation into the Olokun cult in Benin has been well-documented (Nevadomsky 1988), has established a shrine in Long Beach, California.

Mami Wata, an African female water spirit worshiped from Senegal to Tanzania, is currently experiencing a dynamic growth (H. J. Drewal 1988). Mami Wata is a Pidgin English term for "Mother of Water." In her more contemporary transformations, she represents Africans' attempt at understanding or constructing meaning from their encounters with overseas strangers. Mami Wata is an independent, foreign spirit, free of any social system. She is believed to dominate the realm of water and those who come under her sway. She relates to her devotees more as a lover than a mother, and offers rich financial rewards. Africans incorporated the concept of the mermaid, characteristically depicted as emerging from the water, combing her long, luxurious hair as she contemplates her reflection in a mirror (H. J. Drewal, 162).

The many new religious movements (mostly Christian-related), which abound in places like South Africa, Kenya, Nigeria, Ghana, and Côte d'Ivoire, exhibit both continuity and innovation. In the independent churches, women have found important new ceremonial functions. This leadership and responsibility is both an extension of and reinterpretation of traditional priestly roles and spirit mediumship (Jules-Rosette 1987; Callaway 1980). It contrasts with the submission and dependency advocated by the mission-related churches. Several women have founded their own movements, such as Alice Lenshina and the Lumpa Church in Zambia, Christianah Abiodun and the Cherubim and Seraphim movement in Nigeria, Marie Lalou and the Eglise Déimatiste in Côte d'Ivoire, Mai Chaza in Zimbabwe. Indeed, the very first recorded African religious movement was founded by a woman, Dona Béatrice (Kimpa Vita) in the late seventeenth century in the former kingdom of the Kongo (now Zaïre). Because of her challenge to the Portuguese Roman Catholic Church and its doctrinal and liturgical hegemony, and her advocacy of indigenous leadership, she was burned at the stake in 1706. It has been argued, however, that despite their increased ritual participation (in part linked to the fact that healing is a central focus of these movements), women's political authority and public leadership are restricted in the independent churches (often through taboos), short-lived (female successors are rare), and chiefly symbolic (Jules-Rosette 1987; Hackett 1987, 191–208).

Within the mainline churches or the mission-related churches, it is generally not as priests or pastors that women may exercise influence, but as leaders and participants in the various women's associations and prayer bands. These semi-autonomous groups are a feature of many of these churches; they allow women to organize their own religious and social affairs. In many cases, they constitute a powerful voice within the respective churches and a force for church development (women are renowned as effective fund raisers) (Hackett 1985, 259). As a corollary of this, a number of Methodist and Anglican women in Nigeria have built up compound healing ministries. As in the case of "Ma Jekova," a well-known Methodist healer in Calabar, southeastern Nigeria, they see their work as complementary to that of the larger, more official church.

The position of women in African Islam has been largely neglected by researchers or they have been portrayed as absent or marginal within Islam (Coulon, 113). Islam is presented as a male religion; women's involvement is rather in the (pre-Islamic) spirit-possession cults such as *bori* and *zar* (described above). However, several women with special powers or *baraka* have become revered or even worshiped as saints, *marabouts* or *khalifa*. Such an example is Sokhna Magat Diop in Senegal, who took over her father's Mouride community in 1943 (Coulon, 127–29). Information is coming to light about female *shaiks* who were renowned for their scholarship (Boyd 1989). Boyd and Last show how there is more open activity among Muslim women in northern Nigeria in the twentieth century (1985). Based on their research in Sokoto, they describe the activities of formal women's organizations, where women serve as *agents religieux*. Focusing on the actions and thought of learned women, they claim that women have helped transform the character of West African Islam through their encouragement of the use of vernacular languages and the use of popular songs and poetry for religious instruction and devotion.

The New World offers exciting possibilities for the study of continuities and transformations of African women's religious experiences. In Haitian

Voodoo, women possessed by female spirits act out the social and psychological forces that define, and often confine, the lives of contemporary Haitian women (Brown, 1989; 1991, 237). These spirits or *lwa* are derived from African religious traditions (such as Mami Wata) and identified with Roman Catholic saints (such as the Virgin Mary).

This chapter has sought to identify and discuss some of the main areas of women's religious experience and expression in traditional Africa as well as in the newer African religions. Much research remains to be done, not just to enrich and challenge our understanding of the African context, with its rich and varied religious traditions, but also to complement the many valuable studies that have emerged and continue to emerge on women and religion in related contexts.

Bibliography

Afonja, Simi. 1986. "Women, Power and Authority in Traditional Yoruba Society." *Visibility and Power: Essays on Women in Society and Development*, eds. L. Dube, et al. Delhi: Indian University Press.

Amadiume, Ife. 1987. *Male Daughters, Female Husbands: Gender and Sex in an African Society*. London: Zed Press.

Ardener, E. 1975. "The 'Problem' Revisited." *Perceiving Women*, ed. S. Ardener.

Ardener, S., ed. 1975. *Perceiving Women*. London: Dent Malaby.

Arinze, F. A. 1970. *Sacrifice in Igbo Religion*. Ibadan: Ibadan University Press.

Barber, K. 1991. *I Could Speak Until Tomorrow: "Oriki", Women and the Past in a Yoruba Town*. Edinburgh: Edinburgh University Press for the International African Institute.

Berger, Iris. 1976. "Rebels or Status-Seekers? Women as Spirit Mediums." *Women in Africa*, eds. Hafkin and Bay, 157–82.

Binford, Martha. 1989. "Julia: An East African Diviner." *Unspoken Worlds: Women's Religious Lives*, eds. Falk and Gross, 3–14.

Boone, Sylvia A. 1986. *Radiance from the Waters: Ideals of Feminine Beauty in Mende Art*. New Haven: Yale University Press.

Boyd, Jean. 1989. *The Caliph's Sister, Nana Asma'u, 1793–1865: Teacher, Poet and Islamic Leader*. London: Frank Cass.

Boyd, Jean, and Murray Last. 1985. "The Role of Women as 'Agents Riligieux' in Sokoto." *Canadian Journal of African Studies* 19, 2:283–300.

Brown, Karen McCarthy. 1989. "Mama Lola and the Ezilis: Themes of Mothering and Loving in Haitian Vodou." *Unspoken Worlds, Women's Religious Lives*, eds. Falk and Gross, 235–45.

———. 1991. *Mama Lola*. Los Angeles and Berkeley: University of California Press.

Callaway, Helen. 1980. "Women in Yoruba Tradition and in the Cherubim and Seraphim Society." *The History of Christianity in West Africa*, ed. O. Kalu. London: Longman, 321–32.

Coulon, C. 1988. "Women, Islam and *Baraka*." *Charisma and Brotherhood in African Islam*, eds. D.B. Cruise O'Brien and C. Coulon. Oxford: Clarendon, 111–33.

Douglas, Mary. 1960. "The Lele of the Kasai." *African Worlds*, ed. Forde, 1–26.

Drewal, H. J. ed. 1988. "Object and Intellect: Interpretations of Meaning in African Art." *Art Journal* 47,2 (summer).

Drewal, Henry John, and Margaret Thompson Drewal. 1983. *Gelede: Art and Female Power among the Yoruba*. Bloomington: Indiana University Press.

Ezeanya, S. N. 1976. "Women in African Traditional Religion." *Journal of Religion in Africa* 10,2:105–21.

Field, M. J. 1960. *Search for Security*. Evanston: Northwestern University Press.

———. 1937. *Religion and Medicine among the Gã People*. London.

Gaba, Christian. 1987. "Women and Religious Experience among the Anlo of West Africa." *Women in the World's Religions*, ed. U. King, 177–98.

Glaze, Anita. 1986. "Dialectics of Gender: Senufo Masquerades." *African Arts* 19, 3:30–39, 82.

———. 1975. "Woman Power and Art in a Senufo Village." *African Arts* 8,3:20–29, 64–68, 90.

Gleason, Judith. 1987. *Oya: In Praise of the Goddess*. Boston: Shambhala.

Hackett, Rosalind I. J. 1989. *Religion in Calabar: The Religious Life and History of a Nigerian Town*. Religion and Society, 26. Berlin: Mouton de Gruyter.

———, ed. 1987. *New Religious Movements in Nigeria*. Lewiston, N.Y.: Edwin Mellen Press.

———. 1985. "Sacred Paradoxes: Women and Religious Plurality in Nigeria." *Women, Religion and Social Change*, eds. Y. Haddad and E. Findly. Albany, N.Y.: SUNY Press, 247–70.

Hoch-Smith, Judith, and Anita Spring, eds. 1978. *Women in Ritual and Symbolic Roles*. New York: Plenum Press.

Holden, Pat, ed. 1983. *Women's Religious Experience*. London: Croom Helm.

Horton, Robin. 1969. "Types of Spirit Possession in Kalabari Religion." *Spirit Mediumship and Society in Africa*, eds. Beattie and Middleton, 14–49.

Houlberg, Marilyn H. 1973. "Ibeji Images of the Yoruba." *African Arts* 7,1:202–27, 90–92.

Janzen, John. 1977. "The Tradition of Renewal in Kongo Religion." *African Religions: A Symposium*, ed. N. Booth. New York: Nok.

Jules-Rosette, Bennetta. 1987. "Privilege Without Power: Women in African Cults and Churches." *Women in Africa and the African Diaspora*, eds. R. Terbory-Penn et al. Washington, D.C.: Howard University Press.

———. 1980. "Changing Aspects of Women's Initiation in Southern Africa." *Canadian Journal of African Studies* 13:1–16.

Kilson, Marion. 1972. "Ambivalence and Power: Mediums in Gã Traditional Religion." *Journal of Religion in Africa* 4,3:171–77.

———. 1976. "Women in African Traditional Religions." *Journal of Religion in Africa* 8,2:133–43.

Lan, David. 1985. *Guns and Rain: Guerillas and Spirit Mediums in Zimbabwe*. London: James Currey.

Lawuyi, Olatunde B., and J. K. Olupona. "Metaphoric Associations and the Concept of Death: Analysis of a Yoruba World View." *Journal of Religion in Africa*, 18, 1:2–14.

Levine, R. A. 1963. "Witchcraft and Sorcery in a Gusii Community." *Witchcraft and Sorcery in East Africa*, eds. Middleton and Winter, 221–55.

Lewis, I. M. 1971. *Ecstatic Religion*. Harmondsworth, U.K.: Penguin Books.

MacCormack, Carol P. 1979. "Sande: The Public Face of a Secret Society." *The New Religions of Africa*, ed. Jules-Rosette, 27–37.

Mbon, Friday M. 1987. "Women in African Traditional Religions." *Women in the World Religions, Past and Present*, ed. Ursula King, 7–23.

Mernissi, Fatima. 1977. "Women, Saints and Sanctuaries." *Signs* 3,1:101–12.

Nevadomsky, J., with Norma Rosen. 1988. "The Initiation of a Priestess: Performance and Imagery in Olokun Ritual." *Drama Review*, 32,2 (T118) (summer).

Richards, Audrey I. 1956. *Chisungu: A Girls' Initiation Ceremony among Bemba of Northern Rhodesia*. London: Faber and Faber.

Robertson, Claire, and Iris Berger. eds. 1986. *Women and Class in Africa*. New York: Africana.

Shaw, Rosalind. 1985. "Gender and the Structuring of Reality in Temne Divination: An Interactive Study." *Africa* 55, 3:286–303.

Shostak, Marjorie. 1981. *Nisa: The Life and Words of a !Kung Woman*. Cambridge: Harvard University Press.

Smart, Ninian. 1983. *Worldviews: Crosscultural Explorations of Human Beliefs*. New York: Scribner's.

Sojourner, Sabrina. 1982. "From the House of Yemanja: The Goddess Heritage of Black Women." *The Politics of Women's Spirituality: Essays on the Rise of Spiritual Power within the Feminist Movement*, ed. Charlene Spretnak. Garden City, N.Y.: Anchor Books, 56–63.

Spring, Anita. 1978. "Epidemiology of Spirit Possession among the Luvale of Zambia." *Women in Ritual and Symbolic Roles*, eds. Hoch-Smith and Spring.

Strobel, Margaret. 1984. "Women in Religion and in Secular Ideology." *African Women South of the Sahara*, eds. Hay and Stichter, 87–101.

Talbot, D. Amaury. 1968 [1915]. *Woman's Mysteries of a Primitive People* London: Frank Cass.

Tonkin, Elizabeth. 1982. "Women Excluded? Masking and Masquerading in West Africa." *Women's Religious Experience*, ed. Holden, 163–74.

Turner, Victor W. 1968. *The Drums of Affliction*. Oxford: Clarendon Press.

Wenger, Susanne, and Gert Chesi. 1983. *A Life with the Gods: In their Yoruba Homeland*. Worgl, Austria: Perlinger.

Whyte, Susan Reynolds. 1983. "Men, Women and Misfortune in Bunyole." *Women's Religious Experience*, ed. Holden, 175–92.

Wilson, P. J. 1967. "Status Ambiguity and Spirit Possession." *Man* N.S. 3:67–78.

Zahan, Dominique. 1979. *The Religion, Spirituality, and Thought of Traditional Africa*. Chicago: University of Chicago Press, 1979.

Zuesse, Evan. 1979. *Ritual Cosmos: The Ritual Sanctification of Life in African Religions*. Athens: Ohio University Press.

Religion's Chief Clients

Mercy Amba Oduyoye

A woman is in religion as a client.

"Customer, come buy from me,
Long time no see. *Se daadaa*
Awon omo nko ile nko?"
(How are you? How are the children?
How is the home?)

The solicitude of a market woman for the welfare of her customer closely resembles that of a priest of traditional African religion ministering to a devotee of his shrine. The first time I ever set foot in Ibadan's Dugbe market, I was greeted by a perfect stranger with these words. I had glanced at her tomatoes and was moving on when she said in a most pleasant voice, "Aah, customer, come buy from me." How did I become her customer? Why was she inquiring about my health, my affairs, my children, my home? Indeed, market women are like priests or, perhaps, we should say that religion can be like commerce. If the practitioners are good psychologists, they know exactly what their "clients" need to make life meaningful, liveable, even desirable and enjoyable.

The Centrality of Religion in Africa

Given the claim that Africans are incurably religious and the fact that few months pass without feasts and festivals that cannot be divorced from religious symbols, any person who is bonded to culture is usually a regular "customer" at religious houses and of religious ritual rites and priests or priestesses. The primal religions of Africa (known to scholars as African Traditional Religion), Christianity, and Islam all vigorously claim the allegiance of Africans, while African Traditional Religion continues to be a major source of meaning and receives formal acknowledgment as a living religion. All three form the backdrop of this chapter.

In Africa, or at least in the English-speaking parts, this close interlacing of religion and culture is visible in the educational system. Studies in religion are available at all levels and are often supported by national budgets. Religion is regarded as one aspect of culture and is most often included in the humanities, by itself or as part of philosophy. A few universities locate religion

From Mercy Amba Oduyoye, 1995. *Daughters of Anowa: African Women and Patriarchy* (excerpt). Maryknoll, NY: Orbis Books. Reprinted with permission of Orbis Books.

in the social sciences as a companion to sociology. It is not surprising that African scholars of religion have to employ an interdisciplinary approach: given our African holistic approach to life, God is seen as involved in all aspects of the human ordering of life, including politics, economics, or sports. Seen as present in people's lives from birth to death, God is evoked as the source of approval and sanction for human activity, and God is invoked for support and direction along the way.

If we consider the frequency of attendance at churches, mosques, and shrines as an indication of people's dependency on religion, we can describe women in Africa as very religious and demonstrably more religious than men. In this chapter, I want to look at the actual participation of women in religious practices to examine how and why they participate in religion as well as what is distinctive about their religious involvement. I also want to examine religious practices that impact solely on women....

Blood, Body and Community

In the Akan view of life, blood is not only a physiological substance; it is also a theological substance, imbued with meaning for one's being. Sustaining the body, it is the crucial substance of a human being. In pre-colonial days, human sacrifices were understood in religious terms: one life was given up in order to attain more life, either here or in the hereafter. Of course, some Asante writings of the nineteenth century also describe judicial execution, capital punishment for crimes. Generally speaking, any discussion of blood, especially human blood, as a part of the practice of African Traditional Religion is avoided, since no one wants to be associated with the crude and often racist reports of early European travelers. And yet, an understanding of the religious significance of blood is necessary to unlock many of the mysteries of Akan psychology.

Some examples may clarify the significant role of blood. In the holy place of Asantemanso[1] no menstruating woman was allowed to be present and no other form of shedding human blood was permitted; neither was anyone allowed to die there. In another village, Asubenagya, on the other side of the river, these "negative" forces were tolerated. Because no male whose blood had been shed could become an *Chene* (king), circumcision is taboo among the Asante. Similarly, no one who might be described as *wadi dem* (mutilated) could become a priest or king; this included persons with visible injuries that could have caused bleeding or physical handicaps and those whose wholeness of body had been violated. Physical perfection and purity were required for ruling or for being a sacrificial functionary or an object for sacrifice.[2]

Some of the most significant taboos in African Traditional Religion are associated with the blood of menstruation. A woman's blood is a genuine theological symbol, representing the carrying of life, the potential reincarnation of ancestral spirits, and life offered in sacrifice. Menstruation has an unusually strong potency: it seems, therefore, a form of male envy to put menstruation in the same category as a "person suffering from a gonorrheal discharge"[3], sexual diseases represent abnormality, impurity, and inauspiciousness, while menstruation does not.

In the practice of traditional religion, a menstruating woman becomes "untouchable"; she is like a person preparing an offering and she herself is the offering. She is surrounded by the spirits to whom she is being offered; she must be avoided by mere mortals and she herself must avoid the company of others. Women of child-bearing age are both the symbols and the source of continuity of the human community.

In the history of the Asante, women participated in wars, but they had to be past the child-bearing age. Girls who had not reached puberty or women who had reached menopause went to war as carriers and nurses. First, they did not have any menstrual "power," which could render impotent charms, talismans, and other spiritual sources. Second, if these women fell in battle, they would die as individuals and not as potential sources of human life. It is not surprising, then, that old women often undertook courageous acts to defend with their lives the people they had brought into life.[4]

As has been pointed out, it appears that in the past when women were rulers and war broke out, "they were sent for, or when they were required for important meetings, they would say *makyima* [indicating they were menstruating] and they could not perform their duties"[5]; men, nominated by the elders, then took their place. This legend, although reported from a male perspective, does not explain *why* the women could not perform their duties while menstruating; it seems reasonable to surmise that it had to do with religious traditions and taboos. Similarly, "in the olden days" if a menstruating women entered the "Chapel of Stools," she was killed immediately.[6]

In general, menstruating women were not allowed to participate in rituals. One of the strictest taboos applied to the carving of drums, which was forbidden to all women (even the *Chemaa*). Because blood was taboo to the stately *atumpan* drums (one male, one female), women were not allowed to touch them. Although the *donno* is a drum reserved for women, it was generally thought expedient for women to stay clear of drums and drumming.[7] Similarly, most rituals required male cooks, although sometimes the most senior wife of the *Chene* would be responsible. Women past the child-bearing age could participate by fetching water or the white clay often used in rituals.

It is clear that being beyond the child-bearing age eliminates only one factor of femaleness, the capacity to give birth. This does not clarify why such women should be more "acceptable" from a Christian theological point of view. Is it, using western terms, the old Freudian argument that males might be willing to accept a woman because she no longer has a capacity they don't have? These questions are important because Akan men seem to have a deep-seated fear of menstruation and, therefore, of women. This undoubtedly affects present-day relationships between men and women.

There are occasional examples of traditional male-female relationships that might prove helpful today. For example, during an Akan festival called the *Adae*, the *Chene*, the king, sat in state and could not conclude the public celebration until the *Chemaa*, the queen mother, arrived to greet him. This sharing of honor and responsibility was also shown in a ritual related to the Grove of Asantemanso, which was performed jointly by the *Chemaa* and the *Chene*, although the *Chemaa* was the chief priest and custodian of the grove. I believe we can examine such rituals in search of a new paradigm for creating relationships....

Women and the African Instituted Churches (AIC)

Christianity in Africa has been institutionalized in an abundance of ways ranging from the older churches (mission or western churches, such as the Methodist Church Ghana; historical churches, such as the Coptic and Ethiopian Orthodox churches) to more indigenous expressions of Christianity. This latter category—variously called African Instituted Churches, African Independent Churches, or African Charismatic Churches—includes a range of groups from the praying (*Aladura*) churches of Nigeria to the Zionist groups of South Africa. These popular expressions of African Christianity were founded in Africa as a result of particular African charisms.[8]

In these churches, which I shall refer to by the generic name of Aladura, Christianity has evolved from a combination of teachings from the Hebrew Bible, traditional African spiritually and practice, and a theology that focuses on the victory of Jesus Christ over evil and death, arising from the gospel narratives. These church bodies demonstrate a flexible ecclesiology that follows the African traditions of hospitality and respect that enabled Christianity and Islam to thrive on the continent. Even today, new Aladura congregations spring up literally overnight.

The flexible "ecclesiology" of traditional African religion also has allowed believers to establish shrines after participating in an initiation ceremony commanded by the particular divinity. The call may come either directly from the divinity or indirectly through a third person. As such, it is not surprising to find many women-founded and women-headed Aladura churches and congregations. In structure, they often exhibit a symmetrical organization of men and women with the whole church headed by a prophet or prophets. One well-known Aladura church, the Cherubim and Seraphim, has two sections headed by a Baba Aladura and a Mother Cherubim, respectively.[9]

In the Aladura churches, the male hierarchy generally follows the order described in Paul's Letter to the Corinthians, "And God has appointed in the church first apostles, second prophets, third teachers; then deeds of power, then gifts of healing, forms of assistance, forms of leadership, various kinds of tongues" (1 Cor. 12:28) and Paul's Letter to the Ephesians, "The gifts he gave were that some would be apostles, some prophets, some evangelists, some pastors and teachers, to equip the saints for the work of ministry, for building up the body of Christ" (Eph. 4:11–12). The female leadership is based on other biblical themes, primarily from the Hebrew Scriptures. Popular role models are Miriam, Rachel, and Lydia.

Throughout West Africa, such popular Christianity tends to absolutize the Bible to such a degree that any historical-critical approach is viewed with suspicion or simply dismissed. While some African biblical scholars may mouth contemporary hermeneutical approaches to the Bible, they often accept or hide behind "paradoxes," refusing to draw conclusions. Because non-canonical material contemporary to the New Testament is generally ignored, statements on the position of women are usually taken from Genesis, Leviticus, or the New Testament Epistles; such texts tend to constitute a "man's Bible." Here are a few typical expressions resulting from such contemporary "theologizing":

1. The Gospel of Christ has created a new unity in the one Body of Christ. However, the modern philosophy of women's liberation is not biblical; rather, it is a threat to world peace and a rejection of defined role expectations of each sex within the created order.
2. Here in Africa, particularly in Nigeria, both indigenous and established churches *allow* women's participation in their organization (emphasis is mine).
3. Paul established the equality of man and woman before God, but such equality does not remove the physical distinctions given at creation, which have a divine purpose. The modern call for the liberation of women is a replica of the Corinthian women's libertarianism. For women to aspire to become like men and reject their womanhood is not a genuine form of equality. Hence modern women's liberation is not biblical, and is not African.
4. As St. Paul silenced such women, the antinomian libertines (women liberationists) of today should not be encouraged in the church.[10]

These excerpts could have come from any pulpit or scholarly article. In Africa, the debate on sexism in the church has hardly begun....

Notes

1. Eva Meyerowitz, *The Early History of the Akan States of Ghana* (London: Red Candle Press, 1974), p. 217.
2. Rattray, *Ashanti*, pp. 121-32; for information on taboos, see pp. 131-32.
3. John E. Eberegbulam Njoku, *The World of African Woman* (Metuchen, NJ and London: Scarecrow Press, 1980), p. 15.
4. Rattray, *Ashanti*, p. 81.
5. Kofi Abrefa Busia, *The Position of the Chief in Modern Political Systems of Ashanti* (London: Oxford University Press, 1951), pp. 20, 72.
6. Every palace had a room set aside for keeping the stools (thrones function as shrines) of the rulers, both kings and queen mothers. See Peter Sarpong, *The Sa-*

cred Stools of the Akan (Tema: Ghana Publishing Co., 1971), pp. 26–56. See also Rattray, *Religion and Art in Ashanti*, pp. 74–75.

7. One significant example is the *fontomfrom*, a giant drum.

8. A brief overview of the development of these churches may be found in Lamin Sanneh, *West African Christianity: The Religious Impact* (Maryknoll, NY: Orbis Books, 1983; London: C. Hurst, 1983), pp. 180–209.

9. Akin Omoyajowo, *Cherubim and Seraphim: The History of an Independent Church* (New York: NOK Publishers, 1982), p. 200. *West African Christianity: The Religious Impact* by Lamin Sanneh contains an interesting account of the development of these churches (p. 143).

10. Excerpts from O. O. Obijole's seminar paper on "St. Paul on the Position of Women in the Church: A Study of Gal. 3:28, I Cor. 11:1–14 and 34–36: Paradox or Change?" at the Department of Religious Studies, University of Ibadan in May 1985.

Alourdes: A Case Study of Moral Leadership in Haitian Vodou

Karen McCarthy Brown

I have known Alourdes[1] since 1978 and addressed her as "mother" (a traditional title of respect for one's Vodou teacher) for the last five years. This ample-bodied, powerful, moody, loving, difficult, generous woman has taught me much of what I know about Haitian Vodou. It has not all been a simple matter of gathering scholarly data, for there have been broader life lessons learned under her tutelage. Among them have been many that relate directly to what we scholars would call the moral life. Through Alourdes I have glimpsed a deeply-rooted traditional value system that accepts conflict, celebrates plurality, and seeks the good through whatever enhances life energy.

Alourdes immigrated to the United States in 1963. Her brief career in Haiti as a singer with Troupe Folklorique ended when she married a man considerably older than herself, a man who worked for the Haitian Bureau of Taxation. In spite of the fact that he was able to provide her with security and

From John Stratton Hawley, ed. 1987. *Saints and Virtues*. Berkeley: University of California Press, pp. 144–67 (excerpt). Reprinted with permission of University of California Press.

comforts in striking contrast to her previous life of poverty, Alourdes was not willing to tolerate her husband's jealousy and need to control her life. However, living on her own in Port-au-Prince, the largest urban center in the poorest country in the Western hemisphere, proved extremely difficult. Her mother, though a well-known Vodou priestess in the city, was unable to help financially. By the early 1960s, Alourdes, not yet thirty, had three small children and was desperate to find some way to support them and herself. Moving to New York seemed the only avenue of escape, though it necessitated the wrenching decision to leave her extended family behind. On the day of her departure, Alourdes's mother invited her to come to the family altar and pray for the protection of the Vodou spirits in her new life. Alourdes replied: "I'm going to New York; I don't need no spirits there." Each time she tells this story, she quickly adds: "And I was wrong!"

Once settled in Brooklyn, Alourdes went to work, first as a cleaning woman for the Pratt Institute, then as a pressing machine operator for Cascade Laundry. Finally, she began to hire out as a domestic on a daily basis, working mostly for wealthy families on Manhattan's upper east side. In this early period of her life in New York, Alourdes worked with language skills limited to three words of English: mop, pail, and vacuum. During this difficult time she became ill. Obscure and never adequately diagnosed pains in her stomach took her to the hospital three times. The second time a portion of her small intestine was removed. The second and third times she was in such bad condition that a Catholic priest was summoned to administer last rites. A series of significant dreams on the part of Alourdes, members of her family, and friends indicated that the spirits were causing her illness. They wanted her to return to Haiti temporarily in order to be initiated into the Vodou priesthood. In 1966, Alourdes made that journey home. She has had no recurrence of her illness since.

Alourdes understands herself to have been called to the priesthood by the spirits. She believes it was the spirits who made her sick as a way of reminding her of religious and family obligations. (The two cannot be neatly distinguished since one serves the Vodou spirits not just for oneself, but also for one's "family," whether that term is defined narrowly to refer to the members of the household or broadly to include ancestors long dead, as well as the typical Haitian penumbra of fictive "aunts" and "uncles," "cousins," "sisters," and "brothers.") Alourdes also credits the spirits with her current "luck." Although she, like most Haitians in the greater New York area, lives well below the poverty level, she owns her own home. Although, like many Haitian women, she has all the responsibilities of the head of household, she is surrounded by healthy children and grandchildren. Furthermore, since her initiation, Alourdes has been able to support herself without demeaning labor. She now works full time as a "technician of the sacred."

In her cramped and chaotic rowhouse in the Fort Greene section of Brooklyn, Alourdes functions daily as a *manbo*, "Vodou priestess." Nurse's aides, taxi drivers, dishwashers, and a smattering of persons with more lucrative professions come to see her at six-thirty in the morning before their workdays begin, or at eleven or twelve at night after they end. Mostly, though not all, Haitians, they bring to her a wide range of problems: love, work, health, and family relations. She reads cards to diagnose the cause of the trouble, determining first that the problem is nothing that comes from God,[2] for she has no control over illness or trouble sent by God—only afflictions sent by the spirits. Virtually all spirit-sent problems, regardless of kind, are diagnosed as owing to some disturbance in the network of relations among people, often including a person's relationship to family members now dead. Healing is accomplished by ritually adjusting these interpersonal relationships. Alourdes cures through herbal medicine, prayer, "good-luck baths," charms, and talismans. In serious cases she is directed to the proper cures by her dreams and by consulting the spirits in trance sessions. The more recalcitrant cases may take time and extraordinary effort. For example, severely depressed persons, whom she is especially adept at curing, may be brought into her home to live for a period of several months. In addition to this intimate, problem-oriented work, Alourdes also holds several large feasts for individual Vodou spirits each year.

In scheduling these events, Alourdes follows the Catholic liturgical calendar, which dominates in Vodou ritualizing. Catholicism is an overlay on top of the layers of different African religious traditions that came together on the slave plantations of eighteenth-century Haiti to form Vodou. The Vodou spirits have both Catholic saint names and Afro-Haitian names, the latter being traceable in most cases to Yoruba, Dahomean, or Kongo counterparts. So, for example, Dambala the Dahomean snake deity is feted sometime around 17 March, the feast day of St. Patrick, who is pictured in the popular Catholic chromolithograph with snakes clustered around his feet. Each year Alourdes holds elaborate "birthday parties" for Dambala (St. Patrick) in March, Azaka (St. Isidore) in May, Ezili Dantò (Our Lady of Mount Carmel) in July, Ogou (St. James the Elder) also in July, and Gèdè (St. Gerard) in November. In addition she holds others when there is special "work" to be done that cannot wait until her spirits' feast days or involves another spirit with whom she has a less regular connection. Considerable effort and money (hundreds of dollars contributed by Alourdes and the members of her Vodou "family") are expended for each of these events. From late evening until early morning, praying, singing, and dancing go on in front of a "table" laden with the carefully prepared food and drink each spirit favors. Alourdes functions as the mistress of ceremonies, orchestrating the ritualizing throughout.

Almost always at these events it is also Alourdes who serves as the *chwal*, "horse," who is ridden by the spirit. After the brief struggle and confusion that routinely marks the onset of trance, Alourdes's body posture and tone of voice become those characteristic of the spirit called. She is dressed in a costume appropriate to the spirit, and is treated as if she were the spirit. On these ritual occasions the worshippers approach the spirits with the problems of their lives. The faithful are comforted, chastised, and given advice and blessings. Divine-human interaction becomes powerfully immediate as people are hugged, held, and handled by the spirits they serve.

From this brief description of Alourdes's life and her role as a Vodou priestess, it should be apparent that she is a competent, resourceful, and self-assured woman with an established reputation as a sacerdote and healer. It should also be clear that she, and those around her, believe that she was called to those latter roles by the spirits themselves. Yet none of this is sufficient to explain the position she enjoys within the Haitian immigrant community in New York. Haitian women are often strong and independent. In urban Haiti they frequently provide the main, if not sole, financial and emotional support for any number of children. Furthermore, the Vodou priesthood is not an office that guarantees a following. Many of the initiated never become leaders; and all initiates perceive themselves as having been chosen by the spirits. Building the reputation and steady following that Alourdes has requires further qualifications.

People speak about Alourdes as "strong," meaning that she is powerful and effective. They also speak respectfully about her "knowledge." Still, it is unclear how she might be related to the rubric of "saint" or "moral exemplar." Many of the people who are her clients and participate in her large ceremonies would spontaneously speak of her as a "good" woman. By this they mean that she responds readily and sympathetically to those in trouble; does not charge more than is fair for her services; is responsible to family and friends; and will have nothing to do with any kind of spirit "work" primarily designated to harm another person. Yet while this "goodness" is not irrelevant to her leadership role within the Haitian Vodou community in New York, it does not explain it, and certainly would not be sufficient to guarantee it. If we can speak of Alourdes as a moral exemplar—and I think in one sense we can—it will not be because she exemplifies the good in its popular Western incarnations as fairness, humility, and equanimity. I believe Alourdes to be an ultimately fair person, but she is not humble or self-sacrificing, at least not in the way we usually understand these terms. Alourdes believes she has a right to respect and she demands it from those around her. She is not even-tempered. She will not put up with people who are inconsiderate. Her anger can be sudden and fierce, and her humor cutting as often as it is delightful.

There are two possible ways to approach the role of saints or moral exemplars in Haitian Vodou. I propose to pursue both of them here, although each case will require a significant redefinition of terms. The first approach is to examine not Alourdes herself but the spirits—or "saints" as the Haitians also call them—as they incarnate themselves through her. This tack will require that we relinquish the notion that what is saintly is good. The Vodou spirits are not good, but they are not evil either. They are whole—full, rich, complex character types. For example, Ezili Dantò, whom we will encounter later, though identified with two manifestations of the Virgin Mary, Our Lady of Mount Carmel and the black Virgin, Mater Salvatoris, is understood within the Vodou system to be an independent woman who will take lovers but never marry them and a fiercely defensive mother who will kill to protect her children. The second approach involves concentrating on Alourdes's leadership role. People bring life conflicts, many of them easily recognizable as what we would call moral dilemmas, to the Vodou system. In her community Alourdes is in charge of the process by which Vodou addresses these moral dilemmas. This line of questioning will require that we relinquish the notion that a moral leader is there to be imitated in the specifics of action or being. Alourdes is a moral exemplar not so much because of what she does as because of *how* she does what she does. In a deep sense it is a question of style. Moral sensibility and aesthetic sensibility are very close in the Vodou universe of meaning.

I will begin with a discussion of the exemplary nature of the Vodou saints, or *lwa*, another term the Haitians frequently use. Then I will move to an analysis of Alourdes's leadership role as I have come to understand it. Each of these discussions will be built around material from my field journals. In all cases the material will be drawn from events and interactions observed during the annual "birthday parties" for the spirits, since the high level of ritualizing and the presence of a full community at these events make it easier to observe the moral negotiation going on in the sacred context than it otherwise would be. I believe that essentially the same processes are involved in the more intimate and workaday ritualizing that Alourdes carries on, but in those cases the important role of the community is more implicit than explicit. I will conclude with a discussion of the coincidence of the moral and the aesthetic within the world of Vodou.

The Exemplary Nature of the Vodou Spirits

The following is a selection drawn from my field journals describing the appearance of the warrior spirit Ogou in the latter stages of a fete held to honor the ancient and venerable snake spirit Dambala. All the most important spirits are saluted regardless of whose "birthday party" it is. Furthermore, since Ogou is the major spirit Alourdes serves, his actual appearance in one of his various personae is expected at all of Alourdes's Vodou feasts.

> March 14, 1981
> Feast for Dambala
>
> It is Sin Jak Majè [St. Jacques Majeur, St. James the Elder] who comes, not Ogou Badagri, Alourdes's more usual Ogou manifestation. Maggie [Alourdes's daughter] says to me later that she is sorry Badagri did not

come. "Sin Jak is mean! He have a mean expression on his face all the time. He never laugh or play. Sin Jak is hard."

Sin Jak's coming is marked with bravado. The first thing he does is pour rum into both ears. Alourdes's dress is quickly soaked through to her skin. Not long afterward, someone brings out Sin Jak's sword. This one looks like a fencing foil. He grabs it, unsheathes the blade and then thrusts it repeatedly in the air as if attacking an invisible enemy. Then, he lowers the blade and menacingly jabs it toward those standing nearest to him. Wary, though probably not genuinely afraid, most people take a step or two backward. Finally, he points the blade at himself. Resting the tip on his right hip, he pushes it in just enough to make the blade bend slightly—a gesture full of arrogance that hints at self-wounding. Next, he orders rum and then Florida Water [an inexpensive cologne often used in Vodou rituals] to be poured on the linoleum floor and lighted. People plunge their cupped hands into the blue alcohol flames and carry them upward, bathing face and arms in warmth. Sin Jak then directs some of the people to jump over the flames or to walk over them with legs spread apart. These are blessings from Sin Jak designed to raise life force but, like all his blessings, they contain a hint of danger.

Then people begin to queue up to speak with Sin Jak and he deals with them one by one, giving advice and ritualized blessings. For the most part, his blessings now take the form of spewing cigar smoke or rum over their bodies or directly into their faces. People grimace and hold their eyes tightly closed, but they do not turn away. Every once in awhile, Sin Jak rears back, puffs on his big cigar, puffs out his chest, and surveys the crowd with a calculating eye. As Maggie says, "Sin Jak is mean!"

... Several aspects of Vodou ritual and language would reinforce a reading of the spirits as more closely tied to the person whom they "ride." For example, Haitians might remark: "Have you seen Alourdes's Ogou? He is strong!" This tying of person to spirit goes even further in the belief that spirits can be inherited in a family. So when Alourdes dies and her daughter takes over, as she likely will, people may talk of "Alourdes's Ogou in Maggie's head." A similar point is made in the Vodou rituals that give persons access to, and to some extent control over, their protective spirits. These rituals pay equal attention to "feeding" the spirits within the person and establishing repositories for the same spirits outside the person. In other words, the spirits are simultaneously addressed by these rituals as "in here" and "out there."

In the possession-performances of the spirits that occur in Alourdes's rituals, these two perspectives on the divine-human relationship coexist. In part, it is this dual perspective that lies behind my use of the term *posses-*

sion-performance. I am drawing a parallel with the theatrical context in which the individual actor's interpretation of a well-known character is one of the key ingredients in artistic success. However, I do not wish to signal by the use of this term that Alourdes's possessions are in any sense playacting or pretense. Haitians themselves condemn the occasional manipulative priest or priestess who will *pran poz*, "posture" or "act" as if possessed. Rather, this theater language is intended to make a point with which all Haitians would probably agree: some of the vehicles of the spirits are better than others, just as some actors are better at capturing a character than others. Alourdes has a sizeable and faithful following in the New York Haitian community for many reasons, one of the leading reasons being that she is a good *chwal*. People feel they have encountered the spirits and have been addressed by them when "the spirits come in Alourdes's head."

To examine Alourdes's leadership role in her community, I will eventually need to return to my field journals. The selection I will quote, like the earlier one, focuses on possession-performance; however, I wish to use this one for a broader purpose than the first. This time I want to explore the nature of group interaction and the modes of leadership operating within the group. One can handily locate these general, social processes within Vodou by beginning with a possession-performance, and this is as it should be if we are right in understanding the spirits as condensation points for existential complexities.

The interaction of a group of persons around someone possessed by a particular Vodou spirit is difficult to describe in language dependent on the assumptions we make about the nature of leaders and followers in Western, European-based culture. Our understandings of what it means to be a strong individual especially hamper our ability to comprehend a ritual scene such as the one that will be described here. To guard against importing such assumptions into the discussion, I have chosen to work with the passage in relation to an interactional model indigenous to Haitian Vodou culture....

In this passage Ogou, who has possessed Alourdes, is just leaving. A chair is brought for Alourdes as her body collapses, signaling his departure.

July 21, 1979
Feast for Ogou
and Ezili Dantò

Before Alourdes's body has time to fully occupy the seat offered to her, Gèdè arrives. He leaps from the chair with a mischievous laugh; and a murmur of recognition and pleasure goes through the room. Gèdè's tricksterism always lightens the atmosphere and tonight, after more than two hours of Ogou, it is a special relief. Gèdè [spirit of death and sexuality, protector of small children, social satirist] calls for his black bowler and the dark glasses with one lens missing. Then he frolics and gambols around the room pressing his body against the bodies of various women present in his hip-grinding imitation of lovemaking. He remains a long time, passing out drinks of his pepper-laced *tafya* [raw rum] and joking with everyone. Gèdè is merciless with one elegantly dressed young man. After directing him to sit on the floor in front of him, Gèdè asks him over and over if he has a big penis. He steals the hat of another man; and when I try to take a picture, demands money. I give him some change. Later he comes back and tells me that was not enough. I give a dollar and take pictures uninterrupted. Gèdè collects money more or less continuously, appoints one young man treasurer, and every so often goes back to him and demands that he drag the money out of his pockets and count it. Gèdè says he wants to be sure no one is stealing from him. Ten to fifteen dollars is collected and earmarked for Gèdè's own feast in November.

It is five o'clock in the morning; people are restless; they look at their watches. Gèdè keeps singing: "M'ale. M'ale." ["I'm going. I'm going."] but he doesn't. He collapses into a chair, shuts his eyes, and then jumps up again in two seconds, remembering one more thing he has to say. This goes on and on and on. Everyone is aware that Dantò has yet to be called. This feast is for her, after all! Following some discussion with the elders present at the ceremony, Alourdes's daughter decides to begin the songs for Dantò even though Gèdè hasn't left. We sing slumped in our chairs barely able to keep our eyes open, while Gèdè satirizes our efforts and even injects dirty words into Ezili Dantò's sacred songs.

Finally, Gèdè leaves and the singing picks up. In only a few minutes, Ezili Dantò arrives like an explosion and we are all suddenly awake. Alourdes's ample body crashes into that of a man standing nearby. The spirit seems to spread to him by contagion and he, in turn, goes crashing into the food-laden table. Dantò's eyes dart out of her head. She utters one sound over and over: "dè-dè-dè." The pitch and rhythm change but the sound remains the same. A gold-edged, blue veil is brought and draped over her head madonna-fashion so she looks like the chromolithograph of Mater Salvatoris. She goes up to one man standing at the edge of the crowd. "Dè-dè-dè-dè-dè," she says softly. "Yes," he replies, "I will do it for you." She drags another to the elaborate table prepared for her and points to it emphatically: "Dè-dè-dè. Dè-dè-dè. Dè-dè-dè." A woman across the room yells out to the man: "She wants a table. She wants you to give her a party." "Dè-dè-dè-dè-dè-dè," she says to me, soothing, up-beat. Her hand brushes my cheek and she passes on. She strokes the belly of a pregnant woman next: "Dè-dè-dè-dè-dè-dè-dè-dè," she almost whispers and then roughly grabs the hair of the same woman and jerks her head back and forth: "DÈ-DÈ-DÈ-DÈ-DÈ-DÈ." "Your head washed," someone suggests. "She wants you to get initiated," another puts in. "That's right!" says a third and heads nod all around.

... Alourdes, like a good drummer in an African ensemble, is continually stepping aside in order to be seen better. Trance is a particularly dramatic way in which she sets herself aside. Alourdes absents herself and her life concerns for much of the time during her feasts for the spirits. She does this in order that the spirits, through her, can address the life issues of those who come to her "parties." Paradoxically this very absenting of self confirms her presence and reinforces her leadership role within the community.

In a variety of other ways, too, Alourdes serves in order to lead. For example, I spent the day of the feast for Dantò described earlier helping Alourdes. By the time I left, well after dawn of the next day, she and I had spent seventeen hours without a break in preparing the food and feasting the spirits. Yet, while I was slumped in a chair at 5 A.M., barely able to keep my eyes open, Alourdes's body was being led by Gèdè through rambunctious sexual gyrations. Gèdè had emerged directly out of a two-hour possession by Ogou; and Alourdes returned to herself for no more than five or ten minutes after Gèdè left before Ezili Dantò came. These heroic expenditures of energy in the self-effacing service of the spirits ensure Alourdes's reputation as an accomplished leader among the Haitian immigrants in New York.

Furthermore, in Gèdè's reluctant departure that dawn, we gain some insight into the crucial sense of ritual timing that Alourdes must exercise in myriad ways—in and out of trance. In this also she is like the lead drummer in an African ensemble, whose skill can be said, like hers, to reside in a consummate sense of relationships.[3] The goal of all Vodou ritualizing is the presence of the spirits among the worshippers. They will not arrive, Haitians say, unless the group is *byen chofe*, "well heated up." The group that has eyes open, voices raised, hands clapping, and lives engaged with the ritual action is one which is "well heated up." Alourdes's skill as a technician of the sacred lies in being able to play subtly and wisely on the currents of energy that move through and among the persons who gather in her home for ceremonies. Doing so, she uses a variety of techniques similar to those employed by the African drummer.

I will give only one example of the subtlety and specificity of the connections between her techniques of ritual timing and those of the traditional drummers of Africa. Chernoff says,

An African musician is not so much moving along with a pulsation as he is pushing the beat to make it more dynamic. The forceful quality of this orientation has led some people to speak of African musicians as playing their instruments ... with "percussive attack," staying "on top of" the beat and imparting a rhythmic momentum to even the sweetest melodies.[4]

Percussive attack, which can be helpfully compared to the process of ritual heating up, is technically accomplished by delivering an anticipated beat just before or just after the point when it is expected.[5] The resulting tension has two outcomes. It forces the participant-listener into a heightened sense of his or her own metronome beat and also raises the general excitement and energy of the context in which that beat must be maintained.[6] Gèdè's hesitating departures and repeated reappearances performed an alchemical change on the waning energy in the room. By the dramatic technique of false departures the participants were called back to awareness of themselves, which took the form of awareness of time and anxiety about tomorrow's schedule. The expected beat—Dantò's arrival—was postponed long enough so that, when it did come, there was an awakening and resurgence of energy in the room.[7] This energizing in turn guaranteed the success of Dantò's visit. The people in the room were fully present to engage with her. The skill of a Vodou priestess such as Alourdes is rooted in her ability to give dynamic form to life energy. Thus, it might be said that Alourdes is a leader in the New York Vodou community because she is extremely skillful at using power.[8] This power, however, is best described as life energy and it should be noted that Alourdes does not exercise it over people so much as she organizes it around and through them.

One has only to watch Alourdes at ceremonies such as those described here to realize that her authority rests at least in part on the fact that she has an aesthetic sense rooted, not in the mere tolerance of clash and conflict, but rather in the positive enjoyment of it. She enjoys, and is accomplished at, the organization of power, of life energy. This point can be added to those made earlier to give us a fuller image of the aesthetic style that is the key to her leadership. In addition to her pleasure in giving form to energy, her aesthetic skill derives from a consummate sense of relationships and how these may be clarified and subtly changed to achieve a state that is at once dynamic and balanced. Furthermore, what enables Alourdes to do this is her ability to stay steady in the midst of conflicting forces. Many times I have heard her say, "I got plenty confidence in myself!" And it is precisely this highly developed sense of herself, what we have been calling metronome sense, that enables Alourdes to set herself aside in service to the community.

To sum up: in the first part of this paper we focused on the Vodou saints or spirits as condensation points for complex and conflicting truths about different ways of being in the world. In the second part we examined Alourdes's leadership role in the ritual context, and here we saw her as exemplifying a way of staying steady or balanced in the midst of the polyrhythms within and among these various ways of being in the world. Two conclusions emerge from this. First, although we are justified in calling Alourdes a moral exemplar, it is not because the specifics of her life or being (in or out of trance) represent an ideal against which the rest of the community is measured. In her role as priestess Alourdes does not stand over and against her community so much as she embodies it. She exemplifies a general style rather than specific actions or attitudes, and this is in keeping with the deep pluralism—cosmological, social, and personal—of Vodou. As a technician of the sacred, she has certain highly developed ritualistic skills, yet even these are not unrelated to those needed by the ordinary person who must negotiate conflict in life. The key to both a good ritual and a good life is high life energy and a strong sense of self balanced with responsiveness to others. The second and more general point to emerge from this analysis concerns the close relationship between the aesthetic and the moral within Vodou. I turn to this topic by way of concluding the essay.

Aesthetics and Morals in the Vodou Community

If the comparison between music and the social, therefore moral, interaction of Vodou ritualizing is to seem anything more than mere analogy, we must have some idea of how deep the connection is between the Haitian aesthetic and social senses of "how things are" and "how things ought to be." Chernoff notes that African children are soothed in lullabies whose rhythms *cut across* those of the arms that rock them.[9] I have observed the same process with Haitian infants. This intimation of the depth at which this particular aesthetic sense shapes, comments on, and organizes life for the Haitian people led me to stress Alourdes's enjoyment of what she does as well as her skill at doing it. In a deep art form such as Vodou ritualizing, which amplifies the earliest preverbal sense of how the world is, pleasure and significance coincide because art and life coincide there too.

Vodou operates as a moral system, not because it takes up what is good in life and human behavior and accentuates that, but rather because it takes up all of life and intensifies and clarifies it. The inclusive quality of its commentary on life explains why its mood is more generally celebrative than reverential, for there is nothing set apart to "worship." Indeed one of the most startling characteristics of Vodou ritualizing for one like myself, reared in the solemn rites of the Episcopal church, where only certain very selective forms of behavior are acceptable during services, is the degree to which people genuinely enjoy themselves in Vodou ceremonies. They eat, they drink, they joke and laugh, they cry. In short, the full range of emotional life finds play within the world of Vodou. Even sexuality has a place. This is yet another formulation of a by now familiar point: the context and content of Vodou ritualizing are the community itself. Rituals clarify and comment on the vast and complex intermeshing of human relationships represented there.

To the extent that change occurs in human lives because of these ritual processes, it does so through the subtle readjustments in relationships that occur as the individual "dancer" develops the skill of staying balanced within the existential push and pull represented in the rituals. The point is not to make conflict go away but to make it work for, rather than against, life. Cross-rhythms must be organized in just the right way for the baby to be rocked to sleep.

This view of life as defined by conflict is a morally neutral one. From the Haitian perspective, there is no evidence that humans live in a fallen or imperfect state; there is no Golden Age in the past, no Utopia in the future.[10] The moral pull within Vodou comes from the realization that the polyrhythms of life can wound and destroy when not properly balanced; but when balanced, the same polyrhythms become the source of life-enhancing energy. This moral-aesthetic stance accounts for the high tolerance, indeed enjoyment, of pluralism on the cosmological, social, and personal levels. Haitians appear to believe that it is precisely the conflicts within people and the differences among them that make life worthwhile. From this perspective it would seem that there is no essential evil assumed to reside within specific persons or within specific areas of the world.[11] The moral problem is not evil but imbalance, both within and among persons. In the context of this pluralistic and conflict-centered description of life, the moral leader is not one who sets her own life up as a model for imitation. It is rather that person who, as a subtle and skilled technician of the sacred, can orchestrate ritual contexts in which each person discovers how to dance in his or her own way through a process of dynamic balancing with others who dance in their own way.

Bibliography

Chernoff, John Miller. *African Rhythm and African Sensibility: Aesthetics and Social Action in African Musical Idioms.* Chicago: University of Chicago Press, 1979.

Waterman, Richard Alan. "African Influence on the Music of the Americas." *Acculturation in the Americas*, edited by Sol Tax, vol. 2. Chicago: University of Chicago Press, 1952.

Notes

1. I use only Alourdes's first name in this essay to protect her privacy. I hope no one will read this as a sign of disrespect, for I intend none.
2. Those who serve the spirits in Vodou believe in a single god, Bondye, creator of all that is. Following the story from the Bible of the casting out of Lucifer and his coterie, they believe that the spirits were created by Bondye and subsequently banished to earth. However, these spirits are in no way understood as demonic or evil.
3. Chernoff, *Rhythm,* 150.
4. Chernoff, *Rhythm,* 56.
5. Chernoff, *Rhythm,* 96. The discussion focuses around a lengthy quotation from Waterman's "African Influence," 213.
6. Ibid.

7. Speaking of the lead drummer, Chernoff says: "A true master must time his utterances to replenish the dancers' physical and aesthetic energy at the right psychological moment" (*Rhythm*, 66).
8. "Proper performance of African music requires the respect and enjoyment of the organization of power" (Chernoff, *Rhythm*, 167).
9. Chernoff, *Rhythm*, 94.
10. There is no concept of heaven in Haitian Vodou. The souls of the dead, after existing for some time in a sort of limbo state, are "called" back to interact with the living once more, but this time in the form of spirits. *Lemò*, "the dead," though not to be confused with the *lwa*, the major spirits of Vodou, play a similar role in relation to the living. When well served, they guaranteed good fortune; when neglected, they bring suffering and hardship. Some say that the dead take up permanent residence in a land where their daily life is much as it was when they were alive. There is no sense in which this kind of existence is seen as superior to ordinary existence. In fact, it is probably understood as less desirable than being alive.
11. Haitian Vodou is notorious in the world of popular film and literature for its devil figures. Much of this is quite simply misinformation. There are, however, various sorts of negative spiritlike presences—for example, *lugaru, zobop, zombi*, and *baka*. Careful analysis of the stories that surround these malevolent figures, who are at any rate more figures of folklore than religion, indicates that virtually all of their malevolence can be traced to interrelational problems. For example, the *baka* may be the spirit of a murdered person. The disembodied soul of a person known as *zombi* may have been "sent" to do another harm because of trouble between the sender and the recipient. The *lugaru* and the *zobop* are spirit manifestations of living persons who are jealous or power-hungry.

Questions for Discussion

1. Is it possible to generalize about the roles and status of women in African religion?
   - Why or why not?
   - What are some of the important similarities and differences you find among the different African religions discussed in this chapter?
2. What role does magic play in some African religions? Should such practices be regarded as "religious"? Why or why not?
3. How have the introduction of Islam and Christianity influenced African women's religious experiences?
   - Reciprocally, how have the practices of Islam and Christianity been influenced by preexisting African religions?

4. Do you see any significant differences between tribal religions and the institutionlized world religions described in this text?

5. What arguments can you make for or against female circumcision as a "religious practice" that should be protected under principles of the free exercise of religion?

6. What factors help explain why it is primarily women who perform and perpetuate the practice of female circumcision?

7. How did colonialism influence African women's religious practices?

8. How have African tribal religions influenced the religious experience of women living outside of Africa?

References and Materials for Further Study

Books and Articles

Amoah, Elizabeth. 1990. "Femaleness: Akan Concepts and Practices," in Jeanne Becher, ed., *Women, Religion, and Sexuality*. Philadelphia: Trinity Press.

Asogwa, Cecilia. 1992. "A Challenge to the Integrity of Creation: An African Woman's Perspective." *Ecumenical Review* 44: 339-44. Account of a rural African women's self-help group that has created personal and community empowerment for the participants in the context of patriarchal and sexist African society.

Bell, Diane. 1994. "Aboriginal Women's Religion: A Shifting Law of the Land," in Arvind Sharma, ed., *Today's Woman* in *World Religions*. Albany: State University of New York Press.

Brown, Karen McCarthy. 1991. *Mama Lola: A Vodou Priestess in Brooklyn*. Berkeley: University of California Press.

———. 1989. "Women's Leadership in Haitian Vodou," in Judith Plaskow and Carol Christ, *Weaving the Visions: New Patterns in Feminist Spirituality*. New York: Harper & Row.

———. 1987. "Alourdes: A Case Study of Moral Leadership in Haitian Vodou," in John Hawley Stratton, ed., *Saints and Virtues*. Berkeley: University of California Press.

Clancy-Smith, Julia. 1999. "Islam: In Africa," in Serinity Young, ed., *Encyclopedia of Women and World Religion*. New York: Macmillan Reference.

Fandrich, Ina Johanna. 1999. "Afro-Atlantic Religions," in Serinity Young, ed., *Encyclopedia of Women and World Religion*. New York: Macmillan Reference.

Gleason, Judith. 1987. *Oya: In Praise of the Goddess*. Boston: Shambhala.

Grillo, Laura. 1999. "African Religions," in Serinity Young, ed., *Encyclopedia of Women and World Religion*. New York: Macmillan Reference.

Hackett, Rosiland. 1998. "Art as Neglected 'Text' for the Study of Gender and Religion in Africa." *Religion* 28: 363-76.

———. 1995. "Women and New Religious Movements in Africa," in Ursala King, ed., *Religion and Gender*. Oxford, UK: Blackwell.

———. 1994. "Women in African Religions," in Arvind Sharma, ed., *Religion and Women*. Albany: State University of New York Press.

———. 1990. "African Religions: Images and I-Glasses." *Religion* (Special Issue on African Religions) 20: 303-14.

———. 1985. "Sacred Paradoxes: Women and Religious Plurality in Nigeria," in Yvonne Yasbeck Haddad and Ellison Banks-Findly, *Women, Religion, and Social Change*. Albany: State University of New York Press.

Hoehler-Fatton, Cynthia. 1996. *Women of Fire and Spirit: History, Faith, and Gender in Roho Religion in Western Kenya*. New York: Oxford University Press.

Oduyoye, Mercy Amba. 1995. *Daughters of Anowa: African Women and Patriarchy*. Maryknoll, NY: Orbis Books.

———. 1992. "Women and Ritual in Africa." In Oduyoye, *The Will to Arise: Women, Tradition, and the Church in Africa*. Maryknoll, NY: Orbis.

Paper, Jordan, with E. and P. Aijin-Tettey. 1997. "Glimpses of West Central African Religious Yoruba Religion," and "Akan Religion," in *Through the Earth Darkly: Female Spirituality in Comparative Perspective*. New York: Continuum Press.

Sered, Susan. 1994. *Priestess, Mother, Sacred Sister: Religions Dominated by Women*. New York, Oxford. Discusses women's religions among the Black Caribs of Belize, the *zar* cult of northern Africa, the Sanda secret society of Sierra Leone, and Afro-Brazilia.

Sojourner, Sabrina. 1982. "From the House of Yemanja: The Goddess Heritage of Black Women," in Charlene Spretnack, ed., *The Politics of Women's Spirituality*. Garden City, NY: Anchor Press.

Teish, Luisah. 1985. *Jambalaya: The Natural Woman's Book of Personal Charms and Practical Rituals*. San Francisco: Harper & Row.

Tonkin, Elizabeth. 1983. "Women Excluded? Masking and Masquerading in West Africa," in Pat Holden, ed., *Women's Religious Lives*. London: Croom Helm.

Wade-Gyles, Gloria, ed. 1995. *My Soul Is a Witness: African-American Women's Spirituality*. Boston: Beacon Press. Selections by Sabrina Sojourner and Luisah Teish.

Whyte, Susan Reynolds. 1983. "Men, Women, and the Bunyole," in Pat Holden, ed., *Women's Religious Lives*. London: Croom Helm, 1983.

Internet References

Anti, Kenneth Kojo. "Women in African Traditional Religions." Women's Center, Eastern Washington University Web Site: http://cehd.ewu.edu/cehd/faculty/ntodd/GhanaUDLP/ KKAntiAfricanWomenReligion.html.

Hosken, Fran, ed., "Female Genital Mutilation (Fgm)," Women's International Network NEWS: http://feminist.com/fgm.htm.

Isizoh, Chidi Deniz. "Bibliography on African Traditional Religion." African Traditional Religion Web Site: http://isizoh net/afrel/atr_bibliography.htm.

Mbiti, John. "The Role of Women In African Traditional Religion." African Traditional Religion Web Site: http://isizoh.net/afrel/.

The Female Genital Mutilation Education and Networking Project Page Web Site: http://search.dogpile.com/texis/search?q=female+genital+mutilation&geo=no&fs=web.

J.B. Grant International Health Society, Johns Hopkins School of Public Health: Symposium on Female Genital Mutilation: The Challenge of Promoting Female Dignity:
   http://www.jhuccp.org/ fgm/index.stm.
ReligiousTolerance.Org Web site: "Female Genital Mutilation (A.k.a. Female Circumcision)":
   http://www.religioustolerance.org/fem_circ.htm.
Rosalind Hackett's Web Site:
   http://web.utk.edu/~rhackett/.
WHO Female Genital Mutilation Web Site:
   http://www.who.int/frh-whd/FGM/.

Media Resources

Becoming a Woman in Okrika. Video, 27 min. Filmakers Library, 1991. Women's coming of age rituals in a village in the Niger Delta.

Fire Eyes: Female Circumcision. Video, 60 min. Filmakers Library, 1995. Made by an African woman who underwent the practice at age 13.

The Hamar Trilogy. 3 videos, 50 min. each. Filmakers Library, 1996. Rituals of women of isolated Ethiopian tribe.

In the Name of God: Helping Circumcised Women. Video, 29 min. Filmakers Library, 1997. On Ethiopian women hospitalized after infibulation.

Ndebele Women: The Rituals of Rebellion. Video, 52 min. Filmakers Library, 1997. Fertility rituals.

Rites. Video, 52 min. Filmakers Library, 1991. On female circumcision in Africa.

Seven Nights and Seven Days. Video, 58 min. Filmakers Library, 1992. Healing rituals performed for a woman.

Women and
Goddess-Centered Religions

Overview

The last religious "tradition" that we will examine in this text are the so-called "goddess religions," especially as they have emerged as part of the feminist spirituality movement of the last few decades. Goddess religion is in this sense a relative newcomer on the stage of religious traditions, yet it also draws on elements of goddess worship that existed millenia ago in cultures as diverse as Africa, Asia, Northern Europe and the Ancient Near East. Although goddess religion may also be known by names such as "wicca," or "witchcraft," "neopaganism," "the Craft," and so forth, for convenience and clarity, this text will use the terms "goddess religion" or "goddess spirituality" to refer to this religious phenomenon.

Women from a number of different types of backgrounds have contributed to the development of this emerging religious tradition, especially feminist women who are disillusioned with or frustrated by the patriarchy and sexism of established religious traditions, especially Christianity and Judaism. Many of its adherents claim that their religious practices have roots in ancient religions, however, including those cults of goddess worship said to precede Judaism and found in parts of the Hindu, Celtic, African, and other, especially tribal, religious traditions. It might be argued that Catholic devotions to female saints are a latter-day form of goddess worship (see Orsi 1996). The same might be said for devotional practices to the female bodhisattva Kuan Yin in Chinese religions and Tara in Tibetan Buddhism.

Critics argue that the contemporary goddess movement is nothing more than a cult cobbled together from bits and pieces of other traditions without coherence or context. In the view of critics like Mary Lefkowitz, for example, the current worship of the goddess has no historical antecedents and is a completely fabricated spirituality created by feminists discontented with the patriarchy and sexism of the male-dominated world religions—understandable, perhaps, but misguided. However, as Cynthia Eller argues in "The Birth of a New Religion," included in this chapter, goddess spirituality *is* a "new religion" as that term is understood by sociologists. Although practitioners of goddess religion may attempt to draw legitimacy from a connection to ancient goddess worship, the integrity and coherence of their beliefs and practices as "religion" are not dependent upon establishing the validity of that historical connection.

Unlike most of the other religions we have studied here, however, goddess spirituality is largely an "emerging" religion rather than an established one. In particular, the "consciousness raising groups" that developed during the early days of the second wave of feminism brought women awareness of the lack of a spiritual dimension in political feminism, and simultaneously the extent to which traditional religions were hostile to equality for women. Another group of women came to goddess religion after rejecting their Christian or Jewish backgrounds as antithetical to feminist ideals. Yet another group was motivated to develop goddess worship as a necessary alternative to patriarchal religions, based on the rationale that religion is the linchpin to the society: Just as a patriarchal religion provides the authority and legitimation for patriarchal social relations, so can a transformed spirituality provide the basis for egalitarian ones (Eller 1993, 48). For example, feminist Charlene Spretnak observed that "the underlying rationale for patriarchal societies is patriarchal religion" (Spretnak 1982, 384).

Like the other religions we have explored in this text, goddess spirituality is not a single, monolithic entity but encompasses a range of different beliefs and practices that vary from group to group. Any particular group may include both secular and religious elements, among them ancient goddess traditions, Native American, Asian, or New Age spirituality, nature "worship," or at least a pro-environmental protection spirit, holistic and/or homeopathic healing and childbearing practices, feminist activism, lesbian separatism, and so forth. If there is a commonality running through this wide variety of beliefs and practices, it might be characterized as a belief in and commitment to the cultivation and expression of women's spiritual power.

Relationship of Female-Gendered and Feminine Images and Symbols to "Real" Women

Obviously, modern day practitioners of goddess religion see a close connection between the female images of divine and actual women. It is this aspect of the tradition which attracted many of its practitioners to begin with. Carol Christ's essay "Why Women Need the Goddess" provides a psychological and phenomenological rationale for women's practice of goddess worship. In Christ's assessment, the power of religious symbols is so deep-seated that "feminists cannot afford to leave it in the hands of the fathers" but should counter the dominant male-gendered symbols of God and the divine with female symbols of the Goddess.

Women's Relationship to Goddess Religions

Women-Specific or Distinctive Aspects

Unlike the other religious traditions we have explored here, goddess religion might be said to be a religious tradition developed by women for women. Although this may not be true for the origins of the traditions in ancient times, it is self-consciously the focus on women's spirituality which has attracted the majority of present day practitioners of this religion. In fact, all aspects of the tradition, from the very loose organization and structure of goddess worship, to the theology, rituals, symbols, and imagery can be viewed as women-specific and focused.

Gender-Based Segregation and Inequalities

Since goddess religion was developed in response to the patriarchy and sexism of traditional religions, and emerged in part out of the secular feminist movement of the 1970s, it is relatively free from the male-dominated androcentric symbolism, structures of authority, control over liturgy and theology, and so forth that are prevalent in established religions. Since there is no formal or official theology in goddess religion, there is no established course of study or training for becoming a member or adherent. Rather, as Eller describes, there is a loose knit association of women, both individuals and groups, who participate in various aspects of goddess religious worship, rituals, and practices. And since the goddess religion is not highly structured and has no bureaucratic institutions, there is no formal leadership "track" or progression.

Indeed, since goddess religion is founded on feminist principles, the ideal is to have no formal "leaders" or heads of the religion, but to be nonhierarchical, egalitarian, and participatory rather than authoritarian, and inclusionary versus exclusionary. Nonetheless, there are "priestesses" in many goddess worshiping groups, as Eller describes. Some groups also worship a "balance" of gods and goddess energies rather than being exclusively devoted to the female manifestation of the divine.

Access to Religious Training and Leadership Roles

Women's access to religious training in goddess religions depends upon the particular practice involved. Since many of these traditions are female-centered, if not created and established by women, there is no problem in these traditions with women being excluded. In fact, the egalitarian ethos of many goddess religions and groups is to empower women and give them access to authority and leadership. However, in some of the more traditional goddess religions, such as those based on earlier traditions of witchcraft, gender remains an important category for determining who has access to the reins of power and authority.

Well-Known and/or Influential Women in the Tradition

Probably the best-known practitioner of goddess religion in North America is Starhawk, who has written several books and conducted hundreds of lectures and workshops around the United States over the last two decades. Her contributions to the development of goddess worship is detailed by Eller and in the interview with Starhawk in the selection "Reclaiming the Sacred." As the interview illustrates, Starhawk's goddess spirituality has been deeply connected to caring for the natural environment and to her involvement in a variety of political causes. Other prominent promoters or practitioners of goddess religion include Selena Fox, discussed in the selection by Eller; Zsuzsanna Budapest, whom Eller describes as "the closest thing feminist spirituality has to a founder"; Luisah Teish and Sabrina Sojourner (whose essay "From the House of Yemanja: The Goddess Heritage of Black Women" is included here) who have promoted African goddess worship for African-American women; and National Public Radio reporter Margot Adler, author of *Drawing Down the Dark*.

Changes in the Status of Women

Historically

Those who see an unbroken lineage between ancient and contemporary forms of goddess worship, or between Western and non-Western variants, would say that there has been a vast improvement in the status of women within the tradition—as extreme as that between any patriarchal religious tradition and its most feminist contemporary form. In ancient forms of goddess worship, what little evidence there is suggests that these practices were male dominated, and that women were either excluded completely or held only marginal roles. However, as noted above, there is a good deal of dispute about the authenticity of the connection between ancient and modern forms of goddess worship.

Future Prospects

It is exciting to think about the capacity of a woman-centered religion like goddess spirituality to open up opportunities for women's spiritual exploration and expression. However, given the marginal character of goddess religion today, and its continuing marginalization and even oppression and persecution by members of more mainstream religious groups, it remains to be seen how widespread this emerging tradition will become in the future. While Wiccan and other "New Age" spiritual traditions that worship the goddess have largely been accepted, even welcomed, by liberal Protestant denominations, they are considered a threat to more fundamentalist and evangelical Christian religious groups. Backlash organizations by various "men's movement" groups such as Iron John and "The Promise Keepers" also threaten to roll back women's gains in spiritual autonomy and independence. Time will tell also whether goddess religions can move beyond their primary appeal to middle-aged, middle-class white Western women to women from other ethnic, racial, age, and class backgrounds. Although the selection by Sabrina Sojourner suggests that they can, the word is still out.

The Birth of a New Religion

Cynthia Eller

Neopaganism and Feminism

When feminists arrived on the shores of the emergent religious tradition, the initial point of contact was with neopaganism or witchcraft. Spiritual feminists eventually spread out into most corners of the alternative religious landscape, but feminist spirituality's most important base is still pagan. This continuing contact with neopaganism has left its mark on every aspect of feminist spirituality: its theology, ritual, and social organization. Indeed, many spiritual feminists happily call themselves neopagans or witches, though their particular feminist adaptations of neopaganism set them apart from the mainstream of that religion. Feminist spirituality and mainstream neopaganism coexist and overlap, usually (but not always) quite happily, but they are not the same thing.

Neopaganism in America is a movement organized (or not) in much the same way as feminist spirituality. Small groups of practitioners join together on a regular basis, though probably as many practice alone. There are large festivals and retreats, magazines and newsletters, bookstores and occult supply shops, and one effort at an umbrella organization (the Covenant of the Goddess) that serves as a clearinghouse of information and a badge of respectability (and tax-exempt status) for the neopagan community. As with feminist spirituality, variety is the order of the day, and there are numerous schools of thought and types of practice available for the interested seeker, and plenty of interaction between neopaganism and other types of alternative spirituality. The number of people who are affiliated with neopaganism is difficult to estimate, since there is nothing remotely like an official membership roll. However, in a recent attempt to quantify the movement, Aidan Kelly has extrapolated from book sales, mailing lists, and festival attendance to come up with a figure of somewhere from 50,000 to 100,000 "serious adherents" of neopaganism.[1]

Neopagans believe they are reviving (and sometimes creating anew) ancient nature religions. They usually trace their genealogy to Europe, and sometimes even more narrowly to Britain. Many call their religion "witchcraft" as well as paganism, since they believe that when paganism was forced underground by the Christian church, it was passed in secret from

From Cynthia Eller, *In the Lap of the Goddess: The Feminist Spirituality Movement in America.* New York: Crossroads Publishing Company (excerpted). Reprinted with permission of Cynthia Eller.

parent to child (or believer to believer) as witchcraft. Unfortunately, witchcraft was only temporarily and intermittently tolerated by the Christian church, and eventually witches became the object of a virtual genocide in the Middle Ages. The church portrayed witches in terms similar to those that Senator Jesse Helms used in the mid-1980s in his proposed congressional legislation against witchcraft: "the use of powers derived from evil spirits, the use of sorcery, or the use of supernatural powers with malicious intent." Contemporary neopagans give quite a different definition for witchcraft, saying that the word derives from the Anglo-Saxon root *wic* meaning to bend or shape, and that wiccans (or witches) are those who can bend unseen forces to their will. Far from having malicious intent, modern witches say that they—like their persecuted predecessors—are bending unseen forces for the good of all. Time and again they stress that they are not Satanists, and have no interest in or use for the Christian devil, since their religion dates from long before Christianity. Though some neopagans have given up on the word "witch" as too laden with negative connotations, others attempt to reclaim it as a word that rightfully describes a "healer, minister, and wise person."[2]

In spite of its insistence that it dates to ancient times, neopaganism also has a more recent history, dating to 1954, when Gerald Gardner published *Witchcraft Today*. Gardner was a British folklorist, nudist, and occultist, who after his retirement in 1936 joined an occult society with connections to the Rosicrucians and Theosophists. He says that he was initiated into wicca (or witchcraft) by an old woman in 1939, a woman who had herself been initiated by someone else in a line reaching back, presumably, to the Middle Ages if not further. Gardner wrote one book on witchcraft under a pen name, and after the last of the Witchcraft Acts were repealed in Britain in 1951, he wrote two more books in his own name, *Witchcraft Today* and *The Meaning of Witchcraft*. The witchcraft he described included the worship of a goddess and a god, the officiation of a priestess, and communal rituals involving dancing, nudity, chanting, and meditation that took place on the soltices, equinoxes, and the four cross-quarter days that fall between them.[3] All these forms are still common among neopagans today. Gardner himself initiated many individuals into a neopagan practice that came to be called "Gardnerian witchcraft" after him. Some of Gardner's apprentices split from him to create different witchcraft "traditions," and other sects of witchcraft sprang up with little connection to Gardner, giving rise to the tremendous variety found in modern neopaganism.

Gardner is what many neopagans would call "a hereditary witch," claiming to have fallen heir to a tradition of witchcraft that existed prior to the twentieth century. Those who say they are hereditary witches are rare; some practitioners note that their families passed along interesting bits of folklore, but nothing akin to the comprehensive religion that Gardnerian witchcraft purports to be. But especially in its early years, hereditary witchcraft was very important to neopagans as proof that the religion they practiced had a real tradition behind it. Notebooks of charms and rituals called "books of shadows" were circulated as remnants of an earlier European witchcraft, but none were ever authenticated as such. One invocation, "The Charge of the Goddess," was used in the neopagan community for many years as a bit of "traditional" wiccan lore, but it was revealed in the late 1980s that it was the work of Doreen Valiente, a student and colleague of Gerald Gardner, who wrote it within the last forty years.[4]

Wiccan lineages and ancient practices are of less and less importance nowadays, as neopagans feel more secure in the religions they have created (or maybe only more certain that their hereditary claims will be disproved). Modern witches accept, sometimes even revel in the novelty of what they create. Still, the lure of the ancient calls to them. Gwydion Pendderwen does an excellent job of summing up how most neopagans feel about the newness of their religion: "What has come down [from the Old Religion, or paganism] is so minimal, it could be thrown out without missing it. Many groups have received nothing through apostolic succession and do not miss it. Objectively, there's very little that has gone from ancient to modern in direct succession. But subjectively, an awful lot is ancient. It is drawn from ancient materials. It represents archetypal patterns.[5]

Neopagans (who sometimes refer to themselves simply as pagans) agree on little, and count it as one of the advantages of their chosen religion that they do not have to agree. Still, many neopagans have tried to define just what holds them together, and the thing they mention most consistently is nature worship. Selena Fox, a priestess who heads up Circle Sanctuary, a pagan retreat center in rural Wisconsin, offers this description of wicca: "The Wiccan religion is a nature religion with roots that go back to pre-Christian Europe. It's a religion that focuses on communing with the divine through nature. ... Wiccans worship the 'life force' in all people and animals, revere nature and harm no one. We believe that all of life is sacred and we see ourselves as part of a community of life forms on the planet."[6] What Fox doesn't mention is that most neopagans also worship a goddess. This is often coupled with worship of a god, and their gender polarity is frequently seen as expressing an important truth about the cosmos. But following Gardner, the goddess is usually given some kind of primacy,[7] and in some neopagan circles women's presence is required for rituals to occur.

The appeal of neopaganism to feminists newly arrived in the emergent religious tradition must have been tremendous: here were people already worshiping a goddess, naming women as priestesses, and talking about "the feminine." There were no elaborate rites of entry, if one wished to avoid them; groups were small and intimate, leaving ample space for individual experience; and in a religion with no central headquarters, religious hierarchies were unlikely to get in the way.... Feminism and witchcraft seemed a natural match.

But well before feminists discovered neopaganism en masse, the word witch entered the feminist vocabulary in other, highly politicized terms. In New York on Halloween of 1968, a collective of women named themselves WITCH, an acronym standing for "Women's International Terrorist Conspiracy from Hell." This first group was followed by others across the United States, all of whom used the same acronym, but different names to indicate the targets of their rage....

But the most significant aspect of WITCH was its choice of central symbol: the witch. By choosing this symbol, feminists were identifying themselves with everything women were taught not to be: ugly, aggressive, independent, and malicious. Feminists took this symbol and molded it—not into the fairy tale "good witch," but into a symbol of female power, knowledge, independence, and martyrdom.

This latter association with witchcraft, that of martyrdom, was particularly important to early feminists. Mary Daly in her 1973 book *Beyond God the Father,* and Andrea Dworkin in 1974 with *Woman Hating*, laid the groundwork for a feminist martyrology by researching the witch persecutions of the Middle Ages and labeling them "gynocide," the purposeful murder of women. This theme was further developed in Daly's 1978 work *Gyn/Ecology,* in which the witch burnings were portrayed as an instance of the patriarchal "Sado-Ritual Syndrome," a pattern of the abuse of women that Daly locates cross-culturally and trans-historically. For Daly and those who followed her, words like "witch," "hag," "crone," and "spinster" became titles of honor, capturing the proud spirit of those women who remained true to themselves and their sisters even in the face of persecution.[8] This identification of women with witchcraft was not an explicitly religious one. Women were not named witches because they worshiped a goddess in circles in the woods or because they made herbal charms to encourage prophetic dreaming. Women were named witches because they refused to submit to demeaning and limiting roles, even knowing that this rebellion might literally cost them their lives.

Witchcraft was fast becoming a feminist symbol, even a religiously charged one, dealing as it did with ultimate commitment and ultimate value. But it was a symbol without a practice. It still remained for someone to lower the drawbridge and let religious neopaganism out and feminists in. The first to take on this task was Zsuzsanna Budapest, the closest thing feminist spirituality has to a founder. Budapest grew up in Hungary and took her city's name as her own when as a teenager she left for the West to escape the failing Hungarian revolution. Later, after immigrating to the United States and leaving her marriage, she moved to Los Angeles and became very active in the women's movement: organizing protests, attending meetings, helping to form an antirape squad. But, like others, she came to believe that the women's movement needed a women's religion, and she proposed to give it one. In this, Budapest did not come without resources: she claimed to be the heir of a witchcraft tradition at least eight hundred years old, inherited from her mother, Masika Szilagyi. According to Budapest, Masika was initiated into witchcraft by Victoria, a household servant, who in addition to teaching Masika psychic skills, took her into the woods at night to meet with groups of witches who invoked the goddess, sang of ancient shamans, and spat into the fire. Masika communed with the dead in her dreams, and could speak ancient Egyptian while in a trance, a talent Budapest attributes to Masika's previous incarnation as a priestess of Hathor in ancient Egypt. In her *Holy Book of Women's Mysteries*, Budapest includes materials she received from her mother, including her "book of superstitions," "book of dreams," "book of cures," and "book of sorrows."...

If these provided the seeds for Budapest's women's religion, the sprouting and blossoming were strictly her doing, and that of her feminist sisters. Budapest's experiments in feminist witchcraft began in 1971, when she and a few friends celebrated the winter solstice together. They named themselves the Susan B. Anthony Coven No. 1, to stress their commitment to feminism—and, it would seem, to express their hope that others would follow in their footsteps, adding covens numbers 2, 3, 4, et seq. And others did follow, though with names of their own: the Amelia Earhart Coven in New York, the Elizabeth Gould Davis Coven in Florida, the Sojourner Truth Coven in the Catskills, the Jane Addams Coven in Chicago, and the Elizabeth Cady Stanton Coven in Orange County, California. The Susan B. Anthony Coven itself grew rapidly, by its founders' reports, from the six women who met at the 1971 winter solstice, to seven hundred initiated members just nine years later.[9] Women came and went, and there were never seven hundred women meeting at one time, but it is reported that Budapest led rituals in the 1970s where attendance was well over one hundred....

Though Zsuzsanna Budapest was a ground-breaking figure in the feminist move to neopaganism, she was not alone. In addition to the women working with her, there were other women across the country building bridges between feminism and paganism: some by reaching out to existing wicca groups in their areas, some by radicalizing the covens of which they were already members, some by creating new groups with new traditions. By the mid-1970s, resources were beginning to become available in the women's community, and feminists were able to invent their religion secure in the knowledge that there was a groundswell of feminist energy behind them. Interest in witchcraft as women's persecution history broadened into inquiry into ancient goddess worship. The publication of Merlin Stone's *When God Was a Woman* in 1976, a study of representations of prehistoric goddesses woven together with a story of their overthrow in historical times, gave the feminist wicca movement credibility in new quarters, and inspired more women to search out the supposed surviving remnants of ancient goddess worship in neopaganism.[10] Feminist imagery and politics was rapidly becoming feminist spiritually, as women went beyond talking about witches and goddesses as symbols of female power, and started to become them and worship them.

Yet the meeting of feminists and neopagans was not one big happy family reunion, with everyone rushing deliriously into each other's arms. The neopagan movement was small, and feminists entered in numbers large enough to make a real impact. Moreover, they did not usually enter humbly and meekly, asking if they might please be initiated into the wise ways of the witches. Quite the contrary, they flung open the doors, squared their shoulders, and swaggered in, ready to rearrange the furniture. And in spite of substantial areas of shared interest, there were real differences between the newly anointed feminist witches and neopagans of older vintage.

The first point of conflict was that feminists by and large had no interest in sharing their circles with men, and precious little interest in worshiping a god of any sort. With their palate not yet conditioned to savor the new tastes of the emergent religious tradition, they often were impatient with the measured pageantry and role-playing that characterized some neopagan rituals or for the encyclopedic lists of greater and lesser divinities and spirits. They wanted to worship a goddess—a big one, bigger than the god of patriarchy—and they wanted to worship themselves through her. For many traditional neopagans, this was anathema. Polytheism and gender duality were considered essential parts of witchcraft: if true magic were to happen, both male and female deities had to be invoked, and according to some, both women and men had to be present, fulfilling their gender-prescribed tasks. A further conflict was that most neopagans valued secrecy, partly out of fear of persecution, but also out of a love of the concept of hidden lore, of mystical truths that could only be revealed to the initiated few. Feminist witches, in contrast, tended to be more evangelical, wanting to get the good word out to their sisters. Far from insisting on long periods of training and gradual initiation into higher mysteries, feminist witches hearkened back to a phrase from the WITCH manifesto: "You are a Witch by being female ..." They encouraged one another to form covens of the utterly inexperienced, to make things up as they went along, and to publish accounts of what worked for them so that others could draw on their experience.[11]

Another complicating factor was that a number of practicing mainstream neopagans were sexist, a rude surprise to feminists who thought they had left all that behind in established religions. Oceana Woods, an active spiritual feminist, reports her disappointment with the world of witchcraft: "The first ritual of a witchcraft coven that I ever went to, there was a man there who was a witch, who worshiped the Goddess, who owned a bookstore that sold pornography. Now I have a problem with this. I have a real problem with this .... While that is witchcraft, and that is a coven, I don't feel that that ... truly would be considered feminist spirituality."[12] Even women who entered the world of witchcraft before it was in feminist vogue voiced complaints about the sexism of modern neopaganism, complaints more likely to receive a hearing once feminists involved themselves in that world in significant numbers. Lady Miw, owner of a magic and occult supply store in New York, remembers:

> When I got into Gardnerian wicca—which I adore, I am Gardnerian, proud to be Gardnerian—I couldn't understand why just because I was a woman, why I couldn't draw down the moon into another woman. The men didn't like this at all. I thought, well if we're witches, and we're spiritual, and this is a spiritual thing here, then I'm not female and I'm not male. I'm female *and* male. And everybody in this circle is female and male. So does it really matter on a physical plane of consciousness if I sit next to a man or a woman? ... if I'm male and female, and the guy is male and female, the same thing, isn't that sort of like really Baby Wicca 101?[13]

The downside of the feminist/neopagan combination notwithstanding, overall the combination has proved to be a productive one. The success of the relationship owes much to Starhawk, a witch, feminist, and widely read pagan author. Starhawk found witchcraft and feminism around the same time, and though she saw them as having a real compatibility, she was not specifically drawn into one as the result of her interest in the other, as many women were. Having already been exposed to neopaganism, she was introduced to feminist witchcraft in the early 1970s by Zsuzsanna Budapest.[14] Starhawk's covens are not all separatist (men are allowed to participate and be initiated), but her writings are insistently feminist, and it is clear that she regards witchcraft's attitude toward women and the female to be among its greatest strengths. In many ways, Starhawk has served as a translator and mediator between feminists and neopaganism: she has worked with gender polarity, but evolved away from it; she has developed convincing theological justifications for conceiving of goddess as both monotheistic and polytheistic; she has carved out a central, indisputable place for women without excluding men; and she has praised flexibility and creativity while upholding the value of things taken to be traditionally pagan.

Today there is considerably less friction between feminist witchcraft and the broader neopagan movement than there was initially. There are several reasons for this, one of which is that over the past twenty years of cohabitation, feminist witches have become acculturated to the neopagan world. Things that they initially found odd or off-putting—ceremonial tools and language, polytheism, male deities—have become familiar, even beloved to them, and in some cases have been incorporated into their practice. And for neopagans, feminists are no longer angry alien infiltrators in a settled world of happy, naked, dancing nature-worshipers; they have become a part of the scenery. Finally, controversy between the two parties has lessened in part because the feminists won their right to the goddess. By sheer force of numbers and enthusiasm, their success drowned out all but the most hardened opposition. Neopaganism flourishes today, perhaps more feminist and less hierarchical in flavor than it was before, and feminist witchcraft flourishes alongside and to some extent within it. The most determinedly feminist witches are sometimes called "Dianic," and they often prefer their own company to that of the broader neopagan community. Zsuzsanna Budapest originally called her witchcraft Dianic, and the term has been taken over particularly by lesbian witches, but also by women, heterosexual or lesbian, who are separatist in their practice.[15]

In the wider world of feminist spirituality, however, Dianic witches are in the minority, and neopaganism is more of a subtext than a centrally defining feature. The symbol of the witch still plays a role in spiritual feminist circles, if a somewhat less dramatic one than it used to. In an interesting echo of the WITCH movement, another acronym has made its way onto T-shirts and the letterhead of at least one spiritual feminist group: "Wild Independent-Thinking Crones and Hags." A token use of the symbol of the witch can also be seen in some of the songs that are popular in the feminist spirituality movement; for instance, one very bouncy, upbeat tune with these lyrics:

Who are the witches, where do they come from?
Maybe your great-great grandmother was one.
Witches are wise, wise women they say;
There's a lot of witch in every woman today.[16]

But many women find it too difficult to rehabilitate the word "witch" from its negative connotations, and finally pointless. They feel that they can better communicate their identity to others in different words, or are reluctant to label themselves at all. Recently it has become more common to think of the word witch as denoting a practitioner of wicca, and many women avoid applying the term to themselves simply because they perceive their spiritually as being broader in scope. Other women do not call themselves witches because they see witchcraft as a religion that is wholly derived from European roots. (Luisah Teish, for example, explains that spiritual women in the African traditions prefer to call themselves "root woman," "ju-ju woman," or "two-headed woman" rather than "witch.")

In the feminist spirituality movement today, there is a subtle trend away from identifying oneself as a witch. Partly this is a transition into a more free-form type of spirituality precipitated by a growing conviction on the part of feminists that what they are doing counts as religion in its own right, without the added status conferred by an affiliation with neopaganism. As Anne Carson notes in the preface to her bibliography on feminist spirituality, "As the 1980s progress there seems to be less of an interest in witchcraft per se among feminists, at least in terms of ritual practice, as we begin to leave behind one traditional structure in order to create our own visions and philosophies." Dianic witchcraft has acted as a launching pad for a spiritual movement that is now far more diverse, reaching far beyond neopaganism, into Native American religions, other world religions, New Age practices, and even—sporadically—Jewish and Christian feminism.[17]

Notes

1. Covenant of the Goddess, Berkeley. Information on the role of the Covenant of the Goddess in the neopagan movement can be found in Aidan Kelly, "An Update on Neopagan Witchcraft in America" (paper delivered at the annual meeting of the American Academy of Religion, Boston, Mass., Nov. 1987), along with Kelly's estimate of the movement's size.
2. Jesse Helms, quoted in Ann Forfreedom, *Feminist Wicce Works* (Berkeley: Ann Forfreedom, 9987 [1987]), 4; Starhawk, *Spiral Dance*, first ed., 5. See also Starhawk, interview with Stone, "Return of the Goddess"; Anne Marie Lux, "Witches nothing to be scared of, witch says" (interview with Selena Fox), *The Sunday Gazette* (Janesville, Wis.), Oct. 30, 1988; Miw. At a workshop on "Feminist Wicca Philosophy" (FSC Retreat, June 1990), Delores Cole gave a fairly typical disclaimer, saying that one cannot have Satanism without Christianity, that "Satanism is the death side of Christianity," and thus bears no relation to paganism.
3. Adler, *Drawing Down the Moon*, 60–66, 80–84. See also Marion Weinstein, *Positive Magic: Occult Self-Help*, rev. ed. (Custer, Wash.: Phoenix Publishing, 1981), 93.
4. See, for example, Starhawk, *Spiral Dance*, 2d ed., 229; also Miw.
5. Gwydion Pendderwen, quoted in Adler, *Drawing Down the Moon*, 88. See also Starhawk, *Spiral Dance*, first ed., 188.
6. Lux, "Witches nothing to be scared of." For other definitions of witchcraft or neopaganism, see Forfreedom, *Feminist Wicce Works*, 1; Starhawk, *Spiral Dance*, first ed., 2; Weinstein, *Positive Magic*, 68; Adler, *Drawing Down the Moon*, v.
7. Some neopagans worship no deities or a goddess alone, but I have never encountered any who worship only a male god.
8. Andrea Dworkin, *Woman Hating* (New York: E.P. Dutton, 1974), 118–50; Daly, *Beyond God the Father*, 62–64; and Daly, *Gyn/Ecology*, 178–222.
9. Gayle Kimball, "Goddess Worship in Wicce: Interview with Z Budapest," in *Women's Culture*, ed. Kimball, 239; Adler, *Drawing Down the Moon*, 119; Z. Budapest, *The Holy Book of Women's Mysteries*, vol. 1 (Oakland: Susan B. Anthony Coven No. 1, 1979), 82; Rhiannon, interview with author, Los Angeles, Apr. 14, 1983.
10. Jade, "Witchcraft Philosophy and Practice" (workshop at Womongathering, May 1990); Stone, *When God Was a Woman*.
11. Nikki Bado, "Stirring the Caldron: The Impact of the Women's Movement on the Old Religion" (paper delivered at the annual meeting of the American Academy of Religion, New Orleans, Nov. 1990); Jade, *To Know*, 66; Adler, *Drawing Down the Moon*, 22, 171–222.
12. Woods. Also Sackner.
13. Miw.
14. For a description of this encounter, see Budapest, *Holy Book of Women's Mysteries* (1989), xiv.

15. Adler, *Drawing Down the Moon*, 200; Starhawk, *Spiral Dance*, 2d ed., 220. Jade (*To Know*, 64) says that women are more numerous in mainstream neopaganism than are men. However, it seems that there are more mainstream neopagans than specifically feminist witches. Jade lists journals and newsletters of both feminist witchcraft and mainstream neopaganism, and the latter vastly outnumber the former. Information published by Circle Network (Mount Horeb, Wis.) gives the same impression. The term *Dianic witchcraft* is discussed by Jade in *To Know*, 60. Though usually reserved for lesbian or female-separatist witchcraft, the term *Dianic* is also used by a small group of mainstream pagans who worship both male and female deities and draw on the writings of Margaret Murray; they have no relation to feminist witchcraft.
16. Hoffman. The WITCH group with the name "Wild Independent-Thinking Crones and Hags" is located in Cambridge, Mass. I have not been able to discover the origin of the song "Who Are the Witches?" though I have heard it numerous times in different locations.
17. Garawitz; Bjorkman; Foster; Veracruz; Gordon; Washington; Frankel; Otto; Robison; Schulman; Copeland; Whiting; Sackner; Sharp; Teish, *Jambalaya*, 250; Mary Jo Neitz, "In Goddess We Trust," in *In Gods We Trust: New Patterns of Religious Pluralism in America,* ed. Thomas Robbins and Dick Anthony, 2d ed. (New Brunswick, N.J.: Transaction Publishers, 1990), 366; Anne Carson, *Feminist Spirituality and the Feminine Divine: An Annotated Bibliography* (Trumansburg, N.Y.: Crossing Press, 1986), 9; J. Gordon Melton, *Magic, Witchcraft, and Paganism in America: A Bibliography* (New York: Garland, 1982), 131. Emily Culpepper uses the phrase "Woman-Identified Culture" to refer to the broader feminist movement; see Culpepper, "Spiritual Movement of Radical Feminist Consciousness," 224.

Why Women Need the Goddess: Phenomenological, Psychological, and Political Reflections

Carol P. Christ

At the close of Ntosake Shange's stupendously successful Broadway play "For Colored Girls Who Have Considered Suicide When the Rainbow Is Enuf," a tall beautiful black woman rises from despair to cry out, "I found God in myself and I loved her fiercely."[1] Her discovery is echoed by women around the country who meet spontaneously in small groups on full moons, solstices, and equinoxes to celebrate the Goddess as symbol of life and death powers and waxing and waning energies in the universe and in themselves.[2]

> It is the night of the full moon. Nine women stand in a circle, on a rocky hill above the city. The western sky is rosy with the setting sun; in the east the moon's face begins to peer above the horizon.... The woman pours out a cup of wine onto the earth, refills it and raises it high. "Hail, Tana, Mother of mothers!" she cries. "Awaken from your long sleep, and return to your children again!"[3]

What are the political and psychological effects of this fierce new love of the divine in themselves for women whose spiritual experience has been focused by the male God of Judaism and Christianity? Is the spiritual dimension of feminism a passing diversion, an escape from difficult but necessary political work? Or does the emergence of the symbol of Goddess among women have significant political and psychological ramifications for the feminist movement?

To answer this question, we must first understand the importance of religious symbols and rituals in human life and consider the effect of male symbolism of God on women. According to anthropologist Clifford Geertz, religious symbols shape a cultural ethos, defining the deepest values of a society and the persons in it. "Religion," Geertz writes "is a system of symbols which act to produce powerful, pervasive, and long-lasting moods and motivations"[4] in the people of a given culture. A "mood" for Geertz is a psychological attitude such as awe, trust, and respect, while a "motivation" is the

From Carol Christ and Judith Plaskow, eds. 1979, *Womanspirit Rising: A Feminist Reader in Religion*. San Francisco: Harper & Row, pp. 273–287 (excerpted). Reprinted with permission of Carol Christ.

social and *political* trajectory created by a mood that transforms mythos into ethos, symbol system into social and political reality. Symbols have both psychological and political effects, because they create the inner conditions (deep-seated attitudes and feelings) that lead people to feel comfortable with or to accept social and political arrangements that correspond to the symbol system.

Because religion has such a compelling hold on the deep psyches of so many people, feminists cannot afford to leave it in the hands of the fathers. Even people who no longer "believe in God" or participate in the institutional structure of patriarchal religion still may not be free of the power of the symbolism of God the Father. A symbol's effect does not depend on rational assent, for a symbol also functions on levels of the psyche other than the rational. Religion fulfills deep psychic needs by providing symbols and rituals that enable people to cope with limit situations[5] in human life (death, evil, suffering) and to pass through life's important transitions (birth, sexuality, death). Even people who consider themselves completely secularized will often find themselves sitting in a church or synagogue when a friend or relative gets married, or when a parent or friend has died. The symbols associated with these important rituals cannot fail to affect the deep or unconscious structures of the mind of even a person who has rejected these symbolisms on a conscious level—especially if the person is under stress. The reason for the continuing effect of religious symbols is that the mind abhors a vacuum. Symbol systems cannot simply be rejected, they must be replaced. Where there is not any replacement, the mind will revert to familiar structures at times of crisis, bafflement, or defeat.

Religions centered on the worship of a male God create "moods" and "motivations" that keep women in a state of psychological dependence on men and male authority, while at the same legitimating the *political* and *social* authority of fathers and sons in the institutions of society.

Religious symbol systems focused around exclusively male images of divinity create the impression that female power can never be fully legitimate or wholly beneficent. This message need never be explicitly stated (as, for example, it is in the story of Eve) for its effect to be felt. A woman completely ignorant of the myths of female evil in biblical religion nonetheless acknowledges the anomaly of female power when she prays exclusively to a male God. She may see herself as like God (created in the image of God) only by denying her own sexual identity and affirming God's transcendence of sexual identity. But she can never have the experience that is freely available to every man and boy in her culture, of having her full sexual identity affirmed as being in the image and likeness of God. In Geertz' terms, her "mood" is one of trust in male power as salvific and distrust of female power in herself and other women as inferior or dangerous. Such a powerful, pervasive, and longlasting "mood" cannot fail to become a "motivation" that translates into social and political reality.

In *Beyond God the Father*, feminist theologian Mary Daly detailed the psychological and political ramifications of father religion for women. "If God in 'his' heaven is a father ruling his people," she wrote, "then it is the 'nature' of things and according to divine plan and the order of the universe that society be male dominated. Within this context, a *mystification of roles* takes place: The husband dominating his wife represents God 'himself.' The images and values of a given society have been projected into the realm of dogmas and 'Articles of Faith,' and these in turn justify the social structures which have given rise to them and which sustain their plausibility."[6]

Philosopher Simone de Beauvoir was well aware of the function of patriarchal religion as legitimater of male power. As she wrote, "Man enjoys the great advantage of having a god endorse the code he writes; and since man exercises a sovereign authority over women it is especially fortunate that this authority has been vested in him by the Supreme Being. For the Jew, Mohammedaris, and Christians, among others, man is Master by divine right; the fear of God will therefore repress any impulse to revolt in the downtrodden female."[7]

This brief discussion of the psychological and political effects of God religion puts us in an excellent position to begin to understand the significance of the symbol of Goddess for women. In discussing the meaning of the Goddess, my method will first be phenomenological. I will isolate a meaning of the symbol of the Goddess as it has emerged in the lives of contemporary women. I will then discuss its psychological and political significance by contrasting the "moods" and "motivations" engendered by Goddess symbols with those engendered by Christian symbolism. I will also correlate Goddess symbolism with themes that have emerged in the women's movement, in order to show how Goddess symbolism undergirds and legitimates the concerns of the women's movement, much as God symbolism in Christianity undergirded the interests of men in patriarchy. I will discuss four aspects of Goddess symbolism here: the Goddess as affirmation of female power, the female body, the female will, and women's bonds and heritage. There are, of course, many other meanings of the Goddess that I will not discuss here.

The sources for the symbol of the Goddess in contemporary spirituality are traditions of Goddess worship and modern women's experience. The ancient Mediterranean, pre-Christian European, native American, Mesoamerican, Hindu, African, and other traditions are rich sources for Goddess symbolism. But these traditions are filtered through modern women's experiences. Traditions of Goddesses, subordination to Gods, for example, are ignored. Ancient traditions are tapped selectively and eclecticly, but they are not considered authoritative for modern consciousness. The Goddess symbol has emerged spontaneously in the dreams, fantasies, and thoughts of many women around the country in the past several years. Kirsten Grimstad and Susan Rennie reported that they were surprised to discover widespread interest in spirituality, including the Goddess, among feminists around the country in the summer of 1974.[8] *Woman Spirit* magazine, which published its first issue in 1974 and has contributors from across the United States, has expressed the grass roots nature of the women's spirituality movement. In 1976, a journal, *Lady Unique*, devoted to the Goddess emerged. In 1975, the first women's spirituality conference was held in Boston and attended by 1,800 women. In 1978, a University of Santa Cruz course on the Goddess drew over 500 people. Sources for this essay are these manifestations of the Goddess in modern women's experiences as reported in *Woman Spirit*, *Lady Unique*, and elsewhere, and as expressed in conversations I have had with women who have been thinking about the Goddess and women's spirituality.

The simplest and most basic meaning of the symbol of Goddess is the acknowledgement of the legitimacy of female power as a beneficient and independent power. A woman who echoes Ntosake Shange's dramatic statement, "I found God in myself and I loved her fiercely," is saying "Female power is strong and creative." She is saying that the divine principle, the saving and sustaining power, is in herself, that she will no longer look to men or male figures as saviors. The strength and independence of female power can be intuited by contemplating ancient and modern images of the Goddess. This meaning of the symbol of Goddess is simple and obvious, and yet it is difficult for many to comprehend. It stands in sharp contrast to the paradigms of female dependence on males that have been predominant in Western religion and culture. The internationally acclaimed novelist Monique Wittig captured the novelty and flavor of the affirmation of female power when she wrote, in her mythic work *Les Guerilleres*,

> There was a time when you were not a slave, remember that. You walked alone, full of laughter, you bathed bare-bellied. You say you have lost all recollection of it, remember … you say there are no words to describe it, you say it does not exist. But remember. Make an effort to remember. Or, failing that, invent.[9]

While Wittig does not speak directly of the Goddess here, she captures the "mood" of joyous celebration of female freedom and independence that is created in women who define their identities through the symbol of Goddess. Artist Mary Beth Edelson expressed the political "motivations" inspired by the Goddess when she wrote,

> The ascending archetypal symbols of the feminine unfold today in the psyche of modern Every woman. They encompass the multiple forms of the Great Goddess. Reaching across the centuries we take the hands of our Ancient Sisters. The Great Goddess alive and well is rising to announce to the patriarchs that their 5,000 years are up—Hallelujah! Here we come.[10]

The affirmation of female power contained in the Goddess symbol has both psychological and political consequences. Psychologically, it means the defeat of the view engendered by patriarchy that women's power is inferior and dangerous. This new "mood" of affirmation of female power also leads to new "motivations"; it supports and undergirds women's trust in their own power and the power of other women in family and society.

If the simplest meaning of the Goddess symbol is an affirmation of the legitimacy and beneficence of female power, then a question immediately arises, "Is the Goddess simply female power writ large, and if so, why bother with the symbol of Goddess at all? Or does the symbol refer to a Goddess 'out there' who is not reducible to a human potential?" The many women who have rediscovered the power of Goddess would give three answers to this question: (1) The Goddess is divine female, a personification who can be invoked in prayer and ritual; (2) the Goddess is symbol of the life, death, and rebirth energy in nature and culture, in personal and communal life and (3) the Goddess is symbol of the affirmation of the legitimacy and beauty of female power (made possible by the new becoming of women in the women's liberation movement). If one were to ask these women which answer is the "correct" one, different responses would be given. Some would assert that the Goddess definitely is *not* "out there," that the symbol of a divinity "out there" is part of the legacy of patriarchal oppression, which brings with it the authoritarianism, hierarchicalism, and dogmatic rigidity associated with biblical monotheistic religions. They might assert that the Goddess symbol reflects the sacred power within women and nature, suggesting the connectedness between women's cycles of menstruation, birth, and menopause, and the life and death cycles of the universe. Others seem quite comfortable with the notion of Goddess as a divine female protector and creator and would find their experience of Goddess limited by the assertion that she is not *also* out there as well as within themselves and in all natural processes. When asked what the symbol of Goddess means, feminist priestess Starhawk replied, "It all depends on how I feel. When I feel weak, she is someone who can help and protect me. When I feel strong, she is the symbol of my own power. At other times I feel her as the natural energy in my body and the world."[11] How are we to evaluate such a statement? Theologians might call these the words of a sloppy thinker. But my deepest intuition tells me they contain a wisdom that Western theological thought has lost.

To theologians, these differing views of the "meaning" of the symbol of Goddess might seem to threaten a replay of the trinitarian controversies. Is there, perhaps, a way of doing theology, which would not lead immediately into dogmatic controversy, which would not require theologians to say definitively that one understanding is true and the others are false? Could people's relation to a common symbol be made primary and varying interpretations be acknowledged? The diversity of explications of the meaning of the Goddess symbol suggests that symbols have a richer significance than any explications of their meaning can express, a point literary critics have long insisted on. This phenomenological fact suggests that theologians may need to give more than lip service to a theory of symbol in which the symbol is viewed as the primary fact and the meanings are viewed as secondary. It also suggests that a *thea*logy[12] of the Goddess would be very different from the *theo*logy we have known in the West. But to spell out this notion of the primacy of *symbol* in thealogy in contrast to the primacy of the *explanation* in theology would be the topic of another paper. Let me simply state that women, who have been deprived of a female religious symbol system for centuries, are therefore in an excellent position to recognize the power and primacy of symbols. I believe women must develop a theory of symbol and thealogy congruent with their experience at the same time as they "remember and invent" new symbol systems.

A second important implication of the Goddess symbol for women is the affirmation of the female body and the life cycle expressed in it. Because of women's unique position as menstruants, birthgivers, and those who have traditionally cared for the young and the dying, women's connection to the body, nature, and this world has been obvious. Women were denigrated because they seemed more carnal, fleshy, and earthy than the culture-creating males.[13] The misogynist anti*body* tradition in Western thought is symbolized in the myth of Eve who is traditionally viewed as a sexual temptress, the epitome of women's carnal nature. This tradition reaches its nadir in the *Malleus Maleficarum (The Hammer of Evil-Doing Women)*, which states, "All witchcraft stems from carnal lust, which in women is insatiable."[14] The Virgin Mary, the positive female image in Christianity does not contradict Christian denigration of the female body and its powers. The Virgin Mary is revered because she, in her perpetual virginity, transcends the carnal sexuality attributed to most women.

The denigration of the female body is expressed in cultural and religious taboos surrounding menstruation, childbirth, and menopause in women....

The denigration of the female body and its powers is further expressed in Western culture's attitudes toward childbirth.[15] Religious iconography does not celebrate the birthgiver, and there is no theology or ritual that enables a woman to celebrate the process of birth as a spiritual experience....

The symbol of Goddess aids the process of naming and reclaiming the female body and its cycles and processes. In the ancient world and among modern women, the Goddess symbol represents the birth, death, and rebirth processes of the natural and human worlds. The female body is viewed as the direct incarnation of waxing and waning, life and death, cycles in the universe. This is sometimes expressed through the symbolic connection between the twenty-eight-day cycles of menstruation and the twenty-eight-day cycles of the moon. Moreover, the Goddess is celebrated in the triple aspect of youth, maturity, and age, or maiden, mother, and crone. The potentiality of the young girl is celebrated in the nymph or maiden aspect of the Goddess. The Goddess as mother is sometimes depicted giving birth, and giving birth is viewed as a symbol for all the creative, life-giving powers of the universe.[16] The life-giving powers of the Goddess in her creative aspect are not limited to physical birth, for the Goddess is also seen as the creator of all the arts of civilization, including healing, writing, and the giving of just law. Women in the middle of life who are not physical mothers may give birth to poems, songs, and books, or nurture other women, men, and children. They too are incarnations of the Goddess in her creative, life-giving aspect. At the end of life, women incarnate the crone aspect of the Goddess. The wise old woman, the woman who knows from experience what life is about, the woman whose closeness to her own death gives her a distance and perspective on the problems of life, is celebrated as the third aspect of the Goddess. Thus, women learn to value youth, creativity, and wisdom in themselves and other women.

The possibilities of reclaiming the female body and its cycles have been expressed in a number of Goddess-centered rituals. Hallie Mountainwing and Barby My Own created a summer solstice ritual to celebrate menstruation and birth. The women simulated a birth canal and birthed each other into their circle. They raised power by placing their hands on each other's bellies and chanting together. Finally they marked each other's faces with rich, dark menstrual blood saying, "This is the blood that promises renewal. This is the blood that promises sustenance. This is the blood that promises life."[17] From hidden dirty secret to symbol of the life power of the Goddess, women's blood has come full circle. Other women have created rituals that celebrate the crone aspect of the Goddess. Z. Budapest believes that the crone aspect of the Goddess is predominant in the fall, especially at Halloween, an ancient holiday. On this day, the wisdom of the old woman is celebrated, and it is also recognized that the old must die so that the new can be born.

The "mood" created by the symbol of the Goddess in triple aspect is one of positive, joyful affirmation of the female body and its cycles and acceptance of aging and death as well as life. The "motivations" are to overcome menstrual taboos, to return the birth process to the hands of women, and to change cultural attitudes about age and death. Changing cultural attitudes toward the female body could go a long way toward overcoming the spirit-flesh, mind-body dualisms of Western culture, since, as Ruether has pointed out, the denigration of the female body is at the heart of these dualisms. The Goddess as symbol of the revaluation of the body and nature thus also undergirds the human potential and ecology movements. The "mood" is one of affirmation, awe, and respect for the body and nature, and the "motivation" is to respect the teachings of the body and the rights of all living beings.

A third important implication of the Goddess symbol for women is the positive valuation of will in a Goddess-centered ritual, especially in Goddess-centered ritual magic and spellcasting in womanspirit and feminist witchcraft circles. The basic notion behind ritual magic and spellcasting is energy as power. Here the Goddess is a center or focus of power and energy; she is the personification of the energy that flows between beings in the natural and human worlds. In Goddess circles, energy is raised by chanting or dancing. According to Starhawk, "Witches conceive of psychic energy as having form and substance that can be perceived and directed by those with a trained awareness. The power generated within the circle is built into a cone form, and at its peak is released—to the Goddess, to reenergize the members of the coven, or to do a specific work such as healing."[18] In ritual magic, the energy raised is directed by willpower. Women who celebrate in Goddess circles believe they can achieve their wills in the world.

The emphasis on the will is important for women, because women traditionally have been taught to devalue their wills, to believe that they cannot achieve their will through their own power, and even to suspect that the assertion of will is evil. Faith Wildung's poem "Waiting," from which I will quote only a short segment, sums up women's sense that their lives are defined not by their own will, but by waiting for others to take the initiative.

> Waiting for my breasts to develop
> Waiting to wear a bra
> Waiting to menstruate
>
> ...
> Waiting for life to begin, Waiting—
> Waiting to be somebody
>
> ...
> Waiting to get married
> Waiting for my wedding day
> Waiting for my wedding night
>
> ...
> Waiting for the end of the day
> Waiting for sleep. Waiting ...[19]

Patriarchal religion has enforced the view that female initiative and will are evil through the juxtaposition of Eve and Mary. Eve caused the fall by asserting her will against the command of God, while Mary began the new age with her response to God's initiative, "Let it be done to me according to thy word" (Luke 1:38). Even for men, patriarchal religion values the passive will subordinate to divine initiative. The classical doctrines of sin and grace view sin as the prideful assertion of will and grace as the obedient subordination of the human will to the divine initiative or order. While this view of will might be questioned from a human perspective, Valerie Saiving has argued that it has particularly deleterious consequences for women in Western culture. According to Saiving, Western culture encourages males in the assertion of will, and thus it may make some sense to view the male form of sin as an excess of will. But since culture discourages females in the assertion of will, the traditional doctrines of sin and grace encourage women to remain in their form of sin, which is self-negation or insufficient assertion of will.[20] One possible reason the will is denigrated in a patriarchal religious framework is that both human and divine will are often pictured as arbitrary, self-initiated, and exercised without regard for other wills.

In a Goddess-centered context, in contrast, the will is valued. *A woman is encouraged to know her will, to believe that her will is valid, and to believe that her will can be achieved in the world,* three powers traditionally denied to her in patriarchy. In a Goddess-centered framework, a woman's will is not subordinated to the Lord God as king and ruler, nor to men as his representatives. Thus a woman is not reduced to waiting and acquiescing in the wills of others as she is in patriarchy. But neither does she adopt the egocentric form of will that pursues self-interest without regard for the interests of others.

The Goddess-centered context provides a different understanding of the will than that available in the traditional patriarchal religious framework. In the Goddess framework, will can be achieved only when it is exercised in harmony with the energies and wills of other beings. Wise women, for example, raise a cone of healing energy at the full moon or solstice when the lunar or solar energies are at their high points with respect to the earth. This discipline encourages them to recognize that not all times are propitious for the achieving of every will. Similarly, they know that spring is a time for new beginnings in work and love, summer a time for producing external manifestations of inner potentialities, and fall or winter times for stripping down to the inner core and extending roots. Such awareness of waxing and waning processes in the universe discourages arbitrary ego-centered assertion of will, while at the same time encouraging the assertion of individual will in cooperation with natural energies and the energies created by the wills of others. Wise women also have a tradition that whatever is sent out will be returned and this reminds them to assert their wills in cooperative and healing rather than egocentric and destructive ways. This view of will allows women to begin to recognize, claim, and assert their wills without adopting the worst characteristics of the patriarchal understanding and use of will. In the Goddess-centered framework, the "mood" is one of positive affirmation of personal will in the context of the energies of other wills or beings. The "motivation" is for women to know and assert their wills in cooperation with other wills and energies. This of course does not mean that women always assert their wills in positive and life-affirming ways. Women's capacity for evil is, of course, as great as men's. My purpose is simply to contrast the differing attitudes toward the exercise of will *per se*, and the female will in particular, in Goddess-centered religion and in the Christian God-centered religion....

The symbol of Goddess has much to offer women who are struggling to be rid of the "powerful, pervasive, and long-lasting moods and motivations" of devaluation of female power, denigration of the female body, distrust of female will, and denial of the women's bonds and heritage that have been engendered by patriarchal religion. As women struggle to create a new culture in which women's power, bodies, will, and bonds are celebrated, it seems natural that the Goddess would reemerge as symbol of the newfound beauty, strength, and power of women.

Notes

1. From the original cast album, Buddah Records, 1976.
2. See Susan Rennie and Kristen Grimstad, "Spiritual Explorations Cross-Country," *Quest*, 1975, *I* (4), 1975, 49–51; and *WomanSpirit* magazine.
3. See Starhawk, "Witchcraft and Women's Culture," in *Womanspirit Rising*.
4. "Religion as a Cultural System," in William L. Lessa and Evon V. Vogt, eds., *Reader in Comparative Religion*, 2nd ed. (New York: Harper & Row, 1972), p. 206.
5. Geertz, Clifford. 1973. *Interpretation of Cultures*. New York: Basic Books. p. 210.
6. Boston: Beacon Press, 1974, p. 13, italics added.
7. *The Second Sex*, trans. H. M. Parshleys (New York: Alfred A. Knopf, 1953).
8. See Grimstad and Rennie.
9. *Les Guerilleres*, trans. David LeVay (New York: Avon Books, 1971), p. 89. Also quoted in Morgan MacFarland, "Witchcraft: The Art of Remembering," *Quest*, 1975, *I* (4), 41.
10. "Speaking for Myself," *Lady Unique*, 1976, *I*, 56.
11. Personal communication.
12. A term coined by Naomi Goldenberg to refer to reflection on the meaning of the symbol of Goddess.
13. This theory of the origins of the Western dualism is stated by Rosemary Ruether in *New Woman: New Earth* (New York: Seabury Press, 1975), and elsewhere.
14. Heinrich Kramer and Jacob Sprenger (New York: Dover, 1971), p. 47.
15. See Adrienne Rich, *Of Woman Born* (New York: Bantam Books, 1977), chaps. 6 and 7.
16. See James Mellaart, *Earliest Civilizations of the Near East* (New York: McGraw-Hill, 1965), p. 92.
17. Barbry My Own, "Ursa Major: Menstrual Moon Celebration," in Anne Kent Rush, ed., *Moon, Moon* (Berkeley, Calif., and New York: Moon Books and Random House, 1976), pp. 374–387.
18. Starhawk, in *Womanspirit Rising*.
19. In Judy Chicago, 1979. *The Dinner Party: A Symbol of our Heritage*, (Garden City, N.Y.: Anchor Press/Doubleday), pp. 213–217.
20. "The Human Situation: Feminine View," in *Journal of Religion*, 1960, 40, 100–112, and reprinted in *Womanspirit Rising*.

Reclaiming the Sacred

Starhawk
Jennifer Connor

Growing up in the United States, even those of us not part of any official religion are likely to be raised according to Judeo-Christian principles. From this traditional background, we learn about the proper subordinate role of women and the essential maleness of God. Although much has changed in the past decade, with women assuming positions of power in many established religions, and many religions becoming more inclusive of women, it is still true that everywhere we turn, we still see signs indicating that spirituality is a man's domain.

Since the seventies, Starhawk has been challenging accepted beliefs about religion and spirituality. Known primarily for her work in reclaiming ancient Goddess traditions, her work goes far beyond merely reconsidering the gender of the supreme being. Through her work she radically questions not only what and how we worship, but our very understanding of spirituality and the sacred. Traditional Western religious thought accepts as axiomatic a dualistic universe, with soul and spirit superior to body and nature. Such thinking leads both to a model of domination, man over woman, human over nature, and to an unnatural fragmentation of our being into body and mind. In her work, Starhawk calls for an integration of the different facets of our lives, demonstrating that spirituality is not and should not be separate from our bodies, politics, feminism, or psychology. The different facets of our lives are joined by a web of interconnections; when we sever these connections, we are not whole.

The following pages are excerpts from a telephone conversation with Starhawk. Although topics ranged widely, covering areas including political action, writing, and communal living, I have focused on Starhawk's elaboration of the relationships between politics and spirituality and definitions of the sacred and our daily lives. We began the interview by talking about the circumstances which first led her to identify herself as a feminist.

I got involved, not so much in feminist spirituality, but in Wicca, before I knew anything about feminism. Back in the late sixties, I was a freshman at UCLA and I was doing an anthropology project on Witchcraft. I met some

From Starhawk and Jennifer Connor. 1995. *Women & Therapy* 17, 3/4: 469–74. Reprinted with permission of The Haworth Press, Inc.

real Witches who began to talk to me about the Goddess tradition. It was an amazing revelation to me to think about having female images of God, or of the sacred. I was raised Jewish, and female imagery was something very foreign. I had never encountered it before, and found it amazingly liberating.

It wasn't until a couple of years later that I encountered feminism. I was travelling with my boyfriend in Europe, and I was sick with the flu and I spent a day in bed in a youth hostel in Frankfurt reading Kate Millett's book, *Sexual Politics*. The book was a revelation. Suddenly all these lights went on. For example, I was an art student, and at that time the art department at UCLA was about seventy percent women undergraduates, about seventy percent men as graduate students, and about ninety-nine percent men in terms of teachers and professors. There were all of these things that you just weren't supposed to notice, or to think about how they affected you and how seriously you could take your own work. So I came home and joined a consciousness-raising group, got very involved with a women's center, and started to think of myself as a feminist.

At that point it occurred to me that having a religion with a Goddess in it had something to do with feminism and something to say to women who were feminist. But there was very little support for that idea. The only woman who was talking about it was Z Budapest. But as the seventies wore on, the feminist movement began to look at spirituality and religion, both to critique patriarchal religion and also to explore other possibilities.

I would say my major contribution has been articulating questions of the sacred from a feminist perspective, and maintaining that the issues and the questions that feminism deals with are questions of the sacred and questions of the spirit, as well as strictly political questions. In other words, I try to link the spiritual and the political in both directions. One of the great gifts is a spiritual connection, because without it, it's very hard to stay in political action for ten years, twenty years, thirty years, a lifetime. Political action tends to not be very rewarding in the sense that it's rare that you do something and immediately see a result that you want. You don't go blockade somewhere and then have Reagan turn around the next day and say, "Oh, I was wrong about those nukes, here's all these dedicated people, willing to go to jail to express their opinions." It doesn't happen like that, it's a long, long process. And oftentimes you can only see the results many many years after it's over, so you have to do something to sustain yourself. And for me that comes out of the spiritual connection.

I think many people felt such a sense of enormous urgency around all the political issues that it was very easy to say, "Oh, let's put aside our personal lives, let's put aside our own health, our own needs and just do this, or we'll be dead. The world will end, something horrible will happen." And that kind of energy can sustain you for awhile, but again, if you're thinking about political action as something you're going to be engaged in for a lifetime, you can't just suspend your life for a lifetime.

One example of a political ritual is the one I organized with Elias Fara-jaje-Jones at the Holocaust Museum, the same weekend as the big lesbian, bi-sexual, gay freedom march in Washington. The ritual focused on the lesbian and gay victims of the Holocaust. What happened to the homosexual com-munity in the Holocaust was an enormous tragedy. The survivors faced prej-udice when they were liberated from the camps, and many were thrown back in jail by the U.S. forces, who maintained that they were not political prisoners, but criminals jailed for activities that were criminal in the U.S. Many of the victims were so ashamed and so ostracized by being branded as homosexuals that they were never able to talk about their experiences or be reconciled with their families.

For the ritual there were several thousand people in the park. We began with speeches and some education by the people who had done research about the issue for the museum. All the participants had candles and we held them to the four directions, and then we had a litany read by four different voices that described some of the experiences that people had in the camps. It ended with the voice of a man having a vision as he's being beaten to death in the camps that someday the pink triangle that was a badge of shame will become something that people wear with pride, and imagining thousands and thousands of people in the streets. We ended the ritual with each person taking a pink flower and making a huge pink triangle at the steps of the mu-seum.

Reclaiming, the group I work with in San Francisco, always does sev-eral big rituals for Halloween, including a traditional Spiral Dance that may involve over a thousand people. For the last couple of years we've also done a women's ritual at this season. In 1992, we decided to focus on choice as the issue. And so we did a ritual with a guided trance meditation where women were walked through their lives as if their lives were an orchard and they were picking the fruits of their choices from the trees, placing them in a bas-ket, and then taking them to the Goddess as the old crone in the center of the circle and giving them to her, giving to her cauldron, giving her the fruits of their painful choices and the fruits of their joyful choices and the fruits of our confusion, the choices where we're never sure if they were the right one or the wrong one, and the fruits of our rage. Then we transformed that rage into power with our voices, raising power for women's right to choose, to make choices about our bodies. And that was a very powerful ritual.

For about five years I've been working with a multicultural ritual group that looks at issues around racism, and all the different isms in the con-text of creating ritual together. We also do a ritual during the Halloween sea-son to celebrate the ancestors of many cultures. We create altars to represent all our different cultures with art work and candles and food and offerings and cloth and weaving. You get a sense of the real richness of the different cultures as you go around and look at all the altars. During part of the ritual people tell their personal stories, sometimes in poetry, sometimes in music, sometimes very simply, sometimes in very polished forms. We do a guided meditation where we go back and face some of the not-so-nice parts of our ancestors, and clean up the mess they've left us, acknowledging that every culture has ancestors that were oppressors. But every culture also has people we can be proud of, people who struggled against the injustices of their time in whatever way they could. It's important to do both, to know what history gets in the way between us and other people, and also to claim our own pride in our heritage. We give people strips of cloth, which they take from the different altars that represent different ancestries, and we tie them together and make a long, long strip of cloth. And out of that we weave a giant basket, and then dance a spiral.

The multicultural group has been really exciting for me in the last few years. We've learned so much about each other. One of the most important things we've learned is that a ritual has to come out of a living community. We can't meet once a year to make a ritual, we have to meet throughout the year to do ritual together. And so we've begun to feel more like family and community than just a bunch of stray people getting together around this particular thing. I've learned a lot more about dealing with racism and unlearning it from creating ritual with that group than I ever have from any political analysis of the subject.

In my third book, *Truth or Dare: Encounters with Power, Authority, and Mystery*, I look at questions of psychology most closely and extensively. My thesis in that book is that we live in a society that's based on the principle of domination and power over, and that we all in different ways internalize that principle. We internalize it as images, as energy patterns, as ways of thinking and ways that we respond to the world, to ourselves and to each other. And that principle is what makes us sick, what keeps us in distress.

Psychology has focused so much on the individual family level. That's important, but in some ways that focus creates the illusion that there exists this wonderful world of health and normality and your dysfunctional family somehow doesn't fit that. When the reality, I think, is that the whole society is toxic and your family might express that in more or less harmful ways, or even compensate for it. This focus just on childhood and just on families, tends to distract us from looking at the larger issue of our society, and saying, "Is this working? Do our institutions work for us? Is this a system in which people can grow up and be fulfilled and be at peace with themselves?"

One of the analogies I used is that of trying to heal people who live at Love Canal who are ill, by looking at the nutrition that they got as infants. We would probably find that people who were well-fed as infants had more resistance to toxicity, and people who were malnourished might be more susceptible to damage, but the point is that people would still be living in a toxic environment and that's the immediate overwhelming problem. So my focus on healing has moved from looking at our historical pain more into looking at the way we are internalizing structures around us, and discovering what kinds of counter structures we can create that won't be toxic, but will encourage us to respond and to grow in different ways. As human beings, we are collective and communal creatures. We can't heal in isolation, we need a sense of community and connection. That's why in the women's spirituality movement, women's circles, or covens are so important, because they create islands of possibility.

Today we're at a cultural crisis point centered around the question of what is sacred—in the sense of what is most important to us, what defines our values. We've had hundreds of years of patriarchal religions telling us that the sacred is outside the world. Now we have all these different groups rising up and saying, "No, wait a minute, the sacred is in the world." That's a very radical concept, because if you start saying the sacred is in the world, that our bodies are sacred, that the earth is sacred, then you can no longer exploit the earth. Our authority to make choices about our own bodies becomes a sacred authority. The real question around abortion is about who has the authority to make life and death choices about your own body. Is it an external God, or is it inherent in your own living being? And of course if you say it's inherent in your own living being, then there goes the whole hierarchial chain of command.

If the sacred is embodied in the earth, it means that we don't have the right to exploit nature in the ways that we are accustomed to doing. An old growth forest has a kind of value that can't be computed on scales of dollars and cents and profit and loss. Nature has a value that goes beyond the usefulness we find in it. Indigenous people have been telling us this, it is a concept they haven't ever lost in their cultures, but I think the problem is not limited to industrialized society. It just reaches its most extreme form here. The Puritan agrarian society, for example, was in some ways just as disconnected from a sense of a sacred nature. But I do think that people having to live close to nature, having to contend with it, probably had more of an intuitive sense than many of us have today.

If you think about it, even on the purely practical level of food, up until the last couple hundred years most of the time people ate food that they had some kind of relationship with. You walked outside of your house, you saw what was ripe in the fields and what wasn't. Everything you ate literally came from the land, was an expression of your relationship with that land. And now, we're entirely disconnected from the food that we eat. We don't know where it comes from, what it's been through, what's been done to it, who grew it, what conditions it was grown under, what happened to the soil that grew it. And that's just one of the ways in which we've become alienated from some of the very basic processes of life.

Last year a woman in New York was interviewing me and she didn't quite seem to understand why we would go to the risk and trouble of getting arrested for blockading to protect the old growth forest at Clayoquot Sound, where my husband and three of my step-daughters and I got arrested in the summer of 1993. Finally she said, "Well, you know, the thing is, the environment is sort of unreal to most New Yorkers." I laughed, but I think it's very true. And it's exactly why we're in the mess we're in. Not just to New Yorkers, but to people who make the decisions about what happens to the earth, the earth is a kind of an abstraction. It's not something they really have a close personal relationship with.

I think one of the most important, most political and spiritual things we can do is to develop a personal connection with the earth. Whether that's growing a garden or whether that's just getting out of Manhattan, or whether it's learning about things like the falcons that live on the skyscrapers and the pigeons that they eat. Without that, politics is very disconnected from reality, from what actually supports us. And with that understanding I think we also have a connection we need to sustain us in doing political work and working for change.

References

Millett, Kate. (1970). *Sexual Politics* (1st ed.). Garden City, NY: Doubleday.
Starhawk. (1987). *Truth or Dare: Encounters with Power, Authority, and Mystery* (1st ed.). San Francisco, CA: Harper & Row.

From the House of Yemanja: The Goddess Heritage of Black Women

Sabrina Sojourner

It is difficult, if not impossible, to be raised in the United States without hav-ing Christian value judgments invade one's life. Until recent times, it was doubly hard for Black Americans to escape this intrusion because of the in-trinsic political and social, as well as religious, role the Black church has played in our community. It was only as late as my parents' generation that countless Black women and men began leaving the church, no longer believ-ing in the salvation offered by a white god and savior. Now many women of my own generation are discovering that God is not only not white, She has never even been considered male until relatively recently!

Reclaiming Our Spiritual Mother

Seboulisa mother goddess with one breast
eaten away by worms of sorrow and loss
see me now
your severed daughter
laughing our name into echo
all the world shall remember.

—AUDRE LORDE[1]

The lack of information about Black Goddesses in most works on God-dess worship might lead one to believe that such information does not exist. This simply is not so! We of African descent have a rich Goddess and matri-focal heritage. While it is true that many tribes maintained a kingship for cen-turies before the notion of written history, more often than not, the king received his legitimacy from a magic-sacerdotal female clan. In other in-stances, the power of the king was channeled through the figure of a "dowa-ger queen" or wifely queen. With some tribes, the kingship was not a position desired by most men because the king was ritually murdered every six months to a year.[2]

From Charlene Spretnak, ed. 1982. *The Politics of Women's Spirituality*. Garden City, NY: Anchor Press. Reprinted with permission of Sabrina Sojourner.

The information I have gathered about African Goddesses, heroines, and Amazons is a synthesis of bits and pieces of information from a variety of sources. The following profiles are taken primarily from the works of three women: Merlin Stone,[3] Audre Lorde,[4] and Helen Diner.[5]

Yemanja is the mother Goddess of the Orisha and, as such, is related to Mawu. Yemanja is the Goddess of the oceans; rivers are said to flow from Her breasts. River-smoothed stones are Her symbol. The sea is sacred to Her followers. In *Brazil* She is worshipped as *Iamanja* and is honored on the eve of Summer Solstice.

Mawu is known as the creator of the universe. As mother of the Vodu, She is related to Yemanja. Another form of Mawu is that of Mawulisa (Mawu-Lisa), the inseparable twins of the universe. For the Dahomean people, Mawulisa is the female-male, sky goddess-god principle, also represented as west-east, night-day, moon-sun. Where She is known as Mawu, Lisa is called either Her first son/consort or Her twin brother. Other manifestations of Mawu are Seboulisa and Sogbo.

Ala is a goddess of the *Ibo people* of Nigeria. She is called the provider of life and the mother who receives again in death. It is Ala who proclaims the law that is the basis for all moral human behavior. It is a Nigerian custom to have life-size images of Ala sitting on the porch of a small wooden house in the village visible to all who pass by.

Jezanna is the Goddess of the Moshona people of Zimbabwe. Her symbol is the moon and Her high priestess is Her primary representative.

Songi is the Great Mother of the Bantu people of central and southern Africa. A sacred legend holds that Nsomeka, a young woman, met Mother Songi in the forest one day. Songi notched Nsomeka's teeth. That evening, from the notches sprang forth livestock, fruit trees, houses, and shade trees. When the men of the village beat their wives for not producing these things for them, Nsomeka gathered all the women in her field and notched their teeth. None of the men could join them until they had promised to treat the women with respect.

Mboze is the First Mother of the Woyo people of Zaire. Her sacred story expresses women's attempts to keep tradition in the face of betrayal. Mboze has a daughter, Bunzi, by Her son/lover, Makanga. When Her husband, Kuitilkuiti (who had changed his black skin for white), learns that Makanga is the father, he beats Mboze to death. Bunzi grows older to do the work Her mother had once done, rewarding the faithful with bountiful rains and harvests.

Mbaba Mwana Waresa is the Goddess of the Zulu people of Natal. Among Her gifts, this holy Rain Goddess of the Heavens also gave Her people beer so that they might better celebrate their joyous times.

Tji-Wara (or *Chi-Wara*) is said to have introduced agriculture to the Bambara people. A good harvest is assured through pleasing Her.

African Amazons of the Goddess Lands

As with Amazon cultures of Goddess-oriented Anatolia, much of what we know about the Amazons of Libya (a term that once referred to all of Africa) centers around their fierceness as warriors. Through legend, mythology, and historical facts, we know of Merina,[6] for instance, and her peaceful march east through Egypt. Once in Syria, she conquered the Arabs, settlement after settlement. She led her Amazon troops through Phrygia and up the coast of the Mediterranean. In their path of triumph, they founded towns and colonies. Lesbos and other eastern Mediterranean islands are said to have fallen to Merina. Cast ashore at Samothrace after a terrific storm, Merina named the island and erected a temple to the Mother-Goddess (probably Neith), celebrated mysteries in Her honor, built altars, and made sacrifices. These were all in accordance with a vow she had taken during her hour of peril.[7]

The trek to Samothrace had been long and arduous. Their exhaustion benefited Greek forces led by Mompsus, a Thracian, and Sypylus, a Scythian. At their hands Merina was defeated and killed, ending the ferocious nation of Libyan Amazons. Most of her followers returned to North Africa. There they continued to honor Neith. The Libyan Amazons also worshipped Pallas Athena and Pallas Promochos, the Vanguard Goddess, as their goddess. As before the death of Merina, women were expected to remain virgins (unmarried) while in active service.[8]

Revival of Yoruban Theology among Black American Women

The African belief in a pantheon of goddesses and gods did not die when the Africans were brought to the "New World"; it merely changed. Traces of Yoruban culture survive in the West Indies, the United States, and South America. In the late Sixties, transmitters of this tradition began to be sought out by Black intellectuals wanting to reclaim a lost part of their spiritual heritage. Now a third group has emerged: women who are challenging the present patriarchal structure of the religion. It is their belief that half-truths and false taboos have been imposed on them and the Yoruban manifestations of the Goddess, that undue power has been placed in the hands of men, and that it is their duty as the daughters of Yemanja, Oshun, and Oya to restore their mothers as the heads of the House and regain respect for women.

Two such women are Luisah Teish and Robin Pearson. Teish has lived in the San Francisco Bay Area since 1971. She was not born into the Yoruban culture, but does not approach it completely as an outsider; during her childhood in the Delta region of Louisiana, remnants of it were all around her. Her formal interest began in the mid-Sixties when she began dancing with Katherine Dunham. Upon her arrival in the Bay Area, Teish started teaching Afro-Haitian dance. Since much of the dance is rooted in religion, Teish also provided her classes with information about the religious culture. In 1977 she started teaching classes on the Yoruban goddesses, mostly to women.

Teish believes that Oshun, the Yoruban goddess of love, beauty, and female power, has been wronged by contemporary patriarchs of the Yoruban culture. "Oshun is usually depicted as the very delicate, very conceited and jealous female," observes Teish; but many aspects of this goddess are kept hidden. For instance, Teish explains, "We are told that Oshun's bird is the peacock whose only value is its outward appearance. However, if you listen carefully, you may also hear Her associated with the vulture." Teish adds with a sly smile, "And we all know how powerful the jaws and the claws of a vulture are."

Robin Pearson lives in Jamaica Plains, Massachusetts. Like Teish, Pearson was not born into the Yoruban culture. She joined a communal house in the mid-Seventies that is oriented toward female spirituality. Pearson has since left the strictly ordered house and is working on her own. Both she and Teish hope to become priestesses; the complex ceremony of initiation can span five years. Because the initiators have tremendous influence over the outcome, both women hope to go to Africa, make contact with women who keep the old ways, and return to this country to open feminist Yoruba houses, centers that again will honor the Mother and Her daughters.

Redefining Our Spiritual Heritage

I come like a woman
who I am
spreading out through nights
laughter and promise
and dark heat
warming whatever I touch
that is living
consuming
only
what is already dead

—AUDRE LORDE[9]

The Africans who adopted Christianity maintained their African spiritual sensibilities. Thus, with their conversion began the tapestry of Black theology and folk religion, comprised of threads of African religions and culture, Western civilization, and Christianity. It is colored with the practices, rituals, and philosophies of white, Christian theology and the African tradition that religion permeates all aspects of life with no final distinctions between what is secular and what is sacred.[10]

It is the latter aspect that accounts for the spiritual aspect of Black art, theater, music, and literature. This is why, even though raised outside the Church, there is rarely a Black individual who does not understand the Church's significance to the Black culture and community. Black theology and folk religion, like traditional African religions, seeks the power or the spirit of God (Divine Energy) in all times and places and things; without that power, one is helpless.[11] Because the Church has succeeded in providing for its community a "heaven on earth"—a sense of joy in the face of adversity—it has maintained its central position. By attuning yourself to the Spirit, or its manifestations, you become one with that power. Thus, when Black Christians talk about putting themselves in the hands of God, they are generally referring to their need, desire, or ability to tap into a divine source of energy and utilize that energy to push/pull themselves through a situation. This is not much different from the Pagan process of channeling energy, which many women are reviving today.

Perhaps the Amazons who rode into Europe from the Russian steppes were fierce, blonde, blue-eyed women. My Amazons have always been dark. It is not easy growing up in a society whose language and laws fear, despise, and dehumanize the rainbow of people who are of darker hues. It is not easy trusting alliances with women who continue a *status quo* negation of one's racial/cultural/ethnic/class background. The dark-skinned women who rode, thousands strong, across the African continent and through the Arab world are my reminder that I am the ancestral daughter/sister of a powerful nation of women. Whether their battles were merely for the sport and spoils of war or for the preservation of Mother Right is immaterial. It is their fight and strength that I cling to. For me, this image has been an amazing source of courage, conviction, and freedom.

The works of Diner and Stone are a very helpful and encouraging beginning, but there is much more that needs to be uncovered. Black women must tend to this cultural history; because it is our own, we are more likely to intuit the threads of truth that join the surviving facts. Several Black women writers have already begun to explore the mythical/spiritual realm of our existence: Zora Neal Hurston in *Their Eyes Were Watching God* and *Of Mules and Men*, as well as in most of her anthropological writings; Marita Bonner in her play *The Purple Flower*; Audre Lorde in "Uses of the Erotic: The Erotic as Power," *The Black Unicorn, Coal*, and more than can be named here; Toni Cade Bambara in *The Salt Eaters*; Ntozake Shange in *for colored girls who have considered suicide/when the rainbow is enuf*, the short story "Sassafrass," and numerous poems; Pat Parker in *Movement in Black*; and Joyce Carol Thomas in her play *Ambrosia*, a powerful tale of spiritual reincarnation.

The chasm that exists between the matrifocal cultures of yesterday and the brutal subjugation of our African sisters today, which includes widespread genital mutilation, is treacherously deep. Numerous institutions and individuals have been complicit in leading us to believe that the latter is the "natural" way things have always been. What they try to ignore and we often fail to remember is that patriarchal religion and cultural mores are only a few thousand years old—hardly worthy of the term "forever"! Improving the quality of women's lives around the world requires more than economic and/or political theory. It is my hope that as more and more Third World women read Diner, Stone, Lorde, and others, they will begin to fill in the names, rituals, and deeds—the realities—of the Goddess-worshipping and woman-honoring cultures of our ancestors. I long for a discussion of spiritual, as well as economic and political, structures among Third World women, among all women.

Notes

1. Audre Lorde, "125th Street and Abomey," *The Black Unicorn* (New York: W. W. Norton & Co., 1978), p. 12.
2. Helen Diner, *Mother and Amazons: The First Feminine History of Culture* (Garden City, NY: Anchor Press/Doubleday, 1973), pp. 177–181.
3. Merlin Stone, *When God Was a Woman* (New York: The Dial Press, 1976) and *Ancient Mirrors of Womanhood: Our Goddess and Heroine Heritage* (New York: New Sibylline Books, 1979/80).
4. Audre Lorde, *The Black Unicorn*.
5. Helen Diner, *op. cit.*
6. Merina is most widely known as Myrine, her Greek name, but the former is her Libyan name.
7. Guy Cadogan Rothery, *The Amazons in Antiquity and Modern Times* (London: Francis Griffiths, 1910), p. 113.
8. See Rothery, p. 113, and Diner, pp. 108–109.
9. Audre Lorde, "The Women of Dan Dance with Swords in Their Hands to Mark the Time When They Were Warriors," *The Black Unicorn*, p. 14.
10. Joseph R. Washington, Jr., *Black Sects and Cults* (Garden City, NY: Anchor Press/Doubleday, 1973), p. 20.
11. *Ibid.*

Questions for Discussion

1. What accounts for the growing popularity of goddess religions and similar female-centered spiritualities in recent decades, especially in European and North American countries?
2. What would motivate a woman to leave her religion of origin and convert to a goddess religion?
3. Do goddess religions in fact offer women a more empowering basis for faith than traditional male-dominated world religions?
4. Are goddess religions more inclusive of difference than institutional world religions?
5. Is Carol Christ correct that women "need the goddess"?
   - If so, why isn't it possible for women to find spiritual fulfillment in traditional religions?
   - If not, how should women cope with the patrarichal and sexist aspects of their traditional religions?

References and Materials for Further Study

Books and Articles

Adler, Margot. 1986. *Drawing Down the Moon: Witches, Druids, Goddess-Worshipers, and Other Pagans in America Today*. Boston: Beacon Press.

Budapest, Z. 1989. *The Holy Book of Woman's Mysteries*. Berkeley, CA: Wingbow Press: Bookpeople.

Christ, Carol. 1979. "Why Women Need the Goddess: Phenomenological, Psychological, and Political Reflections," in Carol Christ and Judith Plasko, eds., *Womenspirit Rising: A Feminist Reader in Religions*. San Francisco: Harper & Row.

Eller, Cynthia. 1993. *In the Lap of the Goddess: The Feminist Spirituality Movement in America*. New York: Crossroads Publishing Company.

King, Karen, ed. 1997. *Women and Goddess Traditions: In Antiquity and Today*. Minneapolis, MN: Augsburg Fortress.

Lefkowitz, Mary. 1993. "The New Cults of the Goddess." *American Scholar*, 62: 261-28. Critical appraisal of the new goddess movements.

———. 1992. "The Twilight of the Goddess: Feminism, Spiritualism, and a New Craze." *New Republic* (Aug. 3): 29-33.

Lesco, Barbara. 1999. *The Great Goddesses of Egypt*. Norman: University of Oklahoma Press. Traces the development of workship of the six major Egyptian goddesses in the ancient world.

Luhrmann, T.M. 1989. *Persuasions of the Witch's Craft: Ritual Magic in Contemporary England*. Cambridge, MA: Harvard University Press.

Orsi, Robert A. 1996. *Thank You, St. Jude: Women's Devotion to the Patron Saint of Hopeless Causes*. New Haven, CT: Yale University Press.

Puttick, Elizabeth. 1997. "Female Spiritual Leadership in NRMs," in *Women in New Religions: In Search of Community, Sexuality, and Spiritual Power*. New York: St. Martin's Press.

Ranck, Shirley Ann. 1995. *Cakes for the Queen of Heaven: an Exploration of Women's Power Past, Present and Future*. Chicago: Delphi Press.

Raphael, Melissa. 1999. *Introducing Thealogy: Discourse on the Goddess*. Sheffield, UK: Sheffield Academic Press. Overview of contemporary goddess worship in Europe, America, and Asia.

Reilly, Patricia Lynn. 1995. *A God Who Looks Like Me: Discovering a Woman-Centered Spirituality*. New York: Ballantine Books.

Sered, Susan. 1994. *Priestess, Mother, Sacred Sister: Religions Dominated by Women*. New York: Oxford University Press.

Sojourner, Sabrina. 1982. "From the House of Yemanja: The Goddess Heritage of Black Women," in Charlene Spretnak, ed., *The Politics of Women's Spirituality*. Garden City, NY: Anchor Press.

Spretnak, Charlene, ed. 1982. *The Politics of Women's Spirituality*. Garden City, NY: Anchor Press.

Starhawk. 1989. *The Spiral Dance: A Rebirth of the Ancient Religion of the Great Goddess*, rev. ed. New York: HarperSanFrancisco.

Starhawk, and Jennifer Connor. 1995. "Reclaiming the Sacred." *Women and Therapy*. 17, no. 3/4: 469-74.

Teish, Luisah. 1985. *Jambalaya: The Natural Woman's Book of Personal Charms and Practical Rituals*. San Francisco: Harper & Row.

Walker, Barbara. 1983. *The Woman's Encyclopedia of Myths and Secrets*. San Francisco: Harper & Row.

Weaver, Mary Jo. 1993. "Who Is the Goddess and Where Does She Get Us?" in *Springs of Water in a Dry Land: Spiritual Survival for Catholic Women Today*. Boston: Beacon Press.

Internet References

Artemis Reborn: House of the Goddess Center for Pagan Wombyn Web Site:
   http://www. crosswinds.net/~arbhotgcpw/House/Gate.html.
   Links to many fine resources for pagan women's spirituality and goddess worship.

Celebration of the Feminine Divine in Women's Early Music Web Site:
   http://music.acu.edu/ www/iawm/pages/reference/divine.html.

Catala's Resources Web Site:
   http://www.silvermoon.net/catala/paths/resource.htm.
   Annotated collection of sites related to wicca and neo-paganism.

CoGweb Web Site:
   http://www.cog.org.
   Covenant of the Goddess, an international organization of cooperating wiccan practitioners, with links to bibliographies and other neo-pagan groups.

Goddess-Study Web Site:
   http://www.pinn.net/~swampy/gdstudy.html.
   "An educational forum based on studies of women's relationship with Goddess and Moon Lore" for women only.

Neopaganism and Women's Spirituality Bibliography Web Site:
   http://www.rdg.ac.uk/~lkpbodrd/ magbib/neopag.html.

Partially annotated bibliography of books and other materials relating to women's spirituality and neopagan movements.

SisterSpirit: Women Sharing Spirituality Web Site:
http://ethoscape.com/sistersp.
Portland, Oregon-based organization supporting women's spirituality, with an emphasis on goddess religions. Includes links.

The Witch's Voice Web Site:
http://www.witchvox.com.
Educational network about witchcraft, providing news, information, articles, and links to other neo-pagan sites.

Yahoo's Wicca and Witchcraft Web Site:
http://dir.yahoo.com/Society_and_Culture/Religion _and_Spirituality/Faiths_ and_Practices/Paganism/Wicca_and_Witchcraft.
Yahoo's directory of links to sites relating to wicca.

Media Resources

The Changing Culture: The Men's Movement. Video, 29 min. Films for the Humanities, 1998. Profiles the new "men's movement," explores the various reasons why men become involved in these movements, the influence of feminism, and examines the implications for men and women in the twenty-first century.

Goddess Remembered. Video, 55 min. National Film Board of Canada, Studio D, 1989. Exploration of goddess-centered religion, beginning in pre-historic times, from the paleolithic caves of France, to the neolithic subterranean temples of Malta to the mysterious earthworks of ancient Britain, and the palaces of Delphi and of Crete.

The "Kitchen Goddess": The Reemergence of the Village Psychic. Video, 54 min. Films for the Humanities, 1999. Devotees of Wicca and practitioners of tarot, astrology, palmistry, and other arcane arts explain their gifts of divination and healing while reflecting on their efforts to reconcile their unorthodox callings with Biblical injunctions and sometimes hostile skepticism.

The Need to Know: Women and Religion. Video, 47 min., color. Films for the Humanities, 1996. Covers women in early Christianity, the goddess tradition that Christianity supplanted, and Islam's oppression of women.

Index

A
Company
of Fools

Deborah Ellis

ALLEN&UNWIN

This edition published in 2003

First published in Canada by Fitzhenry & Whiteside, 2002

Allen & Unwin
83 Alexander St
Crows Nest NSW 2065
Australia
Phone: (61 2) 8425 0100
Fax: (61 2) 9906 2218
Email: info@allenandunwin.com
Web: www.allenandunwin.com

National Library of Australia
Cataloguing-in-Publication entry:

Ellis, Deborah, 1960– .
A company of fools.

For children.
ISBN 1 74114 306 3.

I. Title.

813.6

Cover and text design by Sandra Nobes
Set in 12½ pt Bembo by Tou-Can Design
Printed in Australia by McPhersons Printing Group

1 3 5 7 9 10 8 6 4 2